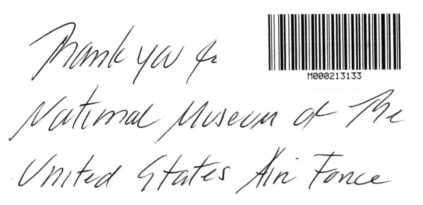

M000213133

# The Last Flight
# of Liberator 41-1133

### The Lives, Times, Training & Loss
### Of The Bomber Crew Which Crashed On
### Trail Peak At Philmont Scout Ranch

*William R. Cass*

i

## By The Same Author

Dick Fellows Photography, Philadelphia

## About the Author

William F. Cass is a suburban Philadelphia marketing communications executive and active Scouter in the Chester County Council (Pennsylvania), Boy Scouts of America, which he serves as Vice President-Program and High Adventure Committee Chairman. He has been a pilot all of his adult life and is an aviation historian of long standing. He and his wife Sarah, a history teacher, graduated from Washington College in Maryland, and are the parents of two grown children. Bill Cass spent his college summers working at Philmont Scout Ranch near Cimarron, in northern New Mexico, where he first became interested in the history of Liberator 41-1133. He is a member of the Philmont Staff Association Executive Committee and the Chester County Council Executive Board.

# The Last Flight
# of Liberator 41-1133

### The Lives, Times, Training & Loss
### Of The Bomber Crew Which Crashed On
### Trail Peak At Philmont Scout Ranch

William F. Cass

The Winds Aloft Press

Library of Congress Control Number:
00-132999

ISBN: 0-9702972-0-3

All photographs, unless otherwise specified, are from the collection of William F. Cass

Illustrations and cartography by William F. Cass

Manufactured in the United States of America

# Dedicated to the Memory of the Crew

Robert O. Redding
Operations Manager, Instructor Pilot
Transcontinental & Western Air, Inc. (TWA)
Captain, Military Pilot, United States Army Air Force Reserve

Second Lieutenant Roland L. Jeffries
Military Pilot
366th Squadron, 305th Bomb Group (Heavy)
United States Army Air Force

Second Lieutenant Charles O. Reynard, Jr.
Military Pilot
367th Squadron, 306th Bomb Group (Heavy)
United States Army Air Force

Jonas G. Ruff
First Officer, Instructor Copilot
TWA

George E. Van Hoozer
Flight Engineer/Aviation Mechanic Instructor
TWA

Corporal Philip E. Macomber
Flight Engineer
18th Squadron, 34th Bomb Group (Heavy)
United States Army Air Force

Corporal Duane M. Peterson
Radio Operator/Mechanic
Headquarters Squadron, 310th Air Base Group
United States Army Air Force

**KIFA**
**near Cimarron, New Mexico**
**4/22/42**

# Introduction

This is the tragic story of how one B-24 Liberator bomber, Army Air Force serial number 41-1133, was lost out of the 490 that crashed in stateside flying mishaps involving fatalities during World War Two (WWII). That airplane, brand new just several months after Pearl Harbor, is now badly weathered aluminum, rusting engine parts, and aircraft components scattered among the trees and rocks near the crest of a 10,242 foot mountain in northern New Mexico.

This particular crash is, in most ways, a microcosm of circumstances surrounding the terribly high number of WWII flying accidents: young men, bad weather, mechanical failures, high performance airplanes, tall mountains, and no margin for error. Yet, it is unique in one respect since it is the most visited crash site of a B-24 or, for that matter, any civil or military aircraft in the world. The wreckage is located on Trail Peak at Philmont Scout Ranch, the principal High Adventure property of the Boy Scouts of America (BSA). Situated near Cimarron, and northeast of Taos, New Mexico, Philmont is the largest youth camping and backpacking facility on earth.

As a college student working summers on the Philmont staff, I visited the crash site twice in 1962 and again hiked up to the top of Trail Peak four times as a regular expedition advisor during the 1990s. Hikes up the mountain were also made in 1997 and 1998 during Philmont Staff Association Rendezvous weekends. What made a major impression on the 1962 climb was not only the wreckage. Rather, it was a sturdy canister attached to a tree amidst the debris. Inside, there was a neatly folded American flag and a somewhat weathered sheet of paper on which was typed the crew roster. Slowly reading the names prompted an almost daydreaming line of questioning as to who those people were, where they came from, what they were like, and how they came to such a violent end. My time on the mountain was limited, so the idle musing promptly ended. Recalling most of the names a week after that first climb would have been difficult.

This book, the foundation for which was an article written for *High Country* (the quarterly magazine of the Philmont Scout Ranch Staff Association), traces its real origin to a phone call from Marty Tschetter, a Philmont training ranger, in July of 1993. Marty was updating the *Philmont Ranger Fieldbook*, wanted some clarification of the Trail Peak bomber crash, and knew that I had done some original research on the B-24 Liberator accident on Trail Peak for my last book, *Return to the Summit of Scouting.*

As with the re-telling of any story, the history of the bomber crash has been subjected to some inaccuracies over the years, so I thought that a well-documented article might be very appropriate for the staff alumni magazine. The two-part article was started in the autumn of 1993 and completed in March of 1994. The article appeared and was reprinted for other media, but there were enough loose ends to prompt "re-opening the case" which was done in late 1996.

The cornerstone of the book's few paragraphs and the much more in-depth article on the crash was the "Form 14" (accident investigation report) which was obtained from the Air Force Aerospace Safety Directorate. The crew's names, now in black and white again, rang familiar — almost as though they had been stored in some little subconscious niche waiting to be re-awakened. There they were once more: Jeffries, Macomber, Peterson, Redding, Reynard, Ruff, and Van Hoozer. It became important to bring those names out from under the cloak of time's passage, and to widely share their identities which had not been done in the previous book.

The accident report was supplemented with newspaper articles, Scouting sources (especially those in Kansas City), telephone conversations, correspondence, and meetings with several of the flyers' surviving relatives and friends who were most generous with their time and cooperation in this project. As the project evolved into a book, emphasis was placed on interviewing those former Army Air Force pilots and instructors who were acquainted with the members of 41-1133's crew.

This book deals with the lives and times of the seven airmen who perished in the crash of their bomber on one of Philmont's major peaks. The "times" are important, and that is why this book contains considerable reference to contemporary life and world affairs from mid-1941 through early 1942. There are substantial discussions regarding the forerunner of Trans World Airlines and the unique role it played during WWII, both in its training of Liberator crews in Albuquerque as well as its role in the wartime Air Transport Command. The Boy Scouting movement forms another major digression because it was not only an element of the civilian response to WWII, but, more importantly, because it is the owner of the property where Liberator 41-1133 crashed. Scouting was also a very significant influence on the life of the pilot flying at the time of the accident. These subjects were considered too important to be banished to chapter notes.

The core of this narrative, however, is Army Air Force pilot training in 1941-42 since the ill-fated flight was the culmination of nearly a year of very intense flight training for the bomber's two recently-commissioned officers. Readers will notice that certain members of the crew are the focal points of more chapters than the other flyers. That in no way should be interpreted as those individuals being more important than the rest of the crew. This book's emphasis on flight training in the Army Air Force Aviation Cadet Program and the scarcity of surviving relatives, friends, and correspondence as research sources for other members of the crew resulted in the book's relatively much stronger emphasis on the two newly-rated Army pilots.

As this chronicle unfolds, readers will share the mystery, frustrations, joy, and fear in the sky as experienced by the crew of Liberator 41-1133, and especially Lieutenants Jeffries and Reynard as they proceed through the Aviation Cadet Program. The two intended audiences for this book, i.e. Philmont-oriented Scouters and those interested in WWII aviation, naturally diverge in their familiarity with the technical aspects of flying. Because this work concentrates on the flight training leading up to the crash on Trail Peak, the complexities of aviation are by necessity a part of the story. Therefore, some readers will enjoy a sentimental journey back to early 1940s aeronautical technology while other readers will be exposed for the first time to the technical details of flight and the planes flown by those pilots who comprise this story.

Some of this book is "speculative," that is, it takes the reader along on what the final flight was assumed to be like. Nobody, however, knows, or ever will know, exactly why the bomber crashed.

The author's opinion as a pilot and the concurrence of certain other pilots (several former B-17 and B-24 aircraft commanders with substantial flying experience over the Rockies) strongly suggest the downburst/wind shear phenomenon as the accident's fundamental cause. Under the circumstances (the freezing level, terrain elevation, and the fact that the bomber had lost an engine), there was very little the crew could have done to avoid ground contact once they were caught in a downburst.

The pictures tell much of this tragic story. A commanding Captain Redding in his pre-war Army Air Corps uniform. A pensive Lt. Charles Reynard in Albuquerque during B-24 transition training as, perhaps, he tries to reconcile his innate compassion for mankind with the inhumanity of the war in which he was about to become a very active participant. In the cockpit of a basic trainer, a solemn Lt. Roland Jeffries who may have been reflecting on how climbing Scouting's trails had helped prepare him for the high, dangerous path he was about to take. A handsome, confident Jonas Ruff, caught up in the excitement of flying in the 30s, the golden age of aviation. The friendly, generous Corporal Philip Macomber whose interest in all things mechanical found a great outlet in the B-24 Liberator's intricate systems. And, George Van Hoozer whose precision with machinery, talent as a teacher, and sense of adventure made him the ideal flight engineering instructor.

Consideration was given to using the journalist's technique of dialogue to more fully bring the flyers back to life and add greater dimension to this chronicle. Other than known checklists, typical comments by instructor pilots, along with the logically derived transmissions between the bomber and control facilities, the significant use of dialogue was ultimately rejected on the basis that the story of Liberator 41-1133 should consist of the facts, not of presumption, no matter how tempting.

The year 1942 was not one of mankind's finer accomplishments in most respects. Yet, the times were marked by a renaissance in such positive virtues as patriotism, cooperation, sacrifice, and other traditional values. Today's young adults might regard the typical 21-year old aviation cadet of late 1941 as hopelessly square at first. After all, the young pilot spoke differently, and might well have said of his airplane, "Gee, it's a real swell ship," or refer to his buddy, the cool dude, as a "good egg."

The aircrews of those days were content to listen to a radio which issued music whose soothing lyrics could be understood; those flyers would have been uncomfortable with the anarchy so commonly projected in today's popular media. That is not to say that America in wartime was without certain moral and economic downsides. However, the youth who answered the call to arms in 1941 would not have been familiar with such terms as crack cocaine, graffiti, skyjackings, schoolyard massacres, and a host of other social and political ills which were essentially unheard of then, but which barely raise an eyebrow today.

Whether or not generations succeeding that of the airmen in this book have been responsible trustees of World War Two's dearly bought victory would make a lively debate subject. Call it nostalgia perhaps, but even in those worst of times during WWII, there was a civility and goodness in mainstream American life that seems somewhat lacking today. Perhaps that nebulous decency is recaptured in this look back at the era and lives of the seven men who perished in Liberator 41-1133's tragic demise.

Trail Peak endures, and now welcomes crew after crew of campers and their adult advisors every summer at Philmont. Almost all visitors to the mountain's summit and those who serve on the Philmont staff have only a limited idea of what the world was like in the spring of 1942 or what it meant to lose a friend or immediate family member who was "killed on active service" or "killed in a flying accident" (KIFA) in the Army Air Force. Hopefully, this book, which originally saw the light of day only as a brief article restating crash report's technical details, will help revive the memory of Liberator 41-1133's crew, their times, and the cause in which they served.


William F. Cass

West Chester, Pennsylvania
April 22, 2000

# Acknowledgments

An unabridged acknowledgments section is found in the final pages of this book. That segment of this work is one of the most important chapters since it represents many of the people who participated in the events described in this effort. They, especially the crew's relatives, contributed their time, recollections, wartime memorabilia, correspondence, and photographs most generously. Others, nearly perfect strangers when this project started, include Scouters from California to Maine, volunteers with museums, historical societies, and archives, and aviation historians, all of whom enthusiastically supported the research required in this undertaking. To say that all of their contributions are deeply appreciated is a monumental understatement.

# About Philmont Scout Ranch

Philmont Scout Ranch, located near Cimarron, in northeastern New Mexico's Sangre de Cristo Range of the Rockies, is the crown jewel in the High Adventure Program of the Boy Scouts of America. With 137,493 acres and a summer attendance averaging 20,000 Scouts, Explorers (including young women), and their adult leaders, Philmont is the largest youth camping operation in the world. Although Philmont offers autumn and winter camping programs, its busiest camping season runs from mid-June through late August. On a typical summer day, 300 people complete their Philmont trek, just as another 300 arrive to go on the trail.

"Camping" is not an adequate description since Philmont's core program is backpacking. Crews hike through a post-frontier, quasi-wilderness within which there are hundreds of miles of trails and over 90 back country, staffed and unstaffed camps which offer a variety of programs emphasizing Philmont's western heritage. Among the many programs are logging, gold mining, Indian lore, fur trapping, western lore, blacksmithing, and homesteading. Those programs are augmented by such contemporary Scouting activities as conservation, archeology, rock climbing, astronomy, wilderness survival, no-trace camping, and crew challenge events.

Philmont is managed by a nucleus of professional Scouters who also direct the summer staff which is almost exclusively composed of college students (approximately 900 young men and women). As might be expected, nearly all of the young men attained Eagle Scout rank when they were active youth members of the BSA. Philmont is very much a working ranch with hundreds of head of cattle and horses, a buffalo herd, and full-time cowboys.

Philmont is a demanding experience for youth and adult alike. Each expedition crew, consisting of seven to twelve persons, including at least two adults, spends eleven days backpacking through Philmont's mountains, alpine meadows, canyons, foothills, and prairie. The crew hikes one of roughly 36 itineraries and sees only a small fraction of the Ranch during its expedition. Access to the Valle Vidale Unit of the Kit Carson National Forest adjacent to Philmont's northern border adds additional trails and program opportunities to the Philmont experience.

Many crews backpacking through Philmont's high, South Country visit the crest of Trail Peak, the 10,242 foot high mountain where Liberator 41-1133 crashed. Since the conclusion of WWII, the several thousand Scouts and their leaders who climb Trail Peak every summer have made that location the most visited military (or civil) aircraft wreckage site in the world.

In the course of their expeditions, crews typically backpack from 60 to 90 miles, and climb to heights nearing 13,000 feet. All of the skills acquired during a Scout's early training are utilized to the fullest extent at Philmont. A young person has every right to be proud of completing a Philmont expedition which is as challenging mentally as it is physically.

In addition to the camping and cattle operations, Philmont is home to the BSA's National Training Center through which 3,000 volunteer and professional Scouters pass every year.

Philmont Scout Ranch was given to the Boy Scouts of America as two separate gifts in 1938 and 1941 by Waite Phillips, a wealthy Oklahoma oilman and philanthropist. The name "Philmont" was derived from combining the first syllable of the Phillips name with a variation of the Spanish word "monte" (mountain).

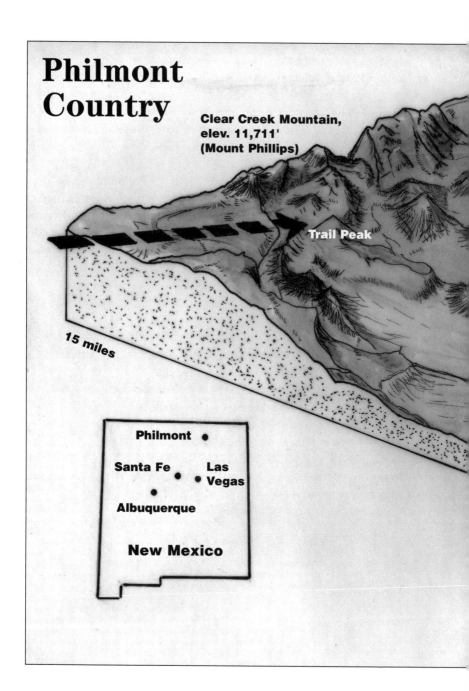

# Philmont Country

Clear Creek Mountain,
elev. 11,711'
(Mount Phillips)

Trail Peak

15 miles

Philmont •

Santa Fe • Las
• Vegas

Albuquerque •

New Mexico

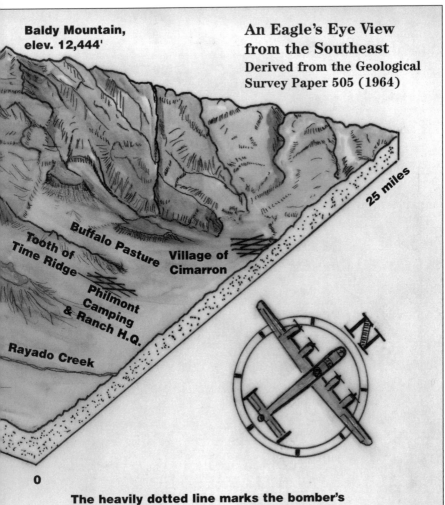

**Baldy Mountain, elev. 12,444'**

An Eagle's Eye View from the Southeast
Derived from the Geological Survey Paper 505 (1964)

25 miles

Buffalo Pasture

Tooth of Time Ridge

Village of Cimarron

Philmont Camping & Ranch H.Q.

Rayado Creek

**N**

0

The heavily dotted line marks the bomber's path in Philmont airspace before crashing into Trail Peak, elevation 10,242 feet above mean sea level. Trail Peak is located in Philmont's high South Country whose principal peak is the 11,711 foot high Mount Phillips (known in 1942 as Clear Creek Mountain).

# Contents

# List of Illustrations

Covers

Front: From the original painting, *The Cruel Sky*, by the author
Back: B-24D Liberator near Albuquerque, New Mexico, early 1942

# PART I

# OUTBOUND

# I

# TO THE HEART OF AMERICA

Screaming the night away
With his great wing feathers
Swooping the darkness up;
I hear the Eagle bird
Pulling the blanket back
Off from the eastern sky.

Iroquois *Morning Invitation Song*

George E. Van Hoozer, the 30-year old flight engineering instructor, arrived at the big bomber just as the ground crew was finishing most of its chores. The Liberator's oil and fuel tanks had been filled as had its oxygen tanks since one segment of this April 22, 1942 training flight, a roundtrip from Albuquerque to Kansas City, would be flown at high altitude. Shortly, two more crew members, both corporals, showed up: the flight engineer trainee, Philip Macomber, and the 22-year old radio operator trainee, Duane Peterson.

Under Van Hoozer's expert guidance, Macomber, in his mid-20s, had easily grasped all of the flight engineer's duties over the preceding three weeks of intense instruction, and would complete the flight engineer's portion of the preflight in the remaining minutes before the pilots arrived. He opened a small access panel on the right side of the fuselage, just below the radio operator's window, reached in, and tugged on a handle whereupon the bomb bay doors promptly retracted.

Macomber stepped up into the bay and checked to see that the bomber had indeed been properly refueled. With 2,100 gallons in the 12 fuel tanks, the Liberator was filled almost up to its 2,348 gallon capacity. Then he opened all fuel valves, climbed up onto the flight deck and quickly looked at the master and ignition switches to make sure they were off. With Macomber's word that the switches were off, the ground crew began pulling each of the propellers through six blades to purge the lower cylinders of any accumulated oil and gasoline.

At about 7:15 a.m., Lieutenants Charles Reynard and Roland Jeffries, both in their early 20s, came walking down the row of B-24s. They had been over at the base operations office getting a weather briefing, planning the flight, and filing their flight plan. Although they had both gone through basic and advanced flight training in the same class, they had not become well acquainted until being ordered to Albuquerque's Kirtland Field and assigned to the same crew almost a month before.

Next to arrive were the instructor pilots, Robert Redding and Jonas Ruff. They, however, were good friends of long standing who had gotten acquainted while flying in Panama nearly seven years before. At age 27, Redding, a six-foot, four-inch tall Nebraskan, was the operations manager of the school in addition to being a first pilot instructor. Ruff, age 34, was a copilot instructor being groomed for a first pilot instructor's slot. Excepting Reynard, everybody was busy loading the paraphernalia of flight into the bomber: pilots' leather-covered navigation kits, a few thermos bottles of coffee, and oxygen masks. There were also several B-4 bags carried on board in addition to aviator's kit bags containing parachutes and the lighter jackets and service caps they would need for their few hours of seeing the sights in Kansas City.

As pilot of the Albuquerque to Kansas City leg, Lt. Charles Reynard was responsible for the preflight inspection of Liberator 41-1133. That B-24 was one of the 16 Liberators assigned to the Combat Crew Training School (CCTS) located at Albuquerque's Kirtland Field. The school, which was staffed by instructor pilots from Transcontinental and Western Air, Inc. (TWA), was charged with transitioning newly commissioned pilots from advanced flying schools into the big, four-engine bomber. The preflight began out at the right wingtip which Reynard inspected to make sure that it and the running light had not been damaged in a taxiing accident.

Reynard continued walking along the leading edge, looking for cracks in the deicer boots, and finally paused in front of the number four engine, but well clear of its propeller arc. Here, he looked for any obvious oil leaks, any nicks or dents in the propeller and to make sure no foreign matter or bird's nest had become lodged between the cylinders.

Quickly turning, he walked toward the fuselage and gave the number three engine the same once over, looking most closely at the leading edges of the props since he knew full well that even a small stone's dent could eventually result in a major problem. As with number four, he looked at the anti-icer slinger ring for security and followed the shiny black rubber boot along the wing's leading edge to the wing root joint at the fuselage.

Then, he turned and walked forward toward the nose, looking up to see that the cloth cover had been removed from the pitot tube. Had he missed this item, only his professional pride would have been poked since there was no rated navigator on board to complain about the lack of airspeed indication at the navigator's station. Reynard rounded the greenhouse-like nose, checking for any cracks. Looking up on the left side of the nose, he noted that the cover on "his" pitot tube had been removed and nothing was fouling the little hole at the tip. Quickly, he popped open an access door in back of the nose to make sure the fire extinguisher was in place.

The nose wheel and gear came next: proper inflation, no bald spots, no bad abrasions, no slippage of wheel on the rim, the right amount of oleo strut showing (about one fist or four and one-half inches to be sure), proper pressure, gear latch in down position, hydraulic lines and fittings secure, and no leaks.

The left wing, engines, deicer boots, and wing panels were similarly observed as the right side had been. Reynard made the turn at the wingtip and walked in toward the fuselage, looking up at the trailing edge to make sure there were no tears or ripples in the aileron fabric. The control surfaces were a throwback to earlier planes and were covered with fabric, dope and paint. Now, he was under the wing, looking up at the panels for any buckling or popped rivets. Here came the heavy duty stuff — the number one engine nacelle for any loose fasteners or excessive oil drips. He paused beneath the engine to look at the turbocharger, examining the wheel for free movement, alignment, and turbine security.

Number two got the same treatment and a bit more because the main landing gear inspection started there. Reynard checked the same things: tire tread, wheel alignment, latch down, secure fittings, proper oleo extension, no leaks, and a good eyeball on the gear for any cracks or buckles. He then walked in toward the fuselage, still peering up at access panels, making sure there were no stains showing fuel leaks. Then he moved out into the sun, looking up at the flaps for alignment, full up position, and freedom from any dents. He next looked up above the wing to check the antenna for security and followed it out in space in back of the wing up to its attachment on top of the right rudder.

He quickly squatted down to look at the belly turret for proper retraction and alignment. This was strictly out of habit, because many of the CCTS planes had been stripped of all guns since they served no purpose in a four-engine transition school. In fact, some of the B-24s had been modified by fairing over the navigator celestial sighting bubble on the nose to improve visibility. In some cases, the top gun turrets were even removed. The blast deflector in front of the left waist gunner hatch was confirmed as closed (there was no waist gun for anybody to fire, so why create any extra drag?). He noted the skid position, and then scanned the tail section for deicer boot security, condition of the fabric on the control surfaces, and proper position of the trim tabs. There were no markings or insignia on the rudders other than the plane's serial number which had been painted in flat yellow — 11133. That number was actually a contraction of 41-1133 in which only the last number of the year of manufacturing contract, 1941, was kept and the hyphen eliminated. Continuing, Reynard saw that the tail turret was facing perfectly aft. Walking around the tail, he popped open a door just in back of the right wing revealing another fire extinguisher.

After securing that, the right wing, gear, turbos, and nacelles were checked. And, he had followed to the letter one of the rules he had first learned as a cadet on the flight line at primary nine months before: he had not walked through any propeller arc. His walkaround inspection was performed from memory. Had he found something he did not like, he would have informed the ground crew chief. His next checklist was printed on a stiff piece of cardboard, and it was not a short one.

He entered the plane through the open bomb bay doors and quickly confirmed a few of the items Macomber had already checked, including the hydraulic fluid level (just at a half-inch below the red line there on the reservoir attached to the right side of the bomb bay). Climbing up onto the flight deck, he definitely confirmed that the hydraulic pump switch was in the off position, that the fuel selector valves were all properly set to the appropriate engines, and that the fuel gauges were reading properly.

Reynard was now effortlessly moving up to the left seat, having learned to crouch while moving forward on the flight deck so as not to knock his hat off on the bottom of the top turret seat. He made sure all were on board, that they were in position, properly equipped, that there was adequate oxygen in the tanks, and that each had a parachute at his station. His aviation cadet classmate, Roland Jeffries, was the acting navigator and had prepared the course they would fly.

Their intended flight plan was not a difficult course to work up. It was a route well known to the instructors because Kansas City was TWA's headquarters. Since this was an instructional flight designed to acquaint Reynard and Jeffries with the B-24's high altitude flying characteristics, use of the autopilot was not allowed. Nor was use of the radio ranges across New Mexico, Texas, Oklahoma, and Kansas. Their route was "Direct." The air routes where Uncle Sam was going to send these young men weren't served by range stations, light lines, or any other navigation aids other than the intensity of anti-aircraft artillery (AAA) and heavily-armed interceptors whose pilots were dedicated to making sure American crews never had a nice day.

No, this course was done the old-fashioned way — the same way it's done today (in case all the gee-whiz-bang electronics falter): true course, magnetic variation, wind drift correction, and compass correction all blended to provide a magic number to chase on the directional gyro, which, if followed diligently, should result in touching down at the desired destination at precisely the estimated time of arrival.

Jeffries had derived the compass heading of 70 degrees using the winds aloft forecast of 30 knots from 190 degrees at their intended cruising altitude, the magnetic variation of ten degrees east, and their B-24's compass correction figure. Coincidentally, the true course to Kansas City also worked out to 70 degrees. With an indicated airspeed of 200 miles per hour (mph), their groundspeed of 230 mph would put them into Kansas City after three hours and a few minutes flying including turns, climbout and their approach legs into Kansas City.

Vapor trails were not the only trails left by an Army Air Force bomber: the paper trails lasted longer and began much earlier. Macomber, being well-taught by Van Hoozer, had already started the paperwork by completing the upper portion of the ubiquitous Form One, of which a supply was always kept in the plane. That portion was devoted to the particulars on the airplane, i.e. date, station, unit assignment, aircraft type, serial number, engine type and serial numbers. Reynard filled in the remaining blanks which consisted of crew names, serial numbers, and functions. To facilitate completion of the form, the CCTS placed a monthly transition class roster by crew in each B-24. Their crew, number 18 out of the 20 on the course, was recorded as:[1]

| 2G-1 | O-438558 | P | Reynard, C.O. Jr. 2nd Lt., 367th Bm. Sq., Salt Lake City |
| 2G-1 | O-438522 | P | Jeffries, R.L., 2nd Lt., 305th Bm. Grp., Salt Lake City |
| 1E-1 | 11029144 | E | Macomber, P.E., Cpl., 18th Bm. Sq., Pendleton Field, Ore. |
| 1E-1 | 6930619 | R | Peterson, D.M., Cpl., Hq. & Hq. Sq., 310th AB Gp. Salt Lake City, Utah |

Reynard would not record the actual flight time until immediately after arriving at the destination.

Macomber also gave Reynard a Form F (weight and balance) to sign. Its computation was quick since many of the variables, such as bombs and ammunition, were not involved. Finally, Reynard was given a Form One-A which summarized individual engine total time, engine fuel and oil service, and any "squawks" relating to mechanical problems. There were no significant complaints, and the only relevant auxiliary equipment inspection was for the radio equipment because 41-1133 was not utilized in a bombing, photographic or other mission profile.

Prior to his preflight inspection, Reynard had obtained his clearance (Form 23) from the Kirtland Field Operations office. He was responsible for three of its five sections of which the last was merely the destination report which was filled out after arrival in Kansas City. Section A was simply the flight's point of origin after which Reynard filled in section B first by writing in his name, rank, Kirtland Field as the station, CCTS as the unit, and the serial number, 41-1133. Then the crew was listed:

| Blackburn, H.F., TWA | Reynard, C.O., 2nd Lt. |
| Redding, R.O., TWA | Jeffries, R.L., 2nd Lt |
| Ruff, J.G., TWA | Peterson, D.M., Cpl. |
| Van Hoozer, G.E., TWA | Macomber, P.E., Cpl. |

He then went to the meteorology office for his weather briefing which forecast decent flying weather that would improve along the route to Kansas City. As the weather briefer was filling in his portion of the clearance, the ceiling was at 7,000 with scattered to broken clouds, wind east at seven knots, temperature 54 degrees F., dewpoint at

43 degrees, and there was some virga (rain falling and evaporating before reaching the surface) east of the field.[2]

Conditions were expected to deteriorate in New Mexico as the day wore on, but marginal flying weather was one of the realities which occasionally came with the territory. While Reynard and Jeffries had only an Army Air Force Certificate of Instrument Proficiency (a "white" card), Redding had the highest rating, a green card, and had recently been the TWA school's chief of instrument flying. Having a white card would not permit the holder to fly solo on instruments. Had conditions gone below visual (or "contact" minima in those days) with Redding on board, it would have been a good opportunity to accumulate some of the actual instrument flight time needed for a green card.

The final step was getting approval from the clearing authority. Since two of the top authorities were on the flight, approval was readily obtained. Next, Reynard completed section D which contained the flight plan he and Jeffries had worked out and which read along these lines:

**RADIO CALL SIGN:** 133; **TYPE OF AIRCRAFT,** B-24D; **PILOT'S NAME:** C.O. Reynard; **POINT OF DEPARTURE,** ABQ; **FLIGHT,** contact; **ALTITUDE,** 21,000; **ROUTE,** direct; **TO,** KCA; **ALTITUDE,** 8000; **ROUTE,** direct; **TO,** ABQ; **AIRPORT OF FIRST INTENDED LANDING,** KCA (municipal); **TRUE AIRSPEED,** 230; **TRANSMITTING FREQUENCY,** 4495 KC; **PROPOSED TAKEOFF TIME,** 0800 M; **EST. TIME ENROUTE,** 7:00; **ALTERNATE AIRPORT,** Topeka; **HOURS OF FUEL (AT CRUISE),** 12; **INSTRUMENT RATING,** (white); **FLIGHT PRIORITY,** D; **REMARKS (SHOW FIXES WHICH WILL BE REPORTED IF INSTRUMENT FLIGHT),** contact; **TOWER FREQUENCIES, DESTINATION/278** KC - **ALTERNATE/278** KC; **WEATHER CODE RECEIVED** (yes); **MILEAGE TO DESTINATION,** 720; **ALTERNATE,** 780; **PILOT,** Charles O. Reynard, Jr. (signed); **RATING,** pilot.

Having signed his signature four times, Charles Reynard was now about to undertake this, his major cross-country flight required for graduation from transition training. Everybody had already pulled on his fleece-lined, winter flying gear: shearling B-3 jackets, heavy A-3 trousers with suspenders, zip-up rubber boots, gloves, and leather flying helmets. They would fly most of the leg to Kansas City at 21,000 feet where the temperature was five degrees below zero.

Just who occupied which positions on that morning is not known for certain, but the following scenario is most likely, considering the fact that a cross country ferrying flight would normally have been crewed by only four men, and a typical pilot instructional flight would have included up to seven men. Yet on this flight there were eight since there was a "passenger." Reynard, as pilot, sat in the left seat. Harold F. Blackburn, the passenger, was superintendent of the school, and certainly not about to be buckled in at a waist gunner's position or stuffed into the cramped nose section. Blackburn took the right seat, the instructor's position, and, in fact, recorded the morning's flight in his logbook as command pilot time. Robert Redding, as the CCTS operations officer, would not have been relegated to any position off the flight deck. He sat on the jump seat in back of Reynard. Corporal Duane Peterson, as the radio operator, was situated in his own cubicle immediately behind Blackburn.

The remaining men had their choice of location, and none could be described as very comfortable. In truth, the flight engineer's role on a heavy bomber was somewhat nomadic, although his nominal post was at the bulkhead by the back of the flight deck. There was what amounts to a small bench on the left side of the flight deck where engineers could be seated. So, Van Hoozer and Cpl. Macomber alternated between that spot and the waist compartment which is where Jonas Ruff, the copilot instructor (or "first officer") spent much of the morning. While drafty and noisy, the waist compartment does have sufficient room for occupants to stand up, stretch and move about, a cheering prospect when compared to being cooped up like the navigator or bombardier for hours at a time. Jeffries spent most of the flight at the navigator's table in the nose. Nobody, however, was permitted in the nose section during take-offs and landings due to the possibility of nose gear failure or the chance of becoming fouled in the gear strut during its travel up or down.

The navigator and bombardier stations were rather cramped, and reaching those positions from either of two entries (through the nose-wheel well or from the bomb bay crawl space) was awkward at best. The view from up front, however, on a D-model Liberator, was not bad since the power front turret would not appear until the E model came along. And, on 41-1133, there was no bombsight in the lower portion of the nose.

These men, now in position, were about to bring life to this great machine. They were not a "crew" in the traditional heavy bomber meaning of the word since they were not going to take this "ship," to use the vernacular of the day to describe an airplane, on anything except a training mission manned by transients. Actually it wasn't their ship anyway; it was just another of the roughly dozen and a half B-24s assigned to their heavy bomber transition unit.

They were, in one sense, practically a "pick-up crew." They had been flying together for only three weeks and had been aloft about a dozen times. They were killing two birds with one stone by getting in a long cross country training flight and flying Blackburn to a high-level management meeting in Kansas City. Within a few days, the trainees would graduate and be scattered to separate squadron assignments. Yet, within this group of eight men, there were some very strong bonds, a few remarkable coincidences, and several striking similarities.

They could very easily be described as an archetypical "All American crew" since they came from the East and West Coasts, the South, the Mid-west, the Northern Plains, the American West, and one quite literally from the heart of America. They came from farms, a ranch, an airline, academia, and a research lab. Several had only recently drifted into flying while others had pursued it fervently since childhood or adolescence. Their accents reflected their geographic diversity. Only four of them were on active military duty.

The words "handy" and "clever" certainly applied: half of them, including two of the pilots, had at one time (or until quite recently) earned a living as airplane or automobile mechanics. Five were pilots, two of them with less than 300 hours, and the other three with their first logbooks long since filled up with entries including everything from Curtiss Jennies and homebuilt gliders to Ford Trimotors and DC-3s. Only one of them would survive that day, and he would go on to fly the oceans hundreds of times in Lockheed Constellations and later in Boeing 707s many years later.

Their roots to the earth ran deep. The flight engineers, Van Hoozer and Macomber, had gone directly from farms into the service. Redding was still a farmer and rancher whose interests in Nebraska were being looked after by his family and in-laws while he was in Albuquerque. Blackburn had grown up in rural Nebraska, was an active 4H member in high school, and would eventually retire to farming. As a youngster, Ruff had worked at his parents' dairy farm in California, and the Reynard family had a hayfield and still kept a milk cow at home. The radio operator, Duane Peterson, had no direct ties to a farm, although he did grow up in a Minnesota farming community. Jeffries was the only city boy of the lot, but he was well acquainted with the great out-of-doors as a result of having become an Eagle Scout in the mid-1930s.

They were a musical crew, and could quite easily have formed a small dance band complete with singers. Indeed, one of their number had been a professional musician and band leader. Other than flying, half of them would describe music and singing as an important part of their lives.

The time had come. Second Lieutenant Charles Otis Reynard, Jr. was about to call the shots. He had been a second lieutenant for approximately 60 days, but in spite of his youthful appearance was not the type to be rattled by the seniorities seated immediately beside and behind him.

Being shorter than the previous pilot, Reynard repositioned his seat forward and upward using the little cranks on the bottom and side of his seat. Then he readjusted the rudder pedal travel by depressing a lever on the right pedal with the tip of his shoe and moving the assembly to a point which best suited him. Blackburn, a trim man of five feet, ten inches and noticeably taller than Reynard, had already finished readjusting his seat and removed the control lock. As he tied the belt-like lock strap off to the overhead panel so it wouldn't flap in their faces, Reynard confirmed the locking lever for free movement. Then, as Blackburn was tightening his safety belt, he heard an authoritative voice call, "Checklist."

Blackburn reached down to the case at his right, and pulled out a checklist printed on heavy cardstock. To the first two items, Form One and One-A, Reynard replied as checked.

"Brakes."

Reynard depressed the brakes by pushing down the tops of the rudder pedals, noting the pressures as being within limits, and finally depressing the parking brake, and calling out, "Pressure OK, parking brake on."

"Chocks."

Both pilots looked out their respective windows and confirmed that the big wooden chocks were in position.

"Pitot covers."

"Removed." Reynard had confirmed them as removed during the walkaround, but each pilot could easily see that the pitot tube on his side of the nose was uncovered.

"Gas caps."

Van Hoozer and Macomber had visually checked the tanks and tied them off with safety wires. Failure to do so would result in gas siphoning out of the system if not being ignited by hot exhaust. He replied that they were secure.

"Flight controls."

Even before Blackburn could finish the phrase, Macomber had pulled the release on the hatch just in front of the top turret, and was now standing with his head and shoulders out of the airplane looking aft. As Reynard hauled the control wheel all the way back, Macomber loudly said, "Up." The procedure would continue through the full travel of rudders and ailerons, at the end of which Macomber would be queried on the fuel and oil state to which he replied in exact quantities.

Next, Blackburn called for a generator check which both he and Macomber did by looking on the panel at the rear of the flight deck. Reynard couldn't view it easily since he would have to turn his head owllike to see it. The generators were left off until immediately before takeoff to eliminate any problems from faulty relays.

"Carburetor air filters"

"Closed," said Macomber. There was no need for them on that morning. Although the wind was out of the east at eight knots, it was too early for dust to be blowing from the construction projects on the base, and there had been some passing showers only an hour before. Actually, it was shaping up to be a pretty decent morning with only scattered to broken clouds at 7,000 and excellent visibility. The barometer, however, was declining slowly, but steadily.

"Main line and battery."

Since they would start using a battery cart, Blackburn turned on the main line master switch, but left the two battery switches in the off position. Just then, there came a sound reminiscent of a lawn mower engine starting. Moments earlier, Macomber had ducked through the bomb bay bulkhead door into the nose section below the flight deck, and started the gasoline-powered "putt-putt," their auxiliary power unit (APU). The manufacturer of the little engine would enjoy a postwar future in lawn, garden and home equipment; the brand name was Homelite. Because the generators wouldn't generate until turned on just before takeoff (and wouldn't generate below 1700 rpm anyway), using the putt-putt was standard procedure even when starting with a battery cart.

"Auxiliary hydraulic pump."

Macomber turned the auxiliary hydraulic pump switch to on. The auxiliary hydraulic pump would come on at 975 pounds and cut out at 1180 pounds to charge the accumulators. Macomber then confirmed both units as, "On."

"Gyros," Blackburn called.

Lt. Reynard crisply pulled the catch on the directional gyro and artificial horizon, and made a mental note to check how quickly the artificial horizon came to life when the engines were started.

"Instruments."

"On number one," Reynard said as he flicked the AC power switch to bring current to the many engine instruments.

"Automatic pilot."

Reynard ran his right index finger over all switches to make sure the autopilot was definitely off. The B-24's controls were heavy enough let alone having to fight an autopilot.

Deicers and superchargers were then checked off as being off.

"Intercoolers."

"Shutters open." Reynard cycled the switches, listened to the motor running, and returned them to open.

"Pitot heat." Blackburn turned the heat on and simultaneously glanced at the voltmeter to see if there would be a sudden drop.

There was, and he quickly turned the switch off. It was only 56 degrees outside, and should they unexpectedly have to fly in cloud, icing was a possibility; hence the assurance that their airspeed data source wouldn't freeze up on them.

"Cowl flaps."

Reynard cycled the flap controls, and each pilot confirmed the flaps as full open on the two engines for his side of the ship. The subject would come up again in a few minutes since the cowl flaps produced such turbulence that the elevator's effectiveness was reduced (not a desirable trait, especially if one wanted to take off).

While Blackburn started to press the propeller pitch controls forward for increased rpm, Reynard again made sure the supercharger controls were in the off position.

Blackburn called "Mixture" and at the same time he placed his hands over the levers in the idle-cutoff position, and said, "In idle cutoff."

He then confirmed that the wing deicers, prop and carburetor anti-icers were in their off positions.

The magic moment had arrived. Reynard and Blackburn pulled back their windows just as the ground crew chief was walking in from the right wingtip, but maintaining a healthy distance from the engines. He was hauling a heavy fire extinguisher. Blackburn and Reynard yelled almost simultaneously, "Clear prop!" Blackburn quickly raised his hand showing three fingers announcing his intention to start number three engine (the right inner — the one which drove the ship's hydraulic pump) after which he told Reynard, "All clear, guard ready."

Upon copilots fell most of the power management duty. Blackburn had more time in Liberators than anybody on the station, several hundred hours in fact, so the starting procedure was very familiar. He turned on all ignition switches. Reynard cracked all throttles open to about one-third of their travel. Each man had spoken his part in this ritual, "Ignition switches on" and "Throttles cracked." Blackburn turned on the fuel pump, saw the pressure rise to about eight pounds, casually announced that the boost pump was on, and then jabbed the priming button six times while simultaneously pushing the starter energizer switch into the "ACCEL." position which produced a distinct electro-mechanical groaning sound. After allowing the engine to grunt for nearly 30 seconds, Blackburn pushed the switch down into the CRANK position.

The right inner prop started turning slowly at first with its "chur, chur, chur" sounds, and suddenly caught, took hold, and belched great clouds of bluish-white smoke from its trailing exhaust pipe. The moment he felt that the engine was running for sure, Reynard smartly moved the number three mixture control into the auto-lean position and stabilized the rpm at 1000. Jeffries, Ruff and Macomber had just been treated to their first morning ration of exhaust smoke which blew in through the waist compartment hatches and bomb bay doors.

Blackburn turned off the booster pump and quickly confirmed that oil pressure was rising to the proper level.

The starting sequence was repeated for the remaining engines in the order of number four (right outer), two (left inner), and, lastly, one. The fuel booster pumps were turned off, the ground crew disconnected the battery cart, and the fire guard departed after the last engine, the left outer, had been started. Reynard made no attempt to start taxiing since

there was still much to do. Manifold pressure, oil pressure, oil temperature, fuel pressure, and cylinder head temperature readings all had to be
confirmed as being in their proper ranges — all done by Blackburn.
He also occasionally glanced at the tachometers to be sure each was
indicating around 1000 rpm, and then dispatched the remaining copilot
duties by checking carburetor air temperature (yes, well above 15
degrees centigrade), hydraulic brake accumulator pressure (taxiing not
recommended below 950 pounds), outside air temperature, gear warning light on, and compass deviation card in place and signed.

The deicer boots were checked by Blackburn who threw the lever
beneath his instrument panel to the right which produced a rippling, pulsating effect beneath the rubber sections on the leading edges of the
wings, rudder, and horizontal stabilizer. He then firmly returned the
lever to the left and operated the anti-icer rheostat just below the mixture levers on the control pedestal. From the circular slinger rings,
Blackburn observed anti-freeze flowing at the propeller hub.

As Blackburn confirmed the instruments, deicers, and anti-icers as
operating, his thoughts may have drifted back to those days ten years
before when he was a copilot and learning the bomber trade by flying in
the right seat, chasing the engine instrument dials, and thinking about
the time when he would be in the left seat.

Reynard then double-checked the little suction gauge at the lower
left side of the panel for proper reading as Macomber switched the vacuum system between the number one and two engines where the vacuum pumps were located. Finally, he caged and uncaged the directional
gyro and artificial horizon, and, noting their stability, said, "Gyros OK."

Blackburn put his head-set on, reached down to the radio transmitter control box on the back of the center pedestal, turned on the radio,
saw that the selector had been left in voice, then quickly looked up at
the cockpit ceiling to make sure the radio receiver switch was in MCW
(voice), and that channel A and the Kirtland tower frequency, 230 kilocycles (kc) hadn't been changed. With "Command" selected on the interphone jackbox at his right, he picked up the microphone and called the
tower for a radio check.

"Army One-Three-Three, time now, 0756, Kirtland altimeter zero-
zero-one, out," came the reply.

Reynard checked the little window on the instrument face and

rotated the knob to the setting to compensate for the change in barometric pressure since the Liberator had last been flown. The altimeter
pointer needles swung to Kirtland's elevation above sea level, 5,300 feet.
Reynard looked at his watch and then pressed the bail-out alarm bell
which produced a quick response from the waist compartment indicating that it had been heard. Reynard and Blackburn then signaled the
groundcrew to remove the chocks.

"Kirtland Tower, Army One-Three-Three, over."

"One-Three-Three, Kirtland Tower, over"

"Tower, One-Three-Three at CCTS ramp for taxi clearance, over."

"One-Three-Three, active runway one-seven, taxi northeast ramp,
hold short runway one-seven, altimeter zero-zero-one."

"One-Three-Three, wilco."

Just short of one-seven, Reynard stopped the ship at the bend in the
taxiway leading up to the runway.

National Archives

*Late spring 1942. Formation flying was the exception rather than the rule at
Kirtland Field's Combat Crew Training School.*

"Crew takeoff positions."

Reynard now started cranking the trim wheels into their takeoff settings: two degrees up for the elevator, three degrees right for the rudders, and ailerons set at neutral. The checklist now came into play again.

"Mixture."

"Auto rich," came the reply as Blackburn moved the four levers into position.

Reynard advanced the throttles again until the tachometers were reading 1500 rpm at which point Blackburn cycled the props from full high to low to high again by moving the gang switch below the lights which winked on and off as full travel was achieved. Reynard slowly advanced and retarded the four supercharger controls just to the left of the throttles. Finally, Blackburn cycled the wing flaps for full travel and confirmed it on his flap position indicator.

"Turbos checked."

"Props and flaps OK."

"Props"

"High rpm."

Reynard nudged the number four engine throttle forward until the tach read 1500 rpm and glanced past Blackburn who now was switching the magneto switch from right to both to left to both, and watching for any significant drop in rpm. Since there was less than a 40 rpm drop, Blackburn said, "Number four mag OK."

Reynard now advanced the number four throttle wide open. While keeping his right hand on the throttle, he moved the number four turbo level forward very slowly until he noted a rise in manifold pressure. Then, he moved it forward again until the manifold pressure read 47 inches, checked that rpm was not more than 2,700, tightened the turbo control lock, backed the throttle off until the tach was reading 1200 rpm, and finally put the mixture into auto lean. The procedure was repeated for the remaining three engines moving from right to left.

Now they were buttoning up the ship. Macomber, who had been looking out the top emergency escape just aft of the cockpit, closed and locked the hatch. Jeffries checked the aft entrance hatch and Reynard closed the bomb bay doors.

"Kirtland tower, Army One-Three-Three, holding short one-seven, over."

"One-Three-Three, Kirtland Tower, position and hold, departing traffic over."

"One-Three-Three, roger."

Liberator 41-1133 was hardly the only ship waiting for takeoff. In fact, Kirtland was a very busy field, not only because the majority of the CCTS' Liberators would be taking off, but also because of the many twin-engine AT-11s based at the Air Corps Advanced Flying School which was located further down the main north-south runway. That school was not for pilot training; it was a bombardier training school. Among the pilots flying the Beech twins were about a dozen of Reynard's former associates who had graduated from advanced flight at Mather Field in California just two months earlier.

Reynard advanced the throttles and moved the ship forward, then quarter turned to his left and taxied onto the main runway turning left slowly until it was aimed directly down the runway. He quickly tweaked the directional gyro knob until the number 170 (the runway's magnetic heading) was centered beyond the heading bug and took another look at the altimeter to see that its reading matched the field's elevation.

"Flaps 20."

"Flaps 20," Blackburn replied after pulling the handle on the left side of the master console.

Macomber was ready for the next command, "Generators on, APU off," and turned on all four generators. He continued past the bulkhead, stepped down, turned, and crawled into the bay beneath the flight deck to turn off the putt-putt.

Reynard continued, "Booster pumps on," and after Blackburn's reply he moved the prop gang switch all the way forward until he got four green lights. Then there was a final check for free movement of the controls during which Blackburn placed the cowl flaps into a position about one-third open (so as to avoid tail buffeting on takeoff). Blackburn was completing the final act before Reynard finished the checklist items by shoving all four mixture controls into auto rich.

Although they were taking off in a crosswind (with a slight tailwind component), it was not a major factor. Pilots preferred one-seven for several reasons. It was the longest runway, and it faced into relatively flat land along the banks of the Rio Grande River, but not mountains or the city of Albuquerque. Losing power on takeoff was always on a prudent pilot's mind, and it was far better to set it down in something other than a city street or rising terrain. Runway eight was avoided for takeoffs since a hospital was located not too far from the end of the runway.

"Takeoff positions," Reynard repeated.

"One-Three-Three, Kirtland Tower, cleared for takeoff, wind now one-zero-zero at eight, over."

"One-Three-Three, is cleared for takeoff. Army One-Three-Three is off at zero, eight, eleven, out"

Reynard's left hand now firmly gripped the control yoke and his right clutched the throttles. His eyes met Blackburn's. The 23-year old newly commissioned pilot and the 40-year old veteran shared a split second bond of boyish glee, deadly determination, awesome responsibility, unbridled enthusiasm, and a sense of heightened awareness that stopped just short of apprehension.

Macomber, poised between the backs of the pilots' seats, knelt on the scratched-up metal surface of the flight deck floor.

Reynard released the brakes and slowly, but firmly, "gave'r the gun," starting each of the four 1,200 horsepower engines to bellow at full fury, and focused intently on the runway ahead. Peterson leaned back in his little stool in the radio compartment cubicle and was craning his neck around to look forward, too. Blackburn was scanning the engine instruments — almost inhaling their many readings in a single breath although there was a wealth of data to monitor and comprehend — all the while stealing frequent glances ahead and to the front quarters of the Liberator.

Had a physician been on board to record blood pressure, the readings would have been absolutely hypertensive.

Outside, the Pratt & Whitney crescendo by then was overpowering. 4,800 Volga boatmen had just been goosed, and they were, in a word, roaring. But, not much, to speak of, was happening yet in terms of motion. Liberator 41-1133 was going to poke along and eat up about a football field or two worth of runway before hitting its stride. And then 2nd Lt. Charles O. Reynard, Jr. would be presiding over a beast that covered territory like a scalded cat.

Had somebody told this young pilot, as little as three years previously, that he would be the skipper of the most lethal bomber in the Army Air Corps and that he would be taking it overseas to drop 8,000 pounds of bombs on enemy targets twenty-five times, Reynard probably would have politely offered an opinion quite to the contrary.

# II

# CHARLIE

Lord, guard and guide the men who fly
Through the great spaces of the sky.
Be with them traversing the air
In darkening storms or sunshine fair.

From *Lord, Guard And Guide The Men Who Fly*
Mary C.D. Hamilton

Most flying actually borders on the monotonous — it's not all aerobatics, takeoffs, landings, or skimming cloud decks in the moonlight. Although pilots do have to monitor the engines and navigation all the time, there is that constant tendency to think about what lies beyond the horizon, especially when it is as featureless as eastern New Mexico, Oklahoma, and Kansas. For Lt. Charles Reynard, extending the east-northeast heading that morning would have come close to taking him home to a small town about 40 miles below Lake Erie's Ohio shore.

Reynard came from Hiram, a remarkable little college town roughly 30 miles southeast of Cleveland. Named for his father, Charles Otis Reynard, Jr. was born on January 31, 1919, placing him eighth in a large family with 13 children. The name is pronounced "Rennerd" with an even accenting of both syllables; not RAY-nard, nor Ruh-NAARRHD.

Hiram is in rolling countryside along the northeast border of Portage County. It is the home of academically well-respected Hiram College, certainly a model of excellence among small colleges. The school dates back to its founding in 1850 by members of Hiram Christian Church (Disciples of Christ). About one in three of its roughly 900 students goes on to graduate school, and it is among the 13 percent of American colleges and universities with a Phi Beta Kappa chapter.

Today, the town is larger than it was when Reynard went away in 1939 — mainly due to the increased college enrollment which, in turn, expanded the number of buildings and faculty which has also augmented the town's population. The first time visitor to Hiram is struck by the little town on the hill having practically no business district. Hiram's buildings are almost exclusively institutional and residential. Strip malls, video stores, fast food emporia, etc. are all located in nearby Garretsville and Aurora which leave Hiram with a unique character, unfettered with typical, municipal impedimenta.

The town is one from which Norman Rockwell would easily have found inspiration and many subjects. On Memorial Day, there is a parade, and, in the cemetery, the roll of those who perished in service to their country is called. The cemetery is located only a few hundred yards from the Reynard home. Along these hills and creeks, "Junior" Reynard played as a child, and followed an older brother's example by becoming a Boy Scout. Summer camp was at the then Western Reserve Council's Camp Skudiweekuik, and there were cookouts and tent camping with fellow Scouts around Hiram, including making their own lean-tos and roasting hot dogs on sticks.

Reynard's brother George became an Eagle Scout, and Junior advanced to Star rank before graduating from Troop 62. He was a very busy young man in high school: a newspaper boy who also delivered laundry, did well academically, and played all sports. It would be very accurate to describe him as "the clean cut boy next door." He was also very bright, and was advanced a grade ahead of his age group shortly after entering elementary school.

By the time college came along, the "Junior" nickname had given way to "Charlie." With sandy hair, peaches and cream complexion, and blue eyes, he was of average height. On campus at Hiram College, he was a big man, very big. In spite of his many accomplishments and collegiate distinctions, he was very down to earth and did not have a raging ego typical of some campus BMOCs.

Reynard would probably have objected to being called a BMOC; humility was one of his trademarks. It was said of him that he didn't have a jealous bone in his body. It is no stretch to say that Charles Otis Reynard, Jr. truly lived his life according to the Scout Oath and Law. The late Ed Radtke, one of Charlie's roommates during primary flying school at Oxnard, California, remembered Reynard as a "prince of a fellow" —

the kind who sadly gives credence to the observation that all too often the good die young, while those less pure in mind and heart survive to old age.

Similarly, another of Charlie's classmates from basic and advanced flying schools, Ralph Lessor, recalls Reynard's loss as "Such a waste of a talented young man. One can only speculate on just what twist of fate took so many, so young, and spared others."

Reynard loved his college and served it well. His father had been on the staff at Hiram, but had left to start an insurance business in nearby Warren. Both of Reynard's parents were Hiram graduates as are most of his brothers and sisters.

The September 30, 1938, issue of Hiram's weekly college newspaper, *The Advance*, carried a bold headline announcing Charles Reynard as the newly elected senior class president.

On page two of the newspaper, there was a prophetic editorial which, in many ways, spoke to all college students across the land and many of the men Reynard would meet as an aviation cadet.[1] The editorial focused on the most likely outcome of the recently concluded Munich talks and exhorted students to pay more attention to world affairs whose outcomes would certainly not bypass Hiram College in its "rustic setting."

At the time, Reynard belonged to a small circle of bright students, an informal discussion group which usually focused on religion and philosophy. One of this group's resolutions was not to take up arms unless the United States was attacked first.

The publication date of the Munich-inspired editorial, September 30, was ironic in that exactly three years later, to the day, Reynard reported to basic flying school, having joined up a full six months before Pearl Harbor.

The 1939 yearbook shows that Charlie was also an officer in nearly all campus service, student government, religious, and musical organizations. A tenor and trumpet player, he was a frequent soloist in college choral groups and with his church choir.

He was a gifted athlete, particularly in basketball and baseball. His size prevented him from becoming a strong football player, but, as a junior, he played on the team anyway in spite of seeing underclassman getting more action on the field while he waited on the bench. It was typical of him since he thought the "discipline would be good for me." He was a very clean-living young man who did not smoke, drink or swear.

He was also an excellent writer of essays and poems. Being observant, inquisitive, adventurous, and enthusiastic were among the qualities that served him well whether he was writing about a hitchhiking trip, some of Hiram's more colorful characters, or the sparkling dew in an early morning meadow. One of his works has become a Hiram classic:

*My Hiram*

Far away amidst the gently rolling
    hillocks of my home
There are many friendly voices calling me,
They enchant me with their laughter
    and their songs fill my soul
Oh, my Hiram, let me live again in thee.

CHORUS:

Oh Hiram, never leave me,
Never leave my mind:
Thy sacred friendly spirit
Be in my heart enshrined.

When sometimes I sit and ponder o'er
    life's relentless drive
And its burden sends away all peace
    and calm.
Then great floods of loving memories
    rush into my troubled soul
Oh my Hiram, heal me with thy soothing balm.

When I come to face the valley of
    the shadow that we fear
When my journey far from home is
    nearly through
May they take me to the resting place
    where life and love are one.
Oh my Hiram, as you held me, keep me too.

His record at Hiram College, from which he graduated with great distinction in 1939, earned him a scholarship to graduate school. At Harvard. His master's degree, earned in June 1941, was in sociology, not surprising considering his interest in people and their welfare. It would have been a good springboard into nearly any field he would have chosen. As he was caught up in the war, his writings reveal a young man, like many others in his circumstances, somewhat uncertain about the future. He was undecided about what would become his life's work, but he did know that it would not be in business management.

About the short term, there was no indecision. While at Harvard, he had met and fallen in love with a young lady from Antrim, New Hampshire, Elizabeth Fellowes.[2] She had entered Radcliffe College in 1935, and had been preceded there by her two sisters. Elizabeth's father followed mining as a career and was a graduate of Bates College in Maine, class of 1902. Her mother had graduated from the New England Conservatory of Music in Boston.

Reynard had also resolved to become a good military pilot, a decision that puzzled some of his contemporaries in Hiram with whom he had engaged in pre-war discussions about the advantages of neutrality.

Reynard had showed no particular, previous interest in aviation and had entered the military well before Pearl Harbor. That the United States would become involved in war was obvious to anybody in 1941. With the draft a reality that year, Reynard had taken the same attitude as thousands of other young college-trained men, and that was to do something about it before Uncle Sam put him in an infantry platoon. As to the broader issue of good versus evil, Reynard quite simply saw serving his country as the right thing to do.

That he chose aviation may have surprised some, but those who knew him best would have recognized another of his traits surfacing: curiosity laced with a sense of adventure. Upon his graduation from high school in 1935, he had an opportunity to take an extended holiday as the traveling companion of his high school principal, a man who used much of his summer vacation for enriching travel.

Years later, Charlie would write of the trip as an opportunity to "wriggle out from under the constrictive influence of parental authority; to face the world alone, with only his hands, feet and his personality to help him." The other reason was to test what some teachers had told him: that high school graduation was a ticket into a gloomy world.

Hiram College Archives

*Charles Reynard '39, President of the senior class, Hiram College.*

Charlie wanted to see if Americans were as hospitable to strangers as he had read people in other lands might be to visitors.

The trip was memorable both for the places they visited and, significantly, how Charlie toured those east coast cities. He was in the company of the older man on such stops as Gettysburg and Philadelphia. The principal had some academic matters to attend to in Washington, and that left Charlie free to roam the city. He attended a Senate session and was listening to Gerald P. Nye when the chamber's attention was diverted by the next speaker, the Kingfish, Huey Long. Charlie was so unimpressed and oppressed (wilting in DC's midday heat and humidity) that he had to get out of town. Hitchhiking was the only way. He returned the next day with the confidence that came from having ridden 252 miles, seen Endless Caverns, earned 50 cents, enjoyed two nice dinners, and made a half dozen new friends.

Charlie soloed New York: took the subway around town and saw Wall Street, China Town, the Bowery, the docks, Columbia University, Broadway, and enough of New York to convince him that he had to get out of town on his own again. He was about to discover southern New England. Sleeping at YMCAs and Travelers' Aid Societies, he visited Cape Cod and Yale University.

He interviewed a Bridgeport journalist whose work he admired and was rewarded with a pleasant lunch. While in Hartford, he had the presence of mind to delve into the records of the Connecticut Land Company which was the original owner of much of his hometown Hiram's real estate.

Charlie's travels extended into Massachusetts where he visited Harvard University before his New England journey took a most interesting turn. He became a barker and traveled with a circus for a week during which time he went as far west as Saratoga, New York. Charlie's memories of circus fare aromas (hot dogs, Crackerjacks, and orangeade) remained with him for years after the experience. That he was a resourceful young man was clear: he left Hiram with $7 in his pocket, and returned weeks later, again with $7.

Reynard took that journey at age 16. His ever youthful countenance gave him an appearance then of not being a day over 14. While at Harvard six years later, and as the European war was into its second year, he looked back on that New England adventure as a parallel to his present circumstances. From a letter to the President of Hiram College:

> You may remember how undecided I was in college as to a vocation, and it was no different in high school. I've never known what I wanted to do as my life's work. Teaching in a classroom has never appealed to me, but neither has the prospect of taking over Dad's insurance business. What's the matter? I wish I knew. It's the same feeling I had on my hitch-hiking trip through New England in 1935 — always wanting to go up the next road whether it's a U. S. Route One or a deserted bi-way. So I see in this work in the Air Corps a chance to take a new road. It may lead to Devil's Den. As long as it doesn't take me over Forty Foot Falls I expect I'll have to be satisfied. I hope it leads to Dingle Dell.[3]

The Liberator started to veer slightly to the left, and Charlie ever so gingerly depressed the right brake pedal to return to a straight heading. Had it happened before he had advanced the throttles to maximum take-off power, he would have shoved the number one throttle ahead of the others to get them back on the runway centerline.

If the drift occurred again, he would have pushed a rudder pedal for correction since they would, at that point, have been going fast enough for the rudders to affect their heading.

Charlie had one hand on the control yoke and one hand on the throttles. Blackburn was monitoring the engine instruments and placing his left hand at the base of the throttle levers to make sure they would not creep backward — they wouldn't set the friction locks just yet.

"Seventy! Eighty! Ninety!" Macomber announced loudly as he read the progress of the airspeed indicator pointer. At ninety, Lt. Reynard slowly pulled the control wheel back, felt pressure, and pulled it back enough to raise the nosewheel off the runway. Here, he held the control yoke in position, and at about 120 mph, the B-24 broke ground. Reynard confidently maintained that attitude until the speed had built up to the point where he was comfortable in lowering the nose slightly for more speed. He cranked the trim wheel to ease the burden of pulling on the control yoke.

Charlie was now starting to glance at some of the primary air data instruments. The vertical speed indicator (VSI) showed a positive rate of climb, his airspeed indicator was moving closer to 150 mph, and the little airplane symbol on the artificial horizon was a fraction of an inch above the horizon line.

"Gear up," Charlie called while giving a vertical hitchhiking gesture with his right hand. As soon as Blackburn pressed the safety button on top of the gear handle and shoved the handle forward, Charlie depressed the brake pedals to stop the rapidly spinning tires as they retracted into the gear wells between the engines.

They were still at maximum takeoff power, climbing at 160, and well clear of the field when Charlie reduced power by pulling turbos one and four back until the manifold pressure read 46 inches and then repeating the procedure for the inboard engines, two and three. Blackburn followed this by reducing revs, and looked over at Charlie who said, "Flaps," while cranking the elevator trim wheel backward to maintain 160 mph.

As soon as Blackburn had retracted the flaps, Reynard asked Macomber to open the bomb bay doors, turn off the auxiliary hydraulic pump, and then close the bomb bay doors leaving only a crack open for ventilation. Blackburn then slowly flicked off the fuel booster pump switches one at a time and, seeing no drop in pressure, then looked at the cylinder head temperature gauges which were running over the recommended 260 degrees C. Being reluctant to open the cowl flaps beyond the trailing position, Blackburn asked Charlie to increase the airspeed which was done by slightly retrimming the ship.

They had a long climb ahead of them, and for the best average rate of climb, Charlie set the power for 43 inches of manifold pressure, called for 2550 rpm, retrimmed for 150 mph, and maintained his runway heading of 170 degrees.

The engine noise, even with the crew wearing earphones, sounded like certain sections of a symphony orchestra at war with each other and the listening audience as well. It was not a monotonous drone (yet), but an aggravating, dissonant roaring caused by the props having not yet been synchronized. The sound was that of the tubas and basses playing a loud, limited, and maddeningly repetitive melody of deep, sour notes that alternately sped up and slowed down. "Ruuuuuuuuuuhm, ruuuu-uhm, ruuuuhm, ruuhm, rum-rum-rum-rum-rumma, rummma, ruuuuuhm, ruuuhm, rumma-rum-rum-rum-rum-rumma, ruuhm, ruhhmma-rum, ruhm." Unless something was done about this, they would all go slightly mad by the time they got to Kansas City.

The remedy was to quickly synchronize the props, another of the copilot's duties. Charlie was about to see the procedure accomplished by the maestro who quickly nudged the prop switches until the tachometer readings were identical and the engines started sounding like they were smoothing out. Blackburn then looked past Charlie to the images of the left engine propeller arcs and started "chasing shadows." Since the outer engine's prop image appeared to be moving inward (or faster than the inboard engine's), Blackburn tweaked the number one engine prop toggle switch until the propeller image appeared to stand still.

*Second Lieutenant Charles O. Reynard, Jr., photographed in Albuquerque, early April 1942.*

Looking to his right, he repeated the procedure and the resulting noise was reduced from a cacophonic roaring to a smoothed out din. Blackburn had nailed it on the first try as only a past master of the trade could. More commonly, once each engine had been synchronized with its immediate mate, the two pairs of engines then had to be synchronized to drive the noisy, nonsynchronous demons away.

Kirtland Field, along the Santa Fe River and within the shadow of the Sandia mountains, was now several miles behind them. Charlie maintained the runway heading to gain more altitude before making a downwind departure to the northeast which would take him right over the Tijeras Pass beacon east of Albuquerque. This departure avoided the heavy traffic which would interfere with a right turn and climbout directly overhead which was also the regular eastbound instrument departure (after making a standard procedure turn off the west leg of the Albuquerque radio range). The heavy traffic was that from Kirtland's bombardier school whose many AT-11 trainers swarmed to the bombing ranges west of Albuquerque day and night.

The Tijeras Pass beacon, at roughly 7,500 feet and usually overflown at 9,500 feet, was located not far from the old route 66 and situated between Sandia Crest and other peaks in the Sandias east of Albuquerque. They were climbing around 750 feet per minute. It would take them all of a quarter-hour to reach their cruise altitude.

"Pilot to crew, coming up on 10,000, going on oxygen now. Fuel pumps." Charlie's intercom call was made just a few minutes before reaching the pass.

Blackburn reached down and flicked on the electric boost pumps. Vapor lock could be a problem with the engine driven pumps at altitude, so the boost pumps would be left on until they were well into their descent for Kansas City. The snow-covered top of Sandia Crest, at nearly 11,000 feet, was passing just off their left wingtip. Soon, they would climb through a thin layer of broken to scattered cloud before emerging into brilliant sunlight.

Once clear of the mountains, Charlie took up the heading of 70 degrees. Soon, he reached his cruising altitude and continued climbing right on up through 21,000. This was not an inadvertent mistake; rather, it was the best way to quickly establish cruise speed. Charlie then shoved the wheel forward to return to 21,000, and the speed quickly exceeded 200 mph. After retrimming, Reynard and Blackburn set up the power for cruise by putting the mixture controls into auto-lean, pulling the turbo levers back for 32 inches, and synchronizing the props again at 2200 rpm.

Van Hoozer and Macomber then started to make the first of seven walkaround inspections of the airplane they would make that morning. Van Hoozer left the flight deck by stepping down onto the catwalk that ran the length of the double-sectioned bomb bay and walking aft, held onto the bomb rack supports for stability.

It was drafty and terribly cold. Reaching the end of the catwalk, he stepped up into the waist gunners' compartment, but immediately had to swing himself around the belly turret support frame which, for all practical purposes, almost blocked entry into the waist compartment. At least he could stand up there and look out the waist hatches for a thorough, visual check of the engine nacelles, turbos, and cowl flaps for any sign of leaking oil, fuel, or hydraulic fluid.

"Pilot to crew. We're at cruising altitude, set regulators for 21,000 thousand. Crew check in."

One by one, they all checked in after setting their regulators for the established altitude. Van Hoozer and Macomber weren't plugged into any outlets. Rather, they were carrying little green, portable oxygen bottles into which they had locked the hoses leading from their oxygen masks. Returning to the flight deck, Van Hoozer again paused in the bomb bay to make sure nothing was amiss. The inspection would have been hampered had the bays been full of their intended cargo, i.e. 8,000 pounds of high explosive. But, since this was a training mission, the bomb bay exposed many of the ship's vital organs and the core of its circulatory system. For here, beyond the maze of hydraulic and fuel system piping, the auxiliary hydraulic pump, hydraulic reservoir, fuel drains, fuel gauge shutoff valves, fuel selector shutoff and crossover valves, and hydraulic pump were located. All was well.

The time was about 8:25 a.m. They were indicating 200 mph, on top of some thin, scattered to broken clouds, and flying a heading of 70 degrees magnetic at 21,000 feet.

The young man in the pilot's seat had less than 250 hours total flying time. The professional aviator to his right, TWA Captain Harold Fredric Blackburn, Superintendent of the Four-Engine/CCTS operation, would record his 7,112th hour of flying time with that flight on April 22, 1942.[4]

# III

# BLACKIE

The man to Reynard's right, the man who was really the aircraft commander that morning, would live a long and very full life. He would attribute some of that to good luck, but much more to working hard at his trade and the discipline that makes great flyers. Harold F. Blackburn, ever the realist, felt that a pilot was not as good as his last landing, but only as good as his next one. He was considered by his peers to be among the very best of flyers.

Harold Blackburn logged over 26,000 hours, crossed the Atlantic more than 750 times, and flew over 6,500,000 air miles in a career which made him one of TWA's best known and most respected pilots ever.[1]

He was on a first name basis with the great names of the Golden Age of American aviation — Jimmy Doolittle, Charles Lindbergh, Roscoe Turner, Amelia Earhart, and many others. No German interceptors' bullets or anti-aircraft artillery ever found his plane nor did he ever put so much as a single dent in any aircraft in a lifetime of flying.

On that fateful April 22, 1942, Blackburn ("Hal" to acquaintances and "Blackie" to close friends) was just a few months past his 40th birthday and poised for a major change in his work with TWA. The impending assignment was partially responsible for the flight to Kansas City since the Army was about to take over all four-engine transition training itself. The TWA operation in Albuquerque was to be shut down in a few weeks, and all aircraft transferred to the new Four-Engine School at Smyrna, Tennessee. The last class of pilots graduated at Kirtland, all 40 of them, were not sent to Combat or Ferry Commands, but to Training Command as B-24 instructor pilots.

That change was about to move Blackburn into a new dimension at TWA: international operations. It would be an interesting path for the slender redhead originally from Urbana, Illinois. He was born on Christmas Day, 1901, the second in a family of four boys. His father, a dentist with an adventurous streak, moved the family to western Nebraska, to the town of Mitchell, between Scottsbluff and the Wyoming border. The elder Blackburn also became a local retail businessman, mayor, postmaster, and school board president.

The drive rubbed off on young Hal who ran a trapline for muskrats, worked as a store clerk, served as a chauffeur for a local physician, and picked up more change as a musician in a band. He started as a piano player and eventually became a drummer. Blackburn also was president of his senior class and a member of the 4-H. Like other members of the crew, Hal Blackburn had a mind for mechanical things, a trait which showed early when he won a 4-H contest with an "automated chicken coop" of his own design.

When he was 17 years old, the flying bug bit, and bit hard. He and a friend had driven to Alliance, Nebraska, to watch an airshow put on by a group of barnstormers — all WWI veterans. Blackburn was enthralled. The loops, rolls, clattering engines, leather jackets, scarves, and whole works made him decide that he had to be a pilot, although he had yet to step into an airplane.

Several months later, his chance arrived when a barnstormer came to Scottsbluff. Blackburn was hooked after his 20-minute flight. Since he had been the last passenger, Blackburn begged the pilot to let him sit in the airplane where he could just soak it in all the more. The barnstormer, a WWI veteran, was none other than "Slonnie," Ira Sloniger, who would become one of the first air mail pilots and eventually the number one seniority pilot at American Airlines.

Blackburn was now possessed by flying, but unfortunately he had to put it on the backburner. First, there was college. That was at Colorado A&M, but his college days were cut short by a dramatic downturn in the elder Blackburn's fortunes. Hal Blackburn now found himself out of college and working in Mitchell to help the family regain its financial footing. Blackburn started working as a mechanic at the local Ford dealership and then, being quite articulate, went into the showroom as a salesman.

Fortunately (or unfortunately), another barnstormer flew into town and then out of town with a hundred and fifty of Blackburn's dollars. From this flyer, Blackburn learned that Curtiss JN-4s (the immortal Curtiss "Jenny") were being sold in their original crates down at Love Field in Dallas for only $500. To sweeten the deal, ten hours of instruction were included. Blackburn promptly resigned from the Ford agency, headed for Dallas, and learned that there was one catch: the engine, at $250, was extra. Returning to Mitchell, he found that prospective backers for his aeronautical enterprise were unimpressed, thus forcing Blackburn to reevaluate his career plans.

The result was his formation of a dance band which operated quite successfully for the next five years. His group played at dances, private parties, and theaters in the mountain states and western plains. Blackburn also daylighted as a clothing store salesman. By 1928, he had continued with flying lessons and prospered to the extent that the time was again ripe to make flying his life's work. He promptly sold the band to his banjo player and set off for Los Angeles to enlist in the United States Army Air Corps, not knowing that only six hundred of the 9,000 who applied annually were accepted.

He passed the physical and aptitude exams, but failed mathematics. Undaunted, and filled with that burning desire for wings, he became a mechanic at Spartan Field in Los Angeles and enrolled at the University of Southern California. While working at Spartan, he also earned his pilot's license. In 1930, with a better grasp of trigonometry, he passed the exams and started primary flight training along with 131 other cadets at March Field, Riverside, California. Of the only 28 cadets who would graduate, Blackburn came out top man.

The balance of his cadet instruction was taken at Kelly Field, San Antonio, Texas, where he met and became engaged to a local belle, Martha Bondurant. She was engaged to a young doctor at the time of their meeting; Blackburn always maintained in later years that it was his

Photo courtesy of *FLYING* Magazine via Wayne Lincourt, Associate Publisher

*The April 1943 cover of FLYING featured a CCTS liberator as flown by Hal Blackburn in early 1942.*

classy uniform with Sam Browne belt that had first turned her head.

At Kelly, he flew the PW-1 pursuit trainer and later the Curtiss P-6 and Boeing P-9 fighters before moving to bombers and the Martin B-5. In June 1931, Blackburn started duty with a posting back to March Field where he flew the B-2 bomber (military version of the Curtiss Condor transport) with the 11th Bombardment Squadron, and also flew the first B-4 Keystone bombers. The 11th Bombardment Squadron was a well-respected unit which had been formed during World War One when it served in France. The 11th was not popular with the Navy since it had been under General Billy Mitchell's command and participated in his highly successful bombing trials against warships in 1923.

Blackburn took part in the relief missions flown to Indian villages in northern Arizona during the terrible blizzards of January 1932. Indian communities were completely cut off, and the only way to get food in was to "bomb" them. Based alternately in Winslow and Holbrook, and with no navigational aids or proper maps, the squadron located the villages by carrying Indian scouts who could point the way. For that work, his squadron was awarded the coveted Mackay Trophy, the Air Corps' highest peacetime award.

Blackburn and Martha were married the following month and were looking forward to gaining a permanent commission in the regular Army in June when his year of active duty was up. But, the Air Corps was shrinking, not expanding, and Lt. Blackburn was granted a reserve commission and placed on inactive duty. He scoured the country looking for gainful, aeronautical employment. The airlines were letting pilots go in droves, so Blackburn leased a Shell service station in California's San Fernando Valley. The Blackburns fixed the place up and grew it to the extent that Hal bought the station in six months. He kept his flying hand in by instructing at a nearby airport, but he still chased the dream of flying for the airlines.

In 1934, the Army started flying the mail, but rejected Blackburn's application for active duty since the service was interested only in pilots with substantial instrument flying experience on their new air mail routes. By 1934, the airlines were starting to grow again. TWA had bought a number of the new DC-2s, forerunner to the legendary DC-3. By 1935, the line had bought ten more DC-2s to supplement the 20 they had acquired in 1934, although they still flew a few Ford Trimotors and single-engine mail planes. Blackburn tried again with the growing TWA through a friend from Nebraska days. TWA, with its modern fleet of passenger planes, was hiring to increase its pilot employment by 50 percent. Hal, anxious for more income since he then had a growing family, was somewhat over the maximum age for copilot hires, but still got the job in mid-1935.

First stationed in Kansas City and then in Los Angeles, he was based at Newark in June, 1936. In 1938, he began the first of the many "special assignments" that would characterize his entire TWA career. Leading off these operations was flying a series of secret, country-wide charters for J. Edgar Hoover and his FBI staff. Although TWA seniority dated from employment date, pilot seniority started from the first flight as pilot-in-command which was July 24, 1938 in Blackburn's case.

In February 1940, a significant promotion came — to check pilot including a change in station, from Newark to Los Angeles. On April 1, 1941, the second special assignment started when he was posted as Superintendent of Instrument Flight Training at TWA's unpublicized training operation in Albuquerque. TWA's Albuquerque school was set up to train civilian ferry pilots in the B-24 Liberator and Lockheed Hudson bombers which were being flown across the Atlantic to the Royal Air Force (RAF). The actual ferry operation was under control of the Royal Canadian Air Force (RCAF). Blackburn was hardly a stranger to Albuquerque and had flown through there regularly as a copilot on TWA's Kansas City to Los Angeles route in 1935.

Hudson and Liberator orientation in Albuquerque ceased several months before America's entry into the war when the Canadians assumed training responsibility for ferry pilots. By then, however, Blackburn had his hands full since the school had begun to train American Army Air Force Ferry Command pilots on the B-24.

Blackburn's talent was recognized with swift promotions. He had gone to Eagle Nest as the instrument flying chief. On September 1, 1941, he was appointed Operations Manager, and in January, 1942, he became superintendent. TWA had bigger plans for him.

Blackburn was managing his flying time wisely in Albuquerque and still learning about navigation. By 1942, he was less involved with the early stages of transitioning pilots to the B-24, leaving the introductory takeoffs, landings, and routine airwork to other instructors. In addition to training his instructors, he frequently flew with students on long cross country flights which he used to learn more about what would later be called "pressure pattern flying." This technique, in which he was a pioneer, involved flying what might not be the shortest route between two very distant points, but using high and/or low pressure systems instead to take advantage of tailwinds.

Thus, on a very long cross country, he might fly with the clockwise winds of a high pressure system for the first leg and then transition to the counterclockwise winds of a low. Rather than fly a straight line, his course would include curves. The B-24, with its superchargers, oxygen system and great range, was the perfect vehicle with which to experiment. The Liberator's great altitude capability allowed him to tap into the high winds aloft which are not always blowing in the same direction as surface winds. Thus, he was not forced to make frequent fuel stops.

Although Blackburn's logbook shows that the flight to Kansas City on April 22nd was not flown near the Liberator's maximum ceiling, his longer flights with Army students to such cities as New York and Washington were frequently flown at 30,000 feet or more.

Liberator 41-1133 droned on. The flight engineers made their half-hourly inspection tours and advised Reynard that nothing untoward had been observed. Blackburn had long since closed the cowl flaps and was

From the Robert Blackburn collection

*After the CCTS ceased operations, Hal Blackburn, shown here in Air Transport Command uniform, became the Superintendent of Flight Operations for TWA's Intercontinental Division in mid-1942.*

making occasional notes on engine readings: oil pressure, temperature, and cylinder head temperatures. Macomber, under Van Hoozer's guidance, recorded the fuel system readings.

This flight was devoid of any idle chatter on the intercom. While a crew which had been flying together for several months in an operational bomb squadron might have used the intercom sparingly for occasional chit-chat or light banter, '1133's radio conversations were all business, and not just because the crew had so few hours in the air together. The school's top brass was on board, and Blackburn, in particular, was known for rigid cockpit discipline.

Their first waypoint was Las Vegas, New Mexico. Here, Reynard transmitted a position report, the first of several he would make to Civil Aeronautics Commission radio range stations and Army Airways Communications Stations along the route. The frequency was switched from Kirtland Tower to 359 kilocycles.

"Las Vegas Radio, Army One, One-One-Three-Three, over."

"Las Vegas, go ahead Army One-Three-Three, over."

"Army One-Three-Three, overhead, time now zero, eight, thirty-two, at twenty-one thousand, estimating Clayton time zero nine ten."

Las Vegas read back Reynard's transmission correctly which Charlie acknowledged. Eastern New Mexico essentially lacks interesting landmarks, and this day was made less interesting by sky conditions. Approaching Wagon Mound, New Mexico, they looked down at an undercast. When they overflew Las Vegas, the weather station there was reporting a ceiling of 700 feet with breaks in the overcast. Raton was no better, although Santa Fe was reporting scattered cloud at 6,000 and Kansas City was off to a nice day with not a cloud in the sky.

The prairie below was still a winter landscape as they flew northeast. The colors were somber hues of tan and gray, not the various shades of green and more vibrant earth tones that would prevail in a few weeks. The flowers that grow where the prairie gives way to the foothills, and the foothills to mountain ridges had not yet blossomed. The ubiquitous Indian paintbrush, scarlet beardtongue and skyrocket would need a few more weeks before their red-orange colors could start dotting the landscape as would the blue-hued harebells, Rocky Mountain iris, and lupines. However, looking to the northwest, into Colfax County toward Philmont, they could just see the tops of the mountains poking up through the undercast: Baldy, Touch-Me-Not, Clear Creek Mountain, Black Mountain .... Trail Peak.

# IV

# FROM THE EAGLE NEST

Blackburn's employment on that April 22nd flight was in his capacity as a civilian airline pilot and not related to his status as an Army Air Force reservist. For many people, it seems initially incongruous that an airline would be running both an Army Air Force pilot transition school and phase training for Air Transport Command, Ferry Division, crews. And, why would the larger, more prominent airlines (United, American, or Pan Am) not be running these schools? To fully understand this requires some in-depth background on TWA, then known as Transcontinental and Western Air, Inc., the youngest of the major airlines. The "Trans World Airlines" as we know it today, would not officially become the corporate name until after World War II.

The forerunner of today's TWA was the result of a merger between Transcontinental Air Transport (TAT) and Western Air Express in 1930. TAT was also known as "The Lindbergh Line" since Charles Lindbergh was among the principals. Heavily involved in the new company's operations was a former army pilot, Jack Frye. He would play a major role in growing the new enterprise, particularly during WWII.

Western Air Express was a holding company which owned a number of regional western carriers. The formation of TAT was inspired by National Air Transport (NAT) which had been formed five years before as an airmail carrier. TAT would be a passenger airline, however, and based on a concept which the U.S. Postal Service had utilized in mail transport: the use of a combination of trains and planes to move the mail.

In bad weather and/or at night, NAT carried the mail between major cities by rail and flew it during the day. This concept was utilized by TAT whose operations headquarters was in Kansas City. If the weather was bad or if there were substantial mechanical problems, passengers would entrain, get off at the next "TAT" city, and then fly again. That cut the time required for a coast-to-coast trip solely by rail from four days to two. It also meant substantial construction for TAT. The company had to build air terminals in cities served by the railroads including the Santa Fe among whose western routes was the very familiar one passing through Albuquerque. Thus, Albuquerque became an important "TWA town."

By 1941, Jack Frye had become CEO of TWA, and the European war was overstraining Britain's aircraft industry. The RAF was becoming a good customer for American aircraft manufacturers. Unfortunately, an alarming number of aircraft ferried "across the pond" weren't getting through — too many were going down into the drink.

General H.H. "Hap" Arnold, the U.S. Army Air Corps chief, met with Jack Frye in early 1941 and requested some help in addressing the problem which was identified as lack of training among the ferrying aircrews. Those crews were composed primarily of American volunteers under contract to the RCAF which had its hands full training its own personnel and those for the RAF. The aircraft involved included the B-17 Flying Fortress, B-24 Liberator, and Lockheed Hudson.

The ferrying crews were a mixture of aerial adventurers, flying soldiers of fortune, former military aviators, and bush pilots. The best pilots for the job, those in Air Corps bomber and transport squadrons or with the airlines, could not be spared. Although a ferry pilot was well paid by the standards of those days ($1,500 per month plus bonuses), the quality of crews was lacking.

That era, flight training and ferrying Hudsons across the Atlantic was portrayed in a movie, *Captains of the Clouds*, which still makes the rounds of late night movie circuits. Jimmy Cagney starred in the film which tells the story of bush pilots training RCAF cadets and subsequent ferry flights to the United Kingdom. The well-reviewed movie, portions

Photo courtesy of Peter M. Bowers

*Late 1941 at Dorval Airport, Montreal. Among the aircraft awaiting transatlantic ferrying flights are several Consolidated Liberators, a B-17 Flying Fortress, two B-25 Mitchells, and numerous Lockheed Hudsons.*

of which were filmed in Canada, went into production just as Eagle Nest went operational, in July, 1941, but was not released until January, 1942. Cagney meets his doom in the cold waters of the Atlantic after intentionally ramming a lone German interceptor in order to assure that the other Hudsons in his flight can proceed safely.

Several reasons had prompted Arnold to turn to an airline for training. He was having severe problems of his own in building up pilot training to meet Army Air Force goals for 1941 (to say nothing about what loomed just ahead). The airlines were major operators of multi-engine aircraft, and many of their pilots were also military reservists. TWA was of particular interest to Arnold because it was the only airline in the world which operated what was then the most advanced, 4-engine land transport aircraft, the Boeing 307 (essentially a B-17 with an enlarged, pressurized fuselage).

Otis Bryan, then TWA's Chief Pilot, was given the task of locating a suitable training site and getting the operation up and running. To survey candidate locations, he took Frye's personal airplane, a Lockheed 14 (from which the Hudson was derived), and narrowed his choice down to New Orleans and Albuquerque.

The school, subsequently known as the Eagle Nest Flight Center, or simply as "Eagle Nest," was operating in Albuquerque at the municipal airport by mid-summer. The name "Eagle Nest" had been selected by Jack Frye who entertained influential friends at a secluded ranch not far from Taos, New Mexico, that is to say, not far from the small village of Eagle Nest. That little community, in the shadow of New Mexico's highest mountain, 13,161 foot Wheeler Peak, is located between Taos and Cimarron, and is easily seen from the summit of Baldy Mountain at Philmont.

The initial aircraft inventory consisted of one LB-30 (export version of the B-24), three Lockheed Hudsons, and several AT-6 Harvard advanced trainers (later known as the "Texan" to Air Force pilots) which were used for instrument training. The Harvards were painted bright yellow in RCAF Training Command colors. The Lockheed Hudsons were in standard RAF day camouflage, i.e. pale gray undersides and mottled green upper surfaces. The school's first B-24s were in conventional aircraft gray and olive drab, but there were a few in desert pink camouflage.

Albuquerque Municipal Airport was soon to evolve into the Army's Kirtland Field, and the school acquired a maintenance hangar along with several pre-fab buildings for instruction and administrative use. The ground school concentrated on familiarization with the aircraft, meteorology, and navigation. The department heads under Otis Bryan, who was the school's first superintendent, numbered men who, in addition to Hal Blackburn, were on their way to becoming prominent TWA pilots including Waldon "Swede" Golien and Frank Busch. Among Swede Golien's duties was recruiting the ferry pilots which he did from offices in New York, Chicago, Kansas City, and Los Angeles.

The flight instructors were all men undergoing training on the Boeing Stratoliner in Kansas City. At first, this was not a popular assignment for the former Stratoliner trainees since it represented a delay in moving to the left seat of the most advanced civil airliner in the world. The pay in Albuquerque substantially sweetened the deal as did the promise that it would only be a temporary assignment.

The staff wore a variation of the TWA uniform. For the coat, there was a braided sleeve insignia that read, "Eagle Nest Flight Center." Pants were dark blue and worn with light blue shirt, dark blue necktie, and garrison cap.

The initial assignment was to give instrument and twin-engine instruction to American single-engine pilots who had been selected for the ferrying operation. The school opened on June 23, 1941, with around 50 employees and ambitious plans to build employment up to a peak of 800.[1] Before instructing, the TWA pilots had to get checked out in the equipment since not all had flown a Hudson. This was done when two of the new instructors, Joe Carr, a former Navy pilot, and Swede Golien checked each other out on the Lockheed at Kansas City's Fairfax Airport. They, in turn, checked out the other flight instructors.

The Lockheed Hudson was used by the RAF in many roles: light attack bomber, photo-reconnaissance, maritime patrol, anti-submarine, special duties in support of the Resistance on the continent, etc. Eagle Nest got the bomber version which proved wildly unpopular among the instructors since this variant was operated without a copilot. Where the copilot's controls would have been was a passageway through which the bombardier

Stephanie Carr Collection

*Autumn 1941. The first Army Air Force pilot graduates of the Jack Frye Four-Engine School at a banquet in Albuquerque just before assignment to Air Transport Command ferrying squadrons. Joe Carr, the flight and navigation instructor, is at far right.*

reached his station in the nose. Once an untoward maneuver, such as a groundloop, was underway, there was nothing the instructor could do to intervene except yell. And, yell he had to since good, sound-dampening insulation was not one of the Hudson's more endearing virtues.

Complicating matters to start with was the fact that the Hudson, being short-coupled (minimal distance between the main landing gear and the tailwheel), had a notorious reputation for groundlooping. Even a well-qualified pilot could have his hands full with a Hudson as the TWA pilots were warned by their peers at Northwest Airlines which operated the civilian passenger version of the Hudson. The Hudson could easily be likened to the occasional fat man on a tennis court who proves deceptively agile — at turning on a dime.

Within fairly short order, all three of the school's Hudsons were involved in groundloop accidents, including one in which the landing gear was completely removed. Unlike a dinged wingtip, the typical result of a simple groundloop, any serious, hard landing accident with a Hudson was potentially quite hazardous since the landing gear could easily be pushed up through the nacelles into the wings where the fuel tanks were located.

Flight instruction at Kirtland posed its own unique set of problems in addition to training young pilots, many of whom had never stepped into a multi-engine airplane. Kirtland's rapid expansion created a steady parade of "temporary" quarters for the TWA operation. The constant earth moving and construction, low humidity, and windy conditions created annoying dust storms which hampered instruction and were hard on the aircraft. The main north-south runway was being expanded to over two miles in length which temporarily made it the longest runway in the United States.

The school was located on the northeast side of the field quite close to the gate with its military guard. Most of the instructors rented houses in Albuquerque to which they could easily bicycle home for lunch. Frank Busch, the chief twin-engine instructor who would eventually rise to TWA VP-Operations, had rented a home on the east side of the Sandia mountains. It became a favorite buzz job target for instructors returning after air work sessions. When reminded that their appointments as Stratoliner pilots could be delayed or they could easily be sent down to a DC-3 right seat, the errant aerialists promptly resumed more conventional approaches to the field.

At $600 a month, the pay was good for men who had quite recently been copilots at $190 per month on DC-3s or $215 on Stratoliners. A particularly well-furnished, three-bedroom house rented for roughly $125 per month and a combination maid and babysitter cost $8 per week.

Just because a man was a good pilot hardly meant that he was also a good instructor. A good captain would bring along his copilot, share wisdom with him, and give the right seater a fair portion of the flying instead of treating him as a baggage-handling, cockpit lackey. Not all line pilots were especially well spoken, an essential skill for instructors. For this reason, a speech instructor was brought out from Kansas City to develop and refine the instructors' teaching and verbal skills. For some men like Blackburn, the former bandleader, or the ebullient Joe Carr, remedial elocution was hardly necessary. Both Blackburn and Carr were particularly articulate and spoke with no hint of a regional accent. When it came to speaking English, Carr was a quick study since he had not spoken a word of the language until age six.

Joe Carr was born in Great Falls, Montana, of Austrian immigrant parents. The family moved to Long Beach, California, after living briefly in Seattle. Carr attended Long Beach Junior College and then Cal Tech, but the depression ended further education, and he subsequently became a naval aviation cadet at Pensacola.

For the other pilots, however, the prospect of speaking extemporaneously for two minutes about a gum spot on the floor was a more vexing assignment than trying to coax a good landing out of a near terminally iced-up DC-3.

Eagle Nest started with just one Liberator on which Swede Golien checked out the first two instructor pilots, Frank Burcham and Ned McKrille. In 1941, the Liberator was considered a lot of airplane. In British registry, the serial number on the first Liberator read AM927. The "AM" stood for "Air Ministry" which the Eagle Nest pilots promptly redesignated, "Air Monster." The ship's manuals were written for British customers, and TWA took some exception to the existing training methods. So, the company rewrote "the book" on the Liberator including converting some of the King's Aeronautical English to Yankee Flyer's English. Thus "windscreen" became "windshield," "undercarriage" became "landing gear," "airscrew" became "propeller," "fine" pitch became "low" pitch, and "cooling gills" became "cowl flaps," etc.[2]

The technical training manual was written by a consortium of TWA pilots and engineers, and editorially blessed by Royce Welliver of the engineering staff and Joe Carr. They were not to know it at the time, but Carr would go on to distinguished wartime and post-war service with TWA while Welliver would perish under tragic circumstances in 1944. Eagle Nest's early Liberators and their teething difficulties, particularly the braking systems, created some problems. Fortunately, Consolidated Aircraft sent a technical crew to Albuquerque, and subsequently remedied the problem in later models of the B-24. Unfortunately, the first Liberator was damaged in a landing accident initiated by the right brake locking up. The right main gear collapsed as did the nose wheel. The big ship veered off the runway and left a trail of bomb bay door remains in the new trench it had just plowed up. It was decided to repair the B-24, but that turned into a six-month project.

Most flying was done in the morning before it got too hot, and included takeoffs and landings. The air work involved approaches to stalls, altitude and night flying, and some formation work. By mid-summer, TWA started to hire qualified outsiders as instructors.

Shortly after Eagle Nest started to graduate pilots, a tug of war began over responsibility for just who would continue training the ferry crews. The RAF was quite content with the civilian training arrangement since any use of RCAF training crews diverted manpower away from the all important task of filling the pipeline from Canada directly into the RAF's Bomber and Fighter Commands. Since it had overall responsibility for the ferrying operation, the RCAF wanted to control the training too.

The RAF lost the battle, and the TWA contract for training ferrying crews was terminated at the end of August. As Eagle Nest wound down, most of the TWA pilots headed back to Kansas City to complete Stratoliner training. It proved to be a very short interlude for some of them.

When it became obvious that the RCAF was going to undertake its own training, Otis Bryan traveled to Washington and successfully proposed that the Albuquerque operation become an Army Air Force B-24 crew training facility. The Eagle Nest Flight Center passed into history and became the "Jack Frye Four-Engine School" or more simply, "JFFES." The curriculum included ground school and 28 hours of flight time for pilots, flight engineers, radio operators, and navigators as individual crews. Many of the first crews were subsequently sent to the Army Air Force Air Transport Command as ferry crews for the B-24Ds which were starting to come off Consolidated's San Diego production line in ever-increasing numbers.

The Army Air Force was glad to have this resource since its number of four-engine qualified crews was quite small and multi-engine qualified personnel requirements anything but minimal. Among those returning to Albuquerque was Joe Carr who was assigned double duty as a flight and navigation instructor based on his experience as a Navy Catalina pilot and supplemental rating as a celestial navigator. In fact, most of the original Eagle Nest instructor pilots were Navy men (Pensacola, 1935-1937).

Navigators were rarely assigned to a ferry crew for flights within the continental United States, but were drawn from a squadron pool for overseas flights. The JFFES also trained the first civilian pilots hired to fly C-87s (cargo version of the Liberator) for the Air Transport Command.

Training flights usually included two or more crews going up in the same Liberator and simply switching positions during the flight in order to minimize downtime. Qualified instructor manpower shortages were starting to show. TWA's domestic schedules were increasing in mid-1941; additional line pilots and flight engineers could not be spared for Albuquerque. JFFES management scoured the country's leading flight and navigation schools for qualified instructors.

The JFFES aircraft inventory was increasing and included LB-30s (early export version of the B-24), a B-24A, and then primarily B-24Ds. The B-24s were stock Liberators right off the production line. The only thing missing was the bombsight; otherwise they were delivered with all of the defensive firepower in place including the ball (belly) turret. The .50 caliber machine guns, still wrapped in protective tape, were frequently removed, and, on many of the '24s, the navigator's celestial sighting bubble was removed to improve visibility for the pilots. Each Liberator was assigned an Albuquerque field number which was painted boldly in yellow on the nose of each ship, and in the case of 41-1133, the line number was "12."

The school very quickly processed nearly all of the Army Air Force's most recently qualified twin-engine pilots, and thereafter found itself giving transition to brand new second lieutenants who had never flown anything more sophisticated than the single-engine North American AT-6 trainer.

The JFFES had its hands full. The majority of the students had just graduated from Air Force advanced flying schools (typically with less than 250 hours total flying time) and were now jumping into the left seat of one of the most advanced bombers of the day. At 250 hours, pilots are just starting to learn about flying.

Part of that problem was due to congressional neglect of Army bombardment aviation (with encouragement from the Navy). Thus, a high percentage of the Air Corps cadets who graduated in the late 1930s were trained as fighter pilots. Most of the JFFES school students had gone through multi-engine advanced schools which had not yet received their twin-engine trainers. It would be late 1942 before multi-engine advanced flying schools had full complements of AT-9s, AT-10s or AT-11s. Thus, many of the just-rated pilots in early 1942 had only a passing acquaintance with heavier aircraft, and were lucky if they even had four or five hours on obsolete bombers such as the B-18 or B-23.

Similarly, many of the radio operators and flight engineers arrived fresh from technical training schools and had never even been up in an airplane. Picture these conditions: noisy B-24s, stuffy crew stations, steep turns, rocking around in thermals, and a brand new flight engineer crawling through cramped quarters. Maybe top it off with the lingering effects of a few *cervezas* and a heavy load of *enchiladas* from the night before. That is to know why JFFES made sure there was an ample supply of burp bags on each flight.

As might be expected, there were a few comic moments to offset the tense ones. As a first officer was carefully balancing his way through the bomb bay on the narrow catwalk, holding onto the bomb rack supports for dear life, it was not unheard of to see the bomb bay doors suddenly retracted by a wildly joking instructor pilot up front. The breathtaking view of a New Mexico desert or mountain top several thousand feet below when seen so suddenly was even more breathtaking, not to mention the tornadic roar of the 200 mph slipstream.

Joe Carr related the story of a 20,000 foot training mission and seeing a radio operator who, rolling and snapping his head and grinding his teeth, was obviously in distress. Thinking the student was having difficulties with his oxygen mask, Joe leaned over and to ask if anything was wrong. There wasn't. The neophyte was popping some peanuts he had put into the mask back into his mouth and chewing them.

There were frightening moments, particularly related to air traffic. Kirtland Field was also used by the airlines and the neighboring bombardier school whose approximately 50 AT-11s shared the same runways. The AT-11's pattern airspeed was significantly lower than the B-24's which made traffic spacing difficult, and night operations complicated matters that much more. The B-24s couldn't really perform the timesaving "touch and go" landings due to the extensive checklist items that had to be performed to reconfigure the plane for takeoff. So they landed, typically on the long north-south runway, made a 180, prepared the ship for takeoff, and roared back down the runway. On several occasions, controllers had cleared an AT-11 at the opposite end of the runway to takeoff. Fortunately, there were no collisions.

There were other incidents including several cases of serious leaks during fuel transfer operations in which raw fuel was seen dripping right past some of the electrical equipment that occasionally threw sparks. There was one instance of a B-24 suffering from extraordinary fuel consumption. Upon landing immediately, it was discovered the a negligent student flight engineer had failed to secure the gas caps before takeoff with the result that gas was rapidly siphoning directly out of the tanks into the slipstream.

At least one crew had difficulty in learning how to manage the turbocharger controls at mile-high Albuquerque. The crew unwittingly took off at a small auxiliary field on a hot day with their turbos so overboosted that the resulting, excessively rich mixture prevented the engines from developing full power. The bomber got off the runway without many feet to spare, and the crew got a good lesson in power management and density altitude.

In the late spring of 1942, four of the TWA B-24s were used in making the movie, *Bombardier.* Released in 1943, the film featured Randolph Scott and Pat O'Brien. Among the co-stars were a couple of up and coming names, Robert Ryan and Eddie Albert. One of the 24s served as the camera plane, and was to photograph a flight of three B-24s led by Hal Blackburn bombing an enemy naval vessel. In reality, the enemy capital ship was a large simulated, wooden structure positioned on the West Mesa bombing range. With a little imagination, filming in black and white, a soft focus, and the right camera angle, the flatness of the mesa passed for a troubled sea. The B-24 crews had picked up three bombardiers from Kirtland's bombardier school and loaded twenty 100-pound bombs whose explosive content had been reduced to six pounds each.

The first run over the "target" had to be aborted because the camera ship was not in place at the right moment, so Blackburn called a go-around. The formation turned, but one of the Liberators had not retracted its bomb bay doors. Another ship radioed the other '24 to roll down the doors, and was promptly appalled to see bombs dropping when the bombardier pulled the wrong lever. Fortunately, the damage below was limited to some less than prime real estate along the west bank of the Rio Grande river.

The Kirtland Field commanding officer was not having a good day on that date which was concluded at the officer's club bar. He predicted that he would never see a general's star because the day's activities included, in addition to the bombing of Albuquerque, the loss of a student bombardier who had fallen out of an AT-11 (or committed suicide by jumping) over one of the bombing ranges. Also, there was the loss of a Douglas B-18 Bolo when it ran out of fuel. The Bolo pilot bailed his crew out, put the plane on autopilot, and started to jump himself. Just as he was about to leap, it occurred to him that he was too low. The B-18 landed itself in the desert with remarkably little damage before he could get back to the cockpit.

By January 1942, JFFES had started to hire "copilot instructors" who were also known as "first officers." These men were recruited from outside of TWA, and although they generally did not have significant, multi-engine time, they were well advanced past the private pilot stage. It was into that category that Jonas Ruff was hired, although he had substantially more than 1,000 hours. The copilot instructors, in addition to flying, also helped in the ground school operation and were responsible for flight scheduling.

Not all of the first pilots were truly cut out for instructing, and there was some turnover. One of the copilot instructors hired in late January 1942 was Harold "Hutch" Thurston, a very capable, young instrument-rated pilot with a Bachelor of Science degree in Aeronautical Engineering from the University of Minnesota. Hutch went to JFFES after working at Honeywell's aviation division in Minneapolis. He tells of a "sweaty-palmed" captain who took out a boundary fence on an excessively short landing and was all set to make a 180 at the end of the runway and promptly take off again without inspecting the obviously damaged landing gear. Hutch and the flight engineer threatened to abandon ship on the spot if it were not taxied to the maintenance line for inspection. The flight was terminated as was, quite shortly thereafter, the hasty instructor pilot.

Hutch Thurston was representative of the young men hired as copilot instructors or "first officers." He was closing in on a thousand hours, had a commercial license with an instrument rating, and was experienced in the heavier, more sophisticated single-engine aircraft of the day. Hutch had gained hours rapidly by flying sightseers around Minneapolis and was part-owner of a Beech Staggerwing, the classic and very advanced, retractable gear biplane of the 1930s. In late January of 1942, he signed on with TWA since it looked like he would have to wait for quite a few months before his applications with Pan Am or Northwest would get any action.

Many of the new flight engineer instructors were recent graduates of civilian aircraft mechanic schools. The new TWA copilot and flight engineer instructors went through the JFFES course immediately upon being hired, right along with Army students, and started teaching the following month. George Van Hoozer, as a regular and very experienced TWA mechanic based at the Albuquerque school, did not fit into that mold. He had transitioned to flight engineer instructor simply because it was an exciting growth opportunity, and became, therefore, one of the most highly qualified flight engineer instructors at JFFES.

The school went through another name change in early 1942 and emerged as the "Combat Crew Training School (Four-Engine) - Division of TWA, Inc.," or simply "CCTS" for short. This reflected the new assignment of serving as a four-engine transition school for the Army Air Force Combat Command. The CCTS introduced the Liberator to pilots, flight engineers, and radio operators who had just been assigned to one of the many bombardment groups then forming.

At this point, the school was operating sixteen B-24s, and providing training in some aspects of flying which had not been emphasized during an aviation cadet's training including oxygen equipment orientation. One long, eight-hour roundtrip cross country was part of the program, and at least two hours of that flight had to be made at a minimum altitude of 20,000 feet in order to familiarize crews with oxygen procedures.

While this was heady stuff for students, it was not easy work. Indeed, there was a lot of strain. Most of the instructors were flying five to six hours a day in conditions characterized by the constant roar of four, very nearby 1200 h.p. aero engines whose decibel level would send today's environmental inspectors berserk; extreme heat; blowing dust; ceaseless, rump-numbing vibration; eternal state of hyper-alertness for student lapses; the never-ending threat of a mid-air; mistrust of brakes, hydraulic systems, and fuel connections; frequent, tooth-jarring hard landings; mind-sapping instrument flying; occasional bone-chilling cross countries at 20,000 plus feet or more; overnight trips extended by thunderstorms or other weather extremes; and, perhaps, the unpleasantness on the flight deck when that doubly green, 19-year old radio operator trainee couldn't reach the burp bag in time.

On top of that, there was the constant pressure to turn out more crews as quickly as possible. When TWA started the school for Air Force crews, each pilot logged 28 hours of left seat time, including a long range cross country. By the spring of 1942, this was down to 12 hours including flying one leg of the long cross country. TWA did its very best to sneak in a few extra hours, but not every young pilot was to benefit from the extra attention. Later in the war, when the instructor pool had grown, B-24 transition lasted nearly three months and put 50 hours in a pilot's logbook. At the Albuquerque CCTS, the B-24 course lasted four weeks, and TWA was running overlapping classes in order to turn out as many pilots as possible within the limited time available, even if each new potential skipper got only 12 hours left seat stick time.

That was not a lot of command time to make the passage from a single-engine, 5,300 pound advanced trainer to a 56,000 pound, four-engine heavy bomber. However, excepting the loss of 41-1133, a few ground-loops in Hudsons, and some very hard landings in Liberators, there were no major accidents during TWA's operation of pilot transition in Albuquerque. Ferry Command flying standardization officers were emphatic in their appreciation of what the school had done for its B-24 pilots. It found systems unfamiliarity and poor operating procedures to be the rule with B-24 pilots trained at sources other than TWA.

The Eagle Nest Flight Center/CCTS was at the right place at the right time. It trained over 1,000 airmen when they were desperately needed and positioned TWA perfectly for the major role it would undertake with Air Transport Command beginning in January 1942.[3] It also produced a cadre of instructor pilots who would move on to other four-engine schools and turn out thousands of additional pilots. Although Robert Redding and Jonas Ruff would not live to follow that route, their skills were the type of which the Army Air Force was in desperate need in early 1942.

# V

# THE RANCHER

Robert Otto Redding had crammed considerable living and accomplishment into his 27 years: husband, father, pilot, farmer, rancher, and entrepreneur. He was born on July 3, 1914 and grew up on his father Virgil's farm just north of Minatare, Nebraska, in a family that included his younger brother Dale and sister Elsie. The "Otto" was in honor of his Uncle Otto Jurgens whose family were German immigrants and Oregon Trail pioneers who liked what they saw in the North Platte Valley and decided to make that area home.

Virgil Redding was a prosperous farmer who grew white beans, russet potatoes, sugar beets, and some corn. The Redding farm also produced wheat, oats, and barley. The Jurgens brothers, Otto, Fritz and Axel, were prominent ranchers in the area, and their holdings included a 40,000 acre spread on which they raised Herefords just across the border in Wyoming. Although he would eventually become a rancher, Robert Redding was consumed by aviation — he ate, slept, and breathed airplanes. He was also a brilliant young man. A broken leg during high school interrupted his athletics, but did not slow down his trumpet playing in the school band. He did, in fact, possess a photographic memory and could completely absorb and retain a page of text in a matter of seconds without ever having to refer back to it.

This remarkable capability was responsible for his advancing through high school in three years at the end of which he faced a dilemma: accept his appointment to West Point and hope for a career in the Air Corps or start flying right away. Higher education was shelved, and Redding headed for Love Field, Dallas, to begin his career as a pilot. Within a few years, he advanced from student pilot to what was then known as an "ATR" (airline transport rating).

He used this to gain employment as an airmail pilot — the youngest in the state of Nebraska and one of the youngest in the fledgling air mail service. At this point, while located in Omaha, he came into ownership of his own plane. His father had loaned another man money to buy an airplane on which the loan was subsequently defaulted. Virgil Redding foreclosed, and young Robert now had an airplane in which he gave lessons to friends at cost.

The Army took over flying the mail in 1934, thus putting Redding out of a job. Airline hiring favored multi-engine, ex-military pilots, and Bob Redding was faced with that perpetual decision of all young pilots who

Photo courtesy of Fred Gray

*At age 18, Bob Redding (at far right) was already giving flying lessons to his friends. He was one of the youngest air mail pilots in the United States.*

aspire to bigger things — where does one get those couple thousand hours of pilot-in-command time on multi-engine equipment? He headed south of the border.

From late 1934 through 1936, Redding flew for *Transporte Aereo Gelabert S.A.* (T.A.G) in Panama as a captain on Fokker Trimotors, sometimes with people as passengers and sometimes with poultry. Other times it was freight and occasionally not just in Panama since the airline regularly flew into Colombia and Costa Rica. The airline owner was Marco "Tito" Gelabert, the father of Panamanian aviation. His airline (flying less than a dozen, second-hand planes bought primarily in the U.S.) was a quasi-military operation based at Paitilla National Airport located just northeast of Panama City. Gelabert had learned to fly in Kansas City at the Porterfield School, got his mechanic's rating in Florida, and studied military aviation in Cuba.

Charter flights took Redding throughout Central America. On one occasion, his Trimotor caught fire in the air, and he had no choice but to put it down at once. Redding pulled off a controlled crash landing in the jungle and, with his passengers, was able to walk to safety several days later.

Panama was an ideal place for a sportsman like Redding, especially for the fishing which was not limited to salt water, big game fish such as the Pacific sailfish. Redding pursued his favorite quarry, trout, even in Panama. Tumbling from the sides of Chiriqui volcano is the Chiriqui Viejo whose chilly waters then supported a lively rainbow trout population.

He had always been tall and very slender, but when he came back from Panama Redding was a bigger man. He flew the cargo, but also loaded it which was responsible for his more imposing physique when he returned.

It was in Panama that Redding met Jonas Ruff. Both were members of the aviation community there and were part of the same social circle of ex-patriate Americans.

By early 1937, Redding had returned to Nebraska, was ranching in Minatare, and would eventually become a partner in a small flying school at the Scottsbluff Airport. The school's trainer was a Luscombe Silvaire, a small high wing monoplane of which there are still quite a few flying today. The Luscombe was, in many ways, ahead of its time with all-metal construction and a design that would be copied by other post-war manufacturers.

Redding attempted to join the Army Air Corps, but was turned down because of educational deficiencies since he could not produce two years' worth of college transcripts. The war crunch had not yet come, and the Army was still only turning out 300 new pilots a year. Redding, burned by the rejection, resolved to gain the requisite 60 credit hours. With the photographic memory that had easily put him through high school in three years, he completed the equivalent of two years of college in six months and successfully entered "flying cadet" training.

Redding's cadet experience was very different from Jeffries' and Reynard's, but much closer to Blackburn's. The Army Air Corps was responsible for all flight training in a program which lasted nearly a year compared to the wartime version. For Redding, primary was taken at Randolph Field, San Antonio, Texas. The primary phase had been taught at Brooks Field in San Antonio, but had become so crowded that primary flight was expanded to March Field in California. By the time Redding entered the program in 1937, the new Randolph Field in San Antonio was responsible for primary and basic flight instruction. Randolph Field was billed as the "West Point of the Air," a reputation it

Photo courtesy of Fred Gray

*At the time of the accident, Bob Redding was an Army Air Force reservist waiting for his July 1942 call-up to active duty in the rank of major.*

would maintain for years to come. The first month at Randolph was known as "hell month" and was for all practical purposes a compressed version of a West Point cadet's plebe year. If anything, getting through the pre-war cadet experience was more difficult than the wartime program: roughly 50 percent of the cadets who entered primary flying school with Redding washed out before basic began.

Redding completed advanced flying school at Kelly Field, but after his year of active duty was not offered a long term commission in the Regular Army. By 1939, he had completed his obligatory one year of active duty, and was a reservist flying out of Richards Field in Kansas City, Missouri. Through his reserve flying, he developed contacts with Transcontinental and Western Air pilots in Kansas City. Quite a few of the growing airline's pilots had also flown the mails in the early 30s and were reservists too; thus he became well-connected with senior TWA pilots and operations management personnel.

Hal Blackburn did his Army reserve flying at Richards Field also. Reservists flew training aircraft for the most part, including the North American BC-1 (an early version of the T-6 Texan) and the North American BT-9 (a fixed gear variant of the BC-1). Even as late as 1940, they also flew the classic, and very outdated, Boeing P-12 biplane fighter and the Douglas O-46. The latter was a large (46 foot wingspan), high wing observation craft whose performance relegated it to reserve units for use in training and utility work.

One of Redding's acquaintances was a high-seniority TWA pilot who would become his business partner in an enterprise nine miles southwest of Wheatland, Wyoming. This was not too far from Laramie Peak, located on the edge of the Rockies. The business was a 7,500 acre cattle ranch, and the partner was Otis Bryan who was to become TWA's chief pilot. There was a large lake on the ranch, and it offered excellent duck hunting, a favorite sport for both men. Redding was an avid outdoorsman, a skilled hunter (especially with a shotgun), and a fervent trout fisherman. He and Bryan frequently traveled to northern Nebraska and into South Dakota, on the Niobrara River, for trout fishing.

The area around their ranch is still wide open country today, but in the 1930s it was not that far removed from what it had been in frontier days. Bob Redding rode on roundups and cross country cattle drives. There was branding in the traditional sense — with their brand, the "Lazy C Bar."

Photo courtesy of Fred Gray

*Bob Redding was an accomplished outdoorsman, skilled duck hunter, and enthusiastic trout fisherman.*

At about the same time, Waite Phillips was deeding the first of two gifts of land on his New Mexico Ranch to the Boy Scouts of America. Bob Redding would have enjoyed Philmont, not just for the hunting and fishing, but probably more so for the ranching aspect of what was then associated with "Philturn Rockymountain Scoutcamp."[1]

On April 15, 1939, Redding married the strikingly attractive Helenjane Gray, a Scottsbluff college student, whose family had moved to Nebraska from Minnesota several years before. Helenjane's father was an animal nutritionist whose employer, the Nutrina Company, had interests in this agriculturally rich area. For Helenjane's young brother, Fred, then age 14, those were exciting times. Fred was on his way to becoming a star athlete, member of a state championship football team, and part-time employee on the Redding farm. And, he was a frequent hunting companion with his brother-in-law who also taught Fred how to fly in the Luscombe.

Redding built a two-story stucco house two and one-half miles north of Minatare in 1939 and started farming there in addition to his Wyoming venture. Redding's son Michael would be born at Minatare in 1940. The home, even by today's standards, was quite modern. The stucco construction was most unusual in that part of Nebraska, and the view from the second floor was a commanding one that took in the entire North Platte Valley. Scottsbluff was visible 14 miles to the west, and a regional landmark, Chimney Rock, could be seen far away to the east.

As the war broke in Europe, Redding was an Air Corps reservist, but more involved with family, ranching interests, and the flying school in Scottsbluff. He had advanced to first lieutenant rank in early 1940 and became a captain by Pearl Harbor.

Through his connections with TWA, his past history as an instructor and air mail pilot, and his substantial civil and military multi-engine experience, he was offered an instrument instructor's job at the Eagle Nest school in Albuquerque and moved his family there in the summer of 1941. His career at Eagle Nest followed in Hal Blackburn's footsteps with a quick promotion to instrument flying chief and subsequently operations manager.

Redding was the first non-TWA pilot hired at Albuquerque, and most of his early instruction was with instrument students on the North American Harvard (the British designation for the AT-6 Texan) with which he was already familiar from his Army Reserve flying. In late September, Blackburn started instructing Redding and Bryan on the Liberator. Redding was checked out as a first officer on September 27th and was being groomed for a first pilot spot. Blackburn flew with Redding at least once a week, and in late October, Redding was logging considerable instrument time in the LB-30. By the end of the first week in November, he was signed off as a Liberator first pilot.

There was a very close bond between Blackburn and Redding: not quite father-son, but probably somewhere between elder and younger brother, or perhaps young uncle and favorite nephew. Redding was Blackburn's protégé. Beyond the flying bond, there were other ties. Both had successfully entered the Air Corps after being thwarted at first, both had done their reserves flying in Kansas City, both were very bright men from small town Nebraska, and both had first been captivated by flying at Scottsbluff. Although originally from Illinois, Blackburn perceived himself as being, like Redding, a westerner.

Redding also had another close friend on 41-1133 in the person of Jonas Ruff. Together, they shared an interesting past composed of flying and adventuring in Central America during the mid-1930s.

# VI

# JONAS RUFF

Is there magic in the heavens?
Can one feel the sky's allure?
Does the roar of power quicken
Heart-beats with a force obscure?
Are men tempted by the beauty
Known only to those who yearn,
While in mystic flights of fancy,
Fires of saddening longing, burn?

From *Earthbound* by C.R. McDonald

Ruff and Redding had become fast friends in Panama during the mid-1930s and stayed in touch over the intervening years. Jonas Ruff was a particularly skilled, intuitive pilot whose flying talents were enhanced by the combination of two uniquely important attributes. He was an accomplished glider pilot and gifted mechanic.

Almost 34 years old and a native of San Jose, California, he was named for his grandfather, and born in the house that his father, George Ruff, had built. The elder Ruff, with his parents and brothers and sisters, had emigrated to America from Germany at age 14. The family operated a dairy ("The College Park Dairy") on the outskirts of San Jose, and, like the Macombers back east, were active members of their local Grange chapter. Jonas was followed by another brother and, in 1911, by a sister. The farm and that of his grandfather were located along the Guadalupe Creek (replaced today by the Guadalupe River Park). Located nearby is the San Jose Airport whose construction pleased Ruff's father who had visions of his son flying home from his many travels.

The young Ruffs helped out on the farm (a scene repeated by Jonas' Liberator crew mates from Missouri, Nebraska, and Maine). Life was good for the Ruffs in the 20s and early 30s. The dairy prospered, and the boys were close and protective of their little sister who loved to tag along with her brothers. At age five, left-handed and bilingual Jonas was sent to the first grade at the nearby College Park School.

When he was in the fifth grade, an event occurred which foreshadowed the development of his mechanical talents. While his parents were away one afternoon, Jonas completely disassembled a wall clock and spread the parts out on the dining room table. The returning parents initially were aghast, but then watched, spellbound, as their youngster perfectly reassembled the clock piece by piece.

Four years later, the Ruff children were each presented with a bicycle and sent to the Jefferson School in San Jose. During summers, the young Ruffs also worked at their uncle's farm in nearby Evergreen, pick-

Photo courtesy of Helen Ruff Crawford

*Jonas Ruff was an accomplished glider pilot before obtaining his single-engine land plane rating.*

ing plums. The year before Jonas graduated from Jefferson School in 1924, his brother George died from pneumonia. The tragedy devastated the parents and brought Jonas and his sister, Helen, even closer. By this time, he was interested in all things mechanical and completed San Jose High School the following year after excelling in metalworking machine shop. His parents were adamant about his attending the University of California at Santa Clara.

Jonas was just as insistent about becoming a machinist. Working was the only way he could afford to take flying lessons. He started working as a technician in a San Jose automotive repair garage. "Automotive" may be a bit narrow since the company also serviced home appliances and refrigeration equipment. Jonas quickly became the specialist on refrigerators, radios, and one of the company's specialties, authorized repairs on Stewart Warner speedometers.

Ruff started flying gliders in the late 20s and became a doubly-rated pilot when he acquired his single-engine land plane rating in 1930 after already becoming a sailplane flight instructor. His interest in mechanics and flying meshed very nicely. Although left handed, his teachers in school forced him to use his right hand; one probable outcome was superior motor skills resulting in exceptional ability to coordinate movement of aircraft controls.

To read Jonas Ruff's logbooks is to take a sentimental journey through the Golden Age of American aviation. Many of the great aircraft names are there: Fairchild, Eaglerock, Great Lakes, Travel Air, Waco, Staggerwing, Stinson, and Ford Trimotor among others. There are a few nearly forgotten names such as Solo Sport and Kreider-Reisner. Classic engines including OX-5, Hisso, Wasp, Cyclone, Siemens, Kinner, Cirrus, and Ranger appear in his logbooks since it was customary then to include the engine type along with aircraft name and registration number.

Ruff was a member of a particularly active flying club, the San Jose Olympic Flyers, and with several other members, he rebuilt a Curtiss Robin, the popular high wing monoplane of the mid-20s. They also produced a homebuilt glider and a light, experimental aircraft (in today's parlance, a sport-homebuilt). San Jose was a good gliding center, and Jonas quickly became a master at extending distances and wringing every last bit of lift possible from his wings. He was a regular contestant in glider meets up and down the California coast.

Once Ruff got his private, powered aircraft license (certificate #

18911), he was flying several times a week, and rapidly building up time including both night flying and cross countries. The commercial and flight instructor licenses quickly followed. Although still employed full-time as a machinist, Jonas was now instructing and flying charters, particularly hunting and fishing parties.

With his flying club, Jonas participated in the "air tours" that were so popular in 1930s aviation circles. These cross country tours frequently involved dozens of aircraft and typically included destinations a thousand or more miles away. His first tour, flown in the Robin, was to El Paso and back which says a lot about Jonas' love of flying. Powered by the Curtiss OX-5 engine, the high-winged monoplane Robin was a boxy, three-place ship which cruised around 80 mph. The flight was flown in early September 1931, and was certainly without the comfort of today's turbo-charged, air conditioned light aircraft. Jonas' father and uncle accompanied him on several of those jaunts, including one to Mexico in early 1933.

Ruff also raced the Robin in the OX-5 engine aircraft category in various meets on the West Coast and took home a few second and third place ribbons from those contests.

Photo courtesy of Helen Ruff Crawford

*Ruff's early flying experience was gained with an especially active club, the San Jose Olympic Flyers.*

The instructing and charter flying continued in 1933 when he flew his sister downstate for a job interview. Helen had graduated from San Jose State University with a degree in elementary education and was being interviewed for a teaching position at a new school near Bakersfield where, in just eight years, Jeffries and Reynard would be assigned to the Air Corps Basic Flying School there. While flying down to the Kern County Airport, the Robin developed a mechanical problem, so Jonas prudently decided to set it down at once which he promptly did at Delano. He fixed the problem himself, as might be expected for a man with his mechanical talents, and Helen arrived on time for the interview which resulted in her getting the job at Keane, near Bakersfield.

From 1932 to 1934, Ruff was flying at least once a week, and usually in the Robin or the OX-5 powered Travel Air, a two-place biplane. In 1934, more time was logged flying cross country charters, as far away as Los Angeles or up the coast. He was also widening his experience by flying more recent model aircraft, including newer Fairchilds. For his own pleasure flying, he occasionally flew two classics, the Eaglerock and Great Lakes biplanes.

He flew all of the air tours, such as those to Boulder Dam or Salt Lake with his flying club, and was instructing regularly in the Kreider-Reisner two-place biplanes. The outbound leg to Salt Lake was nearly 800 miles which, including stops, took 12 hours to fly. Whereas Ruff's cross countries in 1932 and 1933 had been flown in his Curtiss Robin, the 1934 and '35 cross countries were flown in more sophisticated planes including the Stinson Model S, a four place high-wing monoplane. With a 215 horsepower Lycoming radial engine compared to the Robin's 90 horsepower OX-5 engine, the Stinson Model S, introduced in late 1931, was a much more comfortable cross country plane with a cruise speed of nearly 130 mph. The other cross country favorite was the Fairchild 42 which, although powered by the 300 h.p. Wright J-6, had a performance comparable to the Stinson.

Beyond flying, Ruff was also interested in photography and became quite proficient with a movie camera. In addition to filming family events, he frequently took the camera aloft and shot aerobatic sequences in addition to ground and coastal panoramas.

In 1935, Jonas continued working as a precision machinist in San Jose and was not married, although he never suffered from a lack of feminine company. Ruff, five feet, eight inches tall and with blue eyes and brown hair, was a strikingly handsome man who was occasionally mistaken for a movie star. In reality, his personality, while warm and friendly, was anything but that of an egocentric matinee idol. As a bachelor with a good wage, his income allowed him to enter into a partnership with two other gentlemen for the purchase of a highly respected airplane: a Travel Air 6000. That was not your basic J-2 Piper Cub type puddle jumper. Although the Travel Air Company would not survive past the early 30s, one of its principals would go on to build a new company that would become an enduring benchmark of quality in private, business, commercial and military aviation. His name was Walter Beech.

The 6000 was a large (48-foot wingspan) cabin class monoplane with a 300 horsepower Wright Whirlwind engine. In addition to the pilots, the cabin seated four passengers with 150 pounds of baggage. Although the plane was not a speed merchant, it featured insulation, heaters, and automobile-style crank down windows for passenger comfort. The plane's large wings made takeoffs and landings particularly easy which was an important feature since the market bias was still in favor of biplane configuration.

The 6000 was billed as the "Limousine of the Air" and sold well as soon as the first one rolled out of its Wichita plan in late 1928.

From a commercial operator's viewpoint, a Travel Air 6000 could haul a respectable cargo load when the easily-removed passengers seats were taken out. That was a major attraction for Jonas and his two partners because they had entered into a contract to fly gold out of Cali, Colombia.

Jonas and his partners set out in mid-June of 1935 for their new mining transport venture. Left behind was a saddened, lovely blond lady friend, Aileen Smith, who wasn't quite able to get Jonas to settle down. Although the flight south was exciting and included stops in Mexico, Guatemala and Honduras, they had to wait in Panama for their Colombian work permits. To familiarize themselves with their routes, Jonas and one of the partners, who had brought his wife along, took off on an orientation flight that nearly resulted in disaster. The other pilot, whose wife was occupying the copilot's seat, drifted off course in the high *cordillera* between Medellin and Cali. With peaks in the 5,000 meter range, the unsupercharged Travel Air was approaching its service ceiling.

Ruff's partner soon had them boxed in by high ridges with not enough power to climb over the crest ahead and probably not enough

Photo courtesy of Helen Ruff Crawford

*Ruff's partnership in this Travel Air 6000 led him to Panama and ultimately employment with the Department of Commerce in the Canal Zone.*

room to safely complete a 180-degree turn at that altitude. When it became obvious that their demise was imminent, Jonas leaped from the first passenger seat, took over the plane and did the only thing possible: cut the power, split-S'd, and pulled it out on a reciprocal heading, passing unpleasantly close to the valley floor. In fact, they very nearly crashed into the little stream in the center of the valley below, but Jonas' aerobatic experience saved the day. They were, of course, lucky to survive not just the potential impact with the ridges or valley floor, but also the very likely structural failure of the Travel Air which had been designed for transport, not aerobatics.

Returning to Panama, Jonas and his partners languished waiting for the red tape over the permits to unsnarl. From the many ships passing through the canal zone, one had tied up while awaiting experts to repair its faulty navigation instruments. Jonas inquired if he might have a look. With his mechanical talents, he promptly made the repairs, and in doing so, caught the attention of Canal Zone authorities. By this time it had become clear that the gold hauling contract was not going to work out.

That inescapable economic reality prompted Jonas to accept employment as a master machinist/instrument maker with the United States Department of Commerce in the Canal Zone.

For a man who liked aviation, travel and new experiences, Panama was tailor made for Jonas as it had been for George Van Hoozer and Robert Redding before him. Panamanian skies buzzed with aircraft, and not just the Navy patrol bombers from Coco Solo or the Army interceptors from their base at Rio Hato on the west coast. Albrook Field at Ancon, the key American Army facility, was also regularly served by Pan Am, and the principal general aviation field, Paitilla National Airport, was home to many privately-owned aircraft.

Ruff found the architecture in Panama City to be Spanish, but the inhabitants much more international. Along Colon's awning-lined arcades were shops featuring goods from the Orient, the eastern Mediterranean, and throughout Latin America. Open air cabarets throbbed to the beat of the latest American hits and Latin rhythms alike. And there was more merriment at the annual, four-day festival, *Carnival*. English was spoken almost universally, and appeared on most signs. Accents came from everywhere, especially the Caribbean.

The living was good, and the cost of it increasingly high, although that was offset for Jonas since, as a Canal Zone employee, he had access to American government commissaries and stores which sold a wide variety of goods at little over cost.

Jonas enjoyed great mobility since, as a pilot, he could fly from the canal's Pacific terminus to the Atlantic coast and back in little more than an hour. Flights by private aircraft over the Canal Zone proper, however, were forbidden and those by commercial flights severely restricted. Or, he could, as Van Hoozer and Redding had done earlier, take the one and a half-hour train ride to make the trip from one side to the other.

The Travel Air remained in Panama as did one of his partners who also started working there. Jonas used the 6000 commercially for weekend flights to Costa Rica, Mexico, Colombia, and Caribbean destinations. It was through becoming a member of the American aviation community in Balboa, on the Pacific coast, that Ruff and Robert Redding became close friends. Redding, having developed malaria, left Panama in 1936, but the two pilots corresponded occasionally in the years that followed.

Shortly after settling in Panama, Ruff qualified for a Panama Canal Zone Transport Pilot license, a unique license which authorized him to fly as a pilot and/or crew member on regularly scheduled commercial air flights within the Canal Zone. This license and the fact that his work schedule was not a predictable nine a.m. to five p.m. routine were his tickets to more commercial flying and the road to more sophisticated aircraft than the Travel Air 6000.

Although Jonas was away in Panama, his family was a close knit one. A very dutiful son, he never missed a thoughtful remembrance on holidays and birthdays, and always spent considerable time at home in San Jose on his long summer vacations. He also stayed in touch with aviation back in the continental United States through his membership in the Aircraft Owners and Pilot's Association (membership number 1109).

Ruff's movie camera was a regular passenger on many of his flights and land-based excursions. The film has been converted to videotape and provides a marvelous record of Jonas' activities and friends in Panama, including a few frames with a lanky, young pilot from Nebraska, Bob Redding.

Jonas enjoyed Panama immensely and was happy in his work. There was the active social life, excitement of trips to the interior to trade with the local people, the distance an American dollar extended at the commissary, and the opportunity to maintain his flying proficiency. One of the trips to the interior, where natives had not yet traded in their blowguns for shotguns, provided an unwanted side effect: malaria. Still, he enjoyed Panama and his lifestyle which included a cook and maid at the apartment he shared with another bachelor. Already fluent in German, Jonas became tri-lingual as he quickly mastered Spanish even though many Americans never bothered to since English was spoken nearly everywhere.

Jonas, not ready to be tied down at that point and a bit like the sailor with a girl in every port, met the love of his life in Panama, although other attractions would follow. Her name was Fran, she was a schoolteacher, and she would eventually return to Ohio and a happy marriage there after Jonas left Panama in early 1941.

Ruff's former employer back in San Jose had expanded his business, but was at the age when retirement beckoned. The owner had been so pleased with Ruff's work that Jonas was made an attractive offer to buy the business. Jonas turned it down since he was doing well in Panama and the entrepreneurial demands on his time would curtail his flying. As an employee of the Commerce Department outside the continental

United States, he had an exceptional annual leave plan and was able to head north to visit his family every year.

He was flying actively, and on several occasions ferried aircraft to and from the United States in addition to periodic trips to the east coast for product and technical briefings by some of the Department's instrument suppliers. Ruff's flying experience reached a new dimension in Panama. With flexible hours at his Department of Commerce job, he was able to work part-time as a commercial pilot, and in doing so was able to gain valuable experience on seaplanes and both the Ford and Stinson Trimotors.

In these planes, he was also increasingly faced with instrument flying conditions. During this period, he began flying the more powerful, single-engine ships such as the Beech Staggerwing, a cabin biplane with retractable gear and a performance which exceeded that of most military fighters.

Jonas added many new commercial and sport types to his logbook in Panama including later model Wacos and Stinsons. Through a close friend at the U.S. Navy base at Coco Solo, Jonas had unrestricted access to a Stinson Gullwing Reliant. It was a high wing monoplane powered by a 300 h.p. engine with controllable pitch propeller, but the performance wasn't quite that of the Staggerwing. Nonetheless, the Lycoming-powered Reliant was, and is today, considered to be a stylish, well-appointed high quality airplane.

Returning to San Jose on vacations, he continued his club flying on the Kreider-Reisner biplanes and the economical little Porterfield, (similar to the Piper Cub, but with a small radial engine).

1940 was a pivotal year for Jonas Ruff. By this time, he had sold his share in the Travel Air 6000 to one his partners who later returned to the United States and was subsequently killed in the crash of another aircraft. Jonas logged quite a few hours as a copilot/navigator on an all-metal, cabin class monoplane, the Vultee V1-A. Only 27 V-1/V-1As were built, but it remains as a classic design. It was a large airplane with a 48 foot wingspan, a Wright Cyclone engine (usually 750 horsepower), retractable gear, constant speed prop, and an eight-passenger cabin. The plane's owner was none other than Marco Gelabert, Redding's former employer. The big Vultee was also the first ship in which Jonas got an introduction to serious instrument flying.

That particular V1-A was built in 1936 as the only example of a V1-

AD Special for William Randolph Hearst, the California newspaper magnate. Shipped with a 1000 h.p. engine, Hearst later sold it to Gelabert who flew it rather hard before selling it to a Honduran operator.[1]

Using the Commerce Department's very liberal annual leave policy, Jonas journeyed to Michigan in 1940 to take delivery of a new Oldsmobile sedan which he drove back to San Jose. In 1937, he had bought a new Olds from the same Panama City dealer who was also a personal friend. Ruff enjoyed travel immensely, and promptly took off with his parents and sister for a subsequent vacation drive to Vancouver and return via Yellowstone.

He still had a week's vacation left when he arrived back in San Jose, and logged nearly 30 hours of what would prove to be well spent instrument instruction time.

But, by the autumn of 1940, as the Battle of Britain was coming to a climax, he had become restless. Ruff was then 32 years old and very conscious of world events, especially as a number of refugees from the European war had settled in Panama. Jonas was well-read, and subscribed to several American news and general editorial magazines while he was in Panama. He had acquired a shortwave radio and spent considerable time listening to war news (as interpreted by both sides) and Roosevelt's fireside chats. That something bigger was in the wind was apparent, not only from the shipping going through the Canal, but also by construction of new, much wider locks and the buildup at neighboring Army and Navy facilities.

Jonas had occasionally thought about moving back to the continental United States in the previous year, but favored the tropical, maritime climate to the extent that he wasn't sure how well he would react to colder weather up north. Concern about weather passed though, and in September 1940, he made a direct inquiry with the Royal Canadian Air Force for pilot training. Not coincidentally, he spent part of his long annual vacation on the east coast. Prior to leaving for New York, he had gotten in touch with the Clayton Knight Committee, the organization responsible for recruiting Americans into the Royal Air Force via the Royal Canadian Air Force. Some of the young Americans who passed before the Clayton Knight Committee trained in Canada and went on to become part of the RAF's Bomber Command. A larger number went to Fighter Command where they were eventually concentrated in 71, 121, and 133 Squadrons which the world would better know later in 1941 as the "Eagle Squadrons."

Jonas initially appeared to meet the Committee's basic requirements, i.e. age 20-40, a 2S rating (single-engine, land airplane), experience with aircraft having a gross weight of 3,000 pounds or more, and health that matched that required of an Army Air Corps aviation cadet. 400 hours flying time was required in 1940, but that requirement would be reduced as the need for pilots increased. Jonas, at that time, was approaching 2,000 hours in powered aircraft, and, had he reported his additional time in gliders the total would have been closer to 3,000 hours.

In late 1940, an instrument maker vacancy occurred at the Department of Commerce's Weather Bureau research laboratory in Washington, DC. Jonas applied for the job and got it, but was in a quandary about accepting the offer since another opportunity had come his way at the same time. The latter possibility was also for an instrument maker's position in a government facility at a Navy yard in a tropical setting: Pearl Harbor, territory of Hawaii. Jonas chose the Washington job, in part because it would facilitate landing what he really wanted: a full-time flying job, possibly with an airline. He left Panama in late January 1941, and found an apartment near the city limits of Washington, on Sargent Road in what is today's Michigan Park section (bordering

Author's Collection

*The Vultee VI-AD that Jonas flew, shown here in a 1939 photograph taken in San Diego, was sold the following year by the publisher, William Randolph Hearst, to Ruff's part-time employer, Tito Gelabert.*

Hyattsville, Maryland). His work as an instrument maker was not at the Department of Commerce Building near the Ellipse and Washington Monument, but rather at the Bureau's labs in the Washington Navy Yard on the Anacostia River close to the Eleventh Street Bridge.

Immediately, he was receiving very high performance reviews for his work as a senior laboratory technician. Jonas enjoyed the novelty of snow, the first he had seen since leaving California six years before. Even the cold weather wasn't as bothersome as he had expected. And, he was taking in all of Washington in his spare time.

Much of the lab's work was military in nature, especially that done for the Navy. Ruff's work was so valued that the Weather Bureau requested a draft deferment for him early in 1941.

Although his draft status was 1-A, the exemption was not quite what Jonas had in mind. He was using his new location in Washington to expedite his entry into a more active, aviation-related involvement in the war. He was flying as frequently as he could, and had renewed his commercial pilot license before leaving Panama. His flying from suburban Washington in early 1941 was split between aerobatic practice and working toward an instrument rating. There were a few cross country hours, especially to Philadelphia where his work required frequent visits to the Navy Yard. There he met and dated the lovely Daisy Orvall who, like Aileen Smith before her, couldn't quite snare the handsome pilot.

By late April 1941, he was aggressively pursuing a full-time flying job. Over the summer, he applied to several of the major flight instruction schools which were beginning to train large numbers of Army aviation cadets. Among these schools were Riddle (later known as Embry-Riddle), Rankin Aeronautical in Tulare, California, and Parks Air College near St. Louis. From several of these companies, including Parks, he received employment offers which came temptingly early. The fact that he had successfully completed the flight instructor refresher course on PT-18 Stearmans at Parks' Sikeston, Missouri, contract primary field and then finished his instrument rating with Parks in East St. Louis during his 1941 summer vacation would have assured his employment nearly anywhere in the rapidly growing contract primary training business.

Ruff had, however, taught primary flight, soaring and aerobatics for ten years. With the memory of the Vultee V1 and Trimotors very fresh in his memory, he decided to pursue flying something more interesting than Stearman biplanes.

Ruff took to instrument flying like the proverbial duck to water. Not every "natural born, stick and rudder man" does, however. With his instinct for mechanical precision, draftsman's training, work with geometry, tolerances and three-dimensional shapes, mastering the spatial relationships inherent in instrument flying came easily to him. His letters home reveal a fervor for the type of flying which many pilots unenthusiastically approach as a necessary evil and a hurdle to be mastered in order to move to the next, higher level of flying. It must be noted that instrument flying in the 30s and early 40s was a much purer form of the art (or science) than in today's environment with its glide slopes, localizers, and the prevalence of radar vectoring to direct pilots onto final approach courses. Jonas even enjoyed flying Link trainers.

An instrument rating in 1941 was a noteworthy distinction as it largely is today, although the requirements in some respects were then harder, and, in others, easier. The same 200 hours flying time prerequisite was required, but only 20 hours of instrument dual was required in contrast to several times that needed today. Acquiring 20 hours of instrument dual was more difficult then, although much of the test was similar, i.e. the basic airwork of steep turns, climbs, descents, spirals, and recoveries all under the hood. In addition to successfully negotiating a written exam, an applicant in 1941 had to demonstrate familiarity with the radio range system by flying on the airways, holding, identifying the cone of silence, and making approaches into the field where the examination took place. Including instrument flying in Panama and California, Jonas had 71 hours of instrument time when he passed the test in St. Louis which in reality amounted to something between a breeze and formality.

In late summer, Jonas' work at the Navy Yard required him to spend several days at a time in Philadelphia. He put his evenings to good use by practicing on Link trainers at two airports, the old DuPont Airport north of Wilmington, Delaware, and Philadelphia's landmark general aviation facility, Wings Field. He was also able to log 15 hours of actual instrument flying time during that period.

While he was pursuing full-time aviation employment, his automotive fortunes took a major change for the better. He had sold the Oldsmobile sedan to his recently married sister and brother-in-law the previous year. He liked Oldsmobiles, and bought a new, 1941 Olds coupe, one of the first with the "Hydramatic" (automatic) drive.

Airline work proved elusive. Pan American, United and American were not hiring significant numbers of applicants in mid-1941. Airlines preferred copilot applicants to be under age 30; Jonas was 33 at that point. However, as had been the case with Hal Blackburn at TWA, most airlines were willing to bend the rule if only a couple years were involved and the applicant was especially promising. He continued to pursue the Canadian possibility, both the RCAF and its Ferry Command which was partially comprised of civilians. In the latter case, the pay was excellent — 1,000 American dollars per month for a captain and $800 for copilots. In training, it was $10 per day.

Unfortunately, his applications to the U.S. Navy and the Royal Canadian Air Force for flight training were both rejected for the same reason; he was color blind. Although very impressed with Ruff's flying capabilities, United Airlines turned him down promptly on the color vision matter, and he left the Chicago interviews uncharacteristically down in spirits. Still, American Airlines had given him considerable encouragement that an offer wasn't far in the future. His old friend, Bob Redding, had told him that he stood a good chance of becoming an instructor at the TWA operation in Albuquerque.

Jonas was visiting the Library of Congress with a lady friend when the Pearl Harbor announcement was made, and he was in the gallery when President Roosevelt addressed Congress to make the declaration of war. On January 14, 1942, a telegram was delivered to Jonas; Hal Blackburn advised that airline tickets for his interview in Albuquerque were being airmailed that day.

Ruff was subsequently hired as a copilot/instructor at an annual salary of $4,400 from which the cost of his TWA uniform, with its Eagle Nest braid, would be deducted. The letter of employment included a secrecy clause and a proviso that employment would cease if TWA's contract with the government were to be terminated (which either party could do on 30 days notice). Jonas, in his brand new black Oldsmobile coupe, was on his way to the Land of Enchantment where he reported on February 2, 1942. There was no doubt in his (or Hal Blackburn's) mind that he was up to the task of his dreams — flying the B-24 Liberator heavy bomber.

# VII

## THE CONSOLIDATED B-24
## LIBERATOR HEAVY BOMBER

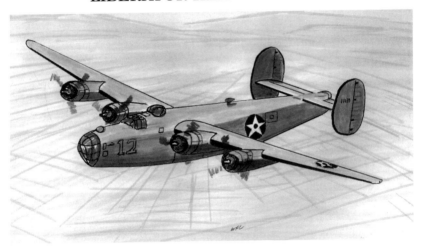

How different Kansas looked to Jonas at 21,000 feet. He had only seen Kansas once before, and that was very briefly in the summer of 1941 after his Army instructor's refresher course in Missouri. Charlie had driven across the state on the way to primary flight training in California. Now, nearly ten months later, Reynard was flying one of those big bombers which had been part of the impressive flyover when he graduated from primary. Looking out along the left wing, Charlie was impressed with the power of this Liberator which some news reporters described as a "giant." Large it was in its day, but it wouldn't have won any beauty contests. It never developed a loyal following among pilots the way the B-17 Flying Fortress did. The '17, as "Queen of the Skies," completely overshadowed the '24, and thoroughly captured the imagination of the press and the public.

The Liberator, however, was built in larger numbers than any other American plane during the war — over 18,000. First built at the

Consolidated Aircraft plant in San Diego and then at the company's plant in Fort Worth, the Liberator was also built under license by three other manufacturers. They were Douglas/Tulsa, North American/Dallas, and the Ford Motor Company in Willow Run, Michigan (the latter not without some teething problems).

In fact, only the German Messerschmidt Bf109 fighter and the heavily armored, tank-busting Russian Ilyushin Stormovik light attack bomber were built in greater numbers. Today, there are only three flying Liberators left in the world. Very few pilots cared for the B-24's handling characteristics. It did not have a reputation as a widowmaker in the Martin B-26 Marauder sense, nor was it a "hot rod" like the Douglas A-20 Havoc. The Liberator was heavy on the controls (not that any four-engine plane with a gross weight of 56,000 pounds was as responsive as a North American B-25 Mitchell medium bomber or the British Spitfire interceptor). The B-24's wing area was substantially less than the other "heavy", the B-17, and with a slightly heavier gross weight, the wing loading was higher which correspondingly resulted in faster takeoff and landing speeds.

The B-24 tended to "hunt," that is, it wandered and would not hold altitude and heading as well as some other aircraft, such as the B-17 which tracked very well. It was as though each of the B-24's big twin rudders argued with the other as to just who was the boss with the result that neither won the argument, and the plane's directional composure was the real loser. The hunting, however, was nowhere near the magnitude to warrant description as lacking inherent aerodynamic stability. This laziness about holding a heading was not unusual since more than just a few multi-engine planes have the same tendency — it is just more pronounced in the Liberator.

The situation might be likened to a large, leashed dog not wanting to walk quite the same course as his master who must constantly remind Fido to stay on the straight and narrow. This shortcoming required attention and re-trimming to maintain the desired heading and altitude. This was not a big deal, let's say on a casual cross country flight involving just one B-24. With a full 8,000 pound bomb load, wallowing around in somebody else's propwash, and trying to maintain straight and level flight in air disturbed by anti-aircraft artillery or rising thermals, it became another matter entirely, especially in a tight combat box formation with five other Liberators in close proximity.

The B-17 begat the B-24, or so the story goes. In 1939, the Army Air

*The first B-24s were manufactured in San Diego by Consolidated Aircraft. No other American aircraft was built in larger numbers than the Liberator during WWII (over 18,000 produced).*

Corps knew it had a winner in the B-17 Flying Fortress, even though it had less than two dozen of the great ships in its inventory. So, the Air Corps went shopping for other aircraft manufacturers to produce 17s under license to Boeing. Even with plants in Seattle and Wichita, Boeing could not produce enough Fortresses for Air Corps needs.

Army procurement officials approached Consolidated Aircraft of San Diego as a potential B-17 manufacturer. Consolidated was well known for its production of large two and four-engine flying boats. Consolidated suggested that it could build a better bomber than the B-17. In January of 1939, the Army Air Corps accepted a design proposal from Consolidated for a bomber that would outperform the B-17. Emphasis was placed on long range, speed over 300 miles per hour, and a service ceiling of 30,000 feet. On operational B-24s, depending on load, the projected altitude was obtainable, but the 300 mph speed was something of an illusion.

The XB-24 flew on December 29, 1939 ("X" for experimental). Both the British and French placed orders for the new ship in addition to the Air Corps' initial purchase of 70 planes. The '24 had some unique features not the least of which was the "Davis" wing, a high lift design whose greatest thickness was well aft which allowed for maximum strength, large fuel capacity, simplified construction, and wheel wells in the wings instead of engine nacelles which was the more common practice. Structural ice was, however, not one of the items at which the Davis wing excelled at lifting.

The Liberator also employed the new Fowler flaps that extended outward from the trailing edge, a steerable tricycle landing gear which was then becoming the standard, and a unique double section bomb bay with doors that rolled up the side of the fuselage. Consolidated's Model 31 flying boat bequeathed the Liberator its characteristic, twin rudder arrangement.

Otherwise, the B-24 can simply be described as a high-winged, four-engine heavy bomber powered by four Pratt & Whitney Twin Row Wasp supercharged engines developing 1200 horsepower each. The wing span was 110 feet, fuselage length 67 feet, height over 18 feet, range of 1700 miles with average bomb load of 8,000 pounds, and the advertised top speed was 300 mph.[1] The bomb load varied depending on how much fuel was aboard, and the speed was rarely seen in any mode except nose down.

To put this into today's perspective, the wing span was comparable to smaller jet transports such as early DC-9s or Boeing 737s, but the fuselage was only about half as long. It would take nearly a miracle to cram 150 people and baggage into a '24 let alone think about taking off with them aboard.

The Liberator flew with most Allied air forces and in many roles: heavy bomber, VIP transport, cargo, tanker, photo and weather reconnaissance, maritime patrol, electronic warfare (radar jamming), and antisubmarine warfare.

When viewed from directly head-on, or directly aft, above or below, the plane looked quite clean and efficient, almost a model of aerodynamic cleanliness (for a heavy, 1940s vintage bomber, anyway). From the side, it looked as though it might have come from some Jurassic barnyard with its beer belly, slab sides and barndoor tails. The Liberator's tendency to wallow on the ground as well as in the air, its portly bearing, and its low-slung demeanor prompted more than just the occasional pilot to preflight one as though it were a somewhat dyspeptic hippopotamus to which the B-24 displayed more than just a passing resemblance.

At first glance, one might think the B-24 to be a roomy aircraft considering its bulky appearance. Such was not the case at all, with the possible exception of the waist gunners' compartment, but even that was cluttered with the .50 caliber machine guns, drop-down windows, ammunition belts and boxes, the ball turret nearly blocking access to the bomb bay, and, after the D-model Liberator, the bulky, ubiquitous oxygen cylinders which replaced the oxygen tanks located in the outboard wing panels on early B-24 models. Tossing in a B-4 bag or two, aviator's kit bags, everybody's chest parachute, a few half empty food ration packs, flak vests, and helmets created an atmosphere which could not easily be confused with a standard room at the nearest Holiday Inn.

Including the front turret gunner on later models, the nose section was shared by the navigator whose station provided a wonderful panorama of the rudder pedals and pilots' feet, and the bombardier whose view, on the D-model, was on par, if not better than that of the pilots and top turret gunner. Unfortunately for the men situated in the nose, their companion was the space-hungry nose landing gear and its attending strut and steering mechanism.

The nose gunner, navigator and bombardier could enter the bomber through the nose wheel well (although they were normally banished from the nose during takeoffs and landings). These men developed the duck-walk to a fine degree since the clearance between the ground and the bottom of the fuselage was minimal. The gear doors were spring loaded, and

National Archives

*One of the 16 Liberators operated by the Combat Crew Training School in Albuquerque. Photographed in late spring 1942.*

in an emergency bailout situation, those in the nose could jump down through the wheel well after pulling the doors' manual release.

Pilots and crews rarely had anything complimentary to say about the Liberator's fuel system because it leaked dangerously. Unlike today's capacitance or ultrasonics-based fuel gauging systems whose data is calculated and displayed digitally, the B-24 utilized sight gauges at the flight engineer's station. The fuel level was read directly through graduated glass columns. Should a thermos jug, flak helmet, or kneeboard accidentally bash the glass column, the flight deck would be filled with spraying gasoline. And, hopefully, the radio operator would not have decided moments before that the time was opportune to enjoy a Lucky Strike.

Excluding auxiliary tanks further out in the wings, the main fuel load was carried in 12 bladders, three for each engine, with a total main fuel capacity of 2,343 gallons. The auxiliary tank system provided another 450 gallons in six additional cells. These tanks were connected by a labyrinthine crossfeed system which allowed fuel to be transferred between tanks. It was in this system where the leaks occurred. The fuel system was subsequently fixed on later models, but it was a problem which claimed more than just a few B-24s. Since the ship accumulated such dangerous levels of fuel vapors, prudent Liberator pilots usually flew with bomb bay doors

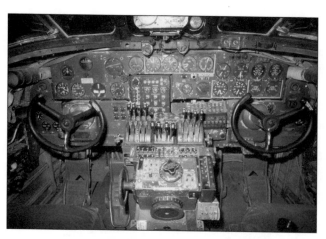

Author's Collection

*B-24D instrument panel. Designers placed all of the air data and navigation instruments on the left for the pilot. The copilot got all of the engine instruments at right.*

opened slightly to clear out the fumes and turned off the radio equipment when transferring fuel. One spark was all it would take.

The B-24's unique bomb bay doors were ideal for clearing out fumes because they did not hang down into the slipstream like most other bombers'. Since the doors rolled up the side of the fuselage, they created minimal drag and cost only a negligible loss in airspeed — a small price to pay for so much explosion insurance.

Like all great round engines that belch fire and cough smoke, the Pratt & Whitney R-1830 Twin Row Wasps each had a taste for oil — perhaps a bit more than a garden variety Ford Taurus. Indeed, each engine was equipped with a 39-gallon metal tank whose oil lubricated not only the engine, but also the turbocharger. The oil actuated the turbocharger regulator and operated the propeller pitch and feathering mechanisms as well.

TWA and the other airlines flying for the Air Transport Command flew the C-87 Liberator Express, a somewhat de-featured cargo version of the B-24 bomber for which the bomb bay was faired over and turned into space for freight. Bereft of retracting bomb bay doors with which to remove gasoline fumes, the C-87 provided extra incentive for those trying to kick the weed habit since lighting up could prove instantly fatal as opposed to providing a lingering, cancerous departure for that great hangar up in the sky.

Merely one little spark from a hydraulic pump, radio, fuel pump, or the flame of a thoughtlessly lit cigarette match could turn a Liberator Express into a flaming explosion. Hal Blackburn often maintained that the Air Transport Command C-87s inexplicably lost on long overseas flights went down not due to poor piloting, but, rather, because most of them quite simply blew up unobserved when accumulated vapors ignited. In 1943, a TWA Liberator Express blew up in mid-Atlantic on the southern route: on course one moment and a fireball the next — from what was surely a fuel vapor explosion. The pilot had been one of the TWA first officer/instructors in Albuquerque when Jeffries and Reynard were going through the school.

Shortly after going operational with the C-87, TWA pilots formalized their complaints about the plane in an engineering white paper which focused primarily on the fuel management and measurement systems, but also suggested specific improvements in the oil, electrical, lighting, and fire suppression systems. No corrective action was ever taken. That failure sweetened the day in mid-1943 when TWA traded out its C-87s for new Douglas C-54s. On the other hand, crews had nothing but praise for the Pratt & Whitney R-1830 Twin Row Wasp engines. It's not for nothing that the motto was bandied about in those days, "Trust in God and Pratt & Whitney." Even today, the corporate tag line is "Dependable Engines." That's about as far as praise went for the '24, however.

This particular airplane, serial number 41-1133, had been built in San Diego and had less than 120 hours on it when it departed Kirtland that morning. It was a very early D model, and produced in a block of aircraft from which many were transferred to the Royal Air Force. Under the Lend-Lease Program, the RAF took delivery of 1,694 new Liberators during the war, and hundreds more, many quite war-weary, were turned over to the RAF and other Allied air forces in the field.[2]

The cost to Uncle Sam was $391,514 for a brand new B-24D.[3] 41-1133 rolled off the assembly line in early March, and immediately went into production testing, a time-consuming process involving acceptance by Consolidated company and Air Force pilots. It could take a week or longer for all of the engine run-ups, system checks, flight checks, compass correction on the compass rose, paint touch-ups, and re-checks for squawks identified in the first round of inspections. The big ship was taken into Army Air Force inventory on March 7, 1942. Nine days later, it was allocated to the TWA school in Albuquerque, and flown there by pilots from the Air Transport Ferry Command base at Long Beach, California. It may have been a homecoming for the crew since nearly all of the Air Force's first B-24 ferry crews had been trained by TWA in Albuquerque.

The D model had the glass-framed "greenhouse" nose and was the first model produced in large numbers — around 2,500 out of the total of over 18,000 Liberators produced.

The RAF chose not to operate the B-24D Liberator as a bomber due to its poor forward firepower (that would be corrected in later models with power front turrets). Except for range, the Liberator did not have the performance of the Royal Air Force's faster, four-engine Avro Lancaster whose bomb-carrying capacity was over twice that of the B-24. Instead, the RAF used the Liberator primarily as a long range maritime patrol bomber and VIP passenger transport. Winston Churchill's personal transport was a Liberator named "Commando." Even though it was an early model, modified with the removal of its bomb doors, and subject to fuel leaks, it was probably afraid to blow up on its cigar-smoking passenger.

Another Liberator was modified for use by President Roosevelt. After a rash of C-87 accidents, it was decided that maybe the Liberator wasn't the best choice after all. Instead, Roosevelt's personal transport became a C-54 Skymaster, and his modified Liberator, which he never did fly in, became transportation for VIPs of a lesser magnitude.

The Liberator was physically demanding to fly for long stretches, and Lord forbid a pilot should lose an outboard engine, number one or four. Even re-trimmed to reduce the tendency to turn into the dead engine, the pilot had to stand on a rudder pedal — maybe for hours. Yet, the ship did have some virtues. The cockpit was comfortable and actually included upholstered seats for the pilots. That was small consolation in a crash landing, however, since the top turret had the distressing habit of collapsing down onto the flight deck right between the engineer's and radio operator's stations thus effectively blocking fast exit through the bomb bay or the nose wheel well which had to be accessed from the rear of the flight deck.

The B-17, while offering less creature comforts, was easier to depart from in an emergency and generally considered to be a structurally more sound aircraft. Yet, the '24 was built in significantly higher numbers. Until the B-29 came along and went into service in 1944, nothing else from American factories could match the Liberator for the purpose to which it had been designed — carrying a larger bomb load higher, faster, and farther than any other operational heavy bomber.

While the B-24 Liberator never quickened an aerodynamic stylist's breath, it had one virtue that was revealed only after the wartime statisticians closed their books on stateside flying accidents. In the continental United States, it was a comparatively very safe machine to fly. During the full three and a half years of direct American involvement in WWII, the B-24 Liberator type experienced an accident rate within the zone of the interior of 35 incidents per 100,000 hours of flying.[4] That was not quite as good as the B-17 Flying Fortress (30 accidents per 100,000 hours), but statistically, significantly lower than advanced trainers such as the AT-6 (55 per 100,000).

To put that into finer focus, the graduating cadet who wanted to live on the edge had only to become a P-39 Airacobra pilot where the rate was 245 incidents per 100,000 hours of flying. Even the much maligned Martin B-26 Marauder's overall wartime accident rate was only 55 (although early in the war before new training and maintenance procedures were initiated, B-26s were having accidents at the rate of 162 per 100,000 flying hours). Still, during the course of the war, there were

Author's Collection

*To be sure, the once-savored, never-forgotten roar of Pratt and Whitney Twin Row Wasps. Photographed aboard the Collings Foundation's B-24 Liberator on a lovely autumn morning over eastern Pennsylvania.*

1,713 flying accidents in the continental U.S. involving Liberators, and of those, 746 were written off as wrecks. All of the dry, safety statistics and all of the plane's laurels are, of course, little consolation to the families of the 165 Liberator crewmen killed in domestic flying accidents in 1942 or the families of nearly 2,700 more Liberator flyers killed in stateside mishaps before the war's end in 1945.

However, in spite of the many disparaging comments directed at its frumpy appearance and somewhat wayward ways in the air, the B-24 was a hardy old bird. Anyone who doubts that would do well to experience a Liberator takeoff wherein, after first getting up its head of steam, the ship becomes a thundering, runway-gobbling beast with enough acceleration to make a firm believer of even the most aeronautically ambivalent.

Yet, on that April 22nd, four miles aloft over Kansas, with the penetrating cold and deafening roar, there was no sense of speed, no rush of momentum, and no thrill of illicitly whizzing past church steeples, mountain crests, building tops, or the fleecy cupola atop some billowing cumulus cloud.

# VIII

# KEEP 'EM FLYING

It was the rare, newly rated-pilot who hoped for assignment to a B-24 transition school. Mechanics and flight engineers had pretty much the same attitude since the machine was not designed with easy maintenance in mind. Thus, pilots valued the services of well-qualified flight engineers and mechanics. In that regard, the five pilots on 41-1133 were blessed with a remarkable amount of talent in their flight engineers and radio operator, beginning with the most experienced man aboard, the flight engineer instructor.

George Van Hoozer was no stranger to Kansas City which had been his residence for several years prior to moving to Albuquerque the previous autumn. Had this fateful flight taken place in early November 1941, Van Hoozer's wife Ruth and baby daughter Carolyn would have come out to meet the plane at the Kansas City Airport and then driven back to their home on Morrell Avenue.

The Van Hoozers had moved to Albuquerque when George was in his sixth year with TWA as an aircraft mechanic. At that time, the number of Liberators at the Jack Frye Four Engine School was increasing from just one B-24A and several LB-30s to over a dozen. With the number of hours flown in a busy training schedule expanding rapidly, the need for mechanics grew dramatically. When the Van Hoozers moved to New Mexico, they were young, it was an advancement for George; the school was contributing to the Allied effort, and George had a curiosity about far away places that Albuquerque would at least temporarily satisfy. In late February 1942, Van Hoozer gave in to that adventurous nature, went through B-24 flight engineer training with the March class, and became a flight engineer instructor in April.

George Van Hoozer stood out in a crowd. Nearly 30, he was just over six feet tall, slender, and had a very debonair appearance capped off with a well-trimmed moustache. "Well-trimmed" are key words because

Carolyn Van Hoozer Fullerton Collection

*George Van Hoozer in Albuquerque, early 1942.*
*Prior to becoming a flight engineer instructor, he*
*had been an aircraft mechanic and maintenance*
*instructor with TWA in Kansas City.*

he was a very meticulous man. The most complicated of repairs or maintenance projects were approached with precision: disassembled parts were laid out in logical order and reassembled in exact sequence. The notes he made on machine repairs or servicing aircraft are models of discipline. It was no surprise when he went into aviation maintenance — he was gifted mechanically. He is remembered as a man who undertook the most complicated, filthiest of jobs and emerged remarkably clean and organized, looking almost as though he were about to initiate the work instead of completing it.

His hometown, Windsor, Missouri, is in a very pretty setting on the Ozarks borders. It had been settled by trappers in the early 1800s and was the site of the first Confederate flag raising in Missouri. The Windsor countryside, southeast of Kansas City, is one of rolling hills, woods, lakes, pastures, and fields. The town has a population of slightly under 4,000 and can legitimately be described as small town America in the heart of America. Although there was no Scout troop in town during Van Hoozer's youth, Troop 632 is one of several activities available to Windsor youth nowadays.

The town's first major employers, a coal strip mine and shoe factory, no longer operate. Today's light industry is secondary to farming in this town which has not changed significantly since Van Hoozer left in 1931. Dairy farming, wheat, corn, soybeans, and milo dominate the agricultural base.

Van Hoozer's father, George, had moved from Tennessee to Missouri where George, the younger of two sons, was born in Leeton in 1912. While his close friends called him "Van," young George was also known in the Van Hoozer family by his middle name, "Emery," to avoid confusion with his father. Subsequently, the family moved to Windsor where the elder Van Hoozer became a produce farmer with a residence in the town itself.

Within George Van Hoozer there was a submerged, audacious nature that first showed up late in high school. He took the academic course and was quite musical. He sang well and played both the harmonica and guitar. He also had a neck cradle for the harmonica which freed his hands to play the guitar simultaneously. He was able to combine his musical and mechanical interests in a way which was an occasional attraction at school assemblies — his combo featured homemade instruments with George Van Hoozer at the "bass fiddle" which incorporated a large, galvanized wash tub.

Since music ran in the family, there were many sessions with George strumming the guitar, singing, and his mother playing the piano. Not surprisingly, George was a member of the glee club and mixed chorus in high school. He also was vice president of the drama club which had started up late in his junior year as well as art director of the school yearbook.

His work in the family produce business precluded participation in school sports, but Van Hoozer was an active player in neighborhood softball games.

In his junior year, the first inkling of a career path surfaced when he built a hang-glider with two friends. They drew lots to see who would fly it from a building roof within sight of the high school yard: George became one of the two unlucky observers. "Lucky" might be a better choice of words since the flight ended in disaster when the unfortunate pilot broke an arm in the ensuing crash landing. But, it clearly kindled an interest that was realized when George enlisted in the Navy for aircraft mechanic training after graduation from high school in 1931.

He finished first in his class at Glenview Naval Air Station just outside of Chicago in 1932. He was in fast company since that particular class established the strongest record of any in the training center's history.

That this young man from the Ozarks would join the Navy as opposed to the Army, where a stateside assignment was the rule, is another indicator of that Van Hoozer wanderlust. The quest for something different resulted in his assignment to the Panama Canal where he served as a seaplane mechanic.

At some point in the mid-1930s, Van Hoozer started flying lessons. Although he did not pursue the instruction to the point of a license, the experience added to his mechanical depth. The desire to fly, then submerged, would surface again after Pearl Harbor.

Not too long after his return from the Navy, he met and married Ruth Kays who was originally from Warsaw, Missouri. They settled in Kansas City where George had gone to work as a mechanic for TWA after working briefly at the shoe factory in Windsor following his discharge from the Navy. Their marriage was kept secret for a while. George sent for Ruth after getting established with TWA, and they moved into an apartment in Kansas City. Later, in 1940, with a baby on the way, they rented the home on Morrell Avenue.

George received regular promotions and by 1941 had advanced to

Carolyn Van Hoozer Fullerton Collection

*George Van Hoozer started working on a pilot's
license shortly after completing military service as
a Navy aircraft mechanic in the mid-1930s.*

maintenance instructor. In 1940, their daughter, Carolyn Kay, was born,
and a year later, they moved to Albuquerque where George became a
mechanic on what was then the latest bomber in the Army Air Force
inventory. Prior to the move, Van Hoozer was encouraged by some of his
TWA friends, military reservists, to renew his ties with the military, but
he chose not to do so at that time. Later, however, when it was obvious
that the TWA school in Albuquerque was going to be folded, the Army
Air Force offered Van Hoozer a direct commission based on his out-
standing performance, and he was planning to accept. Had this become
a reality, Van Hoozer might have become an engineering instructor —
probably on B-24s. It is more likely, however, that he would have been
teaching engineering instructor candidates since the demand for qualified instructors was desperate in early 1942.

By all accounts, George Van Hoozer was an excellent instructor who combined a wealth of technical knowledge with the ability to communicate it well. And in Corporal Macomber, he had a particularly apt student.

## The Downeaster

Philip Emerson Macomber came from rural, inland Maine where his ancestors had lived since colonial times. He was solidly built, of average height, and as you might expect of a man growing up on a farm, had large, powerful hands.

He is remembered as a remarkably friendly and generous young person with a lot of community spirit. He was the type one would treasure as a next door neighbor.

North Jay, his hometown, is one of those many little New England crossroad villages consisting of a post office, two churches, a fire station, grange hall, a service station, and a few homes. Located just several miles above the larger town of Jay, Macomber's hometown is situated in a particularly picturesque part of Maine — where the rolling hills near the coast give way to the mountains of central Maine.

Augusta, the state capitol, is about 30 miles to the southeast (as the crow flies, and a bit longer on today's roads). Although there are numerous meadows and fields around North Jay, the landscape is dominated by forest, lakes, and fast-rushing streams, especially the Androscoggin River on whose banks the area's largest employer, International Paper, is located five miles down Route 17. Farming is still important, but most of the economic activity in the area is located in Jay proper and adjacent Livermore Falls. At one time, North Jay was home for a granite quarry whose output was utilized in many commercial and institutional buildings, not to mention monuments including Grant's tomb.

"Downeaster" accents are thick in this southernmost corner of Franklin County. The Macomber name is pronounced, "Make-em-buh." The Macomber home, long since passed out of the family hands, is very well kept up by its current owners. Originally, the Macomber place was that uniquely New England farm home with <u>attached</u> barn. Between the residence and barn was a large shed through which ran a passageway. A two-car garage now occupies the space once taken up by the shed. The barn has been razed, but beyond that the home remains much as it had been during Philip's lifetime. From the front yard there is a beautiful, mountainous panorama to the south including the apple orchard just across the road, and beyond that, fields and forest. The setting conjures up Currier and Ives-type images of skating on frozen ponds in winter, tapping maple trees for sap in the early spring, and days gone by when sleighs and buggies were more common than automobiles.

The farm was located on Macomber Hill which dominates North Jay's eastern horizon. The Macomber place was a large one with over 70 head of cattle, sheep and work horses. Philip, the second of two children, was born on Flag Day, June 14, 1917. His first few years were typical farm boy — helping with the chores, carefree play on the farm, sledding down the hill with his sister and friends in winter, and attending the one-room elementary school located quite near his home on the road to North Jay which is located little more than a mile away.

Tragedy visited the Macomber family early in Philip's life when his father died in 1925. Philip, with his sister Eloise, worked hard enough to see that his mother, Cora, was able to keep the farm going, although the operation was scaled back considerably when most of the livestock were sold. Still, it was a busy life with the milking, garden, and many chores so typical of family farms. Philip enjoyed high school sports as an occasional spectator, but duties on the farm took up much of his time.

Philip Macomber graduated from Jay High School in 1935, and traveled to Cleveland, Ohio, for a year's course in mechanics at the McSweeney Trade School. Like many a farm boy, Macomber was handy and gifted mechanically. Upon his return, he was employed at Harry Stansfield's, the local garage. As with most young men in North Jay, he hunted deer, brought home the occasional rabbit for dinner, and frequently fished the fast, cold streams for trout.

Macomber wore several hats, and had to be hard-pressed to juggle so many activities. In addition to his regular job, there was the family farm and, of course, any farm is hardly a nine-to-five business. He was also very active in the North Jay Volunteer Fire Department and a very visible member of the Grange.

"The Grange" doesn't have quite the central role in rural America that it once did due to the decline in the number of family farms. But, even today, few rural communities are without the Grange hall, and North Jay is no exception. Still, there are over 350,000 members and over a thousand chapters. Its role as the center of community life is reduced now. However, in Macomber's day, it was the center of activity for which not the least of reasons was its function as the community store.

Eloise Macomber Hatfield Collection

*Philip E. Macomber photographed at home in North Jay, Maine, shortly after his June 1941 enlistment in the Army Air Force.*

In North Jay, the Grange hall is a three-story, rambling white building and still the largest structure in town. How easy it is to picture Philip with a friendly smile and hearty laugh at Grange events, or maybe stopping by the Grange after work to see his sweetheart, Margaret Holt. He was a member of the Grange degree (ritual) team which was quite an honor for one so young.

He had a good job and was comfortable in North Jay, but that little community was not immune from world events and the draft which was shifting into high gear in 1941. Philip enlisted in June at the post office at Lewiston and was first stationed at Westover Field in Chicopee Falls, Massachusetts. In the peacetime Air Corps, aviation mechanics were usually trained at Chanute Field in Illinois, but that field could not absorb the dramatic expansion in enlistees assigned to mechanic schools.

To remedy the situation until Air Corps facilities were able to absorb them, new men were sent to private industry for training much in the same manner as pilots were sent to civilian contractors for primary flight instruction. In Westover's case, men who had just enlisted were sent to east coast aviation trade schools, such as New England Aircraft School, East Boston, Massachusetts, or Roosevelt Aviation, Garden City, New York, for approximately six months before being assigned to a specific squadron.

Between July 1, 1939, and December 31, 1941, the civilian schools trained 6,968 aircraft mechanics, 356 sheet metal workers and 38 aircraft welders.[1] During the same period of time, Chanute Field graduated 17,945 aircraft mechanics. On December 7, 1941, over 15,000 students were enrolled at Chanute and the other two bases which had started aircraft mechanic training programs (Keesler and Sheppard Fields in Mississippi and Texas, respectively). Slightly more than 4,000 were enrolled at the civilian schools on that date.

Philip received 960 hours of classroom and hands-on instruction over a 28-week period in a program wherein the civilian school supplied textbooks, tools, facilities, airplanes and engines. For his education, the contractor was paid $1,113.87. The washout rate, at seven percent, was substantially lower than that for pilot training. Considering the fact that keeping men like Jeffries or Reynard in the air, seven specialists (aircraft mechanics, radio technicians, etc.) were required, the civilian schools for mechanics were established just in time.

Macomber's arrival at Westover in June 1941 coincided with the just completed base receiving its first new aircraft — several B-17s. It would be many months before its resident air units received their full complement of nine aircraft per squadron.

He was assigned to the 18th Bomb Squadron of the 34th Bomb Group, one of the first organizations to become operational with the B-17. The 34th had been activated at Langley Field in Virginia and moved to Westover where they were responsible for anti-submarine patrols. New England accents prevailed among the ground crews, gunners, radiomen, and flight engineers in the group's early days since a majority of its personnel after the move to Westover came from Massachusetts and neighboring states.

Philip and his fellow New Englanders became known as "backyard soldiers" by the old men of the group who started with the 34th in Virginia in December 1940.

The move to Westover was welcomed since the hangars were bigger and the barracks more comfortable. At that stage, in the late summer and autumn of 1941, while Philip was in mechanic's training, the 18th Bomb Squadron maintenance schedule was not too demanding. The 34th Bomb Group had only several B-17s, a few B-18s, and most of the pilots had to settle for PT-17s in order to qualify for flight pay. Flying crews used a target one-half mile west of the field itself as a practice bombing range, and air-to-air gunnery practice was conducted off the coast of Long Island.

There were three other squadrons attached to the 34th Bomb Group; one of them, the Seventh Bomb Squadron, was skippered by a no-nonsense, cigar-chewing major headed for larger commands in the very near future. His name was Curtis Emerson LeMay.

Philip Macomber is remembered today by surviving 18th Squadron mates as a friendly young man who never lost his temper. "Easy-going" and "happy-go-lucky" are phrases repeated when Macomber's name is mentioned. He is also recalled as a mechanic who got around in style since he rode a motorcycle while stationed at Westover. That Philip would become a flight engineer did not surprise his friends for within him there was an adventuring streak. His attraction to engines, speed, power, wind, and motion was well developed before he ever saw the inside of a B-17 Flying Fortress. With his great Harley Davidson, he had motored much further than roundtrips between Macomber Hill and North Jay. Indeed, his vacation in 1940 was spent riding his motorcycle to Florida and back.

German submarines operated quite close to the American coast and well within range of Army Air Force patrol bombers before Pearl Harbor. The sinking of the American destroyer escort *USS Reuben James* in October, 1941, put Westover-based squadrons on an even higher state of readiness and would prepare them for their next duty station and assignment.

All Christmas leaves were canceled in the wake of Pearl Harbor. Civilians were not permitted on the base any longer, and a 24-hour guard was established. Pearl Harbor also prompted a change in stations for the 34th.

Philip had been able to get home twice since enlisting, but on January 22, 1942, he left home for the last time. The New England flying weather had been miserable since late October. The Second U.S. Army

Air Force, based in the Pacific Northwest, was building up rapidly and needed heavy bomber crews. Philip boarded a troop train with the 800 officers and men of the 34th Bomb Group and headed west.

Macomber's talent, training and work experience showed quickly since he graduated from aviation maintenance training among the top three in his class. Aviation mechanic training was highly specialized and involved both airframe and powerplant studies. For those who did well and passed the aircrew aptitude tests, the door was open to subsequent training as a flight engineer.

It was for training as a flight crew member that Macomber was sent to the TWA-operated CCTS. Had he lived, he would have shortly also been assigned to an aerial gunnery course since flight engineers usually functioned secondarily as top turret gunners.

It is most likely that Philip Macomber would not have remained with the 34th Bomb Group. Many of the flight engineers and radiomen sent to the Kirtland CCTS were subsequently assigned to the 305th or 306th Bomb Groups. Fortune favored those who remained with the 34th Bomb Group which stayed in the United States until late spring of 1944 when it became the last heavy bomb group assigned to the Eighth Air Force. Knowing the 34th Bomb Group history is a worthwhile diversion, here, since it sharply illustrates what a difference the simple stroke of a personnel officer's pen could make on a flyer's fortunes.[2]

While it was stationed in the United States, the 34th functioned as a B-24 replacement training group based at Davis-Monthan Field, Arizona, Geiger Field, Washington, and Blythe Field, California. On May 31, 1944, the 34th left the Zone of the Interior for England via the southern ferry route: Florida, Trinidad, Brazil, West Africa, and Marrakesh. Within several months of arriving in the European Theater, the group traded in its B-24Js for B-17G Flying Fortresses, a move that pleased nearly everybody involved.

Ironically, the 34th lost exactly 34 of its planes to enemy fire, but of that number only one was to a German fighter, and that was under very unusual circumstances. Returning from a mission as darkness was setting in over its base at Mendlesham, England, several 34th Group B-24s were attacked by a German intruder aircraft, a Junkers Ju88 night fighter, which shot one of the B-24s down. Thus, the only 34th Bomb Group loss to *Luftwaffe* fighters was right over its own base.

The group, in a year of combat, flew 170 missions, but only experienced about one-fifth of the losses experienced by pioneer groups such as the 305th or 306th Bomb Groups with which Philip Macomber almost certainly would have gone overseas to face daunting prospects for survival.

Philip was a pleasure for Van Hoozer to work with, and would have been a highly valued member of any bomber crew to which he might have been assigned. Unlike so many of the younger enlistees and draftees who had no particular mechanical experience or training, Macomber's profile closely approximated the Air Corps' late 1930s ideal prerequisites for flight engineers in training: at least one year of trade

Eloise Hatfield Macomber Collection

*Philip Macomber with his mother, Cora, and sister, Eloise, while home on leave from Westover Field, Chicopee Falls, Massachusetts. Autumn 1941.*

school, three or more years of practical experience, familiarity with airplanes, and enough time logged in the air to want more.

Flight engineers shouldered the weighty responsibility of making sure all aircraft systems were functioning properly, and if something should fail, it was the engineer's job to set it right — in flight. In the case of the B-24D, Macomber's talents would have been fully utilized since the ship was widely regarded as a mechanical sad sack for its fuel system and, to a lesser extent, for its hydraulic system. There were also problems with the propeller governors, cowl flap motors, and generators. Macomber had to know more about the airplane than the rest of the crew put together.

That's a lot of knowledge considering what is involved: powerplants, fuel system, electrical system, the hydraulic system, the oxygen system, flight controls, the deicer and anti-icing systems, environmental controls, and the emergency and fire suppression systems. Because he came from a heavy bomber squadron, he also had to be knowledgeable about the bombing and gunnery systems, although that expertise was not developed with 41-1133 since many of the Kirtland CCTS ships were essentially stock B-24s of which many were stripped of their .50 caliber machine guns.

Macomber also had other duties. The flight engineer, although he never received flight instruction, was expected to function as a back-up to the copilot (principally for engine management), and he was the designated first aid expert.

But, he did not have to worry about the bulky, complex and, by today's standards, dinosauric communications system (other than its power source). That was Duane Peterson's bailiwick.

### The Northern Plainsman

"High Plains Drifter" would be another way to describe Duane Millard Peterson. At age 22, he was finishing his fourth year in the Army, and had only recently completed radio training. Flying over the flatness of eastern Kansas was reassuring to him since he had grown up on the plains too. Whereas Philip Macomber felt a bit exposed and unprotected by the lack of mountainous bulwarks on the horizon, Peterson was used to the freedom of an unbroken horizon. But, Peterson left very few, if any tracks, in the communities of his youth.

No college remembers him, he is not warmly recalled in a grange or fire hall by a gathering of elderly men looking back to the days of their youth; no Scouting society honors his memory, and no group has ever tried to name something in his honor. His branch of the family has completely evaded the reach of Peterson genealogists in today's southwestern and south-central Minnesota where he grew up. His name appears only on a county memorial to WWII dead and, of course, on his own grave for which the stone's cryptic lettering beneath an outlined cross says only, "DUANE M. PETERSON  MINNESOTA  CPL. AIR CORPS  APRIL 22, 1942." The stone is no longer bright. It now bears the stains of leaves which have fallen, wet, and lingered over Peterson's final resting place.

He grew up in southeastern Minnesota, and although his early high school days were spent in the village of Westbrook, in Cottonwood County, and his enlistment into the Army was from St. James, in south-central Minnesota, his roots and most formative years were from Worthington, the seat of Nobles County.

Very little is know about Duane Millard Peterson today. He is not remembered in Westbrook or St. James, and most of his contemporaries have moved away or passed away. Born on August 21, 1920, he was the second son of Willard V. and Helen Millard Peterson. Willard Peterson had served in the Army in France in WWI, and was a very visible member of his church, First Baptist of Worthington. Subsequently, the elder Peterson would become very involved in the American Legion and eventually serve as the Legion's Minnesota state chaplain. The family lived with Peterson's parents on Sixth Avenue. The Worthington Hospital now occupies the Peterson home's former site.

Willard Peterson went to work for the railroad as a fireman when he came home from military service in France. Worthington was a division headquarters for the Chicago-Northwestern-Omaha Railroad, and Peterson, a forceful sort of man, was gone from home quite frequently.

Today, Worthington is a town of around 11,000 people in a setting still dominated by agriculture: corn and soybeans in particular. The earth is rich — as typified in the name of a nearby town, Blue Earth. Most of the roads run straight. The nearby place names are dominated by British origins: Windom, Butterfield, Jackson, Reading, Brewster, and Rushmore. Earlier, the Sioux left their mark with Watonwan, Waseca, Owatonna, Mankato, Wabasso, and Okabena. The latter name is that of a beautiful lake adjoining the town of Worthington. Here and there are some other place names brought by later immigrants — places like New Ulm which record northern Europe's immigration to America's high plains. In looking at the smiling faces in Peterson's eighth grade picture, many names could have come right from England, but Nordic names dominate: Nelkorn, Larson, Hansberger, Janssen, Heidelbrink, Nelsen, Vestrem, Zevenbergen, Hansen, Hagen, and Sylling.

Yet, Peterson is barely remembered by his surviving contemporaries. The family moved about 20 miles north to the small town of Westbrook in 1935-36, and then another 20 miles east to St. James in 1938 when Duane enlisted in the Army. So, he was never in place long enough to have made a significant impression.

There is some indication that he was not a good student since there is no trace of a high school graduation, and he was almost two years older than his peers in the eighth grade. He was not active in Scouting, although his brother, Marvin, was with Worthington Troop 35. The troop folded, however, at about the time Duane would have been the right age to join, and there were no troops in Westbrook when the family moved there.

Marvin Peterson was stationed in Northern Ireland with the Army at the time of Duane's death. He married after returning from Europe, but his wife, Bette, never met Duane. Marvin perished in an auto racing accident at Brainerd, Minnesota, after the war. What little personal information exists suggests that Duane had a "mellow" personality, was stocky, about 5' 8" tall, and had red hair. Perhaps he was the stereotypical second child, a quiet youngster in his older brother's shadow and dominated by an imposing father.

Regardless of any academic deficiencies, he was clearly not dull, and it may well have been the case that Peterson was a "late bloomer" since training as a radio operator was not an option for the enlisted man of just average intelligence.

Although "radio operator" was the generic specialty code for Peterson's function, the actual rating was "radio operator/mechanic" (ROM), and tapping out morse code was only the immediately visible aspect of his expertise. In 1941, after having originally been stationed at Fort Knox, Peterson "re-upped" and on July 23, 1941, was passed into the Army Air Force Technical Training Command after completing a battery of physical, aptitude, and mental tests. Unlike his peers on Liberator 41-1133 who were Air Force reservists on active duty, Peterson was "RA," Regular Army. Following completion of radio school, he was sent to the headquarters squadron of the 310th Air Base

Group at the Salt Lake Army Air Base for ground duties until being assigned to aircrew training in Albuquerque.

For his own radio training, he was most likely sent to Scott Field, home of the Army Air Force's radio school for six months of intense training. Scott Field was not a hastily assembled facility built to meet immediate war needs; rather, it dated back to April of 1917 when it had become a major training base. Nor was it strictly used for radio training in WWII since it served as a staging base for heavy bombers headed for war zones. Quite a few of Peterson's contemporaries had not been sent to Scott. Consistent with the lack of facilities to serve the tremendous increase in recruits and draftees, many radio operators were trained on the job in the squadrons they were sent to immediately after basic military training.

Soon, the dit, dah, dah, dit, dah, dit, short-long-long, short-short-long would be driving Peterson crazy. Morning, noon, and night, for interminable hours, he sat at cubicles on long tables practicing with fellow trainees until his speed was up to an acceptable level. Radio operators had to be able to transmit and receive 16 words per minute. Make that eight by blinker since he had to be able to work with code visually too. The radioman also had to transmit neutrally, i.e. his technique had to cleansed of any tracks or individuality that could lead to identification of his location.

Developing speed and accuracy was only a part of his specialty since other members of a heavy bomber crew were also trained in code. However, Peterson was the only one with enough skill to repair a radio in flight, and that meant gaining expertise in radio construction. This involved a thorough understanding in the electronic devices of the day, i.e. vacuum tubes, rectifiers, amplifiers, generators, power supplies, crystals, antennas, etc. Peterson also had to understand principles of electricity and radio including voltage, currents, power, wave length, frequency, and magnetism.

One might not have expected a high school dropout to master the complexities of radio theory and maintenance, but Peterson had clearly grown during his first three years in the Army.

The more critical portion of Peterson's assignment was intimate knowledge of radio construction and trouble shooting —assembling the several types of radios and reassembling them blindfolded. A radio operator had to be able to take shot-up radio equipment and cannibalize parts to the extent that one good transmitter and receiver could be built.

Although he wasn't responsible for navigation, Peterson also had to be familiar with the radio compass and be able to locate his aircraft's position using it.

In the B-24, there was a lot of radio equipment — all of it quite primitive by digital standards. Today's completely integrated, combination navigation and 720-channel communications transceivers are packaged in little more volume than that required by one cigar box. To move all of a Liberator's 1940s generation communication and navigation radios from a base stores facility out to the flight line for installation would require the space afforded by a pickup truck.

The Liberator's most frequently used radio equipment was the intercom system which linked all crew stations. This system had 12 outlets into which throat mike and headset jacks could be plugged. The amplifier was located at the ROM's station immediately behind the copilot and the power supply on the floor beneath Peterson's table. Only the pilots controlled the other components, a pair of filters which selected range (navigation), voice or both.

Although the interphone system was just that, i.e. for talk between stations, the crew could listen to the output and reception on the navigation system, and the other two radio systems, liaison and command. This was accomplished by simply switching to the appropriate position on the jack box which also had a volume control. On the intercom box at each station was a final selection simply marked "CALL." This was for emergencies and would override any other channel in use at the time.

For the crew of 41-1133 that day, the intercom was used for its basic purposes: oxygen checks, flight engineer status reports, but probably not much for idle chatter to break up the tedium of flight since that would represent a breakdown in cockpit discipline, especially with the CCTS management brass on board.

The command radio was strictly the bailiwick of the pilots, although it was used only minimally on this April 22nd since its principal purpose was for plane-to-plane communication and with airfield controllers. That equipment, in modules, included two transmitters to cover frequencies in the ranges of 5300 to 9100 kc and three receivers for other frequencies. Those units and their attending equipment (modulators, relays, power supplies) took up a surprising amount of space on top of the wing box aft section and immediately above the bomb bay. The antenna ran from midfuselage on the left side to the top of the left rudder.

Although Peterson was charged with the proper working order of all radio equipment, it was operation of the liaison radio system that he was personally responsible for and for which his crew station had been established. His was not a bad location, right there behind the copilot. He could easily see out through the cockpit and had his own little window, which on the right side could afford him a view, not to southern Minnesota, but to plenty of Kansas farmland. Even better was his view of the two roaring Pratt & Whitney R-1830s just several feet from his face.

The flight engineer's station was on the opposite side of the cozy flight deck, and Van Hoozer or Macomber was standing next to Peterson looking out the hatch just in front of the top turret during the pre-take-off check list or kneeling near Peterson on takeoffs while calling out speeds for the pilot. To add to the crowd, the flight deck was a frequent holding pen or passageway for the navigator, bombardier and, on later B-24 models, the front turret gunner, all of whom had to vacate the nose on takeoffs and landings.

Peterson had a small chair and a metal table beneath which was the liaison transmitter. The liaison system had seven tuning units, of which most were stored over the wing box while others were located at the rear of the flight deck. The remaining equipment was crammed all around Peterson, including the liaison receiver, antenna controls, and his *raison d'etre*, the transmitting key with which he sent the ship's coded messages and position reports.

Had his day ended uneventfully, he would have very soon completed transition training with about 20-30 hours in the air on '24s and almost certainly have been assigned to a gunnery school. Following that, he would have returned to Salt Lake City, his previous duty station, and gone overseas with one of the heavy bomb groups to which Jeffries and Reynard had been assigned.

# IX

# KANSAS CITY

May you wear good moccasins in all your journeys
And may nightfall always find you resting before the
Campfires of Friendship and Warmth.

Chief Lone Bear

Lt. Jeffries was riding in the nose for most of the outbound flight. He had been assigned the nominal role of navigator on this leg, and spending the four-hour flight at the navigator's station in the nose of the B-24 was as uncomfortable as planning the flight from Albuquerque to Kansas City had been simple. His responsibilities during the flight were to confirm their position and groundspeed, to log them at periodic intervals, and advise Charlie of any course corrections. Riding in the nose did have one advantage though, and that was the view from the bombardier's position.

Most of Jeffries' spare moments were spent looking below as Kansas slowly slid beneath the nose. Down there, he could see the occasional small towns with their streets laid out in the same logical patterns — almost like crossword puzzles. The boredom was occasionally punctuated by seeing other planes far below. Most military traffic flew well below 21,000 feet. The many planes flying out of Wichita's factories were rarely flown to their destinations at much more than eight or nine thousand feet.

Since this was a cross country navigational exercise, use of the radio ranges was forbidden except for brief, demonstration purposes, but that was somewhat academic since all but the first and last few miles of the flight were off the airways anyway. As cadets at advanced flying school, Jeffries and Reynard had learned radio navigation, but that was not attempted on this flight since this was their "final exam" for which old-fashioned pilotage was the name of the navigation game. Based on the need to provide new pilots with the "feel" of the aircraft, the autopilot was not used to any significant extent on the long cross country. Charlie was trying to fly a straight line course, and occasionally retrimming the Liberator which, left to its own devices, was somewhat wayward when it came to holding a precise heading.

Periodically, Charlie would call an oxygen check on the intercom, and all positions had to reply that they were OK. Everybody had a continuous flow, rebreather type oxygen mask on and plugged into the nearest regulator on which each man had turned the selector control knob until the indicator pointed to the altitude at which they were cruising.

Prior to takeoff, Van Hoozer and Macomber had checked all regulators for proper operation and confirmed that the oxygen tanks in the outboard wing panels had been filled. Due to the vulnerability of concentrating the oxygen sources in the wing locations and their proximity to the fuel bladders, oxygen supplies were subsequently dispersed beginning on late D model B-24s by using cylinders scattered throughout the fuselage.

By now, both Reynard and Jeffries had learned to retrim the ship largely by reference to instruments, not the horizon. Occasionally, the VSI might show a modest climb or descent in which case Charlie simply pushed or pulled the control wheel until the VSI pointer centered on zero and the little airplane symbol on the artificial horizon settled onto the horizontal bar. Having done that, he cranked the trim wheel slightly to relieve the pressure of holding the control wheel.

The rudders were trimmed by monitoring the directional gyro and turn and bank, and turning the trim wheel until the turn and bank's ball centered and the directional gyro stayed reasonably put (the pilot who can hold a rock-solid course with zero deviation is yet to be born).

Aileron trim was similarly accomplished by releasing the wheel, holding a heading on the directional gyro, and trimming out any wing low tendency seen on the artificial horizon by cranking the aileron trim wheel. The procedure would have to be repeated from time to time when control pressures built up or when leveling off after a climb or descent. Still, the nose tended to wander as was the way of the Liberator kind. Up to a point, it had to be accepted. The alternative was to spend one's life trimming all the day long.

The checkpoints came and went: Liberal, Meade, and Dodge City.

There was work to do. Every once in a while, Charlie looked at his directional gyro and compared its heading to the magnetic compass and, being sure that he was not in a turn, corrected the directional gyro to match the reading on the magnetic compass.

The curse of flying is the boredom that can lull pilots into a false sense of security. Thus, many pilots tend to look at parts of their aircraft when they have finished their last scan of the instruments and sky. There's a speck on the windscreen: a spot of oil or a P-40 way out there on a collision course? That scratch on the navigator's window, how'd that get there? Looks like a loose rivet just this side of the window frame. That thin little streak of oil just in back of the middle cowl flap on number two, it appears to be getting thicker. Was it there when we took off?

Blackburn periodically jotted down the engine instrument readings. April 1942 was proving to be a very busy month for him. He would log nearly 100 hours in April, and some of that was as a TWA line check pilot in addition to his duties in Albuquerque. His cross countries in CCTS B-24s that month took him to New York, Chicago, and Washington among other cities. Some of these flights were at 30,000 feet which would prove to be good preparation for many of his students who would be returning to bomber groups scheduled for departures to the UK in just a few more months.

There wasn't much of interest in that April morning's skyscape so Charlie scanned his primary air data instruments more frequently than he otherwise might have. At roughly 300 miles out from Kansas City, he started the descent by pulling off some power and retrimming the bomber for a 200 feet per minute descent while still indicating 200 mph. After passing Council Grove, Kansas, he called the crew on the intercom to advise of their upcoming descent through 10,000 feet and that they could secure their oxygen gear. As they were descending through 10,000, Blackburn switched off the fuel boost pumps. Nearly 35 minutes later, when they were descending through 2,500 feet, Blackburn tuned the command radio to 278 kc, Kansas City tower's frequency. The ceiling was unlimited, but visibility was occasionally dropping to eight miles in industrial smoke and haze.

"Kansas City Tower, Army One, One-One-Three-Three, over."

"Army One-Three-Three, Kansas City Tower, over."

"Army One-Three-Three, DeSoto inbound, descending through two thousand, landing Kansas City, over." DeSoto, with its fan marker beacon, was a regular approach check point.

Tribe of Mic-O-Say Archives via F. Gail Hixson

*Kansas City Municipal Airport, circa 1937. Airline traffic now flies into Kansas City International, 15 miles northwest. The old municipal airport is now known as Kansas City Downtown Airport and serves commuter and corporate aviation.*

"Army One-Three-Three, plan left downwind to runway one-seven, call Lake Quivira inbound, over."

"Army One-Three-Three, wilco."

Within a few minutes, Kansas City and some of its prominent features were starting to emerge from the haze. This was all unfamiliar territory to Charlie, but home country for Blackburn and Redding who had flown in countless times before.

"Kansas City Tower, Army One-Three-Three, Lake Quivira at one-thousand, six hundred, over."

"Army One-Three-Three, say type aircraft, over."

"One-Three-Three is a B-24 Liberator."

"One-Three-Three, call Kaw River inbound, over," ("Kaw River" was local colloquial for the Kansas River, and the inbound checkpoint referred to a bend in the river along Kaw Drive in Kansas City, Kansas).

"One-Three-Three wilco."

After the passage of a few more minutes, "K-C Tower, One-Three-Three, Kaw River inbound, over."

"Army One-Three-Three, you are cleared for the approach, left downwind to runway one-seven. Call abeam the tower, Kansas City altimeter now zero-one-five."

"Altimeter for Army One-Three-Three is zero-one-five, cleared for the approach, out."

Reynard then went on the intercom to drive Jeffries back to the waist compartment since the nose section had to be vacant during landings.

Passenger comfort is not a hallmark of the B-24, and only the pilot and copilot can be said to be in relatively comfortable circumstances. The waist compartment comes as close to a sitting room as it gets in the Liberator, and although the gunners' hatches were closed to reduce the noise and cold, Jeffries was riveted to the landscape passing by the hatch frame. The view was a familiar one because Roland Jeffries was about to land in his hometown — Kansas City. Their approach took them on an easterly heading right over the Missouri River where Jeffries strained, looking through the plexiglass to see his street, Warwick Boulevard, but it was lost in the maze below and soon gone as Reynard turned north on the downwind leg.

Hidden in the distance amidst the newly verdant land on that late April day, was Camp Osceola, a place that was near and dear to Jeffries. It was the summer camp of the Kansas City Council, BSA, and both institutions meant a great deal to him.

But, all of the larger, familiar landmarks were out there: the Heart of America Bridge; Hannibal Bridge (the Broadway Bridge was still in the future), the intercity viaduct connecting the two Kansas Cities, the stockyards with its landmark Armour packing plant and smoke stack at the river junction, and Penn Valley Park's foliage contrasting the city's industrial bottoms. Kansas City's skyscrapers were passing beneath him: City Hall, Jackson County headquarters, the Federal Reserve Bank, the Fidelity Building, Kansas City Power & Light Building, and the municipal auditorium.

George Van Hoozer was looking just as intently far to the southeast since his hometown, Windsor, Missouri, was just north of what is today's Harry S. Truman Lake, the northern gateway to the Ozarks. He too was looking at the streets below for Morrell Avenue, location of his last residence in Kansas City.

Things were now going into high gear as Charlie got on the intercom to call crew stations for landing. Blackburn had pulled out the checklist and called, "Aux hydraulic pump." Macomber replied, "On," and then eased his way through the hatch leading to the nose compartment where he could check the nose gear travel.

Charlie knew the autopilot was off, but touched all switches to make sure none had been accidentally engaged, and then pulled off more power and retrimmed the ship for 160 mph. They were now down to their pattern altitude of 1,580 feet above mean sea level.

"Gear."

"Gear down." Blackburn shoved the gear selector into the up position, noted the pressure as being within limits and then selected down. That the gear was in travel was obvious, and even more so after the bump heard and felt when it locked down and diminished their airspeed by five mph. Macomber had reappeared and nodded a "yes" to Charlie, indicating that he had visually confirmed the nose gear was down and locked.

"Waist to pilot, gear down OK," from Van Hoozer on the intercom.

"Boost pumps."

Blackburn flicked them all into the on position at once.

"Mixture."

"Auto-rich."

"Intercoolers." Blackburn answered his own question by confirming the intercooler shutters as open, and then checked the deicer selector to be sure it was off before looking at the leading edges of the wings.

Charlie quickly scanned the brake pressure gauge. It was OK at 1050 lbs.

"Props."

"2,400 now." Blackburn pressed the buttons to bring revs up to 2,400.

It was just after 10:35 local time when Charlie called the tower as they rolled into a left turn over the southwestern corner of Riverfront Park on the south side of the Missouri River.

"Kansas City Tower, Army One-Three-Three, downwind for one-seven, over."

"Army One-Three-Three, Kansas City Tower, altimeter zero-one-five, wind one-eight-zero at one-three, TWA traffic now on short final, call turning base, over."

"Army One-Three-Three, wilco."

Charlie motioned with his right hand in an up and down movement, palm down, almost like patting a dog's head, whereupon Blackburn lowered the flaps 20 degrees. Blackburn and Macomber were glancing frequently ahead and to the left to keep an eye out for any unreported traffic across the Missouri River at Fairfax Airport, home to general aviation and military reserve units.

"K-C Tower, One-Three-Three turning base," Charlie said as he eased the bomber into a left turn to roll out on a heading of 260 degrees. Charlie was, however, flying strictly by visual reference to the main north-south runway which was soon at right angles to his line of flight.

"Army One-Three-Three, wind now steady from one-eight-zero at one-three, you're cleared to land, runway one-seven, over."

"Army One-Three-Three cleared to land, out."

Charlie had now brought the power back to twenty five inches. His airspeed had dropped to around 135 mph, and he started a standard rate turn onto the final approach course. The Kansas City Waterworks was now obscured beneath his right wing. When he rolled out, the runway was about 800 feet below him, the city skyline dead ahead, and the river and stockyards just beyond the airport boundary on the right. Charlie pulled the turbo controls back into a position about a half-inch from their rear stops to be sure he would have adequate power in case he had to go around. He then pulled off some more power, down to about 15 inches. The wind was right on his nose, so he had no crosswind to contend with.

"Full flaps," to which Blackburn brought the flaps down to their full, 40-degree travel. They were now indicating 125 mph, although Charlie never looked at the airspeed indicator because Macomber was right at his shoulder, calling out the airspeed. By now, Charlie had the big brute perfectly aligned with the runway. Fortunately, on 41-1133, this was easy to do since the navigator's bubble (used for celestial navigation) had been removed and faired over thus making over-the-nose visibility much improved.

They now had a sink rate of roughly 400 feet per minute, were indicating 125 mph, and gliding in right over the east bank of the Missouri River. Reynard had well learned that landing a B-24 was a bit like shooting ducks — both had to be led. The '24 did not respond as quickly as his single-engine trainers had. Considering the B-24's great energy and momentum, Charlie had to pull back on the controls well in advance which he did in coordination with his next to last power reduction.

He now flared the big ship out, and when he had begun sinking the last few feet down to the runway, he pulled the throttles well back. Simultaneously, Charlie rolled in some nose up on the trim wheel. In less than five seconds, a shudder ran through the ship as there were two, almost simultaneous barking sounds and two puffs of white smoke as the main gear contacted the runway at which point he instantly closed the throttles. His right hand went quickly to the yoke as Blackburn curled his left hand over the bottoms of the levers to prevent their creeping forward. The big Army bomber had attracted the attention of people standing on the terminal building observation deck from which they saw those two puffs of smoke as the bomber touched down at 10:39 local time.

Charlie's feet were firmly on the rudder pedals, but not yet on the brakes as he was still hauling back on the controls, trying to keep the nose gear off the runway as long as possible and using aerodynamic drag for most of his braking. At around 75 mph, the nose started falling, and as soon as he heard the "clonnnk," Charlie almost timidly touched the brakes, trying to feel them out while Blackburn moved the mixture controls into auto-lean. They were rumbling along midfield now as Blackburn opened the cowl flaps fully.

"K-C Tower, Army One-Three-Three rolling out for TWA operations, over."

"Army One-Three-Three, left turn by the terminal, then right down to TWA's ramp, over."

"One-Three-Three, roger."

Charlie and Blackburn now quickly went through some house cleaning tasks by closing the turbos, pressing the prop controls for high rpm, confirming when their lights came on, and turning off the boost pumps. Charlie taxied down to the large TWA hangar located next to the passenger terminal, turning heads in the terminal's restaurant and observation deck in the process, and parked in an open spot, dwarfing several of the DC-3s also parked nearby.

While the engines were still idling, Charlie cranked all the trim handles into takeoff settings. Blackburn shoved all mixture controls into idle-cutoff and, several moments later, flicked the four ignition switches off. Charlie had earlier advanced the throttles to bring revs up to about 1000. Macomber turned off the generators as Blackburn switched off the radios, and, after checking to see that the engine indicators were in normal ranges, lastly turned off all electrical switches.

The ship's systems were definitely shut down, but the Liberator was still making sounds, almost in protest at having been made to leave its natural element and sit in disgrace on the paved earth. There was the soft metallic crackling, clinking sound of hot engine parts starting to cool and the spinning, winding down whine of the gyro instruments. A TWA ground crew was starting to chock the wheels, after which Charlie released the brakes. Blackburn returned the gear handle to the down position from neutral and locked the controls to complete securing the cockpit.

When the bomber was parked, the crew all exited through the open bomb bay doors which had just been retracted. Their flying coveralls and heavy, fleece-lined B-3 flying jackets and pants, and boots were stowed on the plane. Underneath, they were wearing lighter clothing for what was going to be a pleasant day in the big city. For Redding and Ruff, lighter clothes meant a TWA Eagle Nest uniform. George Van Hoozer was wearing civilian clothes, and in his case, they would have had a sporty, distinctive flair. The Air Force men were wearing service uniforms including neckties, service caps, and if not a blouse, then an A-2 leather flying jacket.

Reynard was the last one to exit the Liberator since he had to take a few moments to complete the flight's paper trail by filling out Forms One and One-A. After Reynard stepped down off the catwalk and ducked his way out onto the tarmac, Macomber opened the access panel below the radio operator's window, moved the handle therein, whereupon the bomb bay doors clattered down their tracks into the closed position. Both men stretched and stood tall trying to shake the effects of nearly four hours of being cooped up in a cold, deafeningly noisy aluminum monster. It was nearly 11 a.m. local time and about five hours since any of the crew had breakfast.

The men of 41-1133, singly and in small groups, were about to go their separate ways. Fortunately, after these many years, just what the crew did with their few hours in Kansas City is largely known and can be reconstructed fairly accurately. Hal Blackburn ceased to be a member of the crew, and would return to Albuquerque several days later on a regular TWA flight. He proceeded directly to the TWA offices adjacent to the municipal airport terminal since he was in town for meetings with Jack Frye and Otis Bryan. Their meeting would shortly gravitate to Milleman and Gilbert's, the famed restaurant in the passenger terminal.

The subject of their discussions was the winding down of TWA's CCTS, a development which would have a dramatic impact on Blackburn's career. It wasn't the first meeting about what the future held for the nearly four dozen TWA-CCTS instructor pilots and first officers. Joe Carr, the former navy pilot, had been summoned to a meeting with TWA's top brass only a few months before. Carr had been puzzled by the drift of the conversation which eventually focused on ocean flying, a novel topic for an airline limited to domestic routes. Carr's brains were being picked because his aeronautical credentials were unique: in addition to being a naval aviator, he was a rated navigator who had long range, overwater experience in the Navy's big flying boats.

As Carr outlined what he thought would be required to bring an average TWA line pilot's expertise up to transoceanic standards, he recalled another curious meeting one of his peers had quite recently. Hal Blackburn had been sent on a brief mission, a "fact finding" visit with Pan Am's Pacific Division.

The April 22nd meeting was about TWA's embryonic Intercontinental Division (ICD) gearing up for a major role in the Army Air Force Air Transport Command. TWA's 4-engine Boeing Stratoliners had already been pressed into service for cargo or VIP transport, painted olive drab, and designated as C-75s — all five of them. ICD's initial trip had been to North Africa by the South Atlantic route, and only several weeks before, the first TWA C-75 had flown the North Atlantic.

It was revolutionary for 1942 — the use of landplanes on transoceanic flights. From a logistics viewpoint, the task was monumental. It meant that TWA had to reinvent itself as an international airline and go from five ICD crews in January to more than 100 by December 1942.[1] In the process, Blackburn would play a major role and take many of the CCTS personnel with him. Thus, Blackburn's afternoon was spent in planning sessions with TWA's top management on how to essentially create a new airline from scratch.

The other pre-war TWA employee, George Van Hoozer, walked across the ramp and into the TWA maintenance hangar to say hello to TWA mechanic friends and have lunch with them. He remained at the airport all afternoon, but did make several phone calls to acquaintances in town.

Robert Redding did not accompany Blackburn into the meetings. Although technically a TWA employee, he was also an Air Force reservist who had already received his call-up notice, thus his services would not be available to Blackburn after June. Redding was no stranger to Kansas City, and knew the town and its airfields very well since he had flown many of his reserve duty hours at Richards Field on Fairfax Airport just across the river. With his close friend from Panama days, Jonas Ruff, he quickly walked through the passenger terminal and caught a bus into town.

Likewise, the two corporals caught the same Route 18 bus from the airport into downtown Kansas City on the other side of the Missouri river. The ride cost just a dime (four tokens for 34 cents) and took only a few minutes.

Lt. Charles Reynard, the inveterate metropolitan explorer, tried to hit as many of Kansas City's landmarks as possible in several hours as he had done Washington, Philadelphia and New York before the war. Jeffries would have told him about the important things to see, but not about an annual event that would have captured his interest just a few years before, the Annual Boy Scout Roundup which would be held over the coming weekend at the municipal auditorium.[2] The theme for 1942 was "A Strong America" and featured such enduring Scouting themes as physical fitness, marching and drilling, signal communications, and a salute to Native Americans. Although Jeffries had been one of the most prominent youth members of the Kansas City Council, B.S.A., in the mid to late '30s, he had not been active since his eighteenth birthday, and his registration had lapsed at the end of 1939.

Mary Casey, Jeffries' lovely fiancée, had been waiting at the passenger rail and embraced him warmly after he ran from the bomber to the gate. Then they were off to see their parents using Mary's car to get back to town. With a little extra room in the car, it is likely that they gave Reynard a ride into town and dropped him off where the rest of the crew would independently converge: Country Club Plaza. Jeffries had no intention of sharing the afternoon with anybody but Mary and their parents, but Country Club Plaza was directly on the route to the Casey residence on Morningside Drive.

Knowing his way around Kansas City, Redding probably stopped for lunch at a well known downtown restaurant, the Italian Gardens on Baltimore Avenue. That well-known local institution would soon be changing its name to just "The Gardens" for the duration since Italy was part of the Axis powers. Nonetheless, it was favored by the local scout council executive, H. Roe Bartle, visiting luminaries, and Kansas City's famous and not so famous.

None of the crew would have had time to see the most popular movie in town, *Gone With The Wind* which was replaying at Loew's Midland. An adult matinee ticket was 40 cents and children's tickets just 17 cents. Kansas City was not short of theaters. The Tivoli, Bijou, Strand, Vogue, Orpheum, and dozens of others were playing such hits as *Kings Row* (starring an up and coming young actor named Ronald Reagan), Alfred Hitchcock's *Saboteur* or *The Spoilers* with Randolph Scott and Marlene Dietrich. The Sun Theater was playing *Flying Cadets* with William Gargan, but it was not one of Jeffries' or Reynard's favorites.

Although between them they had seen some city lights in the past year, Macomber and Peterson were still small-town men for whom downtown Kansas City was unique: a big city with an agricultural base. Getting off the first bus, they walked around downtown. Nearby, at Walnut and 11th Street was Emery, Bird & Thayer, Kansas City's premier department store. They could have passed through the men's clothing and furnishings department on the first floor, but probably would have found the merchandise on the other seven floors less relevant to the lifestyle they were about to undertake. The sale items that day were for the ladies and included the newest spring hats for $2, clothes-pin classic seersucker dresses at $3.98 each, and ladies' shoes at 25 percent off.

Macomber, when speaking to a bus operator or store clerk, would have turned heads with his strong Maine accent. Peterson would not have, being a quiet, almost shy soul, but his post-Scandinavian, Minnesota accent would have been noticeable in this city where accents of the American South and West merged.

Kansas City was rapidly going on a war footing. It was an arsenal town, and soon B-25 Mitchell medium bombers would be rolling off Kansas City production lines along with Pratt & Whitney engines and amphibious landing craft. It was a major grain and cattle center. Hog prices were climbing through $14.10 per hundred pounds. The war was expanding dried egg production. Wheat, soy beans, rye, and corn prices were all moving up, and there was widespread concern over the availability of storage facilities for the coming crops.

Economic uncertainties were felt throughout the national economy on that mild, spring day, April 22, 1942. Prices were mixed on the New York Stock exchange. U.S. Steel, GM, Goodrich, Westinghouse, DuPont, and Union Carbide all closed down that day. Much of the concern was based on large industrials fearing a slowdown in orders due to a lack of transportation and energy production not keeping up with demand.

The average citizen was finding it hard to travel by air since military passengers had priority. Still, in late April, a one-way ticket from Kansas City to Tulsa was $11.37, and TWA was advertising regular flights to Washington as taking just six and one-half hours. Air travel was the subject of First Lady Eleanor Roosevelt's newspaper column, "My Day," on April 22nd. Whereas FDR used the radio for his chats with Americans, Mrs. Roosevelt communicated with them in a widely syndicated newspaper column. On that Wednesday, she longed for the pre-war days when airliners' windows were not curtained for security reasons. With the war on and security critical, passengers could no longer enjoy some of the delights of flying such as beholding majestic cloud formations or watching the passages of lakes and mountains below.

The economic impact of the war was spreading. The War Production Board had just directed the cotton textile industry to start converting its lines to war production thus drying up some items such as fine cotton hosiery. The Office of Price Administration outlined plans for sugar rationing which would go into effect on May 5th. Of some consolation was the fact that matters were much worse in Germany, a situation aggravated by the retreating Russians' destroying horses and farm equipment in order to deny the Germans as much harvesting capability as possible.

The war news, other than the April 18th Doolittle raid on Tokyo and other Japanese cities, was not encouraging. Rommel was still a menace in North Africa and would not meet his El Alamein until the autumn. Much beleaguered Malta had just been bolstered by the arrival of 47 brand new Spitfires which had been flown off the American carrier *U.S.S. Wasp* just two days before. After heavy raids by the *Luftwaffe*, over half of the new interceptors had been destroyed or damaged. Still, Malta hung on.

In Russia, the Red Army was making some progress along the Finnish front, but Leningrad was still besieged. American aircraft in the China-Burma-India theater were busy evacuating military personnel and civilians from Burma to India.

The Royal Air Force peers of '1133's crew were beginning an important transition, one that was facilitated by the *Luftwaffe*'s having dis-

persed much of its strength to the Russian front. The RAF was substantially stepping up its bomber operations against targets deeper in
Germany and doing so with new generation, heavier bombers, greater
use of fire bombs, and new electronic aids to bombing. During April,
very successful attacks were carried out on two cities important to the
German war machine: Rostock and Augsburg.

The latter raid was carried out by the RAF's new four-engine heavy
bomber, the Avro Lancaster whose appearance looked like that of a
very streamlined Liberator. The Augsburg raid, involving two squadrons
of Lancasters which plastered the target, was prophetic in terms of what
the American bomber crews would face once they arrived in England:
heavy, heavy losses. Over half of the Lancs did not return to their base
from the Augsburg mission.

There were diversions to the war news. In April 1942, Kansas City
did not have a major baseball team, but at five and two in the new season, the Kansas City Blues were second only to Milwaukee. Baseball
fans were thrilled to have just learned that both the Yankees and
Dodgers would be coming to town in July to play a series of exhibition
games against the Blues at Ruppert Stadium. Both of Philadelphia's professional baseball teams were in the bottom of their leagues. The
Dodgers were on top in the National League while Boston was leading
in the American. Professional sports ranks were starting to thin, though,
as many players were joining the colors.

A quick ride on the #56 street car would have brought Peterson and
Macomber out to Union Station. For the son of a railroad man, Peterson
would have been gladdened to see some of the 300 trains to arrive or
depart Kansas City every day. Just across from the station, they may
have gone to the Liberty Memorial in Penn Valley Park, taken in the War
Relics Museum and visited some of the monuments in a day when the
park was well-maintained.

In separate groups, '1133's crew converged on Country Club Plaza
which would become a very popular attraction for the many servicemen
stationed around Kansas City during the war. The Plaza was within
walking distance of the Nelson-Atkins Museum of Art, an institution
which would have held some interest for Reynard, although a visiting
serviceman could easily spend a full day at the Plaza, which remains to
this day as a landmark in suburban shopping mall design. Begun in 1922,
the Plaza was America's first true mall, and its many shops, restaurants,

stores, and theaters were located over 15 acres. The architecture, walls, murals, courtyards, towers, and fountains are old world Spanish-inspired. It was at Country Club Plaza that Jonas Ruff paused to send his parents a postcard, thus indicating how the crew spent several of its last carefree, leisurely hours.

Changing buses back in downtown Kansas City, Charlie Reynard had enough time for a little sociological "people watching" along Baltimore Avenue, Main Street, and, to the east, Holmes Street. He may have been attracted by the Woolf Brothers window display at Walnut and Eleventh. There, an army officer's blouse sold for $45, slacks for $17, and a pair of Johnson & Murphy low quarter Oxfords were $11.50.

Charlie was responsible for the return leg navigation and was among the first back to the field. After retrieving his pilot's navigation kit containing charts, plotter and flight computer, he walked over to the terminal and climbed the stairs to visit the weather briefing office on the sec-

Tribe of Mic-O-Say Archives via F. Gail Hixson

*The old Kansas City Municipal Airport terminal building. The weather office is on the second floor behind the observation deck.*

ond floor. April 22, 1942, was a delightful day, full of superb flying weather — for those aviating in the eastern half of the country. Looking out the office window, which faced the observation deck, confirmed what a lovely day it was. For the men of 41-1133, flying southwest from the heart of America, the weather forecast was not encouraging. In fact, although not completely known to them, heading into a hurricane could be about the only weather extreme worse than that into which they were about to fly.

By contrast, Kansas City, during the weather briefing, was enjoying a nice, sunny, albeit breezy afternoon. The sky was clear, temperature in the mid-70s, visibility was excellent, and the barometric pressure was dropping at only a barely perceptible rate. Unfortunately, such terms as "wind shear" and "downburst" had not become part of the meteorologist's lexicon nor had the capability of assigning probabilities to their occurrence in specific locations and time periods.

Weather forecasting was not an exact science in early 1942. Technology's gifts of Doppler radar, weather satellites, and weather modeling supercomputers were not available then. Even a complete terminal or area forecast amounted to little more than general "guesstimates," and most of what a pilot could expect consisted of simple sequence reports from the various stations along his route.

That fateful April afternoon was setting up for more than an archetypically classic thunderstorm scenario in New Mexico. It was, quite literally, building the mother of all thunderstorms. The greatest concentration of thunderstorm activity in the continental United Sates is located in an arc that runs the full length of Florida up along the panhandle and westward along the Gulf of Mexico through the southernmost counties in Georgia, Alabama, Mississippi. That region experiences thunderstorms during 70 to 100 days per year.[3]

There is only one other continental U.S. location which experiences thunderstorms 70 days per year, and it is a comparatively small geographic area. At its epicenter are the Cimarron Mountains in the Sangre de Cristo Range of the Rockies which dominate Taos and Colfax Counties in New Mexico and the southern portions of Las Animas and Costilla Counties in bordering Colorado. It includes Wheeler Peak (highest point in New Mexico at 13,161 feet) which overlooks the villages of Eagle Nest and Red River, and, heading north, the Spanish Peaks near Walsenburg, Colorado. Philmont's greatest mountains, of which there are almost a dozen over 10,000 feet, ranging from Trail Peak at 10,242 to Baldy Mountain at 12,444, are at the heart of the Cimarrons. Areas adjacent to the Sangre de Cristos and Colorado's Front Range experience thunderstorms on an average of 60 days a year. Nothing else in the American West even comes close. Indeed, Colfax County, New Mexico, where Philmont is located, has a well-deserved, national reputation among professional meteorologists for the brilliance of its lightning. The Cimarron Mountains experience precipitation (as rain or snow) on an average of 100 days per year, but also enjoy sun on three days out of four which is quite consistent with how rapidly weather can change in that area.

Philmont's major peaks are at once the best and worst places to observe the complete cumulonimbus cycle. From those mountain tops above timberline, visibility easily stretches north, well into Colorado, far out across the eastern prairie, and to the mountainous south and west — a hundred miles or more on a good day. Because the mountains are, for all practical purposes, great rocky lightning rods, they are also the worst possible places to be during thunderstorms. Philmont rangers are quick to make sure campers understand this, and point out the sad fact that lightning has occasionally been responsible for death at Philmont. To catalog all trees hit by lightning at Philmont would be an impossible task. Burned out, shattered trees litter not only the mountain tops, but also ridges, mesas, and passes in countless numbers.

Although a typical summer day at Philmont usually begins with a spectacular sunrise, by late morning, fluffy-puffy cumulus dot a large portion of the sky. By noon, several of these seemingly innocuous balls of aerial fleece have grown much larger, especially in the vertical sense. One of these cumulus clouds has become a cell in which warm air is rising at a rate which exceeds its ability to cool itself normally through expansion. Within this cloud, whose moisture is condensing, heat is generated and rises. The vertical winds are rushing skyward and pluming out in the familiar anvil-shaped top. The condensed, rising moisture passes through the freezing level, and when the droplets have become heavy after coalescing with ice crystals, they start falling in the form of hail and/or rain.

Violent hail storms are quite common at Philmont and can turn a lovely, green alpine valley into a winter-like snowscape in a matter of minutes. Indeed, some of these hailstorms are of such magnitude that it is not unheard of for shovels to be used in mid-summer to remove the heavy "snow" from the walks at Philmont's camping and training head-quarters.

From a pilot's perspective, be he flying a B-24 Liberator or Learjet, the hail, rain and lightning are definitely troublesome, but not as threat-ening as their principal side effect: chilled air falling down through the cell's core which is surrounded by warm air still rushing skyward. This terrible storm machine, which can easily be five miles across and eight miles high (or more), will eventually spend itself, but not before pre-senting the pilot with the prospect of flying through powerful vertical winds flowing in opposite directions in remarkably close proximity.

Were it a simple matter of contending with just one huge "thermo-cumulonimbo" cloud, Lt. Jeffries' task as pilot would have been easy: just fly around that particular portion of aerial blight, and once past the problem, ask Lt. Reynard for a new vector to the destination.

Unfortunately, the great, maturing storm cell sows the seeds of per-petuation at its feet. All around the violent storm's base, cold winds fan out in every direction, forcing nearby warm air aloft in their path. With warm air rapidly rising, new cumulonimbus clouds start forming, some-times in isolation and sometimes in conjunction with their windborne peers whom they join to create sky dragons even more menacing than the original storm cloud. Sometimes, these cells grow over mountains in a string not completely unlike line squalls associated with frontal storms. In northern New Mexico, this effect is readily visible to pilots aloft and to those watching from the crests of Sangre de Cristo peaks.

At Philmont, for the casual observer, who, let us say, is located on the top of what was known at Clear Creek Mountain in 1942, and enjoying the midday sun with nothing but blue sky over him, a glance to the northwest can reveal a row of marching storms over Wheeler Peak just north of Taos. At the same time, and to the more immediate north, a storm may run from Baldy Mountain over Touch-Me-Not Mountain and approach Clear Creek (now Mount Phillips) itself. Other storms can be seen off the Ranch to the southwest near Agua Fria Peak. Far to the north, the great sentinels of southern Colorado, the Spanish Peaks, are obscured in storms of their own. To the north-northwest, the high peaks in the Costilla cluster beyond Baldy, are enveloped in their own stormy shrouds.

The Cimarron Mountains have no monopoly on storm generation. The prairies to the east are constantly visited by cumulonimbus of the more convective variety which can completely dominate a whole quadrant of the sky and produce all of the hail, torrents of rain, and gale-force winds of neighboring mountain storms.

"Just another day at Philmont" is not an exaggeration. Nor is it a particularly vexing problem during a day at the office — if one is working in a San Diego-bound 747 out of Kennedy flying at 38,000 feet and can look down at all of this violence or be vectored around it by Air Traffic Control.

Conditions on that April 22nd couldn't have been more conducive to severe storms. There was a massive high pressure system centered in the eastern half of the United States. That created a beautiful spring day in Reynard's Ohio hometown and was responsible for the day's pleasant weather in Kansas City. With the clockwise flow from the high, winds blowing out of the Gulf of Mexico were heavily laden with moisture. Such winds travel across Texas and start rising with the terrain which generates clouds, especially when those winds bump into the high country. On that day, the surface winds were quite strong and headed for the Sangre de Cristos at nearly 30 knots. Clouds, those magnificent, billowing clouds for which New Mexico's skies are so memorable, then develop into towering cumulonimbus which, in turn, generates thunderstorms. If certain conditions exist in the western half of the United States, a plain vanilla, mountain thunderstorm can become even more evil. A jet stream trough or another front approaching from the west will add potentially lethal fuel to the fire. On April 22, 1942, there was a strong jet stream trough running from the Canadian Rockies down through the western third of the United States. Although the jet stream was unknown in early 1942, its location on that April 22nd has been confirmed by a present day, professional meteorological interpretation of sky conditions, wind, and pressure gradients on the continental surface weather map for that date. Thus, the inevitable thunderstorms on that day were packing plenty of everything pilots try hardest to avoid: torrential rain, hail, downbursts of rain-cooled air, windshears, and blinding lightning.

This is not to imply that the men of '1133 were about to fly off to the southwest completely in the dark. Quite to the contrary. They were made aware of the possibility of thunderstorms along the final segment of their route, and knew that there were some developments already. The weather briefing offices at Kirtland and Kansas City Municipal had access to hourly reports from over 600 reporting stations (mostly North American, but also from international locations including eastern Russia, Greenland and Iceland). Every six hours, those stations prepared a brief summary which went out over teletype.

'1133's pilots read the early afternoon sequence reports which were not encouraging. Sante Fe: scattered to broken clouds at 4,000 feet above the surface, occasional rain, wind from the east at 27 knots, barometric pressure dropping. Las Vegas, New Mexico: overcast ceiling at 1,000, scattered showers, wind southerly at 20 knots, barometric pressure dropping. Albuquerque: broken ceiling at 6,000, wind south to southeast at 22, rain showers, pressure dropping. Raton, New Mexico: sky obscured, estimated ceiling 2,800 with occasional breaks in the overcast, wind south at 27, barometer falling very rapidly.

Jeffries and Reynard were not experienced instrument pilots. Each had about 40 hours of instrument time including roughly 20 hours in Link trainers. Some of that experience was very recent time and included nearly two hours under-the-hood in a B-24. Ruff did have a Civil Aeronautics Administration (CAA) instrument rating and over a hundred hours of actual instrument flying time. The two lieutenants' experience levels would have just qualified them for a CAA instrument ticket. Redding, having been the instrument flying manager at the CCTS, was very experienced and possessed both a military, green instrument card and a civilian airline transport rating. He was no stranger to western mountain storms since he had been flying in Albuquerque for nearly a year. Both Redding and Ruff had experience with tropical storms. Had Redding been leading a flight of basic trainers to the southwest, he would have postponed the flight; but they were buoyed by the confidence in their advanced, heavy bomber complete with its state-of-the-art navigation equipment.

Charlie, faced with the prospect of rainshowers at the least and thunderstorms at the worst, sat down at the table and revisited the flight plan. They would not return at 20,000 feet since they had satisfied the high altitude training requirement on the flight to Kansas City that morning. There was a more practical reason for selecting a lower altitude: what had been a quartering tailwind from Albuquerque had now become a quartering headwind. So, they would fly the return at an altitude that would not require oxygen, but would keep them below the strongest headwinds, yet high enough to minimize turbulence from thermals still rising from the sunbaked fields of Kansas and prairies of eastern New Mexico. In a few minutes, Charlie had worked out the navigation for Jeff to follow. The true course back was the reciprocal of the morning's course: 250 degrees. Cruising at 200 indicated miles per hour at 8,000 feet where the temperature was nine degrees centigrade (almost 50 degrees Fahrenheit) would produce a density altitude of roughly 10,000 feet and a true airspeed of 220 mph. Throwing in a 35 knot wind from 200 degrees produced a course of 242 degrees and ground speed of 190 mph. Adjusted for magnetic variation and '1133's compass correction, Jeff would be advised to fly a heading of 235 degrees. If Charlie detected any significant deviation en route, he would give Jeff a revised heading.

The takeoff must have been the defining moment in Roland Jeffries' short life. If it weren't, it certainly was the proudest day in his nearly 22 years. Watching him fly the great bomber were his adoring fiancée, loving mother, and admiring relatives, including an aunt, uncle, niece, and nephew. The takeoff was past the landmarks of his youth — the TWA hangar where he had attended Scouting meetings and over the skyline of his hometown where he had risen above family disadvantages to become a good student, Eagle Scout, valued employee, and successful entrant into the highly selective aviation cadet program.

# PART II

# THE AERIES

# X

# JEFF, THE EAGLE SCOUT

And this I know when my race is run,
When starlight falls o'er oak-clad hills,
And setting sun bespeaks the end of my life span -
I have been challenged to the best in me,
I have been strengthened by an Eagle's Claw.
I go, Great Spirit, answering Thy call
For it is well - my brothers carry on.

Chief Lone Bear[1]

To say that Jeffries had been looking forward to the April 22nd flight
to Kansas City is an understatement. He returned to his hometown that
day as a changed man: an officer and pilot of the Air Force's most deadly
bomber. This homecoming was a rare luxury because since entering the
service the previous summer, he had enjoyed very little free time, and
had never been away from family and friends for such an extended
period. In the few hours Jeffries and Mary Casey had together that afternoon, they came to a momentous decision. They would be married late
the following week when Jeff was to be given four days leave after completing four-engine transition. Quite a few 42-B cadets had married when
they graduated from advanced, and who knew what the future held for
Jeffries? It might have been months before he could get back to Kansas
City again, and he had no idea where the 305th Bomb Group, the unit to
which he had just been assigned, would be headed in the weeks ahead.

Roland Jeffries, better known as "Jeff" to his friends, had belonged
to a unique circle of young men in his early high school days — not
exactly a gang or club, but more of an informal discussion group. It was
a rather eclectic band. There were a few Scouts, but Jeffries was the
only one from Troop One. They came from different walks of life, different faiths, and different high schools. Aviation was an occasional

topic, and, indeed, a disproportionate number of them became military pilots too. Their meetings were held in an unused room over the garage of one of the boys' parents' homes. They discovered poker playing, but also had in-depth discussions on religion and philosophy. Surviving members of that group remember Jeffries as an easy-going young man and as a "still waters run deep" type who, although not talkative, was worth listening to when he did speak.

Jeffries, born on May 28, 1920, was the youngest in the family which also included his two sisters and a brother. Jeffries came from a broken home. His father, James O. Jeffries, abandoned the family when Roland was about ten years old and never paid any child support. The father was a maintenance man for one of the office buildings in downtown Kansas City when he deserted the family for another woman. Roland's mother struggled at several jobs including work as a seamstress for the

From Roland Jeffries' photo album courtesy of his nephew, Larry McPherron

*Aviation Cadet Roland Jeffries photographed during basic flight training late in 1941.*

manufacturers of the "Nellie Don" label, a popular dress in the 30s, and was able to bring in a very modest income. It was not easy, and the economic stress forced Roland's next oldest sister out of high school to take a job. The Jeffries family had lived in the Marlborough section of Kansas City (around 82nd and Flora), but after the family breakup, Roland, with mother, moved in with an aunt and uncle at 4107 Warwick Blvd. Given these economic circumstances, it was fortunate that Jeffries was able to enter Boy Scouting and stay with the program. Then, as now, Scouting provided the adult male role models, challenges, growth opportunities, and recognition that the missing father could not provide. It was clearly an environment made for the circumstances and one in which Jeffries excelled. Of the seven men of Liberator 41-1133, Jeffries was not the only one to suffer serious family difficulties or traumatic events in childhood. Only Redding and Van Hoozer grew up in families not touched by death or serious adversity. In the other families, however, the primary nurturing influences, such as both parents or close siblings, were present to a far greater extent than they were for Roland Jeffries. Thus, Scouting can quite accurately be described as a second home for him.

To fully appreciate the profound role Scouting played in Jeffries' life requires an in-depth digression into that remarkable institution, the Kansas City Council, Boy Scouts of America, in the 1930s and the unique force which shaped it into the strong organization that it is today. At this writing, both the Chief Scout Executive of the Boy Scouts of America and the Director of Program at Philmont came from the Heart of America Council, originally known as the Kansas City Council. It has historically been a top ten council at Philmont in terms of numbers of Scouts and Scouters participating in the summer camping program, training center, and seasonal staff.

When Jeffries was an active Scout in Kansas City, his council led the nation in all benchmarks: growth, membership, program, advancement, and camping. It still is the powerhouse it was in Jeffries' day.

Scouting took hold early in Kansas City. Fifteen troops were operating in Kansas City in the summer of 1910, the year in which Scouting in America was first chartered.[2] It was a time when records were kept loosely and communication with the national office haphazard at best. It would be two years before there was any significant communication between council headquarters and the new national office in New York City.

By September 1910, the confusion of identifying troops by their sponsoring churches and schools had forced the issue of adopting troop numbers. Some troops had been operating before formal charters were adopted, and that complicated the issue of which troop was indeed, "Troop One." To settle the matter equitably, all parties agreed to a random drawing. Accordingly, fifteen numbered pieces of paper were drawn as a means of assigning troop numbers. Although it was not technically the first to be chartered, Jeffries' unit, Linwood Presbyterian Church's troop, which was founded on September 2, 1910 (two weeks after First Congregational's troop had been organized), became Kansas City Troop One. In the 1920s, Troop One moved to St. Paul's Episcopal Church at 4041 Main where Jeffries became a Tenderfoot Scout in May, 1933.

The Heart of America Council's strengths are due to the efforts of many dedicated Scouters, professional and volunteer alike; but it would not be inaccurate to say that today's Scouters are still working in the shadow of one particular professional, "the Chief." That was H. Roe Bartle (Harold Roe Bennett Sturdevant Bartle).

Had one thought that Kansas City's professional football team, "The Chiefs," was named for some plains Indians tribal council, he would be wrong. They are named for "the Chief," Roe Bartle, who, as mayor of Kansas City following his professional Scouter days, brought professional football to Kansas City. That was hardly his most significant accomplishment, however.

It would be a fair observation, now nearly 50 years after he took office, that Roe Bartle still is Kansas City's most popular mayor of all time. To say that he was larger than life is an understatement. He started big — nearly 11 pounds at birth. Ultimately, he would grow to 375 pounds and six feet, four inches tall. He would remain larger than life for all of his days.

H. Roe Bartle was born in Virginia in 1901, the son of an immigrant Presbyterian minister, and educated at Fork Union Military Academy before going on to the University of Chattanooga. In 1921, after obtaining his law degree, he became Acting District Attorney in Lebanon, Kentucky, where he met the woman he would marry, Margaret Jarvis Rains, a lady who went on to significant achievements in her own right. Importantly, Bartle served as a Scoutmaster while in Lebanon. Although he became District Attorney in Lebanon, law was losing its appeal. Somewhat uncertain of what to do with his life, he moved to Kansas City

Tribe of Mic-O-Say Archives via F. Gail Hixson

*H. Roe Bartle in 1929, shortly after becoming the Boy Scout council executive in Kansas City.*

where, in late 1922, he was persuaded by James E. West, first Chief Scout Executive of the BSA, to accept the position of Scout Executive in either the Central Wyoming Council or Sedalia, Missouri. A tossed coin settled the matter: Bartle would head to Wyoming. On September 26, 1923, Bartle and "Miss Maggie" Jarvis were married in St. Joseph, Missouri, by the groom's father, Rev. Samuel Bartle.

The Scouting program was in evolution, and local council executives were encouraged to devise means of further developing outdoor and leadership skills. Bartle, being located close to the Wind River Indian Reservation, became a serious student of Native American culture.

It became a two-way street. One of the Northern Arapahoe leaders, Chief Lone Bear, an aged chief, had recently passed away. The mantle of leadership was passed to his son from whom Bartle learned much about the Native Americans. The tribe, which also sponsored a Scout troop, welcomed Bartle into its circle, and, indeed, Bartle was inducted into the tribe as a blood brother complete with his sponsor's name: Lone Bear. This special relationship with Native Americans would give rise to the Tribe of Mic-O-Say, Bartle's concept of a camping honor society.

In the two years that Bartle was the Scout Executive in the Central Wyoming Council, the number of troops grew from just five to multiples of that number with over 1,500 youths enrolled.

In January 1925, Bartle moved as executive to the St. Joseph, Missouri, council which already had a camping honor society stratified by three levels: papoose, brave and warrior. During the 1925 camping season, Bartle awarded single eagle claws to the most worthy boys and leaders. From this foundation, the modern Tribe of Mic-O-Say would rise shortly after Bartle's move to Kansas City in January 1929. The program started in 1929 at the council camp, then Camp Dan Sayre, near Noel, Missouri, and would travel the following year to the banks of the Osage River at what began as Camp Osceola (now today's 3,500 acre H. Roe Bartle Scout Reservation).

The words "Mic-O-Say" come from a blend of Shoshone and Northern Arapahoe, and can be interpreted as "Friendship and Warmth." In spirit and ritual, its purpose is to reach down with warmth of heart and help those who are younger and weaker. The program was originally designed for use in the troop setting and meant for the older boys. Service to the camp, in terms of construction, maintenance, camping season preparation and closing, continue as important Mic-O-Say activities. New youth members entered as "Braves" and were given a necklace consisting of a medicine pouch and an eagle claw.

Jeffries became a member of the Tribe of Mic-O-Say in 1935 and was the 479th member to join. Upon becoming a Brave, he took the name "Little Oak." He was elevated to "Hardway Warrior" status in 1936, his second year in Mic-O-Say, and then wore a necklace with two claws, tipped with green paint signifying a second year as an honor camper.

Currently, Mic-O-Say membership is measured in the tens of thousands as opposed to the hundreds as in Jeffries' day. The Tribe also has a presence in St. Joseph, Missouri, although the latter's ritual is different. And, Chief Lone Bear's legacy is still felt in two Order of the Arrow Lodges (in Colorado and Iowa).

It is so easy to overlook one of Bartle's greatest accomplishments nowadays. After the crash of '29 and the ensuing economic depression,

*The insignia of a tragically short life. Roland Jeffries' Eagle Scout Award, Army Air Force pilot wings, and Mic-O-Say claws.*

a scout executive was fortunate if his council even survived. Bartle's council grew and provided a fertile ground for the development of young men like Jeffries who blossomed in strong troops, a busy summer camp, and the Tribe of Mic-O-Say.

A strong council is not Bartle's only Scouting legacy. In 1948, using his own money, he founded American Humanics Foundation which was originally designed to benefit the Boy Scouts of America. Today, American Humanics Inc. is a philanthropy whose college programs educate students for careers with a variety of human service organizations. The program was initiated at Missouri Valley College of which Bartle served as president for several years.

Bartle also was an early president and a prime mover in the growth of Alpha Phi Omega, the 400-plus chapter college service fraternity based on the Boy Scouts of America. Chief Roe Bartle, during his 32-year career as a professional scouter, always donated his salary back into Scouting.

In 1955, the Chief began a new career as the popular mayor of Kansas City through 1963. Along the way, he found time to be of service to the federal government as a regional director of the Office of Price Stabilization in the late 1940s while still serving as the BSA council executive in Kansas City. Serving as a youth movement leader was his first self-perception, but he was also a successful mayor, lawyer, banker, and cattleman.

The cliches "thundering" and "spellbinding" pale as descriptions when applied to Chief Bartle's delivery as an orator whether addressing thousands at convention, a church congregation, or inspiring Boy Scouts around a campfire. Although he prided himself on being a southerner, his speech was essentially without accent. The occasional "R" was rolled, but not for theatrical effect as the first time listener might assume. Bartle's father had emigrated to America from Scotland, and the Chief's growing up in a post-Gaelic household neutralized what would have otherwise been a fine Virginia accent.

He very deeply felt the wartime loss of so many of his young Scouts. The desire to formally honor fallen tribesmen began in 1943 with plans for a memorial building. Construction was funded from within Mic-O-Say and from outside donations. The Memorial Lodge and adjoining chapel are built of sandstone quarried adjacent to the camp property. Groundbreaking was in 1948, and on July 11, 1954, the building was dedicated to "... the memory of those whose claws shall ever hang in immortality ..."

In addition to the paintings, Mic-O-Say insignia, and ceremonial regalia, there is a special album which contains one page for each tribesman killed in action or on active service. A strikingly high number of the 50 pages honoring WWII and Korean losses are airmen — 23 military pilots or naval aviators. Their names are entered in beautiful script.

The memorials are a microcosm of the air war and flight training. Among the poignant remembrances are these phrases:

> "killed over Germany ... lost off the coast of Ireland ... airplane accident near Luke Field, Arizona ... missing in action over Italy ... died as a prisoner of war, received Distinguished Flying Cross ... killed over Tokyo ... died in parachuting from stricken plane ... plane shot down over Duren, Germany ... killed in plane crash off Guam ... killed in action over Truk..."

Jeffries is honored, of course. The "special data" section on his page of the memorial carries his tribal name and notes the Philmont connection. Of all the tribesmen who perished in WWII, it is safe to say that Jeffries is among the most prominent due to Heart of America Council's close involvement with Philmont. It is also well known that Bartle was a big booster of Philmont during and after his professional Scouter days.

Jeffries did well in high school and had time for such extracurricular activities as choral groups and the biology club. His interest in biology extended to another hobby, taxidermy. He was quite proficient at this, and his work was displayed at several local institutions and at Camp Osceola. Photographs of the nature lodge from the mid- to late 1930s reveal an extensive collection of stuffed birds and animals in very professional-looking display cases.

Jeffries was not an athlete like Reynard, but did enjoy bowling and swimming, and obviously was fit enough to earn his Eagle Rank in 1935 at the age of 15. In doing so, he had to earn several merit badges in the outdoor sports category in addition to qualifying for swimming, lifesaving and personal fitness merit badges. He had also gone beyond the minimum requirements and qualified for a bronze palm to his Eagle award. Jeffries advanced very rapidly in Scouting and moved from Tenderfoot through Star at a particularly fast pace. At age 16, he was on the nature staff at Camp Osceola, after having been a camper from 1933 through 1935 and an "Honor Camper" in 1935. As a junior member of the staff, he was unpaid in terms of money but well enriched by the experience nonetheless.

Jeffries' Eagle award was not presented in a typical ceremony at the sponsoring organization with parents, friends, family and troop members watching. Rather, it was held at the American Royal Building with 8,000 boys participating and more than 10,000 family and friends attending on May 1, 1935. It was, in fact, a standing room only event that served as a Scouting pageant in addition to being a Court of Honor for 61 new Eagle Scouts which became the C.M. Vining Eagle Scout Class (Vining was a previous council president). The pageant included a history of American Scouting and included a preview of the 1935 National Jamboree (which would be canceled at the last minute due to a polio epidemic). Chief Roe Bartle presided and was joined by every former president of the council in presenting the Eagle badges and miniature pins for the proud young men's mothers.

Aviation was of great interest to Jeffries long before he applied to become an aviation cadet. He built model airplanes as a youngster, and was acquainted with the municipal airport manager whose wife was a sister-in-law of Roland's brother, James. Although it wasn't the aviation center that Wichita was, Kansas City had a very strong aviation presence. There was some aircraft manufacturing there in the 1930s, and Jeffries had a choice of several airports for plane watching: Fairfax Airport just over the Kansas state line, Kansas City Municipal across the Missouri River to the north, and Richards Field which was located on the other side of Swope Park in Baytown and only a few miles southeast of the Jeffries residence on Warwick Avenue. "Richards Field" actually had three locations during Jeffries' lifetime.

Old Richards Field in Baytown, named for a WWI pilot casualty, Lt. John F. Richards, was the original military reserve base in Kansas City, and although the reserve units moved to the municipal airport in 1927 and then in the 30s across the Missouri River to Fairfax Airport, the reserve squadrons retained the Richards Field name for their portion of the airports at Municipal and Fairfax. Old Richards Field in Baytown again hosted military activity in the '40s since it became a primary flight training center. Kansas City was also a busy hub for both passenger and air mail routes. Thus, any aviation-minded youth found Kansas City to be a rich locale for hanging out at airport boundary fences, watching planes and dreaming about becoming a pilot.

Tribe of Mic-O-Say Archives via F. Gail Hixson

*In 1937, Roland Jeffries was one of the 21 Eagle Scouts selected to join Sky Scout Troop 12 (a forerunner to Aviation Explorer posts). Following the investiture ceremony depicted above, the 21 Eagles went for a ride in a TWA DC-2.*

In late 1937, Jeffries was one of just 21 Kansas City area Eagle Scouts selected for membership in "Sky Scout Troop 12" which was a forerunner of Air Exploring or today's Aviation Explorer Posts. Appointment to this unit was a signal honor in a city which had a very, very strong Scouting presence. This early Explorer unit was sponsored by Transcontinental and Western Air, Inc.; the Committee Chairman was Cliff Mutchler, an operations manager with the airline. The troop investiture ceremony, at which the charter was presented, was well attended. The National Council was represented, and the Council Exec, H. Roe Bartle was on hand. Jack Frye, TWA's CEO, was a VIP guest. A number of TWA pilots who acted as advisors to the unit were quite visible. Council President J.R. Battenfeld read a proclamation from President Roosevelt during the proceedings which were also attended by 100 (shivering and quite likely jealous) Scouts from troops from which the Sky Scouts had been selected.

The hour long ceremony was held on a rather chilly, breezy October night, and upon conclusion, the 21 Eagles were treated to a brief DC-2 ride. They immediately began weekly meetings in one of TWA's maintenance hangars to study meteorology, navigation, flight dispatching, aircraft blueprints, and radio communication. The troop had access to obsolete TWA equipment for use in studying mechanics. They were reading some of the same aircraft maintenance manuals that had been used by a man who had started work as a TWA mechanic only a year or so before, George Van Hoozer.

Those were exciting times for Jeffries and his fellow Eagles who got to sit in cockpits of TWA airliners and be in the company of TWA pilots. Short of having a pilot's license or a degree in aeronautical engineering, a more ideal preparation for aviation cadets would be hard to find in 1937.

Jeffries quite literally enjoyed a landmark vacation trip with the Sky Scouts in the summer of 1938. The troop's members were given TWA passes good for a round trip to Las Vegas where they were hosted by local Scouts for a tour of one of America's latest marvels, Hoover Dam. The trip out took several days since the Scouts had to travel standby, and not all arrived at the same time. They camped in the backyard of one of their hosts until all arrived. Once there, they marveled at the dam whose construction had been completed only two years before. In addition to boat tours on Lake Mead, they climbed the canyon walls, camped in the mountains, trekked up nearby Charleston Peak, and enjoyed the ensuing snowball fights at over 11,000 feet in the summer sun.

Many of these 21 young men ultimately followed aviation as a career. In addition to Jeffries, two of the other original Sky Scouts, both fellow Mic-O-Say tribesmen, would be killed in WWII or shortly thereafter (Robert Mooney as a pilot with the 51st Fighter Group in China and Walter Tarpy in a post-war jet crash at Tulsa). It is believed that a third, Roy Stout, also perished in WWII as a pilot with the Royal Air Force. Of the roughly 16 Sky Scouts who survived military service, four (Ken Cederland, Roy Pell, Barry Bryam, and Bill Brown) had careers with TWA, and at least one more became a pilot with another airline (Jack Powell who flew for Continental).

Tribe of Mic-O-Say Archives via F. Gail Hixson

*"Sky Scouts" enjoyed weekly contact with TWA pilots, aircraft, and maintenance equipment. In lieu of a pilot's license or a degree in aeronautical engineering, Sky Scout experience was ideal preparation for the Army Air Force aviation cadet program.*

Roland Jeffries' days as a carefree Scout were numbered: in 1938, he graduated from Westport High School after turning eighteen and re-registered with Troop One as an assistant Scoutmaster, but soon drifted out of Scouting's orbit.

There was no money to send him to college. He went to work for CSI, Central Surety and Insurance, which was a busy brokerage selling casualty, fire, and theft insurance. He also moonlighted for a real estate firm as an apartment rental agent. At that period of his life, his leisure interests were bowling and music. It was not unusual for the Jeffries family and Roland's friends to gather around a piano and tape their sessions. Jeffries had been quite active in his high school choir, and often entertained friends on camping trips to the Ozarks with some of the Scouting songs he had learned at Camp Osceola.

He was a busy young man. He was also a bright young man and quite conscious of not having been able to go onto college. So, he took night classes. Prior to his second job of renting apartments, he had also worked as a night stockman at the Kresge store in downtown Kansas City. The store manager's daughter was Mary Ellen Casey. It was the proverbial match made in heaven and perhaps proved the point that opposites attract. She was lovely, slender, and had a bright sense of humor in counterpoint to Roland's which was rather dry. She was more outgoing than Jeffries whose personality was reserved. Her smile was captivating, completely. She was well-dressed and frequently wore unique accessories. She too called him "Jeff" as did all of his friends.

Those were the circumstances in early 1941, a time when Roland Jeffries was remembered as "the star" of his family by his surviving nephew, Larry McPherron, a recently retired Kansas City insurance executive. Jeff was gainfully employed, building for the future, and was blessed with the love of the young lady of his dreams.

Across the Atlantic, the blitz was raining down over Britain, the Royal Air Force Bomber Command was giving as good as it took, and Fighter Command was just starting to carry the air war to the continent with growing "hit and run" ground attacks that would build to a more aggressive campaign in the summer.

The draft was on in America, and like thousands of aviation-oriented young men, Jeffries saw the aviation cadet program as an ideal way of satisfying his military requirement while preparing for a well-paying career in aviation once the war was over. First, he had to become a cadet, and because he had less than two years of college, he had to pass an equivalency exam. His night school courses helped in the preparation, but he was not confident about his mathematics. Seeking a tutor, he turned to a young college graduate and radio engineer, Odis Burris, whose fiancée was a good friend of Mary Casey's. Jeffries also felt that he needed some form of physical conditioning as well, so he initiated his own training regimen built around swimming laps at the Kansas City YMCA pool. The preparation paid off: he passed the equivalency exam handily, took off a few pounds, and improved his stamina by early summer 1941.

The past year had been the most exciting in Jeffries' life as it had been for his fellow aviation cadets. They were living in tumultuous times, and the Army's preparation for those times was completely unprecedented.

Tribe of Mic-O-Say Archives via F. Gail Hixson

*Sky Scout meetings included sessions on maintenance, navigation, dispatching, aerodynamics, and aircraft structures. Roland Jeffries is at the rear right with his chin on hand.*

# XI

# THE TRAINING OF AVIATION CADETS

Mister Jeffries, R.L., Ser. No. 17019923
&
Mister Reynard, C.O., Jr., Ser. No. 15069041

> Come on now, all you young men ... you are needed more
> than ever to fill the gap of a generation shorn by the war.
> You have not an hour to lose. You must take your places
> in life's fighting line. Twenty to twenty-five. These are the
> years! Don't be content with things as they are. "The
> earth is yours and the fullness thereof." Enter upon your
> inheritance; accept your responsibilities.
>
> Winston S. Churchill

In the autumn of 1938, with war in Spain and China raging, the Army
Air Corps initiated facilities planning to accommodate an anticipated
major growth in manpower, especially that of pilots and technical support
personnel. General H.H. "Hap" Arnold, the Army Air Corps commander,
overruled his staff which recommended that the Air Corps undertake a
massive construction program to create new bases, in effect, creating
duplicates of its principal training facility at Randolph Field in Texas.

Arnold saw this as taking too much time, and decided that the task
of primary flight instruction would be given to outside civilian contractors while the Air Corps Training Command would concentrate on
basic and advanced phases of flight training. Many of the civilian
schools were using training aircraft similar to those employed by the
military anyway. History confirmed Arnold's wisdom since it was later
estimated that turning primary over to private industry released 100,000
Air Corps personnel for other duties.[1] Avoiding the construction of a

series of little "Randolphs" saved the government almost $300 million a year in construction costs during the war not to mention the immense savings in time.

Entering classes were designated by their year and month of advanced flying school graduation date, i.e. 42-B for February 1942. The designation was valid across all schools, and in Reynard's and Jeffries' case included their peers who were graduating at the same time from the eight other Air Corps Advanced Flying Schools.

In the primary phase, the military student was taught to fly an uncomplicated, light aircraft powered by a low horsepower engine. In basic, he moved up to a more complex airplane, and in the advanced stage learned to fly an aircraft whose performance put it at the lower end of frontline aircraft. Primary, basic and advanced stages each lasted ten weeks in 1941. In the transition stage, the pilot, who had been awarded wings and an officer's commission at the end of advanced, moved on to training in the type of aircraft he would fly in an operational squadron.

For all practical purposes, however, it took roughly a year to bring a cadet through the system, award his wings and commission, transition him to an operational fighter, bomber or transport, and then wind it up with "phase" training (combat tactics with the squadron to which he had been assigned).

The government's return on investment in instructors started earlier since superior pilots with the right temperament usually were sent directly to an Air Corps basic flying school as instructors after their own graduation from advanced. If these men were lucky, they might be sent to the Central Instructors School or be given extra training in instrument flying, but early in the war, the time spent between graduation from advanced and giving a basic student dual instruction could amount to just several days. The only preparation in the latter case was a few hours of re-familiarization with the basic trainer and mastering rear cockpit landings.

Realizing just how limited the Army's resources were, General Arnold brought in representatives of three of the country's best civilian training schools (Boeing, Oakland, California; Parks, St. Louis; and Curtiss-Wright, Los Angeles) to determine the feasibility of private industry conducting all primary flight training.

The Air Corps had ambitious plans. The initial training wave in 1939 was to create 7,000 pilots, and that was to be followed with a 12,000 pilot training program.[2] To accomplish this, nine civilian schools were selected and instructed to be ready for operation in the summer of 1939. An additional nine schools were on stream by August of 1940. In March of 1941, eleven more schools were opened. By Pearl Harbor, there were 41 civilian schools training Army cadets when the 30,000 pilot program was announced. Before the program started winding down late in the war, there were over 60 civilian contract schools instructing cadets in primary flight.

In this plan, most of the flying schools were located in the Sunbelt for obvious reasons and divided into three commands: Southeast, Gulf Coast, and Western. The latter's operating headquarters was at Moffett Field near San Francisco, but would be moved to Santa Ana, California, while Jeffries and Reynard were in training.

Initially, the civilian flight instructors were required to take a brief orientation course at Randolph Field in Texas, but as the program gathered momentum, traveling Army personnel trained the instructors right at the primary field's location.

Even before the war started, the instruction period for primary was cut from 12 weeks to 10 which included 60 hours of flying time. Of the 60 hours, roughly 24 hours were spent in dual instruction, and the balance as solo time, depending on the student's capability. In the pre-war program, the final two weeks were comprised primarily of review, but that was sacrificed in the shortened program. There was a feeling that many of the cadets actually started to regress in the last two weeks, not unlike the golfer who does well in the first weeks of a new season when remembering the basics of the game, but then slumps when bad habits start surfacing again.

Initially, the quality of instruction was quite high since most of the instructors, many of them reservists, had well over 1,000 hours total flying time. The demand for pilots (from various commands within the Air Force, such as the Ferrying Command, from the airlines, and the Navy), created instructor retention problems which would not be alleviated until pilot manpower requirements peaked and declined as the war wound down.

Later in 1942, another stage of training would be added to the program. It actually became the first phase and was known as "Pre-flight" in which the cadet was given preliminary military indoctrination, drilling, marksmanship, health instruction, bivouac and survival, and physical training. There was a preliminary stage preceding pre-flight called "classification" in which cadets were subjected to more testing in order to sort them into pilot, navigator or bombardier tracks. For Jeffries and Reynard, the pre-flight activities were crammed right into primary training. Nor did they have to endure days of stomach-churning suspense at a regional classification center wondering if they would become pilots, bombardiers, or navigators. That they were headed for pilot training had been established when they successfully completed the aptitude and physical exams before induction into the Army.

By 1943, the Army, having developed a backlog of eager young men who had been accepted for the cadet program, started facing two problems. The washout rate was increasing, particularly among those without prior college, ROTC, or flight training, and there was the matter of thousands of young men hanging around for months waiting for their orders to a classification center simply because the training facilities hadn't expanded fast enough to process them. To alleviate the problem of academic deficiency and still maintain its claim on these men (who were also being watched by their local draft boards), the Army instituted the Aircrew College Training Program. In this program, several semesters of liberal arts and, especially, science were taught at over a hundred colleges to which military training detachments had also been sent. Graduating cadets were then sent into the regular pipeline. Those young men, in effect, had two years of college compressed into several months.

Recruiting was a major job since the Air Corps knew that it had to attract four candidates in order to find one who possessed the academic credentials and could pass the physical exam. Thus, the Army's public relations officers prepared brochures which subsequently flooded college campuses. The brochures portrayed cadets, gallantly dressed in flowing silk scarves and goggled helmets, as valiant knights of the air whose post-military service prospects for employment in aviation were excellent. Press releases about newly commissioned pilots were sent to hometown papers.

The Air Corps cooperated with Hollywood in the production of *I Wanted Wings* starring Brian Donlevy as the flight instructor and Ray Milland, William Holden, and Wayne Morris as flying cadets (the term "aviation cadet" would not be adopted until mid-1941). Shot on location at Randolph Field in Texas, the film introduced wartime siren, Veronica

Lake, and went on to become Paramount's biggest moneymaker of 1941. Pearl Harbor changed the tone of recruiting advertising from glamour to patriotism, but, prior to that, the promotion contained the Madison Avenue emphasis on image. Thus, the loveliest of adoring coeds would be shown on the arms of a flying cadet. Army recruiting officers were told directly, in mid-1941, that the recruitment of candidates for aviation cadet training was their number one priority.

In 1941, most of the entrance medical and aptitude testing of candidates was conducted at a military post or Air Corps Reserve flying station near the applicant's home. Reynard's medical exam was completed in Boston while Jeffries' was done at Richards Field in Kansas City. The tests included an exhaustive medical evaluation that paled even a contemporary airline pilot's semi-annual physical. Cadets were spun, poked, pinched, squeezed, scrutinized, questioned, and subjected to specialized tests designed to evaluate depth perception, motor skills, reactions, and endurance. An All-American lacrosse player with perfect 20/20 vision wouldn't pass the medical if he had flat feet. If he had everything else together, but couldn't pat his tummy and rub his head then switch quickly and successfully, he clearly didn't have the degree of coordination needed. If a physician examining cadet applicants accepted one in four, he was having a much better than average day. An acceptance rate of one in ten was not unusual.

Early in the war, cadets could not be under five feet, four inches or over six feet, two inches in height. Potential applicants were encouraged to have a private physician administer a screening exam to catch any potentially disqualifying problems. Corrective measures could be taken in many cases of weight or dental problems, but any condition beyond those was disqualifying.

The formal application to become an aviation cadet was made to the headquarters of the Army Corps area in which the cadet was residing at the time. For Jeffries, that was Omaha, Nebraska, the headquarters of the Seventh Corps Area. Reynard applied to the Fifth Corps Area, headquartered at Fort Hayes in Columbus, Ohio.

Everybody applying had to complete an aptitude test, and those with less than two years of college (60 credit hours) had to take college equivalency exams or the "mental test" as it was called. The aptitude test measured such basics as reading and mechanical comprehension, mathematics, and tabular interpretation, but also assessed such faculties as spatial orientation, dial comprehension, and technical vocabulary. Instead of taking the exams at Fort Leavenworth, Jeffries completed them at nearby Richards Field in Kansas City, Kansas.

For a bright high school graduate or an aspirant who had completed a couple of college semesters, some self-help or tutoring could produce a passing score on the test which, in 1940 and 1941, was given on the second Tuesday in August, November, February, and May. The general subjects included United States history, western civilization history (up to 1492), geography, and English grammar and composition. For each subject, a standard textbook was recommended as a study guide. The sciences included mathematics with emphasis on college level algebra, although trigonometry, plane geometry and arithmetic were included. Physics was in the test, but its proficiency requirement was at the high school level. A score of 70 was passing, and the final grade was the average of all subjects.

The physical and mental hurdles together could require from one to three days, and traveling expenses to and from the test site were the applicant's responsibility.

Beginning in early 1941, the Air Corps sent traveling boards of examiners to metropolitan areas with a heavy concentration of college and universities. Boston, with M.I.T., Harvard, Boston College, and Northeastern University, was prime recruiting country. Reynard and the majority of young men in one of his political science classes were attracted to the idea of flying and subsequently underwent the exams en masse.

Having been eliminated from another service's flight training program was a disqualifying factor. Successful completion of aviation cadet training obligated the new pilot to a minimum of three years active duty (later amended to duration of the war) unless a shorter term was otherwise dictated by proper command.

At each of the primary fields, there was a military cadre responsible for all activities other than the actual ground school and flight instruction. Periodic flight checks were administered by military pilots who also had the final say on whether or not a cadet having trouble learning would remain in the program.

At this point in the war, ground school instruction was not standardized, nor were there integrated study manuals. The schools improvised and used what individual manuals as were available from the Army. It was not until well after Jeffries and Reynard graduated from the program that the Training Command prepared an integrated manual for the military training and indoctrination of aviation cadets.

Jeffries arrived for primary at what was, for manpower, a fairly typical primary facility in mid-1941: Thunderbird Field at Glendale, Arizona, (a suburb of Phoenix) where the military detachment was commanded by a lieutenant colonel whose staff consisted of several captains (adjutant, personnel, cadet captain, flight surgeon) and lieutenants in addition to roughly two dozen enlisted men. There were six junior officers directly involved as check pilots with the flying program.

There were also 20 flight instructors and six ground instructors from Southwest Airways, the civilian contract operator, which had to properly house and feed all personnel in addition to supplying the landing field(s), hangars and other support facilities. To these civilian operations such as Thunderbird, the government supplied airplanes, flight and maintenance clothing, textbooks, and flying gear, including helmets, goggles and parachutes.

Roland Jeffries got $75 per month in pay and Southwest Airways got $1050 for successfully graduating him.

## The Dodo

Jeffries and Reynard, because of the mild dose of regimentation received at summer camp while Boy Scouts, were somewhat better prepared for their military experience than many of their classmates, but nowhere nearly as well-oriented as several of their peers whose land grant college training had included ROTC. Reynard and Jeffries were each called a "Dodo," the name given to all cadets who had yet to solo.

The term, derived from the Portuguese *dodo* (meaning stupid), referred to the flightless, extinct dodo bird, *Raphus cuculatus*, once found on the island of Mauritius in the Indian Ocean.

Some of the civilian schools, including Thunderbird, initially misunderstood the real thrust of the primary program, and proceeded to emphasize getting the cadet to solo quickly. The Army placed more weight on the well-rounded development of the cadet as a precision military flyer, and stressed the importance of maintaining a high standard of proficiency through the entire 60 hours of flying in primary.

Having soloed, cadets faced a series of phase checks at intervals for the rest of their training. Any serious lapse during a checkride could spell the end of their cadet days. For example, 16 of Jeffries' 66 classmates in Cadet Class 42-B at Thunderbird Field, or roughly one in four, suffered the worst cut of all: "elimination."[3]

Periodically, at 20 and 40 hours of accumulated flight time, students were given check rides by a senior instructor. Most cadets passed these phase checks, and at worst, might be advised to brush up in some areas or practice certain maneuvers which needed more precision. Mistakes could result in failing grades, which, if amply collected, usually resulted in dismissal. However, those students who were truly struggling in the air would be visited by a man whose presence was not at all welcome. For all practical purposes, he might have been dressed in a black cape and carried a sharp scythe. His military bearing and countenance brought on the fear of doom. He was known as the "wash rider," an aerial, fifth horseman of the apocalypse named "Failure" whose steed was a Stearman biplane.

The occasional cadet who was struggling might listen to the rumor that each instructor was anxious to see two or three of his charges dropped from the program as a means of reducing the work load. Actually, Uncle Sam would have been thrilled had there been a 100 percent graduation rate so desperate was the need for pilots. The civilian contractor hoped for a high completion rate since he got paid on successful graduates, not washouts. But, for the unfortunate cadet who couldn't get it together, the final test was a rendezvous with the wash rider from whom a "down check" meant immediate dismissal. Once in a while, a faltering cadet would suddenly grasp things and survive his appointment with Flying Examiner Fate. Much more often than not, however, the tension created a bad case of nerves which, in turn, made matters even worse and produced a deficient performance.

All flying exercises were graded. The scale ran from "A" (excellent) to "F" (failing). A "D" was considered satisfactory. If a cadet received three unsatisfactory or three failing grades (or any combination of the two), each of which was accompanied by the proverbial pink slip, he had to ride with the civilian check pilot. If the cadet succeeded, he faced two prospects. He might be sent back to resume instruction or he might be subjected to another check ride with the civilian stage commander. If the cadet survived that ride, he was returned to the fold, but if he botched it, a prompt appointment with an Army check rider was made. If the performance were lacking, the cadet would shortly be found his bags a-packing.

Indeed, Jeffries and Reynard survived a training process that would claim roughly 40 percent of all cadets who entered the program. From

July 1, 1939, through the end of the war, the Army Air Force graduated 193,440 pilots. And, it washed out 124,000, a number that included those who were killed or injured in flying accidents.[4]

Statistically, a cadet was safest while at primary. During the war, 439 cadets were killed in flying accidents at primary schools.[5] At basic flight, 1,175 were killed and the total for advanced jumped up to 1,888 fatalities. The statistics are consistent with the circumstances, i.e. moving from uncomplicated, light planes flown under ideal daytime conditions as opposed to heavier, more sophisticated equipment flown increasingly in tight formations, on instruments or at night.

In terms of accidents of all types per 100,000 hours, basic had the best record at 27.[6] Advanced was 55 and primary was a higher than might be expected 48. The latter figure is primarily a reflection of dinged wingtips associated with how easily a Stearman trainer would ground-loop. Accidents were inevitable in the extraordinarily rapid build-up. In 1938, the Air Corps' total manpower was just 20,000. By 1944, nearly 2.4 million troops, roughly one-third of the Army, were in the Air Force.

To wash out in 1940 meant to be back on civvie street in a few days. With the need for bomber and transport pilots growing exponentially beginning in 1942, there also came a concurrent demand for navigators and bombardiers. So, many of those who weren't cut out for flying as pilots were recycled into navigation and bombardier training if they were not sent to a gunnery or mechanics' school in the rank of private.

The Army Air Force was not always 100 percent accurate in its washout decisions. More than just a few cadets who had to pack their bags and leave went directly to Canada and into the open arms of the Royal Canadian Air Force and therefrom to the Royal Air Force. Many became skippers in Bomber Command or joined fighter squadrons. A few found their way to fame as very successful fighter pilots in the Eagle Squadrons (before the Army Air Force was only too glad to have them back in late 1942).

Jeffries and Reynard were not exactly enlisted soldiers, hence the title "Mister," although their serial numbers at that stage were those of an enlisted man. Their uniforms were similar to those worn by a real officer, but the insignia was different. Although the service cap was the same, the device attached to the cadet's cap was a winged propeller instead of the large eagle with arrows and olive branches, and there was a dark blue band instead of olive or tan. On his dress "blouse" or coat, the cadet did not wear the standard Air Force patch on his shoulder; rather, it was a gold, winged propeller against a blue background. The propeller/wings insignia also appeared on the sleeve and the garrison cap whose piping was light blue instead of the officer's black and gold braid. The lapel insignia, the "U.S." and wings/propeller, were the same for cadets and officers.

Indeed, the rule at some primary flight schools was no insignia worn until a cadet broke the shackles of dododom and soloed. During his infrequent forays into town with his full cadet insignia on, a cadet might encounter a young, inexperienced enlisted man, who, seeing all of the shiny devices on what looked like an officer's uniform, might salute. The observant enlisted man would quickly note the difference, though, since a cadet's sleeve was barren of the ring which indicated officer status, and there were no shiny bars on the cadet's shoulders. The occasionally mistaken status just added to the cadet's identity problem since he was neither enlisted nor commissioned.

Jeffries or Reynard couldn't be called "Lieutenant" or "Sir" because they weren't quite there yet. Nor were they called "Private." They would be called only by one name until the gold bars went on their shoulders at the end of the 30 week program: "Mister."

Here and there within cadet classes were a few already commissioned officers who were going through flight training in grade. These men, including West Pointers and transfers from other Army branches, attended the same ground school and flying sessions, but were spared the rigors of hazing and other more irksome tasks assigned to cadets.

During a cadet's ten weeks in primary, he flew for 60 hours, sat in class for 150 hours, spent 210 hours in the dining hall, did homework for 75 hours, took a minimum of 50 hours of physical training, talked through another 175 hours hangar flying with buddies, slept in well regulated time periods for 560 hours, and had a maximum of 300 hours free time, assuming he walked very few punishment tours which is a safe assumption for Jeffries and Reynard.[7]

Their days began early, Sunday excepted, with first call over the P.A. system at 4:40 a.m. followed by reveille and a bracing morning "walk" around the "campus." Although most bugle calls were played over the P.A. system, 42-B at Thunderbird had to select a bugler, and in this regard they hit paydirt since one of their number was a professional musician who had played with one of the well known big bands of the day. The boogie-woogie bugle boy flatly refused to play on anything except his own trumpet which was fine with the authorities. Thus, 42B'ers at Thunderbird were treated to "bugle" renditions as they never had been (or would be again).

Following the morning run across the field and back (about two miles), there was the matter of preparing quarters for a.m. inspection. Having cleaned his quarters, Cadet Jeffries was marched off to breakfast at 5:45 a.m. by his cadet captain.

At least once during each of his three ten-week periods of training, a cadet could look forward to being the O.D., officer of the day, not to be confused with the other ubiquitous "O.D." which permeated Army life, i.e. olive drab. Serving as the officer of the day or junior officer of the day was a dubious honor since it involved getting up earlier than anybody else, running the public address system, handling a long list of administrative chores, conducting flag ceremonies, completing a variety of reports, fielding visitor inquiries, and the like. In Jeffries' case, if the job hadn't been completed to the satisfaction of Lt. Robert deBusk, Commandant of Cadets, the retiring O.D. would retire to the ramp for an hour's marching.

Breakfast, and indeed all meals at first, were mixed blessings since it was in the dining hall especially that cadets were hazed by their upperclassmen. Cadets endured "square meals" in which they sat at ramrod attention on the front two or three inches of their chairs and ate without looking down at their plates. Their vocabulary, in the presence of upperclassman, had reverted to the only phrases known to a cadet, "Yes, Sir," "No, Sir" and "No excuse, Sir." While Jeffries and Reynard may have occasionally stood at attention as Scouts, their vocabulary was expanded by other position terms including "fall out," "at ease" and "parade rest."

Cadets had to "brace" anytime so ordered by their senior supreme beings. To brace was to assume the extreme at attention posture, i.e. chest rammed out and gut sucked in. To the command of, "Rap it back, Mister," the cadet pulled his chin in to the point of threatening the neck bones, thus creating a collection of chins which only that of his pudgy Aunt Millicent might rival. A flimsy excuse such as, "But, sir, I am at attention, it's just my coveralls that are at ease, Sir," might easily get the cadet "gigged" for which he would spend time on unpleasant duties such as marching in the sun on Saturday afternoon while his more buttoned-down associates were riding to town on an open post weekend. Before enjoying open post privileges, cadets were reminded of their responsibilities: in uniform, gentlemanly behavior, proper saluting, and a list of do nots which included smoking on streets, thumbing rides, and getting drunk.

Cadets learned, if in doubt, to salute properly i.e. within 30 paces but not closer than six paces and always first. After learning to salute all superiors, cadets had to remember that saluting was not required in church, mess halls, buses, squadron day rooms, or on athletic fields.

Hazing was tolerated early in the cadet experience and was said to be essential for creating disciplined soldiers. Hazing by upperclassmen could be physical, i.e. requiring a cadet to duck walk or do push-ups, but the more subtle and beneficial long term effect was mental. Seemingly idiotic exercises forced new cadets to develop appreciation for the value of knowing what time it was without looking at a watch or knowing from what direction aircraft engine sounds were emanating without scanning the sky.

While an aggressively hazing upperclassman could make an underclassman feel lower than the lowest form of vertebrate life, cadets were always reminded that they were at the leading edge of the best army in the world, that they had emerged from a selection process that could weed out nine of ten who started up the trail, and that they should stand tall and look proud.

Although hazing was officially banned in 1943, it didn't completely go away. The comportment of an upperclassman when "instructing" underclassmen could best be described by the current day expression, "in your face." For a few cadets, the hazing was not worth the bother, and they promptly washed out. For the majority though, the desire for silver wings was so intense that they simply decided that no upperclassman, no matter how obnoxious, would ever stand in the way of graduation.

Cadet Reynard looked younger than most, but was slightly older, much better educated, and with the resulting maturity regarded hazing as just "glorified Freshman Days." One of Reynard's closest cadet friends was Wayne Rogers, a Garland, Utah, resident and graduate of Brigham Young University. Like Reynard, Rogers had a way with words, and although he never took formal credit for the following piece, it was attributed to him as a response to his status as a lowly cadet.

### *I Am A DoDo, Woe Is Me!*

If I were king -
   I'd damn well see
That more attention was paid to me.
   By the officers and men of this army.
Why, I'd tremble and roar
   Or I'd be a bore;
Whichever mood - they'd ask for more.
   If I were king.

If I were king -
   I'd have a million men
Trained to stand or stoop or bend
   At a flick of my brow.
On land or sea or in the air
   With equal ease they'd mind my care
If I were king.

If I were king -
   Commissioned officers would have no place
To bark and heckle and take up space.
   All would be equal,
Except ME at the lead.
   Doubters would die as if they were weeds -
If I were king.

If I were king -
   BT and PT would be no more.
They're TB and TP. They're all pretty poor.
   P-38s and Bell 'Cobras for mine;
And stratosphere bombers that take less time
   From open post periods and dates at hand
And such serious business that'd envelop this land
   If I were king.

If I were king -
   Demerits and gigs would go to those prigs
Who spend so much time making their beds,
   And shining their shoes and shaving their heads.
Time for that would be cut to the core.
   Relaxation and rest would be shoved to the fore
If I were king.

If I were king -
   Crosswind and slipstream, those dogs out there,
Would command respect and get more care.
   Their fleas would be banished or they would be dead.
They'd be pickin'em off the dodos instead.
   If I were king.

If I were king -
   Cadets would be made only to fly.
Their duties they do up there in the sky.
   Ground school and drill would be taboo
Except for the officers and dodos who needed to
   If I were king.

If I were king -
   All this and more I'd institute;
And the first who tried to prostitute
   The good, intended by these laws
Would be thrown into the cage with Captain Hawes,
   If I were king.

Mornings were spent flying, on the flight line while waiting to fly, or in other instruction. Most flying was not actually done at the primary school's main field, but took place at satellite fields located several miles away. Lunch was taken with each dodo again maintaining his curiously quiet, stiff posture rather in contrast to his upperclass "friends" who were enjoying a more relaxed, animated dining experience. Following lunch, there was some uncharacteristic downtime devoted to digestion at the end of which ground school convened, to which activity the cadet marched, typically in double time.

Primary ground school subjects included math, physics, meteorology, aircraft construction and maintenance, radio code, navigation, and powerplants.

Upon their return from class late in the afternoon, Thunderbird cadets, for example, reported to the northwest corner of the field where their athletic officer was anxiously awaiting them. "PT" (physical training) in the afternoon consisted of equal bouts of "pain and pleasure" — one period of calisthenics in cadence, a run in the desert, and a final period of individually chosen sports such as softball, football, archery, etc. There was good reason for the PT beyond the obvious need for physically fit soldiers. On the surface, piloting an aircraft may not have seemed to be any more demanding than driving a car. An hour's worth of aerobatics with attending g-forces clearly pointed out the difference.

Late in the afternoon, cadets returned to their quarters and were left to their own devices, i.e. study. The grading system was simple: 70 was passing for any single subject, but the cadet's overall average had to be at least an 85 or he would be history. At 5 p.m. came the retreat formation and inspection: brass polished, shoes polished, faces clean-shaven, hair closely clipped. Failure to present properly, or for any other infraction, resulted in the cadets being gigged which resulted in a little marching practice not at the cadet's leisure (usually during open post on weekends). Giggable offenses ranged from untidy quarters to dirty fingernails. A record of collecting too many gigs could also result in elimination which was how a surprisingly large number of cadets washed out.

There was, of course, some leather burning in the cadet's daily life. "Fall in. Dress right, dress! Steady! Front! Right face! Left face! Forward, harch! Column right, harch! Column left, harch!" The step was a full 30 inches, and the arm swing did not exceed six inches to the front or three inches to the rear (unless one was a Thunderbird-based British cadet whose style was marched to the beat of a very different drummer).

When the colors had been lowered, the cadets marched off to the dining hall. Cadets actually had some free time in the early evening unless they were "dumb dodos" (with academic deficiencies) who were confined for remedial studying. The most unmotivated of dumb dodos were restricted to quarters or stood guard duty on weekends until their academics improved. Tattoo came at 8:45 p.m. and Taps at 9 p.m.

This is not to imply that the cadets never experienced leisure since morale would have suffered without it. There were dances, frequently held at a local hotel to which young ladies would be invited by the officer in charge of the cadets. For Jeffries and the 42-B class, there was a dance within several days of arrival at Thunderbird. What few, well-regulated hours spent off post were usually devoted to swimming and other recreational activities. Communities near the contract schools pitched in to make the cadets feel at home. One of Phoenix's society leaders was one Mrs. Lou Ella Archer who opened her home and large swimming pool to cadets on weekends. Grateful cadets made her an honorary cadet captain for the 42-A and 42-B classes.

Many cadets "got religion" early in their primary training days. To be invited by a local resident to attend church placed the cadet in town for a few hours on Sunday mornings. On holidays, many residents made guests of cadets who could not be home with families on Thanksgiving or Christmas.

### Thunderbird Field
### Glendale, Arizona

Jeffries' was the fourth class to graduate from Thunderbird which had opened in March of 1941. The field had been dedicated on May 31, 1941, amidst aerial bomb bursts and several of the instructors putting on an airshow in Stearmans. Collectively, those first few classes flew 12,500 hours during which period there were no fatalities in the 10 minor accidents that did occur.[8] In July 1941, Thunderbird's primary trainer fleet consisted of 40 Stearman biplanes. There were two cadet classes in session totaling roughly 120 men, and both the numbers of cadets and planes were about to grow by geometric proportions.

Hollywood built Thunderbird Field. Southwest Airways, the civilian contract operator of the field, was directed by Leland Hayward, a leading Hollywood talent agent and producer whose clients' names littered the tops of movie marquees across the country. He had been a director of TWA and was an aviation enthusiast whose interest in flying was passed along to Jimmy Stewart, a client. In addition to Stewart, several of the motion picture industry's biggest names, including Brian Aherne, Henry Fonda, Cary Grant, and the songwriter Hoagy Carmichael became the financial underpinning of Southwest Airways Inc. Hayward's general partner was John Connelley, a prominent test pilot. Connelley had been an Army pilot in the 1920s, and would go on to expand Southwest Airways from the core of the Thunderbird operation

*Thunderbird Field as photographed six weeks before Jeffries arrived to join class 42-B.*

which, during the war, ran a small air cargo service under contract to the Air Transport Command. The cargo airline flew high priority freight to air bases in Arizona and California. Although the Army took over the flying in 1944, Southwest had gained the experience and route structures that would serve it well in the post-war era.

Operating an ongoing Civilian Pilot Training (CPT) Program-certified primary flight training facility was one of the prerequisites for becoming a primary contractor to the Air Force. CPT was launched in mid-1939 as a government-funded, college and university-administered plan by which students could learn to fly. The purpose was to generate an aviation manpower pool which could be tapped in the event of a national emergency. It worked, and roughly 50,000 collegians received varying degrees of flight training. CPT graduates were vigorously recruited by the Army before the program was shifted directly to Army control after Pearl Harbor.

Hayward, Connelley and partners acquired Sky Harbor Air Service, a small (three Taylorcraft trainers) CPT operation in Phoenix, renamed it Southwest Airways, and stepped up training in October 1940 with an enrollment of 50 student pilots. In December, Connelley signed an Army contract calling for Southwest Airways to commence cadet training operations on March 1, 1941.

In the meantime, the base had to be built, auxiliary fields prepared, and fire/emergency facilities set up. Construction of the facility, whose final cost exceeded $1 million, began in early January 1941. Southwest ran ads in leading national newspapers to recruit the support staff which included mechanics and everything from welders to parachute riggers. The mechanics had their hands full since cadets were hard on the airplanes, and the field's rough conditions, particularly the sand, complicated servicing the Stearmans. Even the cadets in the first few classes were required to pitch in and finish construction of the base.

Southwest and the many other civilian contractors were going out on a financial limb; the initial contract was to run for ninety days only, could be canceled with 30 days notice, and all construction and supply costs were the responsibility of the contractor. It was late 1942 before Southwest Airways received its first payment from the government.

Connelley would later reflect on those pre-payment days, "We owed the Texaco Company $200,000, and were using gasoline at the rate of $25,000 per month."[9]

Prior to his own induction into the Army Air Force, Jimmy Stewart was an occasional visitor to Thunderbird which started off as a large, 640-acre field, one mile to each side and located adjacent to Glendale, Arizona, a suburb of Phoenix. Auxiliary landing fields added another 1,000 acres to the total. The Phoenix area was a key training center which was also home to the Air Corps Advanced Flying School at Luke Field. On the day after Jeffries arrived at Thunderbird, ground near Phoenix was broken for two new training facilities. At Mesa, Arizona, Southwest Airways became the contract operator at Falcon Field which was used for primary flight training of British cadets. Falcon Field was originally to be called "Thunderbird II," but the British balked at that, not having any familiarity with any mythical thunderbirds. "Falcon" the British could relate to, and so it became Falcon Field with Thunderbird II being reserved for a second primary training facility for American cadets. At Highly, Arizona, what would become known as Williams Air Force Base was started as an advanced flying school.

Jimmy Stewart usually flew into Thunderbird in his own Stinson Reliant, a popular high wing monoplane, and frequently visited with the cadets. He had more hours than some of the instructors, and within a year would follow the track of many of the cadets he was then visiting. Indeed, Stewart would pass through both Mather and Kirtland fields as an instructor before heavy bomber transition and assignment to the Eighth Air Force in England. There, as a squadron commander, he would be decorated with a Distinguished Flying Cross and the Air Medal with several oak leaf clusters.

Thunderbird, although it did not have the experience of such leading schools as Ryan, Parks, or Cal Aero, was an innovator. Unlike the other schools, it administered an aviation familiarity exam to all incoming cadet classes to assess potential problems in ground school instruction. Those cadets who had pilots' licenses or had been in the CPT program breezed through as did Jeffries considering his Sky Scout days. Invariably, cadets scoring poorly on the test tended to have the most difficulties in ground school.

Thunderbird went beyond the Army's indoctrination of flying instructors by putting its new hires through an additional three week instructor's course. Thunderbird also instituted a new item in the curriculum: aircraft identification. The need for that had been brought up by the growing numbers of British cadets going through Thunderbird. The RAF had been fighting for nearly two years by the summer of 1941, and was in a position to know how difficult distinguishing between friend and foe at 400 mph could be, hence the development of aircraft identification as a ground school subject. Thunderbird's identification course became the model for other primary ground schools.

"Middle America" would be a good way to describe the 42-B Thunderbird cadets' geographic origins since most came from Minnesota, Arkansas, Missouri, Nebraska, and Kansas. There were quite a few college graduates, and some like Jeffries with no college, but the majority had come directly from state universities, teachers' colleges, or junior colleges. Many had just received their degrees and had been deferred from joining until graduation. Like all cadets in 1941, they had to be under age 27, unmarried and at least 21 years old by the time of their scheduled graduation from the 30-week program. In a few cases, married cadets temporarily divorced their mates in order to get into the cadet program and promptly remarried their ex-wives upon graduation.

Several had pilot's licenses or a few flying hours before getting to Thunderbird, but those who did had to "unlearn" their civilian habits and learn flying the Army way. Those cadets who had already started flying in the CPT program also had to adapt their techniques to the Army way of flying.

41-H was the first class to graduate from Thunderbird. They had arrived when the field was still under construction. Facilities included a control tower located between two large hangars, a central administrative center and five barracks with a centrally located mess hall. The barracks, since they were in civilian ownership, were not typical Army in appearance, i.e. a military, two-story affair lined with lockers and cots on both levels.

Thunderbird's design was in the hands of an architect who was charged with capturing a southwest atmosphere in the field's layout and facilities. Indeed, the field was actually configured in the shape of a thunderbird with the front gate forming the head of the mythical bird, the buildings radiating out as wings, and the control tower being one of the central tail feathers. The colors were a blend of cactus green, desert hues of brown, tan, terra cotta, cream, and tomato red. The atmosphere was a unique blend of frontier army post, new world Spanish, and low rise institutional. The walls of the dining hall were emblazoned with murals depicting the Native American heritage associated with the field's name.

For cadet relaxation, there was a lounge with recent magazines and newspapers, tables for cards, several chessboards, and a radio. In mid-July 1941, *Daddy* with Sammy Kay was at the top of the charts, followed closely by *Maria Elena* with Jimmy Dorsey, and the *Hut-Hut Song* under two labels featuring a choice of bandleaders Freddy Martin or Horace Heidt. The Thunderbird cadet lounge also had a piano at which Hoagy Carmichael held court when he was in Phoenix.

Singing was an important part of cadet life, and song formations became an integral part of building team spirit. The *Army Air Corps Song* dominated ("Off we go into the wild blue yonder...") as was *The Spirit Of The Air Corps* ("Into the air, Army Air Corps, Give 'er the gun, pilots true, Into the air, Army Air Corps, Hold her nose up in the blue..."). Other favorites included *I've Got Six Pence* ("Jolly, jolly six pence, I've got six pence to last me all my life..."). Sung to the tune of *Stars and Stripes Forever* was another favored number aimed lightly at the ground-based, tactical administrative officers, *Now Be Kind To Your Web-Footed Friends*.

Prominently displayed in bright red on the hangar gables and roofs was the field's logo, the Thunderbird of Indian legend, the same symbol

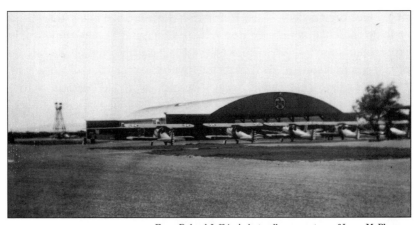

From Roland Jeffries' photo album courtesy of Larry McPherron

*Hangar with Thunderbird logo. The design would also appear later on the hangar roofs, including the hangars built after Jeffries' graduation.*

seen on the undersurfaces of the present-day Air Force Thunderbirds precision flying demonstration team. It is said that the Air Force team picked the name when flying F-84 Thunderjets from nearby Luke Field and saw the Thunderbird art on the hangars below.

As the war progressed, Thunderbird was expanded considerably, and became one of the major American training centers for British and Chinese aviation cadets. The diversity was interesting, especially as the Brits marched with full arm swings and saluted with open palms. Until Falcon Field was completed in late September, nearly 1,400 British cadets underwent primary at Thunderbird as did approximately 700 Chinese cadets during the course of the war. The Royal Air Force cadets were also a bizarre source of amusement for the American cadets. Very few of the British had ever owned or driven cars — not that having driving experience makes a critical difference in learning to fly in the long run, although it does help to develop some of the requisite motor skills. Whether it was for that reason and/or others, the young men from across the seas groundlooped to a much greater extent than the Americans. The Yanks frequently gathered on the field's perimeter to watch their allies groundloop the Stearman trainers as wingtips dug into the field and planes spun around in great, swirling clouds of dust.

Thunderbird became crowded very quickly. When Jeffries arrived, the field's cadet population stood at 275 men of which roughly half were

Royal Air Force cadets. When Jeffries and Reynard became cadets, their schools each had about two dozen instructors, but Thunderbird would grow much more rapidly. Those early growing pains created a shortage of classroom space in 1941, especially with the many foreign students. For that reason, some cadets, especially college graduates or those who already had private pilot licenses, could take the final exam in a subject before the class commenced, and if they passed with a sufficiently high score (92 or above), they were excused from the course, thus creating more room for those who really needed the classroom time.

Although the upper range of temperatures could be extreme, Thunderbird suffered no serious weather-related downtime, although the annual monsoonal moisture season created mud problems. Eventually, the field would be oiled and then paved. In the early days of 1941, however, only the first to take off were not beset by clouds of flying dust. Still, being in the Sunbelt paid off: Thunderbird's record of consecutive flying days topped out at 673.[10] Aircraft utilization hit its stride in 1943-44 with daily hours flown averaging 850.

Not too long after Jeffries graduated from primary at Thunderbird, Hollywood starred the field in an early morale boosting feature called

From the Ed Radtke collection courtesy of Walter Radtke
*Stearman trainers at Mira Loma Flight Academy at the Ventura County Airport, Oxnard, California.*

(not surprisingly) *Thunderbirds*. The flying was good, in Technicolor, but the plot revolved around a predictable love triangle involving Gene Tierney, Preston Foster and John Sutton. When the movie went into production in February 1942, Thunderbird had a few BT-13 basic and AT-6 advanced trainers which livened up the action, but even the movie's director (WWI fighter pilot, William Wellman) was not able to prevent the inevitable mixed reviews by cinema critics.

### Mira Loma Flight Academy
### Oxnard, California

Charles Reynard enjoyed a primary flying school whose facilities bordered on the country club setting for amenities.

Mira Loma was part of the Curtiss-Wright Technical Institute of Glendale, California. That organization's flight instruction unit, better known as Cal-Aero, was under the direction of Corliss C. Moseley, a WWI fighter pilot who had served with the First Pursuit Group in France along with Eddie Rickenbacker. Cal-Aero operated several primary schools and the only civilian-staffed Air Corps basic flying school. C.C. Moseley was a highly respected figure who had also been a test pilot, an air racer in the 1920s, and was the first winner of the International Pulitzer Race trophy. In keeping with the TWA link permeating this story, Moseley was one of the original organizers of Western Air Express Corporation, one of two companies from which Trans Continental & Western Air, Inc. had been formed.

The Mira Loma school itself had only recently been completed as a branch of the main facility at Glendale, and the finishing touches, particularly the landscaping, were in progress while 42-B was in training there.

The school had been in operation for exactly one year when Reynard arrived. Class 41-B had started the previous summer with 17 Stearmans, 18 instructors, and 86 cadets.[11] The school had grown dramatically and by July 1941 included the Army detachment of 11 officers, Cal-Aero's 24 flight and five ground instructors, and many more Stearman trainers. Roughly half of the Air Corps officers were directly involved with flying (giving stage checks) and the other half served in medical, supply and management positions. When Reynard left for basic flight, Mira Loma was growing rapidly and had 93 flight instructors and over a hundred Stearmans on the field with an in-commission rate of 78 percent.[12] Each Oxnard Stearman was flown hard, and on a five-day week basis, averaged 98 hours logged per month.

Photo courtesy of David E. McDonald
*Cadet cottages at Mira Loma Flight Academy, Oxnard, California.*

The Cal-Aero instructors were all very experienced pilots, and most had flown earlier in the Navy or Army. Those without military experience had many hours of instructing and commercial flying time, although as manpower shortages set in, Cal-Aero hired instructors with a minimum of 500 hours if they did well on their qualification tests. Most were college graduates as were the ground instructors of whom the majority were older men who had been active pilots, including two who had flown during WWI. The school was arranged in circular configuration and located adjacent to the Ventura County Airport. It consisted of two large buildings serving administrative, ground school, and dining hall functions while the quarters were composed of 40 cottages. The post buildings were located adjacent to a road on whose other side the airfield was situated. Thus, the morning and afternoon takeoffs and landings were never very far away from an Oxnard cadet. For athletic facilities, the academy had the use of a nearby high school's playing fields to which they were marched daily for physical training.

There were roughly 105 cadets in 42-B at Oxnard, and most also came from Middle America — from Indiana and West Virginia, although a few were from Louisiana, Utah and Mississippi. In fact, the single largest group came from Ohio as did Reynard. They were all college men, an increasingly unique phenomenon, and many represented state schools including Indiana, Ohio State, and Louisiana State. There were a couple

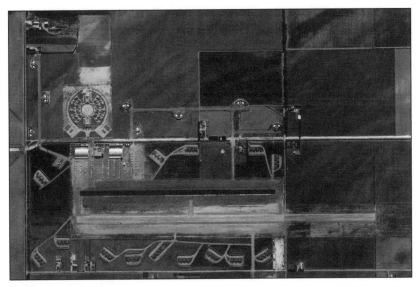

*Ventura County Airport, photographed about a year after Charles Reynard graduated from primary.*

of Ivy Leaguers, but only one Harvard man: Charles Reynard. As he was undergoing primary at Oxnard, Reynard would not have known that of his 41 fellow Buckeyes, six would be eliminated later in training and 12 would be killed, either in flying accidents or in overseas combat.

## The Far Away, Naval Link

Whereas the Army Air Force was not yet at war in the summer of 1941 when the cadets of 42-B first took to the sky, the Royal Air Force was in its third year of operations against the Axis. The RAF had already absorbed all possible pilots from the defeated air forces of Norway, France, Belgium, Denmark, Poland, Czechoslovakia, and Holland, but still faced monumental pilot shortages and training difficulties. To maintain a steadier flow of new pilots, many RAF-bound pilots were trained in Canada, the United States, and in Africa. One of the less-publicized operations set up for the training of Allied pilots was that for Dutch aviation cadets in the Netherlands East Indies. The link between that training and the fate of Liberator 41-1133 requires an explanatory diversion for a glimpse of naval flight instruction on the exotic East Indies setting of Java in the summer of 1941.

By 1939, the Netherlands East Indies had become concerned about Japanese aggression in the Pacific, not to mention the fact that Holland itself was threatened by the Nazis. The Netherlands East Indies government had purchased some Martin and Lockheed bombers before the war, but by mid-1940 decided to step up preparations for its own defense, particularly as Holland had been overrun by that time. Driving this militarization was the fact that Dutch holdings in the southwest Pacific included oil and rubber-rich areas which would certainly become lucrative objectives for the Japanese. In mid-1940, the Netherlands East Indies government selected the Ryan STM aircraft for use in its Army and Navy flying schools on the island of Java. The purchase involved over 100 aircraft including a few naval versions with floats.

The STM was a militarized version of San Diego-based Ryan Aeronautical Company's STA (Sport Trainer, Model A). There are still a few of those beautiful little, two-seater low wing monoplanes flying today, and to see one is to behold the pinnacle of light civil aircraft design in the 1930s.

The Navy flying school was located at Soerabaja and staffed by roughly a dozen American instructors of whom most had military and/or airline backgrounds. One of these airmen was Howard M. Kincheloe who had most recently been a flying boat pilot with Pan American Airways. Based in Miami, Howard had flown Caribbean routes including flights to Havana and Rio de Janeiro. Although from Kansas originally, he had graduated from Pensacola in 1937 after schooling at Wichita State and New York University.

Wichita was the place to be for a young man interested in aviation, and Howard was among the many young teenagers who hung around airfields watching planes take off. He was also active in his Scout troop and attained Life Scout rank (just one grade below Eagle Scout) before the unit folded. Before leaving Wichita he would become personally acquainted with Walter Beech and some of the other men who were building Wichita's name for aviation, including Eldon Cessna and Lloyd Stearman.

The interest in flying remained, and while working at his first job in the printing industry in New York, had, on one occasion, to get proofs on a major job up to a client in Boston as fast as possible. That meant flying, and the most expedient means in that case was through a friend who had a Long Island-based seaplane.

Howard was completely hooked on flying after that flight, and in late

Photo courtesy of Charles O. Cramer, 42-B

*The 41 pilots from Ohio in 42-B at Oxnard. Twelve of them perished in combat or flying accidents before WWII ended. Charles Reynard is at far right, front row, sitting.*

*The Ryan STM-2 was derived from the classic Ryan STA (Sport/Trainer, Model A) and was the principal trainer for Dutch aviation cadets in the Netherlands East Indies during 1941.*

1935 passed through the qualification tests at Floyd Bennett Field on Long Island. After graduating from Pensacola in 1937, he was assigned to the naval air station at Coco Solo, Panama, where he flew Consolidated PBY Catalina patrol bombers during his active duty assignment. Remaining in the reserves after leaving Panama, he signed on with Pan Am.

By late 1940, Howard found airline flying not as satisfying as the prospects offered by the Netherlands East Indies government which was actively recruiting instructors in the United States. For its Navy school, men with flying boat experience were sought and interviewed at the Netherlands East Indies embassy office in Washington.

Howard and his lovely wife, along with four other pilots and their wives, left for Java on a Pan Am Sikorsky flying boat with a layover in Hawaii. Departing Hawaii on December 29, 1940, they were met with such headwinds that the flying boat had to turn back. New Year's Eve was spent festively at Honolulu's Royal Hawaiian Hotel where the pilots' table was joined by the cinema idol, Errol Flynn, and his party.

By mid-January 1941, the STMs were being uncrated and assembled at the Soerabaja base which initially started instruction as a basic flying school. All of the cadets had soloed just before their introduction to the Ryan STM which functioned as their basic, advanced and instrument trainer. The training program was essentially a very compressed version of the training American Navy pilots went through at Pensacola. Once the sleek little STM was mastered, the cadets went on to fly either the floatplane version of the Dutch Fokker T.9 twin engine bomber or the pre-war German Dornier Do. 24 three-engine patrol bomber.

As Jeffries and Reynard were departing for their primary flight training in July of 1941, Howard Kincheloe was busy instructing far, far away,

Photo courtesy of Howard Kincheloe

*Lieutenant (J.G.) Howard Kincheloe earned his naval aviator's wings in 1937, flew PBY Catalinas in Panama, and subsequently flew for Pan Am before instructing in Soerabaja.*

and had no idea of the unique role he would play in the tragedy on Philmont's Trail Peak.

## The Scouting Connection

While Jeffries and Reynard were about to become acquainted with the Stearman biplane, Philmont was being discovered by its third season of campers. Following Phillips' initial gift of nearly 36,000 acres in 1938, facilities consisting of a director's cabin and commissary had been built at present day Ponil (in Philmont's north country). In addition to those at Ponil, cooking and camping shelters were built in Dean Canyon, at Pueblano and Stony Point. Burros and horses were acquired to ensure the "western ranch" aspect of the Philmont experience.

The program was in transition and offered considerable flexibility in choosing between backpacking, burro packing, or using a chuckwagon.

Philmont Museum, Cimarron, New Mexico

*Waite Phillips, the wealthy Oklahoma oilman whose generosity created Philmont Scout Ranch.*

In the first program year, the summer of 1939, expeditions lasted as little as three days or up to 12 days. They also featured trips to nearby attractions such as Mount Capulin or a drive to Taos through the Kit Carson National Forest and the magnificently palisaded Cimarron Canyon. The program was a steal at the rate of one dollar per camper per week (horses, guides, and meals extra).

In contrast to today's camping attendance of roughly 20,000, that first season in 1939 saw only 189 Scouts from Texas, Kansas, and Oklahoma visit the Ranch.[13] In 1940, more councils sent expeditions, and the number of campers quadrupled. Significantly, the Ranch, with its "adventure camping program," was started as a National Office project and, therefore, had full support from the BSA National Executive Staff.

The 1941 season opened with a considerable expansion of facilities in the Ponil area and the construction of a director's residence and training building for conferences that were offered in the spring and autumn.

As Jeffries and Reynard adapted to the cadet's structured daily routine and the exhilaration of flight, Philmont was visited by one of its more interesting expeditions. This was the Philturn Archeological Expedition from Quinnipiac Council in Connecticut. Investigating prehistoric Indian sites in the North Ponil Canyon, the group stayed at Philmont for 14 days and located numerous artifacts in several sites.

Waite Phillips was a frequent visitor to Philturn where he quietly observed how his gift of land and financial support was being used. The impact on Scouting youth, as he observed it, would result in a momentous announcement shortly after Jeffries and Reynard were in the midst of basic flight training.

# XII

# PRIMARY FLYING SCHOOL

**Mother:**
Why are you off in a silver ship,
And must you learn to fly?
What is it calls your heart from me,
And what do you find in the sky?

Patricia Hartnell

Although he was responsible for navigating the return leg back to Albuquerque and constantly staying on top of their position, Charlie had time to reflect on the territory he had covered in the previous ten months as Kansas slowly passed by them 8,000 feet below.

Charlie had joined the other Ohio men assembling in Columbus to be sworn into the service at Fort Hayes the previous July. From there, many took trains to the west coast. Originally, Reynard had been scheduled for primary training in Alabama with the Gulf Coast Training Command, but was switched to the West Coast Command at the last minute. Like Jeffries, he had been notified of his acceptance as an aviation cadet in late April. In mid-June, he and Jeffries received letters indicating that they would be joining the class starting in July, i.e. class 42-B. Two weeks later, both got letters advising them where to report for induction into the Army (the headquarters for the local Army Corps Area).

On June 30, Reynard received a letter with information on the Air Corps Training Detachment, Oxnard, California. At first glance, the letter could be misconstrued as having been written by a travel destination promotional writer. Reynard was advised to bring his clubs if he played golf, not to forget his swimming trunks since ocean swimming was available only two miles from the school, and that appropriate clothing should be brought since the climate was delightful (temperature rarely rising above

85 degrees). Getting to Oxnard would not be a problem since it was well served by Greyhound (two buses a day) and by the Southern Pacific Railroad which made five daily stops. Jeffries received a similar letter, but his was rather skimpy on central Arizona tourist attractions, i.e. the Grand Canyon was closer to 200 miles away than two miles.

A cadet could bring his automobile (but not his motorcycle) if he had appropriate liability insurance and was able to garage it in town. Reynard learned that he would be paid $75 per month and his monthly room and board allowance of $50 would be paid to Cal-Aero. His parents copied down the mailing address and the phone number where their son could be reached, Oxnard 709.

Reynard had nearly a month at home between his Harvard graduation and induction into the Army. Much of that time was spent doing home improvement projects such as painting. The Reynards owned five acres and were self-sufficient in dairy terms because they had chickens and a milk cow. Part of Charlie's vacation was spent "haying it" since his arrival home also coincided with first cutting time. It was, of course, a good way to stay in shape considering the extent to which calisthenics were about to become a part of his daily life. He enjoyed the company of Hiram College friends, went swimming with them at a lake not far from Hiram, and savored a few impromptu songfests.

Reynard's orders were cut on July 10th at Fort Hayes in Columbus, and he was assigned to the first of two groups leaving for California. Other cadets departing the same day were bound for primary training at Ontario, California, and Fort Worth, Texas. Nearly 25 percent of Reynard's group were to wash out. One in four would not survive the war, and of those who would be killed, three died in stateside flying accidents.

Jeffries had given notice to his employer, and was preparing for his departure from Fort Leavenworth for a July 16th arrival in Phoenix. Jeffries took the train and left his '32 Plymouth coupe back in Kansas City with relatives. On the day he reported to Thunderbird, the Germans moved to within 145 miles of Stalingrad. In the Middle East, the Vichy government ceased military operations against Allied units and ended French rule in Syria and Lebanon by surrendering all forces to the British.

Reynard's trip to the west coast was spent productively; he read at length about California, its original Native Americans, the Spanish exploration and missions, and gold rush days. Uncle Sam paid him a per diem travel allowance including a dollar a day for food.

Unlike most cadets who took a train, Cadet Reynard drove out with two other Ohio men, Dave McDonald, who had graduated from Muskingham College several years before, and Earl Evans, an athlete from Baldwin Wallace College. Their trip west via Denver involved a little sightseeing, including stops at Estes Park and Zion National Park. Evans was already a very competent pilot, but would wash out shortly after the 40-hour stage check in basic flight. He was color blind. Evans had been able to negotiate the entry physical and vision test at the beginning of primary and basic on memory alone, but the problem was discovered nearly two-thirds of the way through the program, and he had to leave.

McDonald and Reynard would both pass through primary and basic together, but not in the same flights. McDonald would be sent to advanced single-engine school at Luke Field near Phoenix, went through fighter transition in Mississippi, and eventually became the Deputy C.O. of the 50th Fighter Group. He flew Thunderbolts and Mustangs, and returned from Europe in 1945 with a Distinguished Flying Cross and several Air Medals.

Photo courtesy of David E. McDonald

*Dave McDonald, Earl Evans and Charles Reynard photographed in a Kansas municipal park on the way to California in early July 1941. McDonald later became the deputy commander of the 50th Fighter Group in England.*

Reynard arrived in Los Angeles two days ahead of his July 16th reporting date at Oxnard, so he saw a few former classmates who had moved west from Hiram. He spent one night in San Bernardino and the next night at a Santa Monica hotel after going with his friends to a concert at the Hollywood Bowl.

Reynard's flying school roommates, assigned on an alphabetical basis, were Russell Schleeh and W. Edward Radtke. Actually, they were Reynard's second set of roommates since his first two roommates, one from Toledo and the other from Shreveport, had both washed out during the first few days of primary.

Charlie's longer term roommates would go on to become bomber pilots. Schleeh, who became 42-B cadet captain at Oxnard and then battalion commander at basic flying school, stayed in the Air Force as a test pilot for 20 years and then had a second career with Douglas Aircraft. He completed his combat tour in Europe with the 305th Bomb Group, and later was General Curtis LeMay's personal pilot in the 20th Air Force during the latter days of the war in the Pacific. Radtke would become a heavy bomber instructor and later, in civilian life, was an insurance executive and civic leader in suburban San Francisco.

Both Radtke and Schleeh were Californians who had been added to the Oxnard group at the last minute since several other cadets had just been transferred to the Gulf Coast Training Command.

Jeffries' roommate in primary, Melvin E. Neef, was used to hard work in the sun. He was a farm boy and agriculture major from the University of Missouri where he had run track. Like Jeffries, he enjoyed bowling, but his chief interests were horses and riding. Back home, in Houstonia, Missouri, he had trained riding and jumping horses. His long term plans were to become an airline pilot. Neef's training would directly parallel Jeffries in the ten months ahead. As a B-24 Liberator pilot in the 389th Bomb Group, Neef was shot down during the epic, low altitude Ploesti raid on August 1, 1943. He remained as a prisoner of war in Romania until late 1944, entered the FBI after the war, and later went back on active Air Force duty in security work. He never fully retired though, and was an aluminum company plant manager in Georgia at the time of his death in an automobile accident in late 1995.

Oxnard, California, high summer 1941. Right on the Pacific Ocean. 45 air miles northwest over the Santa Monica Mountains from Hollywood. Spanish place names. New foods, orange groves, and sunny weather. A

From Roland Jeffries' photo album courtesy of Larry McPherron

*Jeff and Neef. Melvin Neef (pronounced Neff) was Jeffries' roommate at Thunderbird. Neef completed B-24 training with Jeffries, was shot down on the August 1, 1943 low-level raid on Ploesti and was held as a POW in Romania until late 1944.*

new life style (not only for Charlie whose daily schedule was markedly different from the occasional civilians he, with a sociologist's eye, periodically observed from afar).

The war was a world away, but getting closer. The nearby Ventura office of the California Department of Employment was actively recruiting for the 1,200 workers San Diego-based Consolidated Aircraft required to build B-24 Liberators.[1] The company desperately needed skilled people to build the B-24s that Charlie and thousands of pilots like him would fly — all kinds of workers: mechanical draftsmen, milling machinists, turret lathe operators, tool designers and makers, sheet metal fabricators, detail and final assemblers, jig makers, engine lathe operators, bolt threading machine operators, tool grinder operators, boring mill operators, and many, many more.

The Chairman of the Senate Military Affairs Committee, Robert Reynolds (Democrat, North Carolina), had just introduced legislation, advocated by General Marshall, the Army Chief of Staff, which would extend the draft and utilize U.S. troops at bases beyond the western hemisphere. President Roosevelt had asked Congress on July 10th for a supplemental appropriation of nearly $5 billion to be spent on ordnance to supplement the $10 billion already allocated for the Army.

In early July, the City of Oxnard began civilian defense preparedness planning since it was believed that the presence of a key primary flying school made the area a strategic target in the event of war. War jitters were accentuated by steady reports of the fighting in Russia which had been invaded only several weeks before by the Germans.

One aspect of the devastating German advance into Russia caught attention in Oxnard: the Red Army's scorched earth policy in which all farm animals and produce were destroyed before the onrushing *Wermacht* could put it to advantage. Much of the surrounding Oxnard economy was based on agriculture, citrus products in particular.

While Charles Reynard was eating institutional, but nourishing "square" meals in the dining hall at Mira Loma, Oxnard residents were enjoying the ripe bounties of local agriculture. At the A&P, four ears of fresh sweet corn cost only a dime. For the same price, four nice cantaloupes or four pounds of fresh peaches could be taken home. Skinned hams, at an average of 10-12 pounds, were sold at 29 cents per pound. For those cadets who imbibed on the rare occasion when safe to do so, many California grocery stores had liquor departments in which a full quart of Kentucky Club sold for $1.60 and beer by the 12-ounce bottle (Buddy, Imperial, East Side Lager, Pilsen Gold, etc.) was just ten cents, plus deposit. Aviation Cadet Reynard was not tempted by hard liquor, and was quite content with a soft drink which cost only a nickel for a seven-ounce bottle.

The Wurlitzer juke boxes in downtown Oxnard's popular Oyster Loaf and other cafes played a song for a nickel. Popular when Charlie arrived in town were *My Sister and I*, *Intermezzo* (from the movie with Ingrid Bergman), and *Maria Elena* with Jimmy Dorsey.

The shortages which would set in by early 1942 were still on the horizon. $142 could buy a deluxe, gas range at Sears where, for the home handyman, jig saws were on sale for $9.99. Numerous apartments and homes were available for rental in July 1941, but in just a few months, their owners would not have to resort to advertising to attract renters.

Cadets who had arrived at Oxnard without wheels ogled the used car ads and might have longed for Hudson dealer Frank Fagan's special, a 1940 Packard Six going for $895. Cadets in 1941, at $75 per month before deductions, would be hard pressed to cough up that much, but could afford another Fagan special, a 1931 Ford DeLuxe Coupe ($95).

Flying did not start immediately, especially since the pre-flight stage of training had not yet been instituted. Reynard, like Jeffries in far away Phoenix, spent several days being physically and dentally examined, inoculated, filling out many forms (including those for the free $10,000 life insurance policy) getting his dogtags, and drawing study materials and equipment. Several cadets washed out at the end of the inoculation line: fainting or a bad reaction was the equivalent of a pink slip. Those not fit enough to withstand the rigors of hard physical exercise, extended running, marching, and standing at attention for long periods in the midday sun also were shown the gate.

Each cadet received blouses, trousers, gloves, underwear, insignia, belts, garrison and service caps, shirts, fatigues, athletic shorts and shirts, rainwear, overcoat, insignia, and two barracks bags. Whether or not Jeff's clothing was too small or Charlie's too large is unknown. They were given several minutes to try on their new garments, and if they did not object to the fitting, they were stuck with what they got.

In Roland Jeffries' case, the clothing included a pith helmet (Phoenix in July could be rather hot). The heat occasionally made it difficult to sleep at night and created aircraft maintenance problems as well. The commander of the First Bomb Wing down at Tucson, Colonel Lackland, had dramatized the problem by showing up at the flight line after lunch with an egg which he had just brought from his refrigerator at home. He proceeded to crack the egg onto an aircraft wing, and within several minutes had a very nicely and thoroughly cooked egg. They didn't refer to the Phoenix area as "The Valley of the Sun" without justification. Hence, the pith helmets were for good reason.

Immediately, cadets started learning the military way of life from Air Corps military detachment instructors and upperclassmen, the cadets of 42-A. From their upperclassmen, they learned precisely what went where in their lockers, how their beds should be made (six-inch turn down and tight enough to bounce a coin dropped in the middle), and how to polish shoes and brass to a remarkable state of reflectivity.

It was not the pants, shirts, or garrison caps which got most of Jeffries' and Mel Neef's attention, but rather, the flying gear: blue flying suit, goggles, silk scarf, parachute, and soft leather flying helmet with Gosport tube (of which more later). The upperclassmen were responsible for some instruction and daily inspections immediately after breakfast or supper. The Air Corps officers were responsible for marching and "SMI," Saturday Morning Inspection.

Before using the accoutrements of aviating, Dodos Jeffries and Reynard had to learn how to salute, march, maintain their quarters, and get a start on such subjects as the structure of the Army of the United States, care and preservation of uniforms, insignia, what to take to the first duty station, exercising command, and the true meaning of the word "mess" (the term applies to those army groups who for convenience, sociability, or economy, eat together).

Reynard and Jeffries also learned about army supply, staff functions, military courtesy, customs of the service, and a subject for which they would be set apart after successful completion of the flying course upon then embarked: pay.

When rated as pilots and getting in four hours flight time a month, they would qualify for flight pay. A second lieutenant, under the U.S. Army pay table effective immediately after Reynard's and Jeffries' cadet graduation, was paid a base salary of $1,800 annually. Flight pay increased that by 50 percent and there were allowances for subsistence and rentals for men with dependents. An officer in an airborne outfit actually came out ahead since he got an extra $100 per month. Jumping paid better than flying.

By contrast, majors with less than 23 years of service who were commanding the military detachments at average-sized primary flight schools had a base salary of $3000 plus a longevity adjustment of $300. Cavalry officers, if they were majors or below, got an annual allowance of $150 if they provided their own mounts. Cavalrymen with influence in Congress died hard. On the other hand, light colonels and above got no allowance for privately owned beasts. Brigadier generals started at $6000 per year plus subsistence, rental, and longevity pay. Yankee dollars went further, a lot further in 1941.

There were other pay nuances relating especially to Air Corps personnel who changed bases frequently: travel expenses. Cadets also learned that their $75 per month already included extra pay for the risks of flying. They received no longevity pay, but did receive a $150 uniform allowance upon commissioning at which time they had the option of paying for the $10,000 life insurance policy for which the government had been paying their premiums during the preceding 30 weeks.

They also learned that a six months pay death gratuity would be paid to their bereaved only in the event that death from wounds or disease had occurred solely as a result of other than their own or their comrades' misconduct. This would not comfort the immediate families of two 42-B cadets who were killed in a joyriding flying accident during the advanced flight training stage. Beyond mortality and insurance, cadets learned about such subjects as promotion policies, foreign service, efficiency reports, and the privileges and rights of officers.

The civilian-run primary schools were patterned after Randolph Field in Texas, which had always billed itself as the "West Point of the Air." The whole thrust of an aviation cadet's training was to blend flight instruction with the equivalent of a West Point plebe year in which aeronautical subjects largely replaced the traditional military curriculum. From two characteristics, no deviations were tolerated: a high sense of duty and honor. The purpose, in addition to creating a pilot, was to take a young man and develop his physical self, mental capabilities and initiative in order to create a junior officer in the fastest growing branch of the Army.

A cadet would visit the barber weekly to remain cleancut. Each and every button on his clothing was to be buttoned, and the zipper on his flight clothing was zippered precisely to a point three inches from the top. His name tag, worn at all times, was printed with bold, block letters and had to be visible from ten feet. The tag, however, did not have to be worn on a leather jacket. If something were out of order, the infraction was remedied by an hour's walking tour around the base flagpole.

A cadet learned how to conduct himself in his cadet flight when approached by an officer, in a room or outdoors, and that the flight was responsible for policing its ready room and assigned areas. He was pleased to learn that coming to attention, saluting, or bracing was not required on the flight line where he could remain at ease in the presence of upperclassmen.

Cadets were marched in class A uniform to the mess hall, and upon entering removed their caps before proceeding to their assigned seat at a table supervised by an upperclassman. The cadet stood at strict attention behind his seat until hearing the command, "Seats," at which time he lifted, not pulled, his chair back. Similarly, when dismissed, he lifted the chair again, and Lord help him if he tried to talk to a cadet at an adjoining table. Had a cadet's table etiquette been somewhat lax before entering the Air Corps, it was promptly corrected.

Cadets were permitted to use the P.X. and recreation hall, but only at certain hours. "Smoke-em if you got'em" was the rule in cadets' rooms, but it was a meaningless privilege for Cadet Reynard since he was not a smoker.

Misters Reynard and Jeffries had to respond unerringly to upper-classmen who might test their knowledge on specifics of the Stearman aircraft, that is its empty weight, useful load, fuel and oil capacities, wing and power loading, speeds, range, takeoff and landing speeds, 50 foot obstacle clearance distances, engine operating parameters, and propeller types and pitches (plural since more than one type of prop was found on the Stearman).

## The Stearman

The instrument by which both Jeffries and Reynard learned to fly was the Boeing Model 75 "Kaydet" biplane, but nobody ever called it that. To the legions of Army and Navy pilots who trained on them in the 30s and 40s, it was known simply and universally as the "Stearman" whether it was a PT-13, PT-17, PT-18, or N2S. The designation differences related largely to the 220 horsepower engines which came from Lycoming, Continental or Jacobs. Those engines drove a roughly nine foot steel or wooden propeller at a maximum of 2,100 revolutions per minute. At gross weight, the trainer topped out at just under 3,000 pounds.

From the Ed Radtke collection courtesy of Walter Radtke

*Stearman designations included PT-13 (shown here), PT-17, PT-18, or, for the Navy, N2S. Engine type determined the designation.*

Outside loops, extended inverted spins, prolonged inverted flight, diving in excess of 185 mph, revs in excess of 2520, and entries into snap rolls and slow rolls at speeds in excess of 106 mph and 124 mph, respectively, were forbidden. Anything else was fair game. The prohibition against inverted flight was based on the Stearman's lack of an inverted oil scavenge system, plus the fact that the gravity fed fuel arrangement would starve the engine anyway.

The Stearman's detractors might say the ship was underpowered and difficult to trim for hands off flight, and the allegations are true since the throttle has no friction lock to prevent creep, and the plane is a study in aerodynamic drag. Stearman-instructed cadets quickly became masters of power management since even the briefest nose up attitude or modest bank significantly reduced airspeed. For most aerobatics, stick forces are moderate, and the roll rate is weak unless well coordinated with rudder.

A minority of the primary schools used trainers other than the ubiquitous Stearman, i.e. the Ryan PT-16 or PT-22 (variants of the beautiful Ryan STA) or the Fairchild PT-19, all low wing monoplanes. The PT-19 was regarded as rather docile whereas the Stearman and Ryans could make the inattentive cadet look bad rather quickly (but better prepared for assignment to basic flying school).

Today, mention the name Stearman to a WWII era pilot and you will see a smile and hear a chuckle as the veteran talks about the Stearman as though it were an old girl friend. It's an affair that can be carried on today since there are still quite a few Stearmans around. The overwhelming majority of pilots, both Army and Navy, trained on Stearmans which traced their origins to Wichita and Lloyd Stearman who resigned from Travel Air to start his own company in the late 20s. From the turmoil of the depression, Stearman Aircraft became a wholly-owned subsidiary of Boeing. Lloyd Stearman had left his company and was with Lockheed when the first Stearman PT-13 went into service with the Army in the mid-1930s. With roughly 8,500 built, it became the most widely produced biplane in the world.

In a day and age when it is easy to become glassy-eyed at all of the avionics contained in even the lightest of contemporary airplanes, the Stearman is a nostalgic retreat to an era when stick and rudder, throttle, needle, ball, and airspeed said it all. In fact, that's about all one got in a Stearman. After all, what more is really needed? Although the Navy ordered a few Stearmans with accessories and electrical systems, the plane is a study in basics. Jeffries' PT-17 and Reynard's PT-13 each cost Uncle Sam $9,120 in 1941 dollars or about one-sixth of the price of the ultimate in wartime, American pursuit flying, the P-51 Mustang (with eight times the horsepower). Today, a well-restored Stearman with a new annual, recent overhaul, and low-time engine sells for about $75,000 (assuming it was never used for crop dusting).

Nobody could mistake an Army Stearman in 1941 — bright blue fuselage, yellow wings and red and white horizontal stripes on the rudder. The engine barked as though a basso bulldog had been grabbed by the tail. Jeffries and Reynard were tantalized by the sight and sound of upperclassmen flying, but nearly a week passed before they got their first flights in late July 1941. Cadets were broken down into flights of about 40 men and then into smaller groups of about six cadets. Each small group was assigned to an instructor who first met informally with his charges to get acquainted and go over the basics of operating the Stearman and how to use a parachute.

In the ten weeks of primary, successful cadets received 60 hours of flying and were expected to make 175 landings. Initial instruction emphasized making the pilot safe enough to solo. In the middle phases of primary, cadets were introduced to maneuvers which developed precision flying including the various "eights" (elementary eights, eights on pylons, and lazy eights) and chandelles. That "accuracy" stage also involved various types of approaches and landings, and the last phase introduced aerobatics with emphasis on loops and various rolls. During primary, dual instruction, as opposed to solo flight, varied between 40 and 50 percent of the cadet's total time in the air. Formation and instrument flying were not part of the program in primary, but would dominate basic flying school, although a cadet near the end of primary could expect a brief, cross country formation hop as a sign of times to come.

Before learning everything a Stearman could do in the air, Cadets Jeffries and Reynard started ground school in which they were taught the principles of flight. In mid-1941, Oxnard and Thunderbird each had six classroom instructors. In the first stage of ground school, aerodynamics dominated study with its emphasis on gravity, lift, drag, and powerplants. In design functions, cadets learned more about lift by studying airfoils in greater detail, and the effects of various types of drag, i.e. active drag, passive drag, parasitic drag, and induced drag. Included in that stage were the effects of angle of attack. The identity of Cadet Jeffries' aircraft structures instructor is lost to history, but Cadet Reynard's is not. That would be Mr. A.A. Fisher, a former Navy pilot, who, as a reservist, kept his hand in by looping amphibians.[2] Fisher is recalled as a serious man who was unimpressed by Cadet Stanley Keller's response on the best way to determine wind direction while in the air ("Take your feet off the rudder bar, and let the plane weathervane itself into the wind.").

Aircraft construction provided cadets with a basic understanding of aircraft components. Some of the terminology has disappeared from today's ground training curricula, but in 1941 wing struts and bracing wires related quite literally to the Stearmans cadets were starting to fly. Having gained an understanding of structures simplified understanding aircraft stability. A seasoned instructor would tell his students to listen to the wires in flight: every airplane talks to its pilot, and the prudent flyer always listens whether his ship is a Stearman or L-1011.

The propeller as a power device was studied in some detail including such nuances as pitch, slip, efficiency, cavitation, propeller drag, propeller thrust, drag ratios, blade camber, and various types of propellers. Some of the ground instructors had grown up as aviation itself did. Reynard's instructor on engines, Mr. L.R. Baas, was no rookie, and had been in the U.S. Army Air Service in France in WWI. He had gone into aviation education after leaving the service, moonlighted as first trumpet with the Los Angeles Symphony Orchestra, and was quite capable of thrashing many of the 20-year old cadets on the tennis court.

Armed with rudimentary, theoretical knowledge, cadets learned that the first step in flying was understanding the plane to be flown and making sure it was, in fact, ready to fly. On the first trip to the flight line, cadets were instructed how to conduct a walk-around preflight inspection. From that day forth, they conducted the preflight. Entry to either cockpit is from the left wing root over which there is a metal strip (aft of the engine firewall, the plane is strictly a fabric-covered job). The instructor reached down toward his knee and withdrew the checklist from its holder. Communication was strictly one-way by means of a maddening device called the Gosport tube, an arrangement by which the instructor yelled into the funnel-shaped device at his end of the tube. His voice, or lack of it by day's end, was carried to the back cockpit where a "Y" splitter tube was attached to the cadet's helmet earpads. Most instructors supplemented communication by the Gosport tube through the use of hand signals.

Before the Stearman was finally ready for flight, the cadet himself had to be preflighted, and for those who had never flown before there were a few moments of fumbling around with what seemed to be an overabundance of straps beginning with the parachute harness. Once that was fastened, the cadet had to attach himself to the airplane as well. That involved getting used to the collection of clamps, pins, snaps, safety locks, one fast-release locking lever, and four heavy belts. Within a few flights, the bewildered butterfingers were confidently harnessing themselves within a few seconds without having to look at the instructor or mechanic as if to say, "Where does this go?"

With the eager eaglet secured into his properly positioned seat, the starting checklist was quickly dispatched with the cadet confirming the ignition switch as off, mixture in full lean, brakes on, controls locked, throttle closed, and carburetor heat set for cold. Fuel state, displayed in quarter tank increments only, was checked by looking at the cylindrical float gauge protruding from the bottom of the wing center section. The fuel selector was moved into the on position and ignition switches reconfirmed as off.

The prop was pulled through several turns to purge lower cylinders of any accumulated oil if this were the day's first flight. Using the checklist, the controls were unlocked by pushing the stick forward and down while simultaneously depressing the left rudder pedal and moving the lock handle into the unlocked position. The mixture was moved into rich. With his seat properly positioned, the young cadet now had to wait for more assistance before the adventure started. The engine was primed from the starter system control panel located outside the cockpit on the front left side of the engine cowling. Four shots in cold weather or two in hot did the trick. Then, two of Mister Reynard's fellow cadets, remaining well clear of the propeller arc, commenced cranking the inertial starter flywheel, each hoping the engine would catch so they wouldn't have to crank it again.

After loudly yelling, "Clear," Reynard engaged the starter and, after one full revolution of the prop, flicked the ignition switch to "Both." When the engine caught, with its barking grumble, Reynard waited a few seconds for the oil pressure to rise before taxiing would start.

Oxnard and Thunderbird cadets took to the air with their instructors for the first time on July 21, 1941. Each cadet may have thought that getting to the active runway would be a miracle, considering how erratic were the instructors' taxiing habits. Here were a dozen Stearmans ziggzagging and fishtailing all over the place. It was not because the instructors had been hitting the bottle, but rather because taxiing in a series of S-turns was the only way to acquire visibility over the nose to avoid hitting something. And, woe betide the cadet who taxied into another Stearman.

During the journey to the head of the runway, cadets were told about the hydraulic brakes and how to use them for turns, but to avoid sudden application since, with enough power on and the stick not held back, the Stearman would pitch forward enough to splinter the prop, and possibly even flip over onto its back.

They were getting close to that magic moment. The pre-takeoff check was used in the last minutes before scanning for traffic and getting a green light from the control tower: controls confirmed unlocked, elevator trim neutralized, mixture in full rich, carburetor heat cold, altimeter set for field elevation (for Reynard, 50 feet was good enough, and for Jeffries, the knob was turned until the pointers showed 1250), and clocks set. The engine was run up briefly for magneto and carburetor heat checks before moving onto the runway. A quick glance at oil pressure and temperature preceded opening the throttle fully.

The crackling roar was what impressed a cadet at first, and a few moments after they started rolling down the runway, the plane's attitude changed as the instructor moved the stick forward. The roar continued, vibration quickened, and breeze stiffened, but at around 60 mph, with the stick pulled back so slightly and the right rudder pedal somewhat depressed, they broke ground and started climbing at 90 mph. Jeffries and Reynard were off on half hour orientation flights which included pointing out the local landmarks. From that day on, each cadet would be flying once a day, five days a week, and usually from 45 minutes to an hour and a half at a hop.

For Jeffries in Arizona, orientation at Thunderbird was based on the nearby White Tank Mountains to the east, the Hieroglyphic Mountains to the north, and the city of Phoenix to the southeast. Reynard, at Oxnard, California, had the Santa Clara River and Pierpoint Bay to the north, the Las Posas Hills to the east, Los Angeles to the southeast, and the Santa Barbara Channel to the west. Unlike their primary cadet peers in other parts of the country where landmarks were few and far between as in the south-central states, cadets at Thunderbird and Oxnard had to work hard at becoming lost.

During the first hour of flight instruction, the basic maneuvers consisting of climbs, turns, and descents, were demonstrated with the invitation for the cadet to follow along by placing his hands and feet lightly on the controls. After that, the cadet tried his hand at these elementary, confidence-building maneuvers along with climbing and descending turns, glides, gliding turns, and rectangular courses. Those cadets with civilian flying experience quickly had to learn the Army way of flying for which one major difference was that the controls, while not slammed about, were moved more vigorously, and that gentle, standard rate turns, were largely a thing of the past. After this first lesson, cadets were responsible for engine management, taxiing, and parking the Stearman.

At some point during the first week, the instructor went through a brief aerobatic routine consisting of a spin, a roll or two, and loops. For the occasional cadet, that was it, the end of the program: the difference between his idea of flying and its reality prompted terror that no amount of practice, instructor's patience, or Uncle Sam's funding could or would overcome. The second week was devoted to stalls, spins, landings, and takeoffs. Because Jeffries' and Reynard's logbooks do not survive, it is not known who their primary flight instructors were. However, it is known that Reynard was assigned to Oxnard's "F Flight" and that one of its eight instructors was a particularly hefty pilot who preferred smaller, lighter cadets in order to balance the total passenger weight in a Stearman.

Since Reynard was one of the lightweights on the course, from a strictly body weight viewpoint, he was almost certainly assigned to Mark Wesley Thompson, the Deputy Flight Commander. Thompson was a civilian, but like the rest of the Cal-Aero instructors, wore a distinctly military uniform complete with company wings and cap insignia. A graduate of Los Angeles City College with a degree in Aeronautical Engineering, Thompson had a reputation as being one of the more demanding instructors who took great pride in the excellent performances his students turned in during their rides with the Army check pilots. Thompson's previous seven years as a commercial pilot and flight instructor could not, however, overturn F Flight's reputation for ground-looping Stearmans more than the other two flights.

The contract primary school graded students, and the list of shortcomings, even for the initial, confidence-building maneuvers was a long one. Such words and phrases as "erratic," "overcontrols," "extremely tense," "forgets ailerons in turns," "leans away from bank," "weak throttle coordination," and "not developing much feel" could be a sign that a wash ride was in a cadet's very near future.

During the last few days of July, Jeffries' and Reynard's pre-solo instruction included S-turns across roads which served several purposes. The turns forcibly taught them how to correct for wind drift which they would need to know in the landing pattern, in simulated emergency landings, and in the airwork that would follow. But, most importantly, S-turns began to develop their "flying sense." With that sense budding, the cadet started using vision, hearing, touch as sensed through his hands and feet on the controls, and the seat of his pants (technically, "kinesthesia" or the feeling that something is awry based on getting "bad vibes" from the plane). When the cadet could integrate all of these with the other important senses, "common sense" and quick headwork, he was well on his way to taking the trainer up on his own.

S-turns were surprisingly difficult for many cadets at first. The Stearman was simply flown across a road and immediately banked so as to have completed a perfect half circle by the time the road was again bisected in a wings level configuration at which time the process was repeated up the road to make a complete "S" (or a series of S's). To the beginner, perhaps bucking a good stiff sea breeze coming in off the Santa Barbara Channel, it was asking a lot on the first try. Keep the nose level, maintain altitude, keep an eye on the turn and bank to make sure he wasn't skidding or slipping, do all of this at a constant airspeed, reef it in a bit on the downwind turn so as not to lose that perfect half circle, and master it after having a few hours of dual instruction is to know why it took a little getting used to.

Pleasing Instructor Thompson was not easy since he didn't want to see mistakes after a flawless demonstration. "Flawless" didn't include choosing a poor road, insufficient or overcorrection for drift, poor trimming, slow reactions, wings not level when crossing the road, or over-controlling rudder. But, there wasn't a lot of time to keep trying to get it right. For the occasional cadet who couldn't grasp it fairly quickly, the Army check pilot was frightfully nearby. For those whose performance was mediocre, there were deficient grades which, accumulated to a certain level, pointed the way out the front gate, suitcase in hand, after disappointing the wash rider.

Cadets who could relax and enjoy flying for what it was, i.e. a game of anticipation and coordination, avoided the criticism that befell their harried comrades who were collecting comments like "mechanical coordination," "hurries maneuver," "insufficient torque correction," "weak planning," or "fights ailerons."

For those who took to it, the solo flight usually came around the tenth hour or during their third week of instruction. The pre-solo stage of primary flying was dominated by normal takeoffs and landings, stall and spin recoveries, and emergency landings. The objective was to get the dodo to solo by 12 hours and give him the wherewithal to get out of the two most likely difficulties he could face during this fledgling stage, i.e. engine failure and a stall developing into a spin.

The preponderance of flat terrain all around Thunderbird and in the very immediate vicinity of Oxnard's Ventura Field made cadets Jeffries' and Reynard's prospects for surviving an engine failure, even on takeoff, quite encouraging. Considering the fact that a two-turn spin in a Stearman could eat up nearly 1,000 feet, the likelihood of getting out of a spin initiated by trying to cut corners on landing was limited at best. Thus, there was considerable emphasis on recognizing what leads to stalls, spins, and how to recover. Recovering from a three-turn spin would be a part of nearly every flight cadets made.

The instructor and the dodo would have just finished some airwork, were practicing landings, and after several good ones, the instructor would have the Stearman taxied to the edge of an auxiliary field where he would get out and tell the student to "Take'er up yourself, shoot three good ones, and don't worry, I'll be keeping my eye on you. Look my way after each landing, and if I want you to come in, I'll wave, OK?" It was, of course, the BIG moment and composed of equal parts of trepidation, determination and exhilaration. No matter how many memorable flights a pilot makes, the one that is remembered most vividly to his dying day is that first solo — the time of day, other aircraft traffic, sky conditions, the instructor's name and the look on his face, his voice, and his words as he climbed out of the plane.

Because the auxiliary fields, where most solos took place, were usually large, square open areas without established runways, the budding aerialist didn't have to worry about a crosswind on his big day (a stiff crosswind could be a problem for anybody flying a Stearman). Shorn of 200 pounds worth of instructor and parachute, the Stearman seemed peppier to most soloing cadets whose typical first solo landings averaged between the best he'd made to date or workmanlike at worst.

Soloing was a cause for great pride and celebration, and in some primary schools there were special antics or traditions to celebrate a fellow cadet's first solo, but such activities were not in place at Oxnard or Thunderbird in the summer of '41.

Failure to solo by 12 hours resulted in an immediate washout. To solo, students had to demonstrate proficiency of fundamental flight regimes including climbs, glides, turns, straight and level flight, takeoffs and landings, spin recovery, and the ability to make an emergency landing.

On the surface, this may not sound difficult, and truly it is not for those who grasp it quickly. Indeed, for those who have been flying for a lifetime, simple maneuvers are not much more difficult than parking a car in the garage. But, they are never, never taken so lightly, for the consequences of a lapse in judgment are infinitely greater. Although instructor pilots will say that no one phase of flight is more important than another, the first obstacle for students and the most trying time of all for instructors is quite literally those moments before the rubber meets the runway.

Landing is a conditioned reflex — like learning how to handle a lacrosse stick or becoming proficient with a pitching wedge on the golf course. At first it is mildly vexing, then frustrating, then infuriating, but after learning the proper relationship between speed, sound, visual cues, sink rate, and after practice with the instructor, most students grasped the proper technique. This usually came after alternating between first flaring out much too high and "dropping in" or nearly flying headlong into the runway before the instructor corrected the attitude. Or, the cadet might have had too much speed with the effect that he ballooned up in the air instead of slowly sinking when he held the stick back only to hear the instructor yelling, "Sit down!"

Jeffries and Reynard soon learned to enjoy that brief interval so close to the landing field's surface when they had done all they could to pull off a good landing. It is in those last few seconds that student pilots feel a blend of giddy uncertainty, apprehension, and hope which turns to unbridled glee when the gentle bump and rumbling vibration join to say that lift has softly surrendered to gravity. Once in a while, the glee went sour in a hurry since it can be said that a Stearman wasn't finished flying until the engine was shut off, brakes set, and controls locked. Many a former groundlooping Stearman student pilot will attest to that.

Much of becoming a pilot, beyond honing proper eye-hand-foot coordination, is learning how to relax and smoothly move the controls, not slam them around. A few never learned to relax. Others could not settle down and overcorrected to such an extent that simply flying straight and level became impossible. Many washed out because they couldn't harmonize control inputs, to move stick, rudder, and ailerons in concert instead of thinking in sequential terms.

Flying, while so natural to experienced pilots, puts the neophyte into a very unnatural environment. It's noisy, very noisy indeed. There's vibration. For students learning at Thunderbird in August, it was hotter than blazes to say nothing about how hot aircraft surfaces got after sitting in the midday sun. With heat come thermals that create turbulence which bumps a trainer around to the extent that straps dig into shoulders and bellies.

There is ample opportunity to be frightened, especially by birds. Both Jeffries and Reynard would be startled by hawks occasionally flying as high as five or six thousand feet or more, and swearing that a collision was imminent, only to have the raptor adroitly roll out of harm's way at the last second. Less clever were the pelicans near Oxnard (they invariably dive) or those great flyers, the seagulls, which frequently don't have the good sense to step aside.

Straight and level flight was only part of the program; other phases of the curriculum were filled with bizarre motions and sensations that only the world's most diabolically designed roller coaster could simulate. Early in his primary training, the aspiring aviator might look out at the horizon over the nose, out at clouds, or up to blue sky and sun while the trainer was heading for the heavens. As things were getting rather quiet, the cadet thought, "Oh Lord, the nose seems way too high." Suddenly, the bottom dropped out just as the plane whipped over onto one side.

He's falling, going down, and in the next moment he's looking straight at the earth, and it's spinning round, and round, and round, and round, and round, and round. There's a singing sound in the bracing wires, then it's a whine and in a few seconds, he's jolted around in his seat as the turning abruptly stops, and some giant hand is pushing him down in his seat, almost trying to stuff his head and neck into his chest. The heaviness recedes within a few seconds followed by the horizon reassuringly showing up again, and then the engine's roaring back to life.

Mr. Jeffries has just been introduced to the spin, and in a few weeks will come other, increasingly complex maneuvers which will test his

From Roland Jeffries' photo album courtesy of Larry McPherron

*Aviation Cadet Roland L. Jeffries shortly after arriving at Thunderbird Field, mid-July 1941.*

abilities and teach him to be the master of his aircraft.

At least several of Reynard's and Jeffries' inner circle of junior bird-men friends lost the tug of war with their stomachs whose contents subsequently decorated the sides of fuselages and tailplane leading edges. That wasn't held against them if limited to just a few early episodes. If it persisted, they too had to say goodbye. In any case, each had to wipe off the disgraceful discharge; then it dawned on them why the instructor sat up front in Stearmans and students in back.

None of the maneuvers came as a total surprise to cadets since the basics had been reviewed on the ground before they were introduced in the air. These introductions were facilitated by the use of blackboards and model airplanes which were never far from the benches and tables that were divided among the various flights and their ready rooms.

Part of their ground school included "Familiarization with Equipment" which, at the primary stage, meant learning just what the Stearman could and could not do, and what the limitations were for specific maneuvers. Stalls in a Stearman are not pronounced and are in contrast to the sharp break Jeffries and Reynard were to encounter in the AT-6 trainers they flew in advanced flying school. Rather, the Stearman tends to mush after stalling, almost giving rise to the observation, "Is that all there is to it?"

As with all aerobatic maneuvers, Jeff was instructed to climb to an altitude several thousand feet above the desert and to make a couple clearing turns. He closed the throttle and started pulling the stick back, back, but did not jerk it sharply back. The Stearman had started to climb, but now Jeff could tell that their speed was dropping. While he had been cruising along at around 80 mph, his speed was dropping back, and the nose, he thought, was abnormally high (actually it was about the same as it would be in landing attitude). His speed fell past 60, and was dropping back through 55 when he felt a light buffet and gentle pulsing running through the stick. Then something happened. The sensation was that of having hit a gentle bump or maybe that something had very gently tugged his plane by the tail, and he felt as though he were sinking. The nose had dropped only about five degrees, and with the plane having been flown on a level keel, neither wing dropped.

"Now, Mister Jeffries, now. Stick forward, let's get some speed. Nose down, come on — just past neutral, power, come on, Jeffries." The procedure was repeated until Jeff's instincts were honed to the extent that he could sense the moment the break occurred at which point he dropped the nose down through the horizon while smoothly coming in with power. Later, his instructor would introduce variations by keeping some power on and inducing a wing drop at the stall to teach Jeff to use the rudder to maintain directional control during a stall.

Once normal, power-on stalls, and partial stalls with and without power were mastered, Cadet Jeffries was ready for spins which were entered like normal stalls, except at the first hint of the break, full rudder, either left or right, was applied. The effect was startling in a rump over teakettle sense of the word which suddenly provided Jeffries with a straight down view of an earth that was now rapidly revolving.

It could be mesmerizing or terrifying. There was one resulting certainty: the airspeed indicator and altimeter pointers were heading in different directions.

"Lead with opposite rudder, then stick forward Jeffries," came the voice through the Gosport tube, "quickly, now, good, right, let's have

Photo courtesy of Mr. and Mrs. Richard Spencer

*Aviation Cadet Charles O. Reynard, Jr. during primary flight training at Oxnard, September 1941.*

some power." Spins were taught not just from a normal entry, but also from climbing and gliding turns as well as steep turns.

Early in their instruction and at unpredictable intervals while flying with an instructor and at heights of about 1,000 above ground (sometimes much less), Jeffries and Reynard were surprised when things suddenly became quiet, very quiet indeed. The instructor had pulled the power back to idle in a simulated engine failure after having sighted several possible emergency landing fields. The cadet, whose blood pressure had inched up a few points, was not usually expected to make an actual landing, but rather to arrive on a short final approach to some promising piece of real estate that would support a reasonably event free landing. Once the landing was assured, the throttle would be quickly advanced and the Stearman would roar up and away. It was not at all unusual to give a cadet several simulated emergency landings in a row, and then tell him the lesson was over and to head for the barn. Not knowing which way the field was after the stress at low altitude produced a weak grade for the exercise.

The most clever of cadets would be ready for the emergency landing drill and had usually scanned below periodically for a likely emergency field. Thus, they could safely glide or spiral down, arriving at the key position with just enough altitude to comfortably assure a landing.

More typically, the instructor would cut the gun when all of his cadet's faculties were focused on something else such as S-turns or elementary eights. Since these maneuvers were usually flown at around 500 feet, cadets had to get it together quickly. The instructor would restore power at 100 feet, and if the cadet did not have a landing assured by then, he was deemed to have failed the exercise. And, the cadet was all too aware of who might be riding in the front seat after a few botched emergency landing approaches. To go on a dual hop without having a simulated emergency landing was an exception to the rule.

During the war years, there were several documented cases of miscommunications between instructor and cadet in which each unforgivably assumed that the other was in charge. Nobody in those isolated cases gave'r the gun at the last second in order to pull up and out of the simulated emergency landing. In one instance, the primary trainer landed all by itself after a fashion. In the others, the planes bellied in, ripped off the landing gears, splintered the props, and prematurely harvested some of whatever had been planted in the field.

By the third week in August, when Jeffries and Reynard completed their 20th hour of instruction, they were ready for a stage check. Reynard, for example, had a few hours of solo flying and had reviewed all of the confidence maneuvers, stalls, spins, S-turns, and landings. He would be waiting in his small group of friends when a voice would come over the loudspeaker located on the flightline, "Mister Reynard, report to Mr. Walters at ship number 137."

Reynard's first stage check was a half hour recap of everything learned to date, and his last flight with Thompson had been the dress rehearsal. Walters was the E Flight commander and a very respected pilot of 13 years who had obtained his Navy wings in 1928. Reynard's interim checks might be with the other flight commanders each of whom had been flying for around ten years. Army pilots gave the graduation check at the end of primary in addition to stage checks and, for struggling cadets, the elimination ride. Most of the Army check pilots were junior officers who had fairly recently completed the instructor's course at Randolph Field in Texas. In early 1942, the luxury of going to instructor's school before becoming an instructor would be another casualty of the war.

Most of the elimination rides occurred during the first 20 hours, particularly in the 10 to 20 range. A cadet getting a solid "S" (for satisfactory) on his 20-hour stage check had good reason to be encouraged. There would, however, be plenty of opportunity for frustration in the next ten hours since this was dominated by learning new types of landings and doing one's best to avoid entry into the "Hall of Shame."

That dubious honor was accorded to cadets who experienced a ground loop in their Stearmans, usually when there was a little crosswind blowing across the field. One moment a cadet could have flared out and assumed he had wired a great landing only to find himself headed sideways seconds later after making a spectacular pirouette midfield, digging in a wingtip, and raising a cloud of dust. Worse yet, he might hear the soul-wrenching crack of structural failure. With its relatively narrow main landing gear, the Stearman has shamed generations of pilots who have thrilled to its other, more endearing, flying qualities since it first flew in the mid-1930s. One anonymous Oxnard pilot/poet expressed it very well.

### *Ground Loop*
**Dedicated to Lewis S. Simon**
**and Gardner Cornwell***

When a pilot's been a'flying for a coupla years or so,
And can kick a plane around and put on quite a show,
It's a thing he takes no pride in, and unless I've been scooped
If he's ever done much flyin', he's at different times ground looped.

When the kaydets get together for a Stage at Oxnard Field,
And you're due to draw a ship with a wobbly old tail wheel;
You come in for your landing and you put her down O.K.
But before you know what's happened, she's headed for the hay.

So you pour the gas into her and she bounds up from the ground,
And you're feelin' mighty thankful for a chance to go around,
Down the base leg you come a'roarin', cut the gun and make the turn,
But you know that they're watching and your ears begin to burn.

You head in for the runway, note the drift and drop a wing.
And you feel the ship a'settlin' as the wires begin to sing.
The ground comes up a'tearin' and you ease back on the stick,
And you bear down on the rudder and you do it mighty quick.

But you can hear the spar a'splittin' and fabric tear apart,
While the terror down inside you takes a death grip on your heart;
Your hands and feet are paralyzed as the dirt goes flying past,
And you duck down in the cockpit as the motor coughs its last.

Then you climb out from the wreckage and your knees begin to shake,
And you feel humiliated for the rubbing you must take.
And all the pilots crowd around you and advice begins to flow
And they tell you how it happened, just as if you didn't know.

They criticize and advise you although they're meanin' well,
You try to laugh it off and tell them to go to hell-
Lots of pilots give prescriptions and enjoy to rub it in,
But there's few that give descriptions of the ground loops they were in.

---

*  Oxnard poet's identity is unknown. The poem was dedicated to Gardner Cornwell, later killed in
   action with the 11th Bomb Group on December 15, 1942, (memorialized in Hawaii) and Lewis S.
   Simon, subsequently killed in a stateside flying accident on June 7, 1945.

# XIII

# "GET ON THE BALL, MISTER!"

**Son:**
The wind might say, if the wind could speak
Or her folk who love the mountain peak;
The birds could tell, for all they know,
Or the arrow flung from a hunter's bow;
But they are mute, and I cannot
Tell you the things my plane has taught,
Except that I want until I die
Weather that's fair and a ship to fly.

Patricia Hartnell

Underclassmen were constantly being reminded of their shortcomings when in the presence of their "betters" who never failed to remind a cadet to "Get on the ball, mister!" Before his first flight, a dodo might not have attached too much meaning to that expression which he simply regarded as a warning to shape up, look lively, or get with it. It was only after he made a sloppy turn in the air, one in which the little marble, the "ball" in the turn and bank indicator, fell out to one side or the other indicating a skid or a slip, that the expression's meaning hit home.

Such a mediocre performance was not lost upon the instructor who quickly reminded the cadet to get on the ball, or "step on it." If the cadet couldn't feel an uncoordinated turn in the seat of his pants, the little black ball's position would tell him which rudder pedal to get on. Very soon, keeping the ball centered throughout all of the turning and rolling maneuvers would become second nature.

Halfway through the ten-week course, Charlie and Jeff became upperclassmen. They had endured a fair amount of grief at the hands of departing 42-A cadets. Within any large group of upperclassmen, there were a few who carried hazing to its unproductive extreme. At Oxnard there were about half a dozen upperclassmen who went out of their way to make life miserable for underclassmen, including zipping through living quarters at the last second before the Saturday morning inspection and leaving cottages looking like a tornado had passed through. Naturally, the underclassmen got gigged and wound up spending most of what might have been open post marching off the hours.

Thus, just before the Oxnard 42-A class was to be transferred to basic flight, and under the cover of darkness, some of the 42-B cadets who had been excessively hazed by the overzealous upperclassmen dug a deep pit just beyond the offending cadets' cottage. The upperclassmen had just gotten to sleep after returning from their graduation dance, and included in their number the 42-A cadet captain, his adjutant and several other ranking cadets. This pit was filled with cold water and what could best be described as farming byproduct matter whose intended use was fertilization of the newly planted landscaping. The 42-B vigilantes descended upon the offenders in the depth of night, carried them bodily to the edge of the reeking abyss, and heaved their tormenters into the vile trough. Members of the swimming party, when later encountered by the 42-B'ers at basic flight, appeared to have matured and mellowed marvelously, and gave no sign of harboring retributive tendencies.

There was another swimming party going on at Thunderbird, one that also placed underclassmen against upperclassmen. This, however, was a regularly scheduled event initiated by 42-B, played every five weeks, and pitted the outgoing upperclassmen against those who were about to emerge from their status as wretched underlings. This was a tug of war across one of the finer landscaping features of Thunderbird Field, an irrigation canal whose modest proportions were exceeded only by the turbidity of its waters. The two sides chose their teams carefully because there was a certain pucker factor associated with being defeated. The entire losing class had to line up, en masse, and kiss the rope by which their team had been dragged through the less than pristine waters. The 42-B'ers carried the day, and thoroughly savored the humbling of the 42-A'ers who would shortly be on their way to basic flight.

The transition to upperclassman at the middle or fifth week of primary brought new challenges in their flight training. Whereas the third and fourth weeks had been dominated by supervised solo flying, take-offs, landings, and flying around the pattern, the fifth week began the "accuracy" stage. Here, cadets learned to make short field takeoffs and landings, spot landings and crosswind landings. The spot landing was made from an altitude of 500 feet at an angle of 90 degrees from the beginning of the approach. The luxury of flaps and power changes was not available, thus the cadet had to learn how to master his airspeed so as to get low and close to the spot just as he was running out of airspeed. The "spot" was usually a line extending from the instructor's position on the ground extending out to the landing lane on one of the auxiliary fields which were not particularly large to begin with.

To undershoot or overshoot twice in a row was considered very bad form and invited a failing grade. In the weeks ahead, accuracy landings would be made using 180 and 360 degree approaches. The more challenging aspect of precision landings was learning to master crosswinds. By learning to land a Stearman in a crosswind, more than one cadet real-

From the Jeffries photo album

*Jeffries by the red and white-striped tail of a Stearman.*

ized that the PT-17 wasn't finished flying until it was both shut down and tied down. Groundlooping as a result of bungled crosswind landings was, by far, the greatest cause of bent Stearmans. The other causes, taxiing accidents, blown tires, ground collisions, and mismanagement of brakes didn't even come close to the havoc induced by groundloops. With its narrow knees and short distance to the tailwheel, the Stearman easily groundlooped in a crosswind for which the remedy ran counter to a cadet's newly developed sense of aerial propriety.

To carry off a proper crosswind landing at that stage of instruction, meant tracking down the final approach slightly upwind of the runway centerline by crabbing into the wind, and kicking out the crab at the last possible split second so as to be aligned perfectly straight down the runway during touchdown and rollout. Failure to perfectly nail the timing automatically resulted in the Stearman arriving at an angle which produced an opposite reaction, wild gyrations, and clouds of dust, if not a bent wingtip, wrinkled fabric, or worse. Cadets were taught that just because the machine was on the ground rolling toward the other end of the field was no reason for complacency; hence, the emphasis on looking at the horizon, glancing quickly out the side to recognize drift, and not to start the S-turns until slowing to taxi speed.

The other technique, taught after crabbing, was to lower the upwind wing and keep the nose straight by applying opposite rudder, i.e. crossing the controls. This initially opposed everything that cadets had been taught about "coordinating" the controls. Once mastered, the Stearman crosswind landing became a source of great pride, but few cadets complained about the prospect of moving onto basic where the main landing gear wheels were spaced luxuriously far apart.

Other airwork in the fifth week involved some review with S-turns and emergency landings, but also introduced two new maneuvers: chandelles and elementary eights.

The elementary eight was an extension of the S-turns which had been taught during late July, and saw the Stearmans almost describing a perfect circle around some point, usually along a road. Rather than close the circle, the trainer headed for another nearby point around which he flew and then headed back to circle the original point, thus the term "eight." The first object was to have the cadet quickly pick out ground reference points which would help him fly perfect circles. The second goal was to further develop the skill to neutralize wind effect since the eights could not be anything except perfect circles around the two points. Sagging or bulging circles invited drooping grades.

As Mr. Thompson would have demonstrated Charlie's first chandelle, "A quick clearing turn, we'll do it right over that road, and power up to 1800 rpm, then we'll lower the nose in a gentle dive to get it up to 110, start a climbing turn right up through the horizon, constant bank, now, full power at the 90 degree point, and start easing off the bank, and we'll roll out at exactly 180 degrees from where we started. And there's our road again. Now you try one."

The simple maneuver was a minefield for bad grades at first: poor airspeed control, excessive or insufficient bank, failure to correct for torque, poor timing, letting go at the 90 degree point, or rolling out off the reference point. Although the chandelle paled in comparison to some of the more exciting maneuvers that would come at the end of primary, the chandelle and lazy eight developed coordination and sense of timing.

The lazy eight is a cousin of the chandelle and requires diving and climbing turns against a reference point at a right angle to the aircraft. Cadets generally enjoyed this maneuver since it involved more activity. The entry is the same as a chandelle with a dive to pick up speed; the nose is raised, a climbing turn executed, and as the speed decays, the nose passes through the reference point. A recovery is initiated to roll out in a gentle dive from which the pull out is made at exactly the same airspeed used on entry. Then the maneuver is repeated in the opposite direction. When viewed from the side, the maneuver looks roughly like a series of figure eights that have been plunked down on their sides with uplifted edges.

Meteorology was introduced at the primary stage, and was of particular interest to Oxnard cadets because their flying was more affected by the weather, especially the sea fogs that rolled in and disrupted morning flying schedules. For that reason, Oxnard cadets alternated their flying and ground school schedules since a cadet consistently scheduled for the first morning flights would never build up hours fast enough to graduate from primary. Cadet Reynard's meteorology instructor typified one of Cal-Aero's real problems. The instructor, Mr. C. A. Moore, was highly qualified, about 26 years old with a B.S. in Aeronautical Engineering from the University of Colorado and an M.S. from Cal Tech. Unfortunately, from Cal-Aero's viewpoint, his services were about to be terminated since he was also a 2nd Lt. in the Air Corps Reserve and soon to leave for active duty. The loss of well-qualified people was not limited just to flying personnel.

Meteorology began with a study of the various levels of the atmosphere, its heating and cooling, temperature gradients, pressure, and moisture. Cloud types and associated weather dominated meteorology along with winds and major phenomena such as the various types of cyclones. Weather maps and forecasting completed the study. With rudimentary cross sectional charts, thunderstorms were discussed, including their formation and composition. The words "microburst" and "downburst" were not yet fully understood by meteorologists and were not part of the curriculum.

A Thunderbird cadet could well wonder what the point was in studying meteorology since Phoenix had cornered the market on sunny flying weather for all practical purposes, although the aspiring pilots would occasionally be confronted by high winds, dust storms, and seasonal, monsoonal rain.

One poetic Thunderbird cadet's view of ground school, especially meteorology, ran like this:

### Ground School Lament

Wobble, wobble, torque and burble
Icing means a lot of trouble.
Engines miss, stall and flutter
Ground loops, spins and a thousand others.

Clouds and fronts and the CCL
Mean effective - what the hell
The adiabatic and the L.F.C.
Why do all of this to me?

It's the same old song they sing,
A cadet has time for everything.
Why teach us this - we never face it?
Well, it will help you when you get to Basic. *

---

\* Poem by Lt. Raymond C. Walton, killed in action on May 1, 1943 with the 98th Bomb Group. Memorialized in North Africa.

Aviation meteorological science was not well developed in 1941, and even an airline pilot briefing was sketchy compared to today's. Cadets quickly mastered reading sequence reports with their little symbols indicating station of origin, type of report, ceiling, sky conditions, visibility, temperature and dewpoint, wind direction and velocity, altimeter setting, and any significant weather at the time of the observation (thunderstorms, lightning, etc.).

Cadets learned the various types of fogs and clouds, and more importantly, what they signaled. Considerable emphasis was placed on the structure of a thunderstorm, various types of fronts, and what to do when encountering such adverse phenomena as cold fronts and related line squalls. Prophetically, rated pilots and cadets were told to always avoid cumulonimbus, and that the best procedure was to locate a nearby airport, land and sit it out. If for some reason, they had to continue, flying over the storm was preferred. That approach was not always an option, so flying around or between major visible storm centers was always preferable to barreling on through a cell, under one, or entering a greenish colored section (usually the most turbulent, highly-charged area of all). Even flying toward a lighter-colored area in a storm had its perils: it could lead to a dead-end blocked by another storm. By the time that peril had become obvious, storm cells may have closed in and blocked a retreat.

The list of storm flying "Don'ts" taught to cadets reads like a prelude to the tragedy that overtook Liberator 41-1133. Don't proceed unless you can see blue sky ahead. If you can't, turn 90 degrees and fly around the storm. Once you've blundered into a big cell, don't make a 180 because you'll just have to fly through the rain, hail, lightning, and turbulence all over again. Flying immediately below the freezing level will keep you from icing up, but also places you in the zone where lightning is at its worst. Don't try to fly underneath a storm in mountain ranges.

Icing was a very important subject in meteorology. Cadets learned how ice could form in the carburetor on a nice day even when the outside air temperature was well above freezing. They were thoroughly indoctrinated on the hazards of structural icing, its origins, what it could do to a plane in flight, the several types of icing, how to avoid icing, and how it could be removed on the more advanced aircraft in the Army's inventory.

Ground school continued with another central subject: propulsion. Cadets would not gain the intimate knowledge of an engine's innards as would an aviation mechanic, but the subject was a major one early in cadet ground school. Here Cadets Jeffries and Reynard learned all about various fuels and their properties, combustion, drive mechanisms, simple engines, and four-stroke cycle engines of the type used on their Stearmans (Lycoming and Continental radial engines). Valves and cylinders were key topics as were cylinder arrangement, crankshafts and connecting rods. The balance of engine component study was devoted to cams, cooling, lubrication, and advantages of various types of oils.

Ignition, carburetion, and electrical systems followed. Cadets were tantalized by one subject that would not have much relevance until after advanced: supercharging. Before their final exam on powerplants, the last topic, engine problems, got everybody's attention. This was not strictly textbook and blackboard learning, but was enhanced with some "touch and feel" since engines and engine parts were displayed on classroom tables.

All of the common symptoms were drilled into cadet minds: engine fails to start, rough running, low oil pressure, excessive or inadequate oil temperature, hot engine, engine missing or knocking, engine not turning up properly, sudden failure, vibration, or pre-ignition. And, of course, so were the remedies.

In the air, by the seventh week, Jeffries and Reynard learned the remaining precision stage maneuvers, the last of the "eights." Eights "on" pylons (as opposed to elementary eights or eights "around" pylons) are also flown down in the weeds, but with the object of having the cadet discover the pivotal altitude for a given degree of bank. From above, the maneuver looks like a figure eight superimposed over a road with the circles placed around two points along the road. Because the maneuver was flown largely with eyes usually glued to the pylons, cadets necessarily had to use their senses of vision, hearing and feel in order to maintain control.

In the Stearman, the maneuver was taught using a 45 degree bank with an entry altitude of 580 feet above the ground. The instructor took the Stearman around several turns showing the effect of altitudes that were too low and too high, then turned the matter over to the student, and warned him against becoming fixated by the pylon. Very early, cadets learned to place the pylon at the center of a wingtip and fly around it by adjusting their altitude depending on which direction the wingtip seemed to be moving relative to the pylon. With the pylon stationary on the wingtip, the pivotal altitude was attained. If the wing moved forward, a little back pressure was indicated to get up to the pivotal altitude. A wing that seemed to be losing the race indicated the need to descend slightly. Eights on were fun — up to a point, but couldn't be compared to the exhilaration of real aerobatics.

When they could see the light at the end of the primary training tunnel, Jeffries and Reynard were getting into the more interesting aspects of airwork: serious aerobatics which were taught in the last two weeks of primary. To many cadets, the simple loop appeared at first to be the easiest of maneuvers: after all, one only had to pull the stick back and hold it there until the plane, assisted with power during the climb, traced a perfect circle in the sky. How could one go wrong with something so simple?

Those cadets quickly learned that they could easily make mistakes of not leveling their wings on entry, not having sufficient entry speed, being too shallow or steep on entry, coming in too early or too late with power, not carrying enough rudder to counteract torque at full throttle, not backing off the power at the right moment on top, losing their original ground reference, failing to stay level, and/or allowing the speed to become excessive before the maneuver was completed.

Charlie's introduction to the loop was initiated by following through with the instructor's example which was preceded by a couple clearing

Photo courtesy of David E. McDonald

*Dave McDonald about to take off from Oxnard for some dual instruction.*

turns to make sure nobody else was near and by selecting a road below to use as a reference point. He shoved the nose down to pick up the airspeed, quickly confirmed that he was level, and pulled back on the stick to bring the nose right up past the horizon. As soon as he reached the vertical, he smartly pushed the throttle to its stop and applied some right rudder to keep the nose on its original heading. Soon, Charlie was approaching the inverted, craning his head backwards to see the horizon coming into his field of view.

"Look back, Mister Reynard, look, keep looking, where's the horizon, the mountains, keep looking. Don't let go, Reynard, keep pulling. Don't forget that right rudder, keep looking, it's all blue sky, wings level, keep your hand on the throttle, yes, there it is, the horizon again even if it's upside down."

Then, Charlie eased off some of the back pressure on the stick as they came over the top of the loop, which he followed by closing the throttle and applying more back pressure on the stick as the nose fell through the horizon, but now all he could see was the earth — straight down, filling his vision in addition to his instructor's head, the wings' trailing edges, and the engine's exposed cylinder heads. In a few seconds, the horizon finally started acting right with the blue sky in the upper half and the blue-gray horizon in the bottom half. Properly executed, Charlie had pulled nearly three Gs during the maneuver which he was gratified to discover was completed on the original heading right over the road he had picked as his reference point. To the Ventura County residents below, that Charlie was practicing successive loops was obvious — there was the unmistakable roaring of the Continental engine at the climbing stage of each loop.

The first roll taught in primary, the slow roll, proved least popular. Failure to have an adequately fastened seat belt and parachute would produce the one mistake a cadet could not possibly make twice (lack of G forces in this maneuver would easily dump an ill-prepared cadet right out of the Stearman when the roll reached the inverted point). Unlike other rolls where the plane's nose traces a circle around a point on the horizon, the slow roll is performed with the nose pinned to a reference point on the horizon.

A gentle dive preceded the slow roll in order to pick up some speed followed by pulling the stick back to put the nose on the point and start a roll, let's say to the left. When Charlie's Stearman was at a right angle to the earth, he gave it more aileron, but also pushed the right rudder pedal in to keep the nose on the point. As the ship went inverted, he held in some forward elevator pressure to make sure the nose pegged on the point. As the plane rolled over the top, back pressure was reinstated as was left rudder. The controls were neutralized when he had returned the straight and level flight with the nose still stuck on that point out on the horizon.

Done the first time, the slow roll, with its lack of G forces, was an unsettling maneuver for cadets because they had never hung in their harness straps before. Nor had their feet ever fallen off the rudder pedals or had they ever seen dried mud, dead bugs, loose items in their pockets, pebbles, and any other trash rising from the floor and disappearing in the slipstream while flying inverted. More than just a few cadets bruised their shins on the bottom of the instrument panel at the beginning of their first slow roll, but they soon learned to flex their legs and tighten their straps before slow rolling.

"Put your feet lightly on the rudder pedals, and gently hold the stick, Jeffries. I will demonstrate an Immelmann, then you can try it. Let's just make a clearing turn and take a look around to make sure somebody doesn't ruin our day by mid-airing us."

Scanning the sky was constantly stressed as an essential self-survival technique considering the many trainers nearby. Everybody also knew that after not too many more months and in some other locales, graduated cadets would have to strain to keep a lookout for other pilots on a converging course. The "other" pilots would have had the most malevolent of intentions, and if they spoke English, it would only have been as a second language.

"You ready? OK, I am going to dive to pick up some airspeed, get it up to over a 120, now pull the stick back, start it just like a loop, now give'r the gun, keep on pulling, don't forget a little right rudder to kill torque, right here, nose just above the horizon, stick forward, and half slow roll it - stick left, and a little opposite rudder to keep our heading. Now we're on a reciprocal heading, and we'll bring the power back. Don't forget to pick up speed before trying this, or you won't have enough steam for the roll out on top."

Jeffries' instructor explained that the Immelmann turn was named for a German fighter ace from WWI who used the maneuver to escape a British or French opponent by suddenly gaining altitude and changing heading. The maneuver failed, however, to ensure Max Immelmann's own survival into 1916.

Taught at the same time was the double first cousin of Immelmann, the half roll, or as it was more widely known later, the "split S," in which the Stearman was slow rolled through 180 degrees, power eased off, and concluded with the second half of a loop and the airplane headed in the opposite direction. To avoid overloading the Stearman, Jeffries was reminded to slow the Stearman down to around 70 before entering the split S in which many cadets hurried the maneuver by rolling too short or too far and trying to finish the pull out too soon.

The snap roll, introduced late in primary, is a violent maneuver, but, when perfected, the cadet's orientation and sense of timing were substantially enhanced. A typical cadet's response to his first snap roll demonstration was one of "Wow, what happened!"

"Reynard, things will go quickly, so don't be surprised if it's over before you know it. Just watch the controls, look and listen. I'll take us through a couple and then it's your turn."

In less times than it takes to relate here, Thompson, who had raised the nose slightly at 90 mph, sharply pulled the stick full back and then immediately applied full left rudder. The Stearman reacted at once by quickly flipping directly around its axis, and when about three-quarters of the way around, Thompson centered the stick, and gave it right rudder to recover. Charlie learned that timing and not being timid were the keys to avoiding sloppy gyration, premature recovery, or a finish that wasn't right on the original heading.

At some juncture, prior to primary's midway point and well before they had gotten to the aerobatic or last stage, both Jeffries and Reynard crossed a bridge, and although there would be trials and frustrations ahead, they ceased to be outsiders at odds with their craft. They no longer had to think about what to do — they did it quite spontaneously. The transformation was one of union, a joining of the Stearman's control system with their emerging pilot's sense. It was no longer a matter of, "I want to be there, so what do I do to get there." Instead, their hands and feet made the control inputs automatically, subconsciously. The aircraft and the cadet became one while in flight. Jeffries and the young man from Ohio with whom his destiny would fuse had become soaring birds, able to climb, dive, turn, roll, and glide at will. As eagles, and even Thunderbirds, they had left the nest.

The Stearmans' wings became extensions of their arms, the engines their muscles, the landing gears their legs. Had they been driving a car regularly at this point when flying daily, their first instinct at seeing a stone or bad bump in the road ahead would have been to start tugging back on the steering wheel in an effort to clear the obstacle.

They had no more than to think and a maneuver was done with remarkable ease. What was once a nervous confrontation with a check pilot who was to evaluate their aerobatics became, instead, a fluent routine, something a seagull or hawk would have enjoyed immensely as a passenger in the front seat. And it was fun to boot! This "oneness" with the airplane had a certain dual quality, almost like a split personality. In the air, they were one. In time, on the ground, an airplane, whether a Stearman, AT-6, Liberator, Lightning, C-54, or Spitfire, became a separate, but intimately close entity.

For that reason, Lindbergh referred to the Spirit of St. Louis and himself as "We." With the same logic, pilots, from time immemorial, have tended to assign human characteristics to their aircraft. Watch pilots preflight their airplanes. They tend not to pat planes as the duck hunter might pat his Labrador or a cowboy slap his Palomino's flank. Rather it borders on a caress as a flyer runs his hands over the metal skinning of a stabilizer or the fabric on a Stearman's rudder during a preflight just as Roland Jeffries might have gently run his fingertips over Mary Casey's outstretched arm.

The relationship between pilot and plane, as three of Jeffries' and Reynard's classmates would tragically learn within six months, requires nothing less than absolute devotion, attention and respect. Like the proverbial black widow, in her brief tryst with a suitor, an airplane can be ruthlessly unforgiving of a partner's straying from the straight and narrow or suffering the slightest lapse in judgment or memory. Thus, Jeffries and Reynard each learned to respect the aircraft which they approached, not with fear, but with a unique blend of enchantment and caution.

Counterbalancing the ecstasy of flying was the continuing reality of ground school. Basic mathematics as taught in primary was a very fast review of everything a cadet had learned in high school plus college freshman level math. Liberal arts majors and those without college quickly learned to use slide rules and played catch up in algebra, geometry and trigonometry. There was a method in this madness, and when cadets arrived at basic flight they would find several practical outlets for their newfound ability with numbers and slide rules.

To avoid mathematics in flying is difficult, if not impossible. Numbers on dials have to be read, freezing levels have to be estimated, centers of gravity must be computed, cargo weight vs. fuel weight decisions have to be made, and fuel exhaustion must be predicted among the many other circumstances requiring mathematical finesse not to mention basic navigation. Charlie's class at Oxnard was composed solely of college-trained men, a difference quickly noticed by the ground instructor staff which quickly enhanced the algebra and trig portions of the curriculum.

Navigation would be a key subject in both basic and advanced, but the groundwork was laid in primary. In Reynard's case, the instructor was another very experienced man, Mr. Delaplane, a WWI fighter pilot who had remained on active duty in the Air Service into the 20s as a flight instructor. Delaplane had been an instructor at UCLA, and was yet another man whose services would be lost to Cal-Aero since he also held a commission as a major in the Air Corps reserve. Navigation in primary encompassed the essentials; application of the knowledge would come with basic flight. Subjects in primary navigation included various types of charts and maps, latitude/longitude, the compass (and its shortcomings), bearings, deviation, wind correction, federal aids to flying, and practice flight planning.

Instrumentation was a subject in ground school, and enhanced by actual instrument panels placed on special stands. Most of the instruments were easy to relate to since they were similar to those in cars, i.e. fuel quantity, tachometer, speedometer (airspeed indicator), etc. At the primary stage, cadets were most concerned with the "huff'n'puff" instruments (the pitot-static system group) and the engine instruments. Although they studied gyro instruments, the actual use of such "new" devices would not take place until basic flight.

One subject stayed with cadets throughout training: Morse code. This was practiced both visually and aurally. Although cadets might only infrequently have to send code messages later in training or after graduation, they would be on the receiving end throughout their flying careers. This was especially true in navigation where the radio range station identifiers were all in Morse code as were the blinking lights identifying airway beacons.

As a corollary to code, cadets also learned the phonetic alphabet to avoid any confusion when using a spoken letter, but what was in practice in 1941 was not today's familiar ICAO phonetic alphabet consisting of "alpha, bravo, delta, echo, foxtrot, golf, hotel, India. etc." Rather, in 1941, "able, baker, dog, easy, fox, George, haw, and item" were in use ("Charley" for "C" survived the transition).

Another subject initiated at Thunderbird would be reviewed even after graduation: aircraft recognition. The aircraft silhouettes on posters and flash cards were studied for instant, positive identification, because in the momentary heat of battle, it could be all too easy to shoot at a fleeting target which was thought to be a Japanese Tony only to discover that it was an early model, similar-looking American Mustang.

Swimming was part of the athletic program; cadets had to qualify by swimming the length of a pool. This was second nature to most cadets, but was a fearsome challenge for those who had never had the opportunity to learn before. Through coaching and practice, the beginners made it across the pool, and were encouraged to become stronger swimmers during the remainder of their cadets days. The swimming posed no problems for Jeffries, who had been doing a lot of swimming to toughen up for cadet training, or for Reynard who was a talented athlete to start with.

Reynard was hardly the only former college athlete. Since nearly all intercollegiate sports were represented among cadets, there was considerable interest in what was going on in the professional sports world of 1941. Just as 42-B started training, the Washington Redskins had signed Sammy Baugh to a lucrative contract, reportedly the highest in professional football. Several of golf's biggest names, Gene Sarazen, Lloyd Mangrum, and defending champion, Byron Nelson, lost to a newcomer, Vic Ghezzi, at the 1941 PGA Championship which had concluded in Denver on July 14th. Professional baseball was dominated by the New York Yankees and their headlong rush toward the American League championship. Softball was popular with cadets and the Phoenix community whose active league also played, and frequently beat, some of the local military base teams.

Korrick's, the large Phoenix department store, was in the midst of its annual dollar day sale which featured deep cuts on linens and summer clothing.[1] Its large space newspaper ads dominated another well-known Phoenix retailer, Goldwaters ("Since 1869, The Best Always") which was having a clearance sale on Manhattan shirts and pajamas. Goldwaters' discounts ranged as high as 40 percent, but refused any returns or exchanges. The Goldwater family had a son in the Air Corps; in fact, he was a lieutenant based at Luke Field where he had just been assigned as the new supply officer. He would soon be a rated pilot assigned to the Air Transport Command, and assume a higher profile in the post-war years including rising to a general's rank in the Air Force Reserve.

On August 20, Oxnard was visited by Major General Barton K. Yount, the new commander of Air Corps forces on the west coast. He arrived in a silvery Lockheed C-57 Lodestar, a less powerful, poor relative of the Lockheed A-29 Hudson light attack bomber. The 57-year old general was a West Pointer (class of 1907), WWI veteran, and most recently had been Air Officer Commanding at McDill Field in Florida. Based at Moffett Field near San Francisco (and soon to move to Santa Ana), he was on one of his frequent base inspection tours. After inspecting the troops and having lunch, the white-maned general officer amazed the cadets with his mastery of the machine gun pinball game in the cadet lounge. As he was leaving, the general claimed to be very impressed with Mira Loma, especially the brand new crop of just arriving dodos whom he described as "good looking boys."

42-C had indeed arrived at Oxnard and Thunderbird. In the latter's case, it was 63 young men, including everything from lawyers to laborers and shoe clerks to accountants. The new dodos were largely from the heart of America too: Missouri, Kansas, Nebraska, and Arkansas.

Exactly one month later, Yount's silvery Lockheed was parked amidst the blue and yellow Stearmans at Thunderbird. Phoenix was gearing up for war in more ways than serving as the location of key training bases. On August 21, 1941, ground was broken for the construction of the new Goodyear Aircraft Corporation plant: the tire company was to manufacture aircraft parts in Phoenix. Later in the war, Goodyear would build planes under license from other manufacturers. While most people remember aluminum and scrap metal drives as part of the war effort after December 7, 1941, they actually began before American direct participation in the fighting. Glendale, Arizona, conducted its first scrap metal drive in mid-July 1941, and Scottsdale had one in late July.

In Washington, the Offices of Price Administration and Production Management were becoming much stronger, and had already told the Detroit auto industry to plan on substantially less steel. Truck production was to be increased, and the 1942 model year car and major household appliance production would be cut in half according to Washington announcements. That in turn produced jitters about massive unemploy-

From the Jeffries photo album

*Jeffries going through the pre-flight check in a Stearman at Thunderbird.*

ment. Partially in response to that concern, the Office of Production Management announced a plan to spread a significant portion of defense contracts around to smaller companies in order to minimize unemployment. Nonetheless, business was good in Phoenix during the summer of '41. The Phoenix Chamber of Commerce tracked a record number of bank transactions and commodity sales throughout the summer.

Although Yount may have been impressed with the growing strength in the Phoenix area, Allied forces elsewhere were not in such good shape on the day of his visit. The Russians, under Marshal Semyon Budenny, were falling back, and had destroyed the Dneiper Dam in the Ukraine to cover their retreat. Marshal Klementi Voroshilov, on the northern front, had called on civilians to form into militia units to help defend Leningrad against the onrushing Nazi juggernaut. Iceland, which had been garrisoned by America in July, was the subject of a visit by a German bomber. The sortie was rebuffed by Royal Air Force pilots flying American-built P-40s.

When finished with his inspection of the primary school, General Yount was off to the advanced flying school at Luke Field. Yount would assume responsibility for the entire Air Force Training Command before the war was over, and come back to the Phoenix area and Thunderbird Field in a unique post-war role. Luke Field's cadets, flying more advanced trainers, ranked somewhat higher on the local social scale than the neophytes at Thunderbird. The cadets at Luke flew an airplane with several times the horsepower, the North American AT-6. Luke was also home to a handful of North American P-64 fighters which resembled a stockier, single-seat version of the AT-6 with much more horsepower and a three-bladed prop. The P-64 was obsolete and had been developed for the export market. Between the Americans at Luke and British cadets at Falcon Field, the P-64s were rather quickly written off in accidents.

The British cadets were on an even more accelerated program than the Americans. The Royal Air Force had no equivalent of the basic flight stage, so British training in the American Southwest was conducted in 20 weeks. The British pilots did receive additional training, primarily in gunnery, when they returned to the United Kingdom where they went through several weeks at an operational training unit (OTU) before assignment to a frontline squadron.

The Royal Air Force wing commander, squadron leaders and flight lieutenants stationed in Phoenix were especially popular on the local lecture circuit. Speaking to women's and men's service organizations, the British pilots could convey first-hand what America was gearing up for. They were in the vanguard of a new British public relations invasion. Several months later, the RAF sent a liaison mission to America for a tour of key air bases. That mission did not visit training fields such as Thunderbird, but the pilots in the group included Britain's leading aces and bomber captains. Although the RAF pilots were collectively unimpressed with the majority of the frontline aircraft they found in American squadrons, they were impressed with what was just starting to emerge from the production lines and especially with the quality and spirit of young American pilots and their leaders.

Slang was naturally a part of the cadet experience, and while the Americans devised colorful slang, it was never as well developed as that of their Allied peers in the Royal Air Force. Still, Jeff and Charlie received regular "sugar reports" (love letters) from their fiancées. VIPs, such as General Yount or even a battalion commander were "big dogs."

"Gunners" were not only those occupying gun turrets, but cadets who, at the dining table, made sure the serving plates and bowls were always full. "Rats" referred to balls of lint which might accumulate on the floor. Too many rats resulted in the Mister being gigged. "Raunchy," which gravitated into civilian slang, referred to that which was dirty or disorderly. The "washing machine" was the training squadron commander's airplane which most assuredly was not one of the sad sacks on the flight line. Based on the way it washed cadets out, some writers have described the entire aviation cadet program as the "washing machine."

By the sixth week into the ten-week primary flying stage, Reynard's outlook on the inevitable war had become more focused. He was a very high-principled, religious young man who was offended by life's inequities (not just those in the military) and impatient with politicians and writers who tolerated business as usual.

That he thoroughly loved flying and was exceptionally good at it is certain, but unlike the vast majority of his associates, Reynard considered it more as a means to an end instead of an end in itself. The average cadet had joined because he was excited by airplanes, thought becoming an Army Air Force pilot was much better duty than digging foxholes while not carrying a rifle on his shoulder, and also viewed it as perfect preparation for a good career in aviation.

Charles Reynard quickly saw another dimension because he was vehemently opposed to the Nazis and firmly committed to their defeat. This attitude was not based on the rising tide of propaganda movies or training films, but as the outcome of his own deliberations based on his upbringing and a sharp, well-trained intellect. His letters home, months before Pearl Harbor, reveal one great reservation in his cause, and it troubled him immensely. That was the cost of destroying so many communities, innocents, and institutions in the process of overcoming evil.

Charlie would have liked to create a better world for all peoples, and in that regard he was, perhaps, not quite a utopian, but certainly included egalitarianism and humanitarianism in his personal, guiding philosophy. He had reflected on this conflict, concluded that what he was preparing for was quite simply the right thing to do, and hoped that the cost to civilization wouldn't be too prohibitive.

As Charlie mailed the letter containing his outlook on the war, the Russians continued to lose ground and had just evacuated Novgorod. Only the weather was their most helpful ally; the Germans had been slowed down by heavy rains during the last week in August. On August 25th, the British and Russians had joined to occupy Iran as a buffer in order to deny Germany additional sources of oil. It was feared that the Germans would very quickly look beyond their advance through the oil rich Caucasus considering their advance in the Russian Ukraine. Occupying Iran opened up a valuable line of communications with Russia from the Middle East, and it would eventually serve as a Lend Lease conduit to the Red Air Force and Army.

By mid-September, Jeffries and Reynard were flying their last few hours, reviewing and perfecting their aerobatics. A couple of weeks earlier, each had successfully negotiated the 40-hour stage check whose successful completion was a good indicator that they would become pilots and officers in February. That they were headed to basic was obvious since they were getting a few hours in the front seat and had flown a short dual cross country in formation.

The war news was dominated by the precarious situation in Russia as the *Wermacht* broke through the outer ring of forts defending Leningrad. Kiev was also under immediate threat of occupation. Only a year before, the Royal Air Force had triumphed in the Battle of Britain, but had nearly spent itself in the process. A year later, the RAF had recovered and was strong enough to send a fighter wing to Russia. Some of the war news was coming closer to home. That an Axis raider, probably a heavily armed merchantman, was at large near the Panama Canal was obvious when several vessels passing through the Canal on September 14th reported that they had heard distress signals while at sea during the previous week. Several British and Dutch ships were overdue from New Zealand and Java.

In early September, there had been an action between the *U.S.S. Greer*, a destroyer, and a Nazi submarine roughly 200 miles southwest of Iceland. Berlin reported the American destroyer as the aggressor, an allegation denied by President Roosevelt who indicated that the U-boat had opened the encounter by firing two torpedoes at the American destroyer. The *Greer* promptly depth-charged the submarine, although neither vessel was damaged. It would not be the last encounter between American naval units and the Germans subs before war was declared three months later.

The 42-B graduation dance at Thunderbird was held in conjunction with 42-C's change in status from underclassmen to upperclassmen. Held in the Fiesta Room of the Westward Ho Hotel, the music was provided by the Cecil Armstrong Band. The 118 cadets and newfound lady friends danced until midnight. Jeffries and his fellow 42-B'ers had done well. Collectively, they had flown a total of nearly 3,400 hours. Of the 66 entering Thunderbird, 50 graduated for a completion rate of roughly 76 percent (two cadets had moved back to 42-C since minor injuries precluded finishing the course on time). In fact, of all of the 42 year classes, only 42-C would finish with a higher completion rate: 81 percent.[2] Anchor classes were 42-G and K with completion rates of 60 percent each. Of the 29 Oxnard F Flight cadets who were to graduate with Charlie in 42-B in February 1942, 11 would not survive to see the end of WWII.

Charlie finished flying at Oxnard around September 24th and spent the last few days wrapping up ground school. The final dress parade at Oxnard was capped off with speeches and a flyover by several B-24s. On September 26th, Charlie got his orders to report to the Air Corps Basic Flying School at Bakersfield, California, on September 30th. He wasn't looking forward to being an underclassman again, but assumed that the grief from upperclassmen probably wouldn't be as intense as it had been during primary.

His last weekend as an Oxnard cadet was spent in Los Angeles enjoying a movie, attending the Southern California-Oregon State football game, and visiting tourist attractions in the city.

Photo courtesy of Walter Radtke

*Toward the end of primary, Oxnard cadets flew a short cross country.*

Thirty-four cadets completed primary with F Flight at Oxnard. All would be posted to Bakersfield for basic, most of them would complete advanced at Mather Field, five either washed out or washed back a class along the way, and several would follow the same road to heavy bomber transition schools as Reynard did. There were no fatalities while Jeffries and Reynard were in primary. However, in early September, a 42-C cadet suffered minor injuries when he wiped out the landing gear and broke a prop on an Oxnard Stearman in a spectacularly hard landing at one of the auxiliary fields.

The Army was pleased with Cal-Aero's work. Charlie's class graduated with a lower than average number of washouts, but the Mira Loma personnel had some reservations about what they were teaching. The flight instructors felt that too much time was spent on elementary eights and S turns across roads, and that adding another week to the course would be beneficial as would more emphasis on aerobatics. They also suggested that the Army do a better job of screening cadets in order to weed out those who were more interested in avoiding the draft as opposed to those who genuinely wanted to fly.

Meanwhile, at Thunderbird, Special Orders number 53, dated September 15th and issued on September 19th, directed Roland Jeffries and the 49 other successful cadets of 42-B to report to the Aviation Cadet Administration Building at Bakersfield not later than noon on September 30th. A few lucky cadets who had cars drove to Bakersfield from Phoenix, but Roland Jeffries, like the vast majority of his fellow Thunderbird graduates, rattled westward in a troop train that left Phoenix on the evening of September 26th. That was just after selecting a tug of war team which saw to it that the 42-C class kissed wet rope. It was a very rewarding experience for the 42-B'ers since the first seven men on the 42-C side of the canal were recent graduates of West Point and among the first commissioned officers to go through flight training.

# XIV

# BASIC FLIGHT

Sunward I've climbed, and joined the tumbling mirth
Of sun-split clouds, and done a hundred things
You have not dreamed of — wheeled and soared
And swung high in the sunlit silence ....

Pilot Officer John Gillespie Magee
412 Squadron, RCAF[1]

In March, 1941, what became Bakersfield Army Air Field was a stubble-filled wasteland through which just one highway traversed. On March 31, 1941, the tractors and graders arrived to start building a facility which would graduate over 11,000 cadets from basic flight during the war years.

When aviation cadets Jeffries and Reynard reported at Bakersfield Army Air Field on September 30, 1941, the paint had barely dried on their new barracks. It wasn't even called Bakersfield yet, but was more commonly referred to as "Lerdo," the name of a road which passed by the site located about 15 miles northwest of the city of Bakersfield, population then about 30,000. Lerdo was hardly an appropriate name for this beehive of military aviation; in Spanish, *lerdo* means slow, heavy, lumpy, obtuse, or dull.

Very shortly before 42-B left Bakersfield, the installation was renamed Minter Field in honor of a local officer, Lt. Hugh Minter, a WWI fighter pilot who was killed in a flying accident at March Field, near Riverside, California, in 1935. Lerdo lingered, however, as the "L" pre-fix identifier in Bakersfield-based trainer field numbers which were painted boldly on fuselage sides.

The junior college in Bakersfield and nearby Kern County Airport had actually served as facilities for the first cadets to arrive, those of 41-

*Bakersfield Army Air Field as photographed four weeks before the cadets from 42-B arrived on September 30, 1941.*

H and 41-I, until the new Basic Flying School was ready to receive 42-A. When the Army pulled out of Kern County Airport, a few primary and advanced trainers (PT-17s, AT6-As, and Cessna T-50 Bobcats) remained on the field for the use of a completely separate training operation. Earlier in 1941, Bakersfield's Kern County Airport had become one of the California airdromes where the Royal Air Force set up a refresher course for American volunteers joining the RAF.

For the RAF candidates, college training was not a prerequisite, nor was passing an educational equivalency exam. A satisfactory medical exam, 200 hours of flying time, and passing a screening flight check put young Americans into the program which amounted to a very compressed version of the Army Air Force's advanced flight training. Americans starting RAF training at Bakersfield in the summer of 1941 later went to Britain for final polishing at an OTU, and were being assigned to operational squadrons at about the same time 42-B graduated from advanced in February 1942.

When Jeffries and Reynard arrived, the field's electrical and lighting systems had not been completed. The base fire department was in place, though, and it was equipped to deal with aircraft fires. Because many aircraft components contained magnesium, which has explosive tendencies when sprayed with water during a fire, the crash trucks contained special chemical mixtures. Base firemen had the latest crash trucks, fog nozzles, and insulated fire suits. The base fire suppression system was endowed with several wells, numerous hydrants, and a pressure enhancement system.

The initial paving, grading and oiling of Bakersfield's rough fields created runways, ramps and parking surfaces that were the equivalent of 30 miles of conventional highway.[2] The steel hangar measured 200 by 121 feet and was the largest structure on the 954-acre base. The Western Training Command was building a major facility that would serve much larger cadet classes later in the war. When 42-B started training, only a portion of the 171 buildings had been completed. When finished, the operation included several mess halls, 45 barracks (housing 63 men each), nine auxiliary fields, and numerous administrative and storage buildings.

Jeffries, Reynard, 292 other cadets, and the 116 Vultee BT-13 Valiant aircraft were supported by the 327th School Wing. This was a major organization of 200 officers and roughly 1,500 enlisted men whose purpose was to see that each cadet successfully passed through his ten weeks at basic. All personnel were under the command of Colonel Carl Pyle, a 48-year old veteran of WWI who had been educated at the University of Washington, the Massachusetts Institute of Technology, and the Air Corps Tactical School. Jeff and Charlie's contact with Pyle was minimal since cadets more frequently encountered the Assistant Commandant of Cadets, First Lieutenant Lester Hess, a recent pilot graduate and West Pointer.

In addition to the crew chief, several men were required for the proper care of a BT-13: a propeller mechanic, instrument technician, and an aircraft mechanic. In addition to the daily care of each trainer, mechanics conducted routine checks at every 25 hours with a minor overhaul at 50 hours. Every 100 hours of flight time put on a "BT" required a more substantial check and maintenance.

While not flying, marching, engaged in physical training, or in ground school, the cadet at Bakersfield could enjoy a number of on-base conveniences. There was a recreation hall, 350-seat movie theater, a complete post exchange, and a base chapel with a new organ. Training squadron day rooms were well supplied with magazines, newspapers and radios donated by Bakersfield residents. In the early evening, cadets could listen to the popular radio shows of the day including such light comedy fare as "Bringing Up Father," "Amos and Andy," the "Bob Hope Show," or the popular mystery, "The Shadow," but most cadets tuned into KNX, the NBC station, which featured Glen Miller from seven to seven-thirty. Glen Miller had a big hit going when the 42-B cadets checked in at Bakersfield: *Chattanooga Choo Choo*, but Freddy Martin was at the top of the charts with the *Piano Concerto* followed by Horace Heidt with *I Don't Want To Set The World On Fire*. The re-arming of America had started to creep into the music world by early October. Coming along in juke box popularity was *'Til Reveille*, a harbinger of the war years' many hits blending patriotism, romance, melancholia, and hope.

For those who enjoyed comic strips, the *Bakersfield Daily Californian* carried "The Gumps," "Gasoline Alley," "Boots and Her Buddies," and "Buck Rogers, Twenty-Fifth Century, A.D." (Buck, on September 30th, hearing a twig snap had just shot at a death ray gun-armed sniper in the forest's depths).

From the Jeffries photo album

*A Bakersfield BT undergoing periodic maintenance. Note the "L" pre-fix for "Lerdo" in the aircraft field number.*

If a cadet wanted to enjoy the bright lights of Bakersfield, he had to be free of demerits or any duty assignments. If he did not have his own car or a ride with a friend, the bus to town cost only 15 cents. Once in Bakersfield, he found a town that was anxious to please, and one that had reduced rates for servicemen at swimming pools, bowling alleys, and other leisure centers. It was not a frequent pleasure. Cadets did not have a lot of free time. Getting up at daylight, a.m. inspections and formation, flying, being critiqued by the instructor, attending classes, athletics, walking off demerits, special assignments, and studying did not leave a lot of time for enjoying the scenery.

When 42-B reported to Bakersfield on that sunny, last day of September, 1941, President Roosevelt and Secretary of State Cordell Hull were drafting proposed changes to the Neutrality Act. Tensions were rising in the Far East and new U.S. troops were arriving in Iceland. *H.M.S. Nelson*, the Royal Navy's giant battleship had just been torpedoed in the Mediterranean. Although heavily damaged, it did not go down as did 13 of the attacking Italian torpedo planes.

Winston Churchill, in an address to the House of Commons, raised hopes of the British by announcing that shipping losses had declined dramatically in recent weeks and that the Royal Air Force was gaining the upper hand in the air. There was truth in that, but much of the *Luftwaffe* had been diverted to the Eastern Front where the *Wehrmacht* was closing in on Leningrad and still advancing in the Ukraine and Crimea. Indeed, RAF heavies had pounded Hamburg and Stettin for two nights in a row, and Bomber Command's heavily escorted, short range daylight raids to the channel ports of Dunkirk and Calais had been very successful. Not all of the *Luftwaffe* had left for Russia, though. While the 148 cadets of 42-B went to sleep in new barracks on the night of September 30, the British residents of Aberdeen, Hull, Newcastle, and Ramsgate spent their night in terror as German bombers came over in much stronger than average numbers. A year earlier, to the day, the RAF had launched a trickle of night bombers to attack Berlin, Bremen, Hamburg, Hanover, and Cuxhaven. Then, the Battle of Britain was winding down as the Germans started giving up daylight raids and turned to night bombing of British cities.

In Washington, Senator Gerald P. Nye was continuing his investigation of the motion picture industry engaging in propaganda. There was little question of where Hollywood's sentiments were in the autumn of 1941. In downtown Bakersfield, *A Yank in the RAF* with Tyrone Power and Betty Grable was playing at the Fox Theater through Wednesday October 1st, and *Sergeant York* with Gary Cooper was opening the next day.

War was not on every Kern County resident's mind, though. In nearby Maricopa, the two leading ski clubs had merged and were planning a new ski hut and rope tow for Mount Abel. Montgomery Ward was advertising Redhead 12 gauge skeet loads at 82 cents a box (25 shells). At Western Auto, $6.59 (plus an old tire) bought a 6.00-16 "Giant Traveler" with staggered biting edges and extra-wide running ribs for silent, non-skid safety and more mileage than ever before. In a few months, tire advertising would disappear for several years, and the recapping industry would grow rapidly.

In Bakersfield, the Kern County Livestock Show had just concluded. The Luer Packing Company paid $500 for the grand champion steer, an Aberdeen Angus raised by Future Farmer of America (FFA) member, Ronald Hutchings. The Kern County Wool Growers Association purchased the grand champion lamb from Bakersfield FFA'er Duncan McLean. 4-H Club member Duane Spillsbury received 88 cents per pound for his grand champion hog, the highest price paid to date for a prizewinning porker.

Airline passenger priority was still in the future. United Airlines was flying four flights a day to Los Angeles and back — 40 minutes either way. Cadets wanting to get to Los Angeles on an open post weekend could ride the Santa Fe for $3.05 roundtrip, or $7.80 roundtrip to San Francisco.

The new 1942 model year radios had just been stocked at Witham & Booth (located in the Fox Theater Building) where the deluxe, 10-tube radio and automatic phonograph was on sale for $179.95. A new battery-powered radio was selling for $39.95, and a top-of-the line Zenith was going for $600. More popular were garden variety radios which started at $18.95.

The last new model cars to be seen for several years had gone on sale in Bakersfield. Plymouth, with a 95 h.p. engine, was delivering ten percent more power. The new, 1942 sedan featured concealed running boards, a low center of gravity with a "marvelous ride — smooth, steady, sure-footed on curves." If you wanted to learn more about the driving economy, low upkeep, and beautifully tailored interiors, you had nothing more to do than visit a local dealer, or tune in to a Chrysler-sponsored radio show such as "Major Bowes' Amateur Hour" on the CBS network.

Yet even in its national consumer print advertising, there were signs of the times to come. Tucked away in a box was a listing of Chrysler Corporation products: passenger cars, trucks, marine and industrial engines, oil-tight bearings, Airtemp heating and air conditioning, Army tanks, anti-aircraft guns, Army vehicles.

For the economy-minded, the new 1942 Studebaker Coupe was billed as the "Top quality car of the lowest price field." Prices ranged from $810 for the Champion model to $1,342 and up for the President Eight.

Most economic news of interest in Bakersfield related to local agricultural or mining industries. However, Churchill's speech about the fortunes of war starting to turn in favor of the Allies was credited for stocks closing higher in New York on September 30th. Most industrials were up a point or two in New York while such food stocks as California Packing and Honolulu Plantation led the way on the San Francisco exchange.

The big news as 42-B settled in at Bakersfield was not military or economic-related. It was the World Series. While Jeff and Charlie were settling into their new barracks, Yankee Stadium saw the Dodgers fall to the Yankees. A record crowd of 68,540 watched the first game as Red Ruffing's brilliant pitching and Joe Gordon's batting prevailed over the Dodgers, three to two.

Sports heroes Kirby Higbee of the Dodgers and "Joltin' Joe" DiMaggio of the Yankees were spokesmen for one of the popular smokes of the day, Camels, whose slower burning tobacco contained "28 percent less nicotine." DiMaggio claimed, "You bet I smoke Camels. Along with all that flavor, Camels are extra mild." The opening game was prophetic; the Yankees went on to take the series four to one.

When the 42-B cadets moved into Bakersfield for their ten-week stay, the city was hosting a different military group overnight. The Seventy-Eighth Coast Artillery Anti-Aircraft Battalion was spending the night encamped at the Lynn Baseball Park. The unit was traveling from its home base near Los Angeles to a military pageant in San Francisco. Its modern weapons and searchlights were on display and lit up by lights on the field. It had been a very pleasant day for their exhibit: sunny with daytime temperatures in the upper 80s.

There was no denying a military buildup. New bases were springing up all over California. In addition to the big base at Bakersfield, there was the nearby basic flight installation at Taft, also in Kern County. And at Lemoore, another basic flying school was being built. Another 42-B

From the Jeffries photo album
*42-B cadets outside a squadron day room, about to head for the flight line.*

contingent consisting of 128 cadets also started basic flight at Gardner Field. The Gardner Field cadets had come from the (Tex) Rankin Academy at Tulare and the balance had come from the Ryan School at Hemet, California. The latter was a branch of the well known Ryan School of Aeronautics in San Diego. The parent company had built Lindbergh's Spirit of St. Louis, the trainers in which Howard Kincheloe was instructing so far away in the South Seas, and also operated both civilian and army flying schools at its San Diego facility.

When the 42-B cadets arrived, they were greeted by the new upperclassmen of 42-A. The preceding upperclass had just departed Bakersfield with a small contingent going to Luke Field in Arizona for single-engine advanced training and the majority heading to Stockton, California, for multi-engine training.

On October 4, 1941, Waite Phillips outlined his plan to make a second donation to the Boy Scouts of America. The scope of this second gift was staggering. It included an additional 91,538 acres; the beautiful Villa Philmonte (his mansion near the present day Camping Headquarters); all ranch buildings, livestock and farming equipment; and the Philtower office building in Tulsa whose annual rentals of $130,000 would provide a substantial endowment.[3]

The gift of what is today Philmont's midlands and south country entailed a number of historic buildings including the Rayado complex which had once been the home of the frontiersman, Kit Carson. It also embraced the lodges that would become landmarks to generations of Philmont campers: Rayado Lodge at Fish Camp, "Old Abreu" and Cimarroncito Hunting Lodges, and Crater Lake Lodge (a lovely stone building located in the shadow of a brooding Trail Peak).

Executives from the BSA National Office in New York visited the Ranch during the second week of October. Their mission was to initiate the planning that would realize Phillips' dream of Philmont becoming a national resource where Scouts could enjoy a growth opportunity in a combination wilderness and western ranching experience complete with horses, wagon trains, and food served up from a chuck wagon.

Aviation cadets ate well, and to the local grocery and produce wholesalers, Bakersfield Army Air Field was an important customer. Officers, cadets and civilian employees initially took meals in the enlisted mess since it was the first to be completed. The budget for a cadet meal was 80 cents, substantially higher than that allotted for other armies. Cadets did not put on weight at Bakersfield due to their physical training and drilling, but new enlisted men did (an average of six to ten pounds during the first month according to medical records).

A typical breakfast consisted of fresh fruit, waffles, syrup, dry cereal, and a variety of beverages. There was no "lunch," rather, it was "dinner," and might consist of rolls and butter, chicken fricassee, mashed potatoes, carrots, creamed cauliflower, salad, fruit punch, pies, iced water, milk, and coffee. For some cadets, not used to a heavy midday meal, a very brief siesta was in order, and the only place a cadet might enjoy such a luxury was on the bench at the flight line if his were one of the latter flights of the afternoon. A representative supper was bread and butter, meat loaf, fried potatoes, summer squash, spinach, salad, chocolate pudding, ice cream, milk, coffee, and iced water.

Whereas the frugal homemaker could get by on spending $40 a month at the grocery store, Bakersfield AAF was spending nearly $45,000 per month with Kern County provisioners.

Officers and enlisted men could enjoy the 3.2 beer which was sold along with sodas at the post exchanges. Cadets could drink only the soda, however, since their daily flying required clear heads. Basic flight was a stage with significant, mental demands placed by three new activities: instrument, formation, and night flying.

Cadets still put in long days which started at 4:30 a.m. Unfortunately, their talented bugler had been eliminated at Thunderbird, thus the musical jump-start to the day's activities commenced on a lower note since a suitable replacement was not available. Ground school, 96 hours of it during basic, continued with emphasis on meteorology, navigation and radio. Another 70 hours went to military training, and each cadet did five hours of guard duty.

The 148 cadets of 42-B, all from Oxnard and Thunderbird, were formed into a battalion of four companies. One of Charlie's roommates from primary, Russell Schleeh, became the cadet battalion commander, and Charlie was appointed as a lieutenant in D Company. Their first week was spent with physical examinations, drawing equipment, and refresher courses on military etiquette. There was no new clothing issue at Bakersfield upon arrival. As winter started to set in, that which had been suitable wear for high summer Arizona or coastal California started proving inadequate. A visiting inspector noticed that the cadet commandant was dressed in a woolen uniform while the cadets' cotton uniforms were insufficient. The inspector gave the commandant two days to produce winter clothing, and reminded the officer that cadets and the officers addressing them would be clothed in the same class of uniform.

From the Jeffries photo album

*Morning formation at Bakersfield.*

From the Jeffries photo album

*Every cadet at basic pulled a mini-
mum of five hours of guard duty.
Roland Jeffries, October 1941.*

Among the items of equipment were .30 caliber Springfield rifles
with which cadets spent considerable time cleaning off the protective
Cosmoline coating. There was a certain expediency in cleaning off the
environmentally unfriendly Cosmoline since rifles had to be spotless by
morning inspection or the unfortunate owner of anything less than a
pristine rifle would be doing some extracurricular marching. The
Springfield rifles along with bayonets in scabbards promptly became
part of drilling, guard duty, and marching off hours. The Springfield grew
much heavier than its original ten pounds as cadets marched off demerits at the rate of one hour per demerit.

Many of the cadets had never handled a rifle in their lives. Although
they had marched in primary, they were still novices at this much more
military oriented stage of their training. Fortunately, the ROTC graduates
saved the day by bringing their peers up to speed as quickly as possible.

To this military determination came a curiously humorous, canine
counterpoint. The base had become home to numerous stray dogs that

knew a good handout when they saw one. The dogs prospered on the
dining hall overflow, and never hesitated to show up for calisthenics at
6 a.m. or for marching practice either. When "Lady," one of the half
dozen dogs affiliated with 42-B, came into heat, the cadets were hard-
pressed to maintain their military bearing and cadence in sight of the
wild, canine abandon going on in their midst. The fact that the amorous
party's participants ranged in size from mongrel Labradors to pint-sized
terriers made the spectacle that much more hilarious.

The dogs never went away, but the Springfields, destined for Lend
Lease transfer to the British, did, but not before cadets applied a new,
heavy coat of Cosmoline.

Cadets were anxious to start flying because their new BT-13s were a
quantum leap forward over the Stearmans they had flown in primary.
Although they had not been up in a BT-13, both Jeff and Charlie had seen

From the Jeffries photo album

*With its new gyro instruments and
additional air data and engine indicators, the BT-13 cockpit was a major
step up from the Stearman's spartan
panel.*

the occasional BTs at Thunderbird and Oxnard. When settling into the more sophisticated BT-13 cockpit for the first time, at the end of the first week of October, the more imaginative cadets easily pictured themselves sitting in a P-40 Warhawk or P-39 Airacobra. In fact, the front cockpit of a BT-13 was reasonably similar to the advanced pursuit ships of the day. There was a full complement of air data instruments, two of the new gyro instruments (artificial horizon and a directional gyro), full electrical panel, flaps, fuel selector switch, fuel pump, radio, and a propeller pitch control.

The vacuum-driven gyro instruments were not received with open arms in all quarters. Some old-line instructors did not trust them because they weren't without problems, and felt that flying "whiskey compass, needle, ball, and airspeed" was a lot safer than trusting instruments with a bad reliability record (along with their attending, solitary vacuum pump). Not caging a gyro before aerobatics tumbled the device. Of greater concern, to maintenance officers, was their being operated with excessive suction or being sent in for unnecessary maintenance for reasons of improperly perceived excessive drift or sluggish response.

The BT-13, with a 450 h.p. Pratt & Whitney engine, had twice the horsepower and nearly double the speed of a Stearman, was basically all metal, and served for most of the war as the standard basic trainer for both the Army and Navy. If anything, it was a bit too easy to fly. As the war progressed, the Army Air Force phased it out, and students went directly from the Stearman into the North American AT-6 trainer. Indeed, by war's end, students in the multi-engine track went from Stearman to AT-6 and, at advanced, into a B-25 Mitchell medium bomber.

The BT-13, BT-15 (same airframe, but with a Wright Cyclone engine of the same horsepower), and SNV (naval version of the BT-13) were built in large numbers: roughly 11,500. There are a few still flying, but they are nowhere near as commonly seen as the AT-6/SNJ advanced trainers.

The BT-13 was produced by Vultee Aircraft which had been founded in 1932 by Jerry Vultee, an engineer who had worked with Jack Northrup on the Lockheed Vega. Funding for the new company came from none other than Everett Cord of automobile fame. Through the 1930s, Vultee primarily produced advanced, single-engine transport aircraft and, for the export market, light attack bombers. In 1943, Vultee would merge with Consolidated Aircraft and eventually become

Convair, later General Dynamics, and ultimately a predecessor of present day's Lockheed Martin.

In 1939, Vultee produced a fighter design which featured a tightly cowled Pratt & Whitney R-1830 engine (same as that used on the B-24). Cooling problems forced the use of a more conventional cowling, and, although the machine performed well, the P-66 Vanguard, as it was known, was produced only in small numbers. Many of them went to the Chinese Air Force, and the balance were taken on by the Army Air Force as advanced trainers.

From the Jeffries photo album

*Roland Jeffries with a "BT," the Vultee BT-13 Valiant basic trainer. The plane was more commonly known as the "Vibrator" since the canopy sections rattled loudly during aerobatics.*

Much of that basic design survived as the BT-13 Valiant which first flew in late 1939. The cockpit, landing gear, engine, and wings were different, but many of the basic lines remained. Nobody called it the Valiant. Most cadets simply called it a "BT" if they didn't refer to it as the "Vibrator" in reference to the way the canopy sections rattled so loudly during stall/spin exercises and aerobatics. For those who still enjoyed the engine's undiminished roar and slipstream's breezy blast, the canopy sections could be left wide open or closed partially as desired by simply rotating the locking lever at the front of the canopy section and pushing or pulling to the desired location.

One of the BT's more endearing features to cadets was the ultra-wide track landing gear. While the narrow landing gear on the Stearman almost invited groundloops, the BT's wide-legged stance almost appeared as anti-groundloop insurance.

At $20,000 a copy, it cost nearly twice what a Stearman did. The BT-13 grossed out at a little over two tons, and had a wingspan of 42 feet.[4] Cruising at 160 mph, the range was 725 miles with an absolute ceiling of 21,000 feet, although cadets rarely flew them higher than 10,000 feet since there was no oxygen system. When a good BT-13 changes hands these days, which isn't very often, the asking price is in the $70,000 range.

First, Jeff and Charlie had to become familiar with the BT-13 by reading its technical manual and memorizing the "do's and don'ts." Outside loops, extended inverted flight, inverted spins, snap rolls entered in excess of 115 mph, slow rolls above 168 mph, and spins in excess of three turns were prohibited. Red line speed was 230 mph and maximum diving rpm was limited to 2750. Then came cockpit familiarization including a blindfold check in which they had to touch each indicator and control as it was called out. One never knew when the lights might fail on a night flight, and best to know exactly what to push or pull quickly without having to scramble around reaching for the mandatory flashlight which had to be carried on night flights.

Although Charlie and Jeff had arrived at Bakersfield on September 30, 1941, another week would pass before their first flight in a BT. Then came a mandatory six hours of dual in the airplane before solo flight was permitted. Those early flights, which began on October 6, 1941, were essentially a reprise of first flights in the Stearman and emphasized takeoffs, landings, stalls, forced landings, spin recoveries, and auxiliary field orientation.

Before his first BT hop, Jeffries determined that the BT had been properly serviced and was safe for flight after the walkaround inspection. Once aboard, he then released the control lock, and after adjusting his seat and rudder pedals, fastening his shoulder harness, and releasing the brakes, turned the ignition switch to the battery position, and saw the fuel pressure warning light come on. Carburetor heat control in cold, prop control in high pitch, oil cooler in open position, and fuel on the fullest tank were read off the checklist and confirmed. After priming, he then turned on the fuel pump, shoved the mixture into full rich, cracked the throttle and yelled, "Clear!"

Jeff energized the starter which promptly emitted a moaning whine, flicked the magneto switch to "both," then pushed the starter switch to the right, into the "engage" position, and watched the oil pressure indicator start rising after the engine caught. The extra work was about to begin, starting with all of the radio equipment which filled the entire right side of his cockpit. And there was a lot of it: separate units for the transmitter, receiver, tuner, master switch box, and intercom controller. The cockpit was crammed with equipment compared to the Stearman. Beneath the radio was a map case and ahead of that was the fuel control chart.

Fuel? It was not a problem in the Stearman; just turn the selector on, and the gas flowed by gravity from the single tank in the upper wing below which a simple sight gauge indicated fuel quantity. In a BT-13, there were three tanks, one four-position selector valve control, a dual-tank fuel quantity indicator, fuel pressure warning light, an engine driven fuel pump, and an emergency, hand-operated fuel pump.

The electrical system was light years ahead of the Stearman, and not devoted just to engine starting. Compared to the Stearman he had flown, Jeff's BT could be lit up almost like a Christmas tree since there were running lights, left and right landing lights, cockpit lights, and instrument lights. Pitot heat, voltmeter, ammeter, and the cockpit lighting rheostat were also located on the electrical panel.

The instrument panel contained the familiar faces of a few old friends including the airspeed indicator, altimeter, turn and bank indicator, tachometer, and magnetic compass. But they were in the minority, and had been joined by many new indicators and gauges which were essential to basic flight's emphasis on instrument and cross country flying. New were the vertical speed indicator, outside air temperature gauge, cockpit ventilation controller, and more complicated engine system indicators. Here too were the first gyro-stabilized instruments Jeff would use, the directional gyro which took the leading and lagging swings out of a compass and the artificial horizon which told him if the plane were turning, climbing, descending or maintaining straight and level flight. Most cadets quickly adapted to the new complexities, and the washout rate fell sharply once in basic flight. Jeff and his fellows were flying about an hour each weekday, and most were going solo by October 10th which was followed by six hours of practicing takeoffs, landings, stalls, and spins. Cadets no longer flew from the rear seat as in the Stearman — now they were up front and the instructor was in the rear.

After receiving taxi instructions and fishtailing down the taxiway, Jeff held short of the runway for the runup which consisted of a throttle check at 2000 rpm, carburetor heat operation, and magneto check at 1500 rpm with maximum allowable drop of 100 on either magneto. He then quickly checked for full travel of the controls, neutral trim, mixture in full rich, prop control into forward position (the BT had only a two position prop), and fuel on the fullest tank. With a clearance from the tower, the flight to an auxiliary field was on. Flaps were not used for takeoff at Bakersfield since they were prone to damage from the many pebbles and stones on runway surfaces. Only on short field takeoffs and landings were flaps employed, and they had to be retracted before taxiing to the ramp.

Once airborne, Jeff climbed out at 90 mph, and when he had gained 400 feet of altitude throttled back to 2,100 for normal climb, occasionally checking cylinder head and oil temperatures.

The first lesson was spent practicing stalls and spins in which the BT gave plenty of warning through wing buffeting, vibration, and mushy controls. The stall came at 75 mph flaps up and at 65 flaps down without any tendency to drop a wing. Spins, in which the rudder had to be held into the spin, were conventional and recoveries effected with opposite rudder and then stick full forward until rotation stopped whereupon the controls were neutralized.

On October 21, 1941, far away in Soerabaja, Howard Kincheloe was enjoying some late afternoon, off-duty refreshment with several other instructor pilots at the Oranje Hotel's open air bar called the Hollendorn. That afternoon, the *S.S. Boschfontein*, a small motorship, had docked at the harbor after nearly five weeks at sea from San Francisco. The passengers included a number of China-bound missionaries, some businessmen, a few pilots who were about to fly for KLM, and some other gentlemen who were not missionaries or businessmen.

Several of the latter group, obviously Americans whose knowledge of aeronautical matters was not just casual, walked in off the street to the Hollendorn. The new arrivals were also headed to China, and like Howard, they were in the employ of a foreign government. The Kincheloes entertained several of these gentlemen at their home that evening, but the guests were shortly off to Bali while their ship was being refueled and supplied for the next leg of their trip which would take them to Singapore and Rangoon. Before the *Boschfontein* left at the end of the month, they were given a going-away salute by one of the STMs which buzzed the ship several times. Within a couple of months, the world would know those visiting Americans as the Flying Tigers.

Howard enjoyed his work in Java, and today looks back on it as the equivalent of a year long, idyllic paid vacation. He was used to the climate after having served in Panama, lived in Miami, and flown Caribbean routes. His salary went a long way in Soerabaja where he had rented a lovely home with servants. There were exotic getaway weekends to Koda Beach on Bali and trips to cities such as Batavia (now known as Jakarta). The flying was good, and a typical day involved airwork along the Java Sea just to the north of Soerabaja. Cross country flights, using the flying boats, took Howard to such places as Timor, 700 miles to the east, or Sumatra, 700 miles to the west.

A major change in emphasis for Jeffries and Reynard came around October 22nd when instrument flying was introduced. Some of the BT-13s were instrument trainers, and had blind flying hoods which pulled down over the seat positions. Of the roughly 70 hours of flying in basic, nearly ten would be spent learning instrument flying, and that was built around a syllabus consisting of ten lessons and a final review.

Ground instruction emphasized the importance of trusting the instruments instead of their physical senses. Prior to the first instrument flying sessions, all of the indicators, and their shortcomings, were reviewed on the ground.

The blind flying hood was not used in the first lesson which was devoted largely to understanding the artificial horizon and the impact that various control movements, speeds and basic maneuvers had on the instruments. Cross-checking instruments was stressed as the BT was put through climbs, glides, and turns. The following lesson was similar to the first, except Jeff and Charlie were under the hood and flying the basic maneuvers strictly by reference to their instruments. As the instrument lessons progressed, the maneuvers flown became more complicated and involved more cockpit indicators, especially the directional gyro. At the halfway point in the instrument instruction, they were making climbing and gliding turns to assigned headings. Shortly thereafter, cadets started flying patterns involving turns and legs flown at different airspeeds. To make it interesting, the patterns might be flown using full panel (all instruments) or partial panel (needle, ball, airspeed), the latter to develop the cadet's ability to fly under the hood without reference to the gyro instruments. To test the ability to control the aircraft smoothly, steeply banked turns (much steeper than the gentle standard rate instrument turns used thus far) were introduced.

By the eighth lesson, cadets were flying more complex patterns involving 270 and 450 degree turns linked by legs at different airspeeds and flown occasionally without reference to the artificial horizon.

Once this was mastered, recovery from unusual attitudes was introduced. If an instructor had a diabolical side, giving a cadet unusual attitude recoveries was a great outlet in which the plane would be flown through basic aerobatic maneuvers as a warm up for the student to whom the controls would be turned over at some delicate moment, perhaps halfway through a sloppily entered chandelle.

"Mr. Jeffries, it's your airplane!" Mr. Jeffries, having been riveted to the instruments, could see that the airspeed was falling off, they were in a climb, turning, and for some reason, the power had been reduced, and that unless something was done quickly, there was a very real possibility of stalling out and spinning. In moments, Jeff had the nose lowered, the power back on, wings leveled, the speed building up, and in a few more seconds had the BT stabilized in straight and level flight with the speed increasing.

A few minutes later, the airspeed indicator pointer might be heading for the redline, the vertical speed indicator going counterclockwise, and the turn needle pegged far to one side. To get all three responses to such a situation was not enough: they had to be in the right order. The cadet who raised the nose, under the latter circumstances, before leveling the wings would get a good lecture on overstressing the plane and an opportunity to get it right the next time.

Near the end of the instrument sessions, cadets were introduced to another, more detailed pattern which required 16 minutes to fly. This

involved flying straight legs, climbing or descending at different airspeeds to assigned altitudes, climbing turns to specific headings, and
doing so at specific rates of climb or descent. The final session was a
complete review in which a failing grade could be expected if the
assigned altitudes, rates, and speeds were off by more than just a few
feet, seconds, or miles per hour.

"Buddy rides" were introduced in basic flight. Because they had
demonstrated basic competency in the airplane by late October, one
cadet would ride with the other as the instrument safety pilot while the
other cadet practiced flying under the hood for the instrument check
ride that was soon to come.

At the end of October, another dimension was added: night flying.
For many pilots, the introduction to night flying was not a welcome
event. For others, it was a delight. In truth, night flying has certain
advantages and is generally much smoother than day flying due to the
lack of thermals rising from the sun's beating on the earth's surface. The
first night flying session lasted for an hour and a half, and was composed
of takeoffs and landings including a half-hour of night solo. Unlike basic
in the Gulf Coast Command, Bakersfield cadets never got the experience of overflying an unlit auxiliary field, dropping a flare for illumination, and then landing.

Not all of the apprehension about night flying came from worrying
about putting the BT down in one piece. Actually, that was the least of
their worries since BTs had landing lights. Along the sides of the oiled
runway, flares were placed at intervals (although each cadet would
make a few landings on a lit runway NOT using his own landing lights).
Rather, fear came from the traffic. The night sky seemed to be lit up
almost like a fireworks display with all of the red and green running
lights. BTs were taking off and landing at frighteningly brief intervals.
Actually, night flying was well controlled by radio and assigning BTs to
specific holding zones and altitude bands. Very long distance night cross
countries were not flown at Bakersfield, but would be completed later
in advanced.

Charlie and Jeff spent the last few days of October concentrating on
night solos and instrument practice. Ground school continued with
some of the same subjects, but meteorology and navigation were no
longer introductory subjects. Navigation would shortly be put to the
practical test. Cadets used regular Civil Aviation Authority (CAA) maps

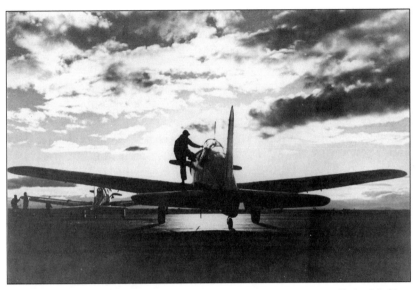

*Night flying was introduced at basic flying school.*

in training. Those maps are strikingly similar to today's sectional aeronautical charts in some respects and outrageously archaic in others, but certainly make for much easier reading. The old maps could still be used for navigation by pilotage, but that would be about all since radio navigation facilities from 1941 have disappeared with the exception of a few marker beacons and the occasional non-directional beacon.

In the early 40s, many pilots flew by what they described as IFR (what a contemporary pilot would call instrument flight rules). But, to the 1941 aviation cadet, "IFR" could mean "I follow roads." The meaning of "roads" extended beyond highways to include those of the rail variety. Not surprisingly, 1941 sectionals showed roads and town names very clearly, and it was a time when even experienced pilots were known to occasionally swoop low over a town to read its name on a water tower or prominent building. In fact, making low passes over communities in order to read the names on water towers, buildings or train stations was a part of the emergency procedures curriculum in basic flight, but was never allowed for normal cross country flying.

While radio navigation would be a key subject in advanced, navigation in basic flight was done the old fashioned way using two devices that looked as though they belonged on an engineering department drafting table instead of a cadet's desk. They were the flight plotter and what was becoming known as the E6-B flight "computer," a circular slide rule adapted for navigation. With this marvelous device, Jeffries and Reynard could, in a matter of minutes, derive the proper heading for each leg of an upcoming cross country. They were bewildered by the computer at first, but quickly became accustomed to obtaining their true course from the plotter and map, revising that with the magnetic variation associated with southern California, taking that figure, and tossing it into the pot along with the other variables (altitude, aircraft's compass correction, indicated airspeed, temperature, and the winds aloft report) to arrive at the desired heading to be flown and estimated time enroute.

Early in the first week of November, 42-B cadets got to apply what they had learned in ground school to the real thing: their first cross country. They were not expected to land at the various waypoints in their triangular courses, but just called in when they were over the checkpoint. At first, these were short hops such as from Bakersfield northwest to Lost Hills, northeast to Corcoran and return. Yes, some cadets did get lost at Lost Hills. For the navigationally-challenged, there were incentives to get up to speed quickly. Any cadet getting lost was decorated with a sign which hung over his back reading, "I got lost on a cross country." The counterbalance, worn over the chest and attached to the sign with two strings, was a chamberpot.

It was during the first stage of cross country flying that cadets became well acquainted with a couple of remarkable characters only briefly introduced at primary flying school. This duo consisted of one Mister Neodd and his very close associate, Mr. Sweven, both of whom would have a lasting influence on cadets. Surprisingly, neither was a flight or ground instructor; nor were these memorable personalities of Scandinavian descent. Rather, they were navigational, memory-jogging acronyms of the first order. Mr. NE-Odd reminded cadets to fly at odd thousands of feet when flying headings to the North or East while his compatriot, Mr. SW-Even, held sway over those flying South or West headings which had to be flown at even thousands of feet. Ultimately, both Messrs. Neodd and Sweven would go into partial retirement when airspace eventually became carved up between high altitude/low altitude routes and instrument/visual flying with only west and east becoming the principal altitude arbiters.

The second cross country also took about two hours and was flown during the first week of November further up the San Joaquin Valley to Visalia, Coalinga and return. Although Jeff and Charlie were rapidly building up solo time spent maintaining their airwork skills, there were

National Archives

*Toward the end of basic flying school, cadets were taught formation flying.*

periodic check rides with the Army instructors who could be relied upon to give an emergency landing exercise, stalls, spins, aerobatics, and more instrument flying.

Aerobatic flying was not emphasized to the extent that it had been during the late stages of primary, although the Bakersfield area offered one improvement over Oxnard and Thunderbird when it came to flying eights on and eights around. The corners of agricultural fields and orange groves were replaced with the pylon-like oil production derricks in one of Bakersfield's practice areas.

At the end of the first week in November, Charlie and Jeff once again became upperclassmen as the cadets of 42-A headed to advanced schools: 63 went to Mather Field at Sacramento and a large number, 75, went to the single-engine advanced school at Luke Field near Phoenix. That new primary schools were coming on stream was obvious from the influx of new cadets to Gardner and Bakersfield. In addition to Thunderbird and Oxnard, the new aeries included such California schools as Ontario, Tulare, and King City. To the two basic flying schools, 206 new cadets arrived, along with 80 brand new second lieutenant/instructor pilots. Bakersfield Army Air Field's population had just risen to 2,403 or roughly two-thirds of its planned capacity. Total cost for base construction in 1942 dollars was $3,468,000.

In mid-November 42-B cadets flew their last cross country from Minter as it was then called. It was a three-hour roundtrip, and for many cadets it was from Bakersfield north to Merced and return via Avenal. In the fourth week of November, a new phase was started: formation flying. Starting with dual rides in two-ship formations, cadets would progress to the point of making three-ship formation takeoffs in less than two weeks. Once a cadet could hold a position relative to his leader, positions were swapped. When a cadet was comfortable with forming up, maintaining close quarters in the air, and moving from one position to another, three-ship, vee formations were introduced.

Then the focus moved from changing formations from a vee to an echelon, and then stepping a formation up or down. Other than several hours of instrument time and a half-hour aerobatic check ride, the last third of basic flight was dominated by formation flying including night formation takeoffs. Fortunately, the BTs' radios simplified formation training and limited the rate at which the instructors, most in their early 20s, grew gray hair. Many cadets were fearful of tucking it in really tight while others created visions of mid-airs, chewed-up wingtips, and dented fuselages.

In case a radio failed, cadets learned to communicate by waggling their wings or fishtailing (meaning assume normal formation or open it up, respectively). More complex were the hand signals including one for failed radio (finger pointed to headset and then hand moved up and down in front of the face). There were signals for the forgetful: hand moved in a clockwise circle meant retract flaps, or, counter-clockwise, to lower flaps. At this stage, formation flying was almost exclusively confined to three-ship flights with an occasional nine-ship formation. The large squadron-size formations of 12 and 16 planes would not be learned until phase training.

From the Jeffries photo album

*Open post frequently meant a trip to Los Angeles where Roland Jeffries enjoyed a weekend in November 1941.*

By the third week in November, Charlie and Jeff successfully completed their 40-hour basic flight stage checks — a reliable sign that getting their wings and lieutenant's bars in another three months was pretty well in the bag. That important stage check coincided with an open post weekend for which the Hollywood USO Club had gone all out to show some hospitality to Bakersfield aviation cadets among other military units in the greater Los Angeles area. The Saturday evening event to which several dozen 42-B'ers had been invited was held at the West Side Tennis Club.

There is no indication that Cadets Jeffries or Reynard attended, but for those who did, it was quite memorable if for no other reason than the shower of greater and lesser stars in attendance. Such leading ladies as Claire Trevor, Gene Tierney, Veronica Lake, and Jean Arthur were there along with a supporting cast of young starlets and UCLA co-eds. It was a dry dance party (upstairs, anyway). Spirits were reportedly both high and flowing down in the locker rooms, though. As if to keep an eye on

Photo courtesy of Trent Wells, 42-B

*Cadet Roland L. Jeffries as photographed in early December 1941 by Ed Radtke using Charlie Reynard's camera.*

his investment in aviation cadet fortunes as personified in nearly a third of 42-B's Thunderbird graduates who were attending, Hoagy Carmichael played on well into the night which itself merrily went on and on. Most of 42-B's party animals just barely made it back to Bakersfield in time late on Sunday.

Early in December, cadets were photographed for the yearbook, *Echelon*. At many bases later in the war, the portraits were taken by the base photo department, but at Bakersfield in late 1941, the photo department was not yet a reality. 42-B's most avid shutterbug was none other than Ed Radtke, one of Charlie's roommates from primary. Radtke, being between cameras, borrowed Charlie's, and photographed the entire class, one by one, next to a BT-13 rudder.

Unfortunately, Charlie blinked as the shutter snapped. Although nearly 23 years of age, his ever youthful appearance was retained. The roughly six months of the cadet program showed in Jeffries' face, however. His December 1941 image clearly shows the progression from youth to a man strengthened by a half year of discipline, physical training, and the blossoming drive that was turning him into a superior pilot.

By December 6, 1941, Class 42-B cadets at Bakersfield had almost completed basic flight and were winding up their 70 hours of instruction with more formation flying. Many had gone into town to see a movie on Sunday, December 7th — as upperclassmen they had more privileges. A few, including Roland Jeffries, were relaxing at the base on that fateful Sunday. When the radio was turned on that afternoon, it was not playing *Chattanooga Choo Choo* or a new song that was catching on fast with west coast audiences, *Blues in the Night*. Rather, the normal programming had been interrupted by a news broadcast of the most important kind.

Charlie had been given a weekend pass, and had buzzed off to see Hiram College friends in Los Angeles where he arrived midday Saturday. He spent the afternoon in Santa Monica shopping for a Christmas present for his fiancée, Elizabeth. After dinner, they took in a late show. On Sunday afternoon, like the rest of America, Cadet Reynard hardly moved from the radio that brought news of the most cataclysmic event in 20th century American history. The same radio and announcer also provided Charlie with his orders, "All military personnel will report immediately to their stations."

His weekend hosts worked at Douglas Aircraft which they found, on Monday morning, guarded by soldiers and anti-aircraft artillery. Charlie was, as were many others, relieved, in one sense, since the suspense was over. It had happened. Now there was a well-defined purpose for the nation and the men of 42-B. Like multitudes of other young people in love, Jeff, Charlie, and their fiancées had to think about the wisdom of a wartime marriage — to postpone a wedding based on all of the uncertainties of their circumstances or to realize their dreams while they had the chance.

At Bakersfield, the base went into overdrive. Other cadets who were returning from off base got the word from the gate guard. Supper that Sunday night was hurried. There was fear of invasion or aerial attack. Should they get the planes off the field and dispersed up in the high Sierra? Cadets were ordered into flight clothing and told to report to their ready rooms prior to further "operations." All cadets passed the night on the flight line. Rumors were as rampant as speculation was wild. Dawn came and an uneasy calm prevailed. Trying to relocate several training squadrons of BT-13s flown by cadet pilots to the Sierra's alpine meadows in fading light would have been a more effective way of destroying them than leaving them prey to hordes of strafing Japanese Zeroes.

Guard duty was intensified, and even primary training fields located near the coast, such as Ryan in San Diego or Charlie's Mira Loma above Los Angeles, were ordered to build revetments to protect planes from aerial attack. Cadets who had just washed out suddenly found themselves guarding gates and Stearmans. Barbed wire and sandbag bunkers appeared practically overnight. Cadets were advised to use their radios sparingly while on training flights.

Just before Pearl Harbor, Howard Kincheloe traveled to Manila to bring some new planes back to the school. They were a type in which he had nearly 1,500 hours — the Consolidated PBY Catalina. The school would not enjoy using the PBYs for very long since they were quickly flown to Australia after hostilities commenced.

Near the end of basic, 42-B cadets were asked if they had a preference for the type of advanced training they preferred: single or multi-engine. There was no guarantee that any wish would be granted since assignments were made primarily on the needs of the service, ability of advanced flying schools to absorb new classes, and the instructors' assessments. A few cadets, usually aviation career-minded men who weren't aerobatically inclined, preferred multi-engine training. The majority hoped to become single-seat fighter pilots and go for single-engine

Photo courtesy of Robert H. Van Riessen

*Charlie Reynard photographed a friend, Bob Van Riessen, flying during formation training. Van Riessen became a basic flight instructor pilot, later a training standardization officer, and finished the war flying fighters.*

advanced training at Luke Field in Arizona. Those wanting to go the pursuit route had been tantalized by a flight of P-39 Airacobras which had overnighted at Bakersfield in late November. The glamour was with the pursuit ships, but that was not the reality of where most of Bakersfield 42-B cadets would report for advanced flight training.

Graduation from Luke Field was no absolute guarantee that a front-line fighter such as the P-38 Lightning, P-39 Airacobra, or P-40 Warhawk was in a cadet's future. The P-47 Thunderbolt and P-51 Mustang definitely were not in a 42-B cadet's near future since they were only starting to emerge from their factories. Ultimately, less than 30 of Luke Field's roughly 175 graduates in 42-B were sent to fighter transition schools. The balance of Luke's 42-B graduates either went directly to bomber squadrons as copilots or went onto first pilot bomber transition schools. Of Bakersfield's roughly 145 graduates in 42-B, about a quarter were sent to Luke for advanced, and of them only eleven became fighter pilots after graduation. They didn't know it at the time, but being among those eleven pilots was, indeed, a rich blessing. They all survived the war.

In mid-December, Charlie and Jeff, along with the majority of Bakersfield's 42-B class, were ordered to report to the commanding officer at Mather Field's Advanced Flying School near Sacramento. For Charlie, getting to Mather was a pleasant excursion since he drove there with roommates from Oxnard: Russell Schleeh and Ed Radtke. The trip upstate, through the Sierra, was somewhat novel for Charlie's coastal California friends who had rarely experienced snow.

# XV

# ADVANCED

Named for Lt. Carl Mather, who had been killed in a mid-air collision with another Curtiss Jenny pilot near Ellington Field in Texas, Mather Field was a pre-war installation dating back to WWI. Located 12 miles southeast of Sacramento, it was comprised of nearly 800 acres (three miles by three and a half miles) with auxiliary facilities located nearby including a large bombing range. Although Mather Field was subject to winter fogs, the flying weather was generally very good. The field drained well, and there were no major ground obstructions nearby.

Unfortunately, when the February 1941 decision was made to upgrade Mather into an advanced flying school, the base was languishing as a satellite facility of Hamilton Field in San Rafael, California. The last active flying unit, the 31st Bomb Squadron, had left in 1936. Commencing in April 1941, Mather became the subject of a $4 million plus improvement program which was still ongoing when Jeffries and

Reynard reported.[1] The first construction crews arrived in early May, and described the installation as being little more than "some old foundations and plenty of trees and grass."

Much there was to be built: 50 barracks, four messes, 16 squadron day rooms, six officers quarters (40-man capacity each), and various administrative, ground school and supply buildings. The first cadets

Photo courtesy of Walter Radtke

*Charlie Reynard drove from Bakersfield up to Mather with his two roommates from primary, Ed Radtke and Russell Schleeh. Radtke became an instructor pilot, first on basic trainers and later on heavy bombers. Following military service he was an insurance executive, a civics leader in suburban San Francisco, and a founder of the Cadet Class 42-B Association. Schleeh, pictured here with Charlie, survived his 25 missions over Europe with the 305th Bomb Group, became General Curtis LeMay's personal pilot in the Pacific, went on to become a prominent military test pilot after the war, and retired after 20 years with Douglas Aircraft.*

graduated in August 1941 after tolerating some rough conditions since the construction program was just getting underway (tent living, no showers, etc). Even the early flying was hampered by incomplete runways, poor lighting, and inadequate radio facilities. 42-B cadets, however, were housed in new barracks that harkened back to the luxury of Oxnard. Mather cadets were quartered four to a room, unlike the Bakersfield barracks and their rows of cots.

The physical plant was not the only challenge. Mather faced monumental personnel problems in generating an effective staff to support the several hundred aviation cadets just as Bakersfield had during roughly the same timeframe. Key personnel needs alone included officers for purchasing, technical inspection, parachute department, transient aircraft engineering, cryptography, medical department, signals, quartermaster, mess, ordnance, facilities engineering, fire marshall, intelligence, judge advocate and provost marshall, finance, morale, athletic, and communication. Not to mention flight and ground instruction.

Mather, in June 1941, became the site of the first navigation school on the West Coast. Twelve Beech AT-17 trainers were based at Mather, which actually had more navigation cadets in training than flying cadets in the beginning (570 to 308). The flying cadets of 42-B, although they had been selected for multi-engine training, would not get their hands on the Beech twins — the Army Air Force quite simply didn't have enough twin-engine trainers to go around in late 1941. Like many of their peers at nearby Stockton and other advanced schools, Jeffries and Reynard went through a multi-engine advanced curriculum on a single-engine airplane, the North American AT-6A.

Mather Field started to receive its first twin-engine advanced trainers, Curtiss AT-9s, just a week before 42-B arrived. By the time 42-B graduated from Mather, the field had over 20 of the little twins, but even if they had a hundred of them, they would not have been used immediately for instruction because practically none of the instructors had been checked out in one. When the first AT-9 arrived in December, there was only one instructor on the field qualified to fly it, and that was only because he had been on detached duty briefly at Wright Field in Ohio and had flown one there.

The AT-9 was exceptionally noisy and had a terrifically high wing loading which produced an approach speed of 120 mph with touchdown at a bare minimum of 110. The problem of qualifying instructors who were also expected to maintain their AT-6 instruction schedules precluded any involvement by 42-B with the airplane, although a few cadets wangled rides in them. Thus, only a minority of 42-C cadets was introduced to the AT-9, and training in it was discontinued in May 1942. Considering where they were headed, an introduction to the AT-9 would have been very useful for Jeffries, Reynard, and several dozen of their Mather classmates.

By the time Jeffries and Reynard arrived just after Pearl Harbor, the flight training program was beginning to recover from its start-up problems, and the construction was well on its way to completion. Many of the instructors were brand new graduates of two recently graduated classes, 41-H and I. Since experience had shown that they needed extra training to become effective instructors, the men teaching 42-B had gone through a quick, 30-hour instructor's course at Mather.

Counting the 42-A upperclassmen, there were roughly 300 flying cadets and 122 flight and ground instructors on the field. Cadets were assigned to instructors in groups of five on an alphabetical basis, thus Jeff and Charlie were in the company of old friends. There were quite a few new cadets since some of the missing faces from Bakersfield had been replaced with cadets from Taft, the other basic flying school located down in Kern County. The Mather base commander, Col. Leland Hewitt, felt that the number of instructors was dangerously low, especially in light of the approaching day when Mather would become a *bona fide* multi-engine school. Hewitt was no amateur in the matter of flight instruction. A Tulane graduate, he had been in France during WWI as an instructor, had served in training and training management positions between the wars, and was a graduate of the Command and General Staff School.

Hewitt had gotten his eagles when Jeffries and Reynard were about halfway through advanced. At the same time, General Barton Yount, commander of the West Coast Air Training Center, was transferred to Washington for a larger role in the Training Command.

For flying instruction, Mather was equipped with 97 AT-6As and 37 BT-13s. The latter were used for some of the early phases of instrument instruction, although the majority of hours logged by 42-B was in the AT-6.

Whereas ground school in primary and basic had prepared cadets for how airplanes fly and how to manage airplanes once airborne, ground school in advanced addressed the subject in another dimension: the military. Ground school was held in one of the large, new buildings which featured six spacious classrooms.

Although Mather was rapidly becoming a complete base, the same could not be said of educational materials. Concurrent with the dramatic increase in the numbers of aviation cadets, such basics as aeronautical charts became short in supply. In partial response to the problem, Mather started making its own maps complete with a drafting department which also prepared sample teletype messages for such reports as winds aloft and air terminal data.

Lecture dominated most of ground school since textbooks were either scarce or non-existent. It would be well over a year before standardized texts on such subjects as basic instrument flying became available. The shortages extended to personnel, and it was not until long after Jeffries and Reynard passed through Mather that an adequate number of ground school instructors was employed.

Complicating matters was a lack of ground school standardization. Although the cadets starting at Thunderbird had been exposed to aircraft recognition, the subject was not taught at Mather until 42-D started in late February, just as Jeffries and Reynard graduated.

Ground school in aeronautical subjects emphasized weather and navigation, especially dead reckoning. Tests were primarily the true-false or multiple choice types. Navigation problem solving was not stressed until 42-B departed Mather. In addition to thorough understanding of the AT-6A technical orders, the full ground school curriculum during 42-B's ten weeks at Mather also included world geography, maintenance engineering, tactics and techniques of air fighting, anti-aircraft and warning nets, squadron duties, combat orders, armament, gunnery and tactical fire, and, inevitably, code. Radio code, administered in a room with visual lights and 80 headsets and keys, continued to be an important subject. To graduate, cadets had to be able to take ten words per minute. All subjects were graded except code which was conducted on a pass-fail basis. While washouts from ground school deficiency or health problems were unusual in advanced, "washbacks" were more common, particularly in the case of minor injuries.

Physical training was not neglected at Mather, but it was not accentuated as it had been at primary either. To a certain extent, winter weather impacted on PT as did a lack of equipment. Initially, one hour of calisthenics and cross country running was required daily. By the time 42-B arrived, basketball, baseball, football, volleyball and track facilities had been completed. When Jeffries and Reynard reported in December 1941, they were tested in the 75 and 150-yard dash, broad jump, chinning, and leglifts. They were re-tested in the same events near the end of the term, and most showed an improvement. Some did not, and that was related to the particularly resourceful mess officers.

42-B, along with most of the other early cadet classes, was not well trained in some subjects that would be introduced early in subsequent cadet classes: oxygen orientation and firearms training. Although Jeff and Charlie were familiar with the manual of arms and marched with rifles in basic flight, they would leave Mather without having shot a .45 automatic Colt pistol at a range or fired a rifle at any target. By 1943, cadets were placed in altitude chambers and quite clearly shown the effects of oxygen starvation.

Mather 42-B'ers had to learn the effects of hypoxia on the job since their oxygen training was minimal, and consisted of little more than a classroom orientation on the mask and regulator followed by a short "altitude hop." Most members of 42-B, spread out among nine advanced flying schools, got less oxygen training since only Mather and Stockton in California and Luke Field in Arizona were set up for oxygen orientation in the entire Western Training Command.

Compared to their two previous stages of flight training, advanced was much more relaxed. The stress of hazing had almost been completely removed. One of the 42-B cadets who would go on to become an instructor and later a Mustang pilot in the ETO, Trent Wells, recalls advanced as a time when cadets could "get off the ball" in contrast to getting on the ball which had been the credo of primary flight. Open post weekends were the rule, not the exception, and upperclassmen also had Wednesday evenings off. Inspections were less frequent, and cadets walked to the mess halls instead of marching.

Dual instruction didn't go away because cadets had to learn radio navigation and go through stage checks, but instructors weren't riding in back as much as before.

Jeffries and Reynard found themselves in a land of plenty when they arrived at a Mather mess hall. The food was the best yet, and a cadet could always help himself to more which created a problem for the flight surgeons. A not insignificant number of 42-B cadets began to put on weight as well they might have considering the dining opportunities and more casual atmosphere. About a dozen 42-B cadets exceeded the weight limits to the extent that they had to be placed on a diet and required to spend extra time in the gymnasium.

When Charlie and Jeff arrived at Mather Field in mid-December, the initial shock of Pearl Harbor had not yet worn off, and the war news was not in the least encouraging. Secretary of the Navy Frank Knox had just released the full accounting of the Japanese sneak attack, and indicated that six capital ships had been sunk and that nearly 2,800 servicemen had been killed.[2] News on the war in Russia and North Africa was overshadowed by events in the Pacific where the Japanese were threatening Hong Kong and pushing the British out of Malaya.

The exception to Pearl Harbor dominating news coverage on December 15th was a solemn, rainswept ceremony held on the *U.S.S. Constitution* in Boston Harbor. It was a memorial service honoring those killed on the *U.S.S. Reuben James*, the destroyer sunk by a German U-boat west of Iceland just two months before.

In a sign of California times to come, Sacramento police broke up a marijuana ring that day. Four men were arrested and ten cans of the weed were confiscated (total value, $195). More significantly though, entry into the war was impacting the man in the street in ways which might not have been imagined several weeks before. Blackouts were initiated. Air raid drills became part of every school's activities. Race tracks and major public events were threatened since gatherings of more than 10,000 people in one place were expected to be banned. The Rose Bowl game on New Year's Day was going to be moved east to Durham, North Carolina, where Duke would play Oregon State. Since military authorities did not want such a large gathering of people all in one stadium, Rose Bowl officials had to refund over $264,000 to 60,000 ticket holders. Many of California's fairgrounds and even Santa Anita Racetrack were offered to the government for military use.

The Office of Civilian Defense had assumed more prominence, and among its duties was public education on the importance of heeding sentries' orders, especially during blackouts. In the preceding week, several guards at California defense plants had fired at those who did not respond to a challenge. One Los Angeles woman motorist was shot dead when she failed to stop at a plant gate.

The war had yet to fully impact the airlines. United had just offered a new daily flight to the east coast from Sacramento. The sleeper flight takeoff was shortly after 6 p.m. with arrival in New York City after lunch the following day.

In New York, advancing stocks were dominated by armaments, aircraft, rails, and steel. A total of 1,100,000 shares was traded on December 15th. Boeing, Douglas, U.S. Steel, United Aircraft, Sperry, Bethlehem Steel, Phelps Dodge, Westinghouse, and Union Carbide were among those gaining two points or more.

Many aspects of daily life had not yet changed significantly, though. Sports went on, and in Sacramento there was pride when a local man, a former Stanford University star, led his new team, the Chicago Bears, onto its fifth straight western division NFL title. Byron Nelson successfully defended his first place finish in the Miami Open by defeating Ben Hogan and Sammy Snead. Nelson took home $2,500 for finishing four rounds in 269 strokes.

With Christmas less than two weeks away, Sacramento shoppers could buy an Admiral automatic radio phonograph at the Hale Brothers appliance store on Kay Street for just $59.95. It was a real value, and could change up to 12 ten-inch records automatically.

Montgomery Ward was offering its six cubic foot refrigerator for $138.95 and a deluxe gas range for $142.95. For the kids there was a folding doll cart at $4.89 or a cowboy outfit at $1.19. For those wanting to follow the war by listening to broadcasts from Europe, Ward's had a nine-tube radio for $49.95. At Brueners, the department store, the Hamilton Beach vacuum cleaner cost $32 (plus the old cleaner). The store featured General Electric too, and its six foot deluxe refrigerator retailed for $153.65 or $7.50 monthly.

Traditional movie theaters were experiencing competition from the Sacramento Newsreel Theater. The popular commentator, H. V. Kaltenborn, was featured on coverage of the Pearl Harbor disaster. Ten complete newsreels played coverage of 54 national and world events. Flown into Sacramento daily, the news could be seen, any seat, any time, for just 25 cents.

Since flying wasn't to start for a few days after his arrival at Mather, Charlie had a few moments to write letters. Now that the war was on, his future with Elizabeth was much in his thoughts. He wrote to his sister Mary with an idea that was not, however, to materialize. He was thinking of buying his brother George's car, and having Elizabeth and sister Mary drive it out to the west coast in time for his graduation from advanced flying school.

Among the letters Jeff received while at advanced flying school was one that had been sent from the offices of the Kansas City Council, Boy Scouts of America. It was a mimeographed newsletter from the Chief. During the war, Roe Bartle made every attempt to know the whereabouts of his many Scouts who were in the service. To those who responded with a written thanks, Bartle penned a personal response.

Flying started on Friday, December 19th, a day that was another bad one for the Allies in the Pacific. Hong Kong was invaded and British forces in Malaya were in full retreat. In Washington, the Senate passed a measure requiring the Selective Service registration of all men between the ages of 18 and 64. Only those between 20 and 44 were to be eligible for the draft. For the 42-B cadets, the 20th was memorable since flying continued over the weekend and because the Training Command issued orders to graduate cadets ahead of schedule.

The flight training curriculum at advanced contained nothing new with the exception of radio navigation. It was a time when cadets were expected to perfect what they had learned at basic, i.e. instrument flying, cross country navigation, and formation flying. Taking off with an instructor in back was the exception, other than the first six hours of mandatory dual when qualifying on the North American AT-6A.

At first glance, the North American AT-6 advanced trainer had the simple appearance of being a beefier version of the Vultee BT-13. The wing spans were comparable, about 42 feet each, but the gross weights weren't: roughly 4,500 pounds to 5,300 pounds. For some reason, however, the wing spans do not appear comparable, and the Six gives the impression of having smaller dimensions from the cockpit. Other than the Six's retractable landing gear, the planes did look similar, but the performance was markedly different. When Jeff and Charlie first climbed into the front cockpit, it looked quite familiar. In fact, the layout was almost identical to the BT in which they had each logged 70 hours. The throttle quadrant was at their left, and the radio equipment on the right. The instrument panel was similarly configured. The trim wheels and flap handle were in about the same location.

But there were several striking differences — differences which reminded them that a more dangerous future awaited just a few short months after graduation. Whereas the Stearman could easily be confused with any number of sport biplanes and the BT had no military systems on board, the top of the AT-6 control stick had two, new protuberances. One was a machine gun trigger and the other was a bomb release button.

And down there, at the lower left corner of the instrument panel was the electrical control panel whose meters, lighting switches, generator, and battery disconnect switches were very familiar. The right third of the panel was all new: it contained selector and safety switches for the guns and bomb release mechanisms. As cadets in the multi-engine track, Jeff and Charlie actually would not have an occasion to use these systems. A few of their classmates, such as Dave McDonald who had been sent to single-engine advanced flying school, would be using the Six's armaments. Those pilots would receive more aerobatic training and shoot at towed sleeve targets. There was no aerial gunnery involved at Mather whose cadets spent more time in navigation, cross countries and formation flying than their associates from basic who had been sent to Luke Field.

A compact man like Reynard might not have noticed another difference between the BT and the Six as quickly as a big guy like Jeffries would have: the Six cockpit was definitely cramped. The BT was roomy, almost spacious in comparison. The BT's cockpit rails were lower which created more comfort and better visibility.

Should one ever engage a former Army Air Force aviation cadet in conversation just as a T-6 happens along, one will undoubtedly note that the dialogue tends to drift off as the older pilot gets a glint in his eye. He will then cock his head at an angle with which to better hear what is approaching. He will have identified the ship long before it comes into view because the T-6 sound signature is overlaid with a most memorable, pulsating throb. The Doppler effect heard when a T-6, with its 650 h.p., nine cylinder Pratt & Whitney R-1340 radial engine, passes by is unmistakable. Some writers have likened the sound to a small chorus of hoarse, unmuffled, two-cylinder Harley Davidson motorcycles roaring past.

The AT-6 and its navalized version, the SNJ, trace their origins to North American Aviation's success with the BT-9 basic trainer of the mid-1930s. The T-6, or more appropriately AT-6 ("A" for "advanced") was essentially a BT-9 with metal fuselage skinning, as opposed to fabric, retractable landing gear, and a 650 horsepower engine. The design proved to be a best-seller, and the air forces of British Commonwealth countries became major customers. In Canada, the T-6 started as the

*A Mather-based AT-6A parked at Moffett Field near San Francisco in early 1942.*

Yale, and in the RAF, it was the Harvard. The Australians, not following the lead of naming American-built trainers after Ivy League schools, called their license-built version the "Wirraway." The AT-6's official name, "Texan," did not become popular until well after WWII. Most Army pilots just called it a "Six." Nowadays, T-6s are regulars at airshows where warbirds congregate. Nearly 16,000 T-6s were built, and quite a few are still flying, unlike the BT-13s of which most went west to aircraft graveyards for transmogrification into aluminum ingots. The flyaway cost to the Army Air Force for an AT-6A in 1941 was roughly $30,000. Should one's good fortune include having $150,000 in loose change lying around the house today, a well restored, later model AT-6 or, for those of the naval persuasion, an SNJ, could be owned tomorrow.

The performance was a step up from the BT. The 200 additional ponies in the Six put the top speed up to nearly 200 mph, and the range made for realistic cross countries. The additional horsepower was most noticeable on takeoff; the tail came up quickly and the machine broke ground in little more than three football fields (assuming no wind, average temperature and a modest load). The aerobatic characteristics were excellent and the landing speed was a not so taxing 56 mph with gear and flaps down.

The Six afforded Jeffries and Reynard with a few luxuries not available on the BT: a retractable landing gear, a fully variable pitch propeller instead of the BT's two position prop, and hydraulically operated flaps. On the other hand, cruise speed in the Six was only 15 or 20 mph faster than the BT, but the stick forces were still relatively light. Putting that into focus, control force pressures are comparable to that of the contemporary Beech Bonanza Model A-36 (6-place, 300 h.p., stretched version of the straight tail Bonanza). Fabric covered control surfaces, good balancing, and relatively low speeds made the difference. Ponderous controls were still in Jeffries' and Reynard's future.

There was one other, immediately obvious difference when flying a Six. It was not a hands-off flying machine. Properly trimmed, the BT would merrily fly on and on, hands off. Trying that in a Six put a cadet all over the sky. The Six had to be flown all the time.

With cadets getting their first orientation flights in the Six on December 19, 1941, Charlie approached the big trainer already having read its technical orders. After checking Forms One and One-A, he started the walkaround preflight by removing the left wing gas cap, checking the level, and securing the cap before checking the wing itself. Moving to the engine cowling, he looked into the intakes, peered into the inspection plates, and ran his fingers over the propeller to check for dents or scratches. The ship had just been flown so pulling the prop through ten turns was unnecessary. Charlie could see over an inch of shiny steel on the landing gear oleo struts so he knew their inflation was proper. Tires looked good and the wheel wells were unobstructed. The walk continued along the left wing where the pitot tube was checked to be free. Rounding the tip, Charlie checked the aileron for movement, made sure the baggage compartment was secure, walked back by the tail, and checked the control surfaces for movement and tension before looking at the tailwheel. After the right wing and fuel tank were checked, Charlie strapped on his parachute and climbed aboard with the instructor.

Form One was signed off and given to the crew chief. Charlie, being shorter than most cadets, had to adjust the seat and rudder pedals before unlocking the controls and checking for free movement. Then came the ubiquitous checklist-driven items: controls free, parking brakes on, fuel quantity checked and selector set on reserve tank, landing gear handle confirmed as down, hydraulic pressure checked, carburetor heat cold, oil cooler shutters open, manifold pressure drain gauge closed, electrics and radios off, altimeter set to field elevation (Mather Field was just 87 feet above mean sea level), and gyro instruments uncaged. Charlie stowed the checklist card, and quickly shoved the mixture full forward, moved the prop back to low rpm, and opened the throttle, slightly.

"Switches on," he announced as he flicked the master, generator and ignition switches on. After a few shots of priming, he yelled, "Clear!" as he energized the starter by depressing the heel end of the starter pedal. The Six just sat there emitting a sound somewhere between a grunt and hum, but after ten seconds, Charlie pressed the pedal's toe to crank the engine which promptly started after several blade turns. Reynard advanced the throttle to bring revs up to 500 and turned on the radio. In a few seconds, oil pressure climbed past 50 pounds, so the prop control was moved fully forward. With oil and cylinder head temperatures OK, they were ready to taxi.

With a burst of throttle, he started taxiing the Six whose over-the-nose visibility was poor compared to the BT. The instructor in back rolled his canopy shut, but Charlie's had to remain open while they were taxiing and S-turning their way to the warm-up pad. The ship was idled at 1000 rpm, run up to 2000 rpm, and backed off to 1500 for the last checklist items including proper readings on the ammeter, voltmeter, temperature gauges, and suction gauge. The trim wheels at his left elbow were cranked until the indicators showed 11 o'clock on the elevator and two o'clock for the rudder. With stick back and feet on the brakes, Charlie alternately moved the ignition between right, both, left, and both noting that the resulting drops were within the allowable 75 revs. Cycling the prop control quickly back, then as quickly forward, introduced a slashing "whoosh" sound and momentary drop in rpm indicating the propeller pitch mechanism was functioning. Had a printed checklist not been available, Charlie would have used the takeoff checklist memory jogger, "CIGFTPR," an acronym standing for Controls-Instruments-Gas-Flaps-Trim-Prop-Radio.

Flying control cleared the Six for takeoff, Charlie acknowledged the clearance, and with a last looksee in every direction, taxied into position on the runway. There he locked the tailwheel, quickly reset the directional gyro to the runway heading, and then firmly advanced the throttle to full power. He had been warned not to rush the matter since the Six produced much more torque on takeoff than the BT. Because the Six isn't like your grandmother's tricycle landing-geared Cessna 172, takeoffs are more interesting, and require undivided attention to the rudder pedals due to the torque and any crosswinds. After the tail came up (typically taking less than five seconds to do so), the Six broke ground about 900 feet further down the runway while accelerating through 80 mph.

Charlie remembered the instructor's warning not to forget to brake the wheels before retracting the gear. When it was obvious that they had eaten up enough runway that putting the Six back down on it would be impossible, Charlie pushed the hydraulic control lever and flipped the gear switch into the up position. As the gear retracted, the speed was increasing, and when they had gained two hundred feet, Charlie brought the power back to 32 inches and revs to 2,200.

Soon they were turning and heading out for a review of basic airwork beginning with climbs, turns, and descents to quickly get a feel for the plane. Stalls and spins followed immediately. Whereas the Stearman and BT mushed or broke gently in a stall, the Six break, although preceded by plenty of warning, was much sharper and could involve a wing dropping. A poor recovery could waste, in a few moments, several hundred feet of altitude or more than enough to prove fatal in an attempt to take shortcuts on a botched final approach. Once power off and power on stalls with gear and flaps up and down and accelerated stalls were mastered, spins and recoveries were introduced. Although well-trained in spins by this point, each 42-B cadet would get spin exercises every time an instructor rode with him, which wasn't actually that frequently in advanced.

After about six hours, each cadet was sent off solo in the Six. In those first few hours, they also flew the accuracy and rolling maneuvers learned in primary, had the throttle suddenly pulled for a simulated emergency landing, and logged slightly over two hours under the hood for basic instrument flight. The Six would not be their only instrument trainer, however. Some of their instrument training was also gained in BTs, but a significant portion was obtained in a remarkably truncated craft introduced immediately after soloing the Six.

The groundbound "craft" that would enhance their instrument flying was none other than the "jeep," a popular nickname for the Link Instrument Flying Trainer which is the progenitor of today's digitally whiz-banged, panorama-wrapped flight simulators. Unlike contemporary simulators which combine virtual reality terrain images and carbon copy cockpits of the planes for which they simulate, the Link trainer was a study in generic basics. The jeep could almost qualify as a terribly overgrown, fabric covered model airplane in which a cadet was uncomfortably ensconced. The contrivance was mounted on a pedestal, capable of limited movement in pitch, roll, and yaw axes, and had a coffin-like canopy which closed down over the cadet's head. Instead of simulating a real aircraft's roar or slipstream sound, the jeep brought forth an electro-mechanical hiss. Before advanced was finished, cadets would log roughly 15 hours each in the jeep.

In contrast to today's military and airliner simulators which are essentially big boxes on multiple stilts, the Link trainer sprouted stubby wings and a tiny tail unit — almost as though a soapbox race car designer had become aviation-minded at the last minute. In charge of

National Archives

*The AT-6 was a particularly good aerobatic trainer. Its narrow undercarriage called for more attention on landings compared to the BT-13 with its wider track landing gear.*

the performance was a controller seated at a nearby desk. In an attempt to make it user-friendly, most Links were painted in trainer colors of the day, i.e. red and white striped rudder, blue fuselage, and yellow wings.

The Link trainer was unpopular with most cadets for several reasons of which the most fundamental was a lack of understanding about what the machine's real purpose was. It was not a substitute for flight in true instrument meteorological conditions. Rather, its purpose was to develop a cadet's instrument consciousness, i.e. the ability to comprehend the full panel's indications and not to focus on just one instrument. The baseline goal was to understand the aircraft's attitude by comprehending the correlation between the various instruments and then, using that insight, to perform coordinated maneuvers directed by the controller. To a lesser extent, the jeep was also useful in maintaining proper radio phraseology. Cadets who did well with the trainer usually had fewer difficulties with actual instrument flying and radio navigation which was a major emphasis in advanced flying school.

Unfortunately, early Link trainer instruction suffered from several flaws including poor maintenance, improperly trained instructors, and bias against the Link on the part of instrument flight instructors and cadets alike.

Nevertheless, when Jeff and Charlie reported to the Instrument Flying Trainer Department, they were informed of the differences between the Link and real aircraft before being given an orientation in the cockpit. The most notable differences, other than the obvious ones of aircraft configuration, were in the sensations of flight, i.e. stick pressure, sound, centrifugal force, acceleration, deceleration, and the Link's relatively faster response to control inputs.

Their performance was graded, although not in a numerical scale as with other ground school subjects. Instead, a quasi-pass/fail system was used in which they were rated as "above average," "average," or "below average."

At this stage of their training, Jeffries' and Reynard's introductory sessions in the Link were limited to nine exercises consisting of climbs, descents, straight and level flight, and turns. When proficiency had been gained on these elementary maneuvers, timed turns, climbing turns, and descents to assigned headings and altitudes were practiced before the final session which was a wrap-up review. Throughout the Link sessions, any observed sloppy technique, involving skidding or slipping turns, poorly timed turn entries or roll-outs, or altitude over or undershoots, was made abundantly clear to the cadet through the interphone. The Link had a full panel including gyro instruments, although the cadet's first few minutes of "flying" were done on a "contact" or visual basis just to get used to how the jeep responded to control inputs. Starting a Link was done by the simple expedient of turning on the ignition switch. Going through the real drill of flicking on multiple switches (master, fuel pump, magnetos), priming, cracking the throttle, advancing the prop control, energizing, and finally cranking weren't part of the jeep program. Fluorescent lights illuminated the instruments, but the cadet had to turn on the cockpit lighting manually for reading maps. When the controller was satisfied that the cadet was comfortable with the jeep, a spin was demonstrated and repeated until the student was competent at recovery. Indeed, any prolonged inattention on the cadet's part could easily result in a spin. One thing any cadet could appreciate about the Link — it was a ship from which even the worst crash could be walked away in good health.

Once the spin demonstration was completed, the instructor closed the cockpit hood, returned to his desk, and, through the interphone, directed the cadet through the first exercises beginning with straight and level flight at 160 mph after first using the artificial horizon to arrive at the straight and level mode. Throughout the exercise, the instructor at a nearby table monitored the cadet's progress on a recorder chart whose pen registered every triumph and tragedy. The first nine exercises went quickly, and required, on average, only a couple of hours at most. The maneuvers were very familiar since they were, in fact, a reprise of their "under-the-hood" exercises that they had already learned on the BT-13 back at Bakersfield. There was no set number of Link hours in the advanced flight curriculum. A particularly clever student would spend about 12 hours in the jeep, and a cadet for whom instrument flying did not come easily might spend 18 hours in it.

For the occasional student hesitant about radio procedures, the Link controller quickly reinforced the cadet's vocabulary with all the key passages including "roger," "wilco," "repeat," and "that is all." Ground station call signs such as "tower," "airways," and "radio" became part of the cadet's lexicon as did how to identify himself and enunciate numbers as in altitudes and times.

On Saturday, December 20th, Mather's new cadets were guests of honor at a tea dance given by the Chamber of Commerce and the

Sacramento Charity League. The gathering was held at the Senator Hotel, and also attended by 75 young ladies including many college girls home for the holidays. It was the first of many cases where local citizens tried to make the cadets feel at home. Most cadets were able to spend Christmas day with local families. The library at Mather was growing with books supplied by local citizens and Sacramento's public library.

Mather Field, like most training bases, was practically a community unto itself. There was a base theater which played, if not first run features, such fare as *Tarzan's Secret Treasure* or *Four Jacks and a Jill* (the latter with Ray Bolger). These daily shows included comics and newsreels like any downtown Sacramento theater. Aviation cadets did not have to rely solely on newspapers, newsreels, or the radio for important developments; all training squadron day room bulletin boards were posted with current events summaries and war maps.

The recreation hall was the setting for amateur theatricals put on by local theater groups and, occasionally, base personnel. Mather had several bands which provided the music at dances held on base (young ladies were shepherded to Mather under the auspices of the Sacramento YWCA).

In addition to physical training of aviation cadets, the athletic training office coordinated a substantial number of intramural activities. While 42-B was at Mather, there were several basketball leagues, and the base team also played local colleges. For former wingfeet, there was winter track, and for the less hardy, a ping-pong league.

Although there were isolated cases of good pre-Christmas news coming from the Pacific war, the Japanese were gaining ground everywhere. Dutch pilots hit several Japanese cruisers off Borneo and the Flying Tigers shot down a number of Japanese planes attacking the Burma Road, but a Japanese fleet of 80 ships had landed a force of over 100,000 men on Luzon in the Philippines. The war was coming closer to home; four ships had been attacked by a Japanese submarine just off the California coast. Later in the week, the tanker *Montebello* would be torpedoed and its four lifeboats full of survivors fired upon. Another tanker in the same area, the *Doheny*, would escape.

On December 30, 1941, Waite Phillips signed the property transfer agreement, and created Philmont Scout Ranch as a property of the Boy Scouts of America. Pearl Harbor shelved any immediate development of the property, and Scouting activity during the war years was minimal. In

*AT-6As in a stepped-up, echelon right formation. In advanced, Mather-based cadets perfected their basic skills which included long, cross country formation flights.*

1942, slightly over 1,300 Scouts came to Philmont. In spite of restrictions on travel and lack of manpower, much was done during the war years to ready the Ranch for an anticipated post-war camping attendance of 10,000 youth.

On that December 30th, orientation on the Six was extended to formation flying. By New Year's Eve, each cadet had logged nearly two and a half hours of dual instruction in formation flying. New Year's Day 1942 was a Thursday, and for Jeff and Charlie it was another working day since cadets went on their first cross country. The first cross countries for Mather cadets were short circuits in which they were sent off at intervals and differing altitude bands. A standard, early cross country was one flown northeast to Auburn, then north to Marysville, west to Williams, and back to Mather via Roseville resulting in an hour and 45 minute entry into logbooks.

Just as Jeffries and Reynard were being invited to get off the ball, they were told they would soon have to "get on the beam." This came as no surprise since ground school lecture and blackboard exercises were preparing them for it. The "beam" referred to the radio range system which formed the basis for the country's airways system. The United States was then dotted with several hundred directional radio facilities known as radio ranges. Each sent out four signals in a pattern roughly shaped like an X or a cross. The signals were sent in Morse code and limited to just two letters, A and N. The horizontal segments of the cross might carry the A signal and the vertical segments the N. The upper arm was rarely pointing north, however. Rather, the arms, or pie slices, were arranged based on their use as hubs connecting cities and routes between the cities in the network not unlike an interstate road system.

Cadets learned to navigate by flying on the "beam" that was created when the A and N signals overlapped. Unlike radio direction finding, of which he would learn more in a few weeks, or the VHF omnirange system which evolved after WWII, the beam system was strictly an aural program in which the cadet's earphones pointed the way to go. If the Six were on the beam, he was in a narrow corridor formed by the overlap of the A and N signals and would hear only a solid tone in his headset.

As he drifted out of the beam, he would start to pick up the A or N signal, dit-dah or dah-dit respectively. When he was well off the beam, he would hear only the A or N. As the cadet approached a station, the signal became stronger, and when he passed over a station, known as the "cone of silence," all became quiet for a brief interval. Using this system in weather fair or foul, the nation's airlines had been flying from city to city and making approaches to airports since the early 1930s. 42-B cadets at Mather had no shortage of range stations with which to learn the system. There were five airways in the area, and from them and their range stations approaches could be made to the military fields within easy flying distance, including McClellan Field near Sacramento proper, Hamilton and Moffett Fields on the outskirts of San Francisco, and Stockton Field about 60 miles down the valley.

# XVI

## SILVER WINGS

Although some people say he's just a crazy guy,
To me, he means a million other things. For he's
The one who taught this happy heart of mine to fly.
He wears a pair of silver wings.

And, though it's pretty tough the job he does above,
I wouldn't have him change it for a king.
An ordinary fella in the uniform I love.
He wears a pair of silver wings.

From the song by Maschwitz & Carr,
popularized by Dinah Shore in 1942

Jeff's first session on beam flying was not in the jeep itself, but at the controller's table where the instructor demonstrated signals through a headset. Seated beside the operator, Jeff heard a clear, repetitive dah-dit, dah-dit, dah-dit when the operator's airplane (a point on the controller chart) was in the N quadrant. The operator moved the point closer to the beam and Jeff heard a background sound against which the dah-dit was becoming less pronounced. The controller then moved the plane out of this bi-signal zone and directly onto the beam whereupon a solid monotone filled Jeff's headphones.

The operator continued across the beam at right angles toward the A quadrant. Moving through another bi-signal zone and into an A quadrant produced a blend of background tone through which a dit-dah could be heard which eventually gave way to a clear series of dit-dah, dit-dah, dit-dah. So far so good.

As Jeff and the operator started returning to the beam they had just crossed, the signal changed to a Morse code identifier of several letters: the station identifier code, something which would be very important to confirm, especially in the Sacramento area where there were several range stations. When the identifier had been broadcast, they were in the bi-signal zone, essentially a sound with dit-dahs giving way to a stronger, solid tone once the beam had been reached again. Jeff and his operator quickly turned outbound from the station when they were firmly established back on the beam. Jeff was warned not to readjust the volume control since interpreting the build and fade intensity of the signal was an integral element of using the system. And, he should never select automatic volume control when flying the beam. As they flew away from the station, the obvious happened; the signal slowly began to fade.

Jeff was then shown what happened when the pointer made a 180 degree turn and tracked inbound. The volume increased. Soon, they would fly over the station, and when they got close, there was a rapid build up of the signal, fast fade, then another build up, followed by a fade. They had just flown over the top of the station, or passed through the "cone of silence." Jeff was also shown the sequence of signals that would occur when he flew a circle around the transmitters.

Jeff then got into the jeep, turned the station selector switch to range and set the volume control to the audible minimum. The operator then took Jeff through essentially the same exercise by telling him to fly certain headings and asking him where he thought he was.

Up to this point, the exercise had been simple — the best of all worlds since the subject of wind had not been addressed. The inbound and outbound headings of all range legs were printed on maps, but could not be flown except in a dead calm. To quickly compensate for wind, Jeff had to learn beam bracketing which would be one of his first exercises aloft in the Six. Beam bracketing was a deductive matter of determining which heading off the known bearing of a range would keep the cadet's plane solidly in the beam. In practice it amounted to a quick series of zigs and zags off the known course until that process of elimination produced a heading which did not drive the plane into the bi-signal area. If Jeff's actual inbound leg to a range station might have been 60 degrees, he may have experimented with 40 degrees and 46 degrees before finding that 52 degrees was just right. In practice, he would also learn that flying dead-center on a beam was not the accepted technique, but flying slightly to the right of center was preferred for traffic spacing reasons. Rather quickly, Jeff learned to bracket the beam by sound alone without mechanically resorting to the numbers.

The second subject after beam bracketing and its variations had been mastered was making procedure turns off range legs. These turns would form the basis for holding patterns and instrument approaches to airports. The value of all the BT-13 under-the-hood time, with its turns to assigned headings, timed turns, and descents, quickly became obvious. Completing a good procedure turn consisted of nothing more than turning 45 degrees off the beam, holding that heading for a minute, making a standard rate turn away from the station for one minute, rolling out on a heading reciprocal to the turn just made off the beam, and then intercepting the beam and flying toward the station.

More often than not, an instrument approach to a field would not involve a straight-in track to a runway. The typical approach would be a circling one, assuming that at the end of the timed descent the field could be seen. If at the end of the approach, the field could not be seen, cadets were taught how to miss the approach and return to the airway to hold.

Armed with the sure-fire means of identifying a range station by its Morse code did not preclude the possibility of a cadet becoming confused as just where his position was in location to range transmitters. Hearing an "N" only told Jeff that he was in one of two N quadrants. He was expected to quickly make his way to the station by the most efficient means possible.

To do that, he was taught several techniques including the most practicable, the average bisector/true fade method whose success required only a good ear and some fast arithmetic. Using the range station at Williams, which he had overflown on his first cross country, Jeff looked up the frequency (326 kc), tuned it in, heard the identifier, dit-dah-dah/dah-dah-dah, and averaged the inbound courses on the legs bordering the two N quadrants. The resulting heading, 245 degrees, would take him straight to the station. Or, directly away from it. Jeff would be able to tell whether his heading was to or from by the signal's gaining strength or fading.

In the navigationally imperfect real world, the radio range system possessed a few inherent flaws as the cadets were about to discover. Due to the weather, quirks of individual range stations, proximity to cities, mountains, or magnetic deposits, beams could bend, undulate, split to create multiple courses, or momentarily disappear or fade.

In 1941, the United States airway network was built around roughly
275 range stations.[1] Many of the newer range facilities included a fifth
transmitter and were known as Adcock stations. They had voice transmission capability and, in addition to communications with aircraft, also
broadcast weather reports on regular intervals. Most of the range stations close to Mather Field (Sacramento, Oakland, Williams, Red Bluff,
and Reno) were Adcock facilities.

Armed with the basics of flying the beam, the first 42-B cadets went
for their first dual orientation on radio navigation in the BTs on New
Year's Day afternoon following their cross country up to Williams that

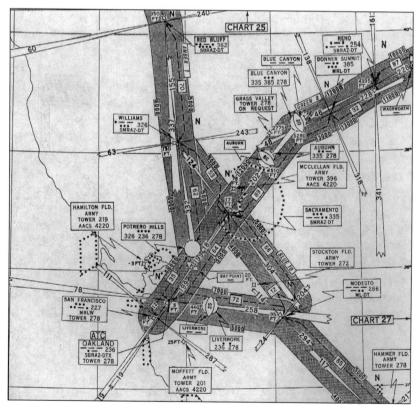

National Archives

*Early 1942 equivalent of a current San Francisco Terminal Area chart show-
ing airway radio facilities available to Mather cadets.*

morning. The pace was picking up. A longer, dual cross country from Mather to Corning, Colusa and return was flown over the weekend in the Six using range stations at Williams, Red Bluff, and Sacramento. Night checkouts on the Six started after the weekend and consisted of one hour dual followed by three hours solo. Their Link sessions in January were exercises utilizing their new beam flying skills. Since the Jeep could be "programmed" in a rudimentary sense, cadets might be told to "fly" up to Reno via the Green Eight airway. To do so in the Six would require a climb to 11,000 feet to get over the Sierra, but at 87 feet above sea level in the Link, they could fly from Mather to the Sacramento range station, fly outbound on the northeast leg, tune in, identify and intercept the Donner Summit range station, and do the same for the last leg into Reno. To make it interesting, the Link operator could have had Jeff hold ten minutes east of the Auburn fan marker to wait for further clearance.

The second week in January was devoted largely to solo formation flying; Jeff and Charlie had received a quick refresher on formation flying with an instructor in the backseat between Christmas and New Year's Day. By mid-January they each logged 12 hours formation flying in the Six and had flown a roundtrip up to Redding using the radio facilities at Williams and Red Bluff. It was during this period that Charlie was able to reprise his cadet experiences in a remarkable, printed letter to friends.

Air Corps Advanced Flying School,
Mather Field, California
January 11, 1942

To my friends everywhere:

In desperation, I turn to the mimeograph to cut the Gordian knot of my correspondence problem. To those whose Christmas cards, Christmas presents, cards of inquiry, letters that have not moved as rapidly as Uncle Sam has moved me, and to those who, though perhaps not recent correspondents, yet in the past have seemed interested in what I am doing and thinking — I send my warmest greetings.

With some of you, this letter will seem too impersonal and distant. Please understand that with the war, a speed up in our schedule has naturally occurred, and the resulting jumble of plans, formulations, rumors, orders, and schedules has severely cut down on the impulse to do things like writing letters which normally come from leisure time well spent.

Much of what I could tell you consists of an aviation cadet's routine as he moves onward through the training program. All this you have seen, or if you haven't, you can see in the various movies, books, and articles about this branch of the service. I shall not bother you with this material. Another phase of our life that many of you would like to know about consists of the rougher side, the things that drive a man in the army to become what everyone expects a soldier to be. The details are comic, tragic, lurid, gory, noble, boisterous, disgusting or pathetic — as you wish.

I will not write about this, even though it is a part of being in the Army that must appeal, in a way, to any fellow, or to those whose interest may be secondary without being at all desultory. Plenty more could be said about this gangling, growing, changing organization as seen from the inside during some of its most turbulent years. I can say but very little of it though.

There are a few things that have occurred to me as being of special interest to the outsider, things that perhaps you haven't heard yet, or haven't heard properly. Please excuse me now, while I ramble on about several phases of the Army Air Corps training program as one member of Class 42-B has felt them. Few of you know a great deal about the sensations of flying; that is, of the pilot himself. I shall introduce you to some of these.

The takeoff, that moment when the throttle is being opened gradually to its full forward position, is an exciting moment, one of power and tension. The airplane, you see, is a creature of two mediums. King of the air, it deigns to stay on the ground only through condescension to petty physical needs. The takeoff is its last snort of disdain as it springs forward, shortly climbing into its rightful place in the air. Once there, it settles back, becoming once more what it will admit to be on the ground — small fry. Somewhat akin to the lesser fleas, every plane sooner or later must dip a wing to a larger plane or formation. Even the B-19 would be forced to yield to a formation of Flying Fortresses.

The takeoff is one place where speed is a definite sensation. Yet speed alone is not nearly the strain on one's nerve, as speed is in the presence of other speeding objects — the difference, say, driving along the Pittsburgh — Harrisburg

Dream Highway and coming out of New York City on the Pulaski Skyway during the Saturday afternoon rush hour. This last is comparable to the end of a flying day when forty or fifty planes are all trying to land on the same field or runway. Naturally, all traffic is organized; nevertheless, as one takes his plane into the crowded pattern, he becomes part of a giant swarm returning to its hive, with a thousand things to do with his hands, feet, eyes, and ears as he attempts to keep out of the way of other planes trying to get in and, at the same time, prepare his plane for landing. Every homecoming becomes an event.

One question asked by every non-flying person of the pilot is, "Have you ever blacked out?" There is something deliciously sinister in the question. The same question in another day, one feels, would have been, "Hast thou slain a dragon, Sir?" To answer the first question — yes, as have most or all of my classmates. A blackout is a matter of degree. In any maneuver where the pilot's body is thrown toward the floor of his plane by centrifugal force, the blood will begin to leave his head and he will begin to black out. It is similar to the last few tenths of a second before a faint. Your body becomes very heavy; you have to strain to hold your head in the right spot — otherwise it will be pulled forward, backward, or to one side.

Visually, the effect is much like a fadeout in the movies — the sky turns from blue or white to a grayish color, then this gray deepens, depending on the degree of the blackout. A partial blackout is much more interesting than a complete one since, in the latter, one is unconscious for a few seconds and so loses the continuity of the experience. If repeated too often, of course, it can be a physically harmful experience.

The reverse experience — I know of no name for it — is quite as peculiar, but never the object of inquiries. This is that condition where a steady and firm forward pressure is applied to the stick. It is the speedier counterpart of going over a small hill in the car, or even over the high spot in a roller coaster. If done violently, the sensation is nothing but an uncomfortable upward jerk.

Done smoothly, however, the pilot's body gradually lifts off the seat until the resultant upward and the downward force is zero. The body is then, as it were, weightless. I have never been a ghost, but I know now how one feels. By placing an object in one's hand, one can multiply the peculiar results of this "light out" phenomenon. The objects will float in the air just above the palm, moving neither upward nor downward, as if controlled by some supernatural force. I've never tried an outside loop where upward forces are comparable to the downward forces it takes to produce a blackout are exerted on the body.

Unquestionably the most esoteric of our experiences are those with the clouds. For the earth bound hoi polloi, clouds are things that you look at from a distance. Like celebrities, they are to be gaped at, admired, and talked about, but that is all. The pilot can be much more intimate with them. Boswell-like, he cannot materially affect their development, but he does become part of their inner workings and revels in the infinite variability of their changing contours.

We younger pilots are not yet on speaking terms with the high silky or fleece-like clouds that hover five and six miles above the earth. Nor are any but the most foolhardy or unfortunate among us intimates of the towering cumulonimbus, the Wotan of the skies, the dangerous thunderheads. Practically all other rain cloud types, however, are within our immediate circle of acquaintances, none more so than those puffs of cotton you see floating around — the delightful cumulus of fair weather.

If a large cloud bank has broken up into these numerous small clouds, one can buzz around them, like a hummingbird or yellowjacket in a field of daisies. If the parcels of clouds are larger, the effect is more like that of a pigeon in lower Manhattan. I might say that all such buzzing of clouds is against flying regulations, but there are few cadets or instructors who haven't yielded to the impulse to do so once in a while.

Solo, it is a glorious experience. First, circling around to make sure another plane isn't in the vicinity, one can zoom up over the peaks, slither through the canyons and crevasses, bank around the outer edges, attempt to cut off the tops of the isolated pillars only to find out that the plane has no visible effect, and generally get the feeling of speed and movement which, on clear blue days, is nearly absent because of the lack of semi-stationary references.

Even more beautiful, in a fantastic sort of way, is a rat-race in the clouds. A rat-race is a game of follow-the-leader, used as an intermission on long formation flights to relieve the tedium of formation work, and is most enjoyable when done over one of those large cloud continents that may stretch for forty or fifty miles in all directions and vary in thickness from a few hundred feet to perhaps twenty thousand feet. The leader will take the formation over the cloud bank and peel off, the other planes following in succession at five second intervals.

There follows a furious race in and around the cloud. Almost beyond description, one gets the impression of monstrous eagles in their wildest moments ever played like this — with snap rolls and half rolls over the cloud peaks, slow rolls and Immelmann turns up through the narrow cloud canyons, speeds of from sixty to three hundred miles an hour as these seemingly irresponsible silver devils turn and swerve and bank and zoom, striving to keep in line with each other while they thread their way around the bulging whiteness of this enormous playground, this dazzling Valhalla.

Please do not imagine that any but a small part of our work as aviation cadets consists of such veritable flights of fantasy as these. I tell you simply to let you know some of the high spots, the creme de la creme, of our work.

I had planned also to include in this letter some reflections on army life with special reference to the sociological side — the problems of morale and organization. Moreover, I wanted to tell you how I feel about this war (thinking you might be interested in a view of the feelings from inside the army), and particularly how I believe it affects the problem of the California Japanese, or in its larger aspects, the development of the American spirit. Each of these, I now see, is a letter in itself. All three have rankled in my breast for several months and I know I shall not feel comfortable until I've gotten them out of my system by reducing them to writing; but not here.

Again, I beg your indulgence for resorting to the mimeograph to reach each of you — I can only plead that you have, collectively, swamped me before I could catch my breath. It has only been through the kindness of the W.S. Brant family, who invited my roommate and me to dinner one night, and the use of the machine in Mr. Brant's office in the Weaver Tractor Company Building in Sacramento, not to mention the aid of his daughter, Sue, that I have been able to do this.

This letter has been written during odd moments on the flight line, while fog or the vagaries of the flight schedule have kept me on the ground. We are all trying hard to get in our time, in spite of sunny California's winter fogs, hoping to be ready to graduate and receive our commissions on February twenty-third.

You don't know how much I would like then to make the rounds of my friends and show them my uniform, my gold bars, and most of all, my wings. Actually, I'm wondering if I can show them to my fiancée; for along with many other cadets, I have to hope for marriage soon, not plan on it. But, there's work to be done, so many things will have to wait.

Till such a time I can see you and talk with you, please accept my warmest greetings. And do keep writing (at Hiram, if you're unable to follow me around very closely), won't you?

My best to you all,

Charlie

Six days after Reynard sent that letter, morning radio listeners heard some bad news, and for TWA and the Jack Frye Four-Engine School the news was terrible. TWA's Flight Three had crashed into Mount Potosi 35 miles southwest of Las Vegas the night before with all souls lost. What made the disaster particularly newsworthy, from the American public's viewpoint, was one of the passengers: actress Carole Lombard, wife of the cinema idol, Clark Gable.

The reason for the DC-3's crash has never been determined. Lombard was returning to Burbank from a spectacularly successful war bond tour and resisted being bumped off the flight which had passed through Albuquerque. As a result of being on the bond tour, she had a high priority since she was traveling on direct presidential orders, the highest priority of all. Several other passengers were removed, but not a group which also had a high priority: that party consisted of recent graduates of the Jack Frye Four-Engine School. Those pilots and their crews were on their way to the west coast headquarters of the Ferry Command, and would have very shortly been flying B-24s from San Diego to squadrons all over the country.

By mid-January, cadets were building solo time with short solo hops to Oroville and Woodland plus longer cross countries downstate to Merced and Madera. Some of the day solo time qualified as instrument hours since they were under-the-hood buddy rides with the guy in back serving as a safety pilot. Redding, Fresno and Merced were destinations for the first formation cross countries and night solo cross countries.

Airways, like the interstate highway system, were all coded by number, but also had a color designator. Both Redding and Fresno were on

*Although photographed over Texas later in the war, this shot shows why Charlie exalted in AT-6 rat races.*

the Amber One airway, but cadets were taught alternate means of night navigation in case their radios failed. That back up system was the network of "light lines" which was superimposed over the airways. At intervals marked on aeronautical charts, there were symbols for rotating white beacons. If the pilot were on course, he would also see a red light blinking in Morse code every ten miles. There was a sequence in the code consisting of W, U, V, H, R, K, D, B, G, and M. Naturally, cadets quickly picked up the memory jogger for the light lines which ran, "When Undertaking Very Hard Routes, Keep Direction By Good Methods."

For the occasional cadet who panicked or became disoriented at night, airfields were marked by rotating beacons which alternated between green and white lights. If the white light were split, appearing as two flashes, it represented a military airport with which California's central valley was becoming well populated by early 1942.

Although radio navigation and cross countries dominated advanced, aerobatic flying was not ignored. The T-6 was a particularly good aerobatic trainer which didn't require diving to build up entry speeds, and many 42-B cadets reveled in looping and rolling as an end unto itself. Aerobatic practice was essential since all of the basic maneuvers learned at primary were the subjects of stage checks with instructors.

The Link trainer also introduced another dimension of radio navigation: the radio compass. A needle, against a 360 degree dial, pointed at the transmitter to which the aircraft's receiver had been tuned. If Jeff

National Archives

*Sixes at six o'clock. Class 42-B cadets at Mather went through a multi-engine curriculum on a single-engine airplane, the AT-6A advanced trainer, because twin-engine trainers were not available in sufficient numbers in late 1941.*

had his Six aimed directly at the station, the pointer remained on the zero indication. Tickling the rudder pedals produced deviations of a few degrees in either direction. Passing over a station resulted in the pointer promptly rotating and coming to rest at 180 degrees. By keeping the pointer on zero, Jeff would eventually fly to the transmitter. In reality, he might not arrive there in a straight line unless a wind correction angle had been introduced, but that was easily mastered, not unlike bracketing the beam had been several weeks before. And, instrument approaches were much simpler and more precise due to the azimuth card in the radio compass indicator. Radio compass navigation was, however, little more than an introduction at advanced since flying on the beam completely dominated navigation instruction. Practical use of the radio compass would become an important aspect at transition school after graduation from Mather.

There was a welcome benefit to radio navigation. The T-6 receivers picked up not only the conventional range transmitters, but commercial broadcast stations as well. Thus, while practicing aloft, Mather cadets could tune in most of Sacramento's stations (KFBK, KPO, KGO, KROY, or KFRC) and listen to such early 1942 hits as Tommy Dorsey's *This Love of Mine*, *You Made Me Love You* with Harry James, or the latest news commentaries.[2]

Five hundred air miles to the north from Mather Field, on January 27th, Philip Macomber's troop train reached its destination: Pendleton, Oregon, which was home to the newly built Pendleton Army Air Field. The 34th Bomb Group arrived at its new base, located on a high plateau west of town, at the end of a record setting cold spell.[3] The group's new B-17s were about to start anti-submarine patrols off the Oregon coast.

When Philip Macomber got off the train, Irish Prime Minister Eamon deValera had just issued a statement protesting the arrival of a second contingent of American troops in Northern Ireland. On the other side of the world, in the Philippines, American troops were in retreat, and the Japanese were within 40 miles of Singapore. The naval battle of Maccassar Strait, however, had produced some encouragement for the Allies. Postwar analysis of Japanese records would show that American claims of 28 Japanese ships sunk were wildly inflated. But, in Burma, the Flying Tigers had just severely mauled a 40-plane Japanese bombing formation as it approached Rangoon.

In North Africa's see-saw battles, the British were in retreat again

Photo courtesy of Eloise Macomber Hatfield
*Philip Macomber with his mother, Cora, and
dog, Fritz, when he left home for the last time
in January 1942.*

after having taken Benghasi in the last week of December. The only
bright spot in Britain's North African operations was the most raided
place on earth: Malta. The island fortress was still hanging tough on
January 27th after enduring its 1,300th air raid in two years.

At the Pan American conference in Rio de Janeiro, a development
which would directly affect nearly a dozen of Jeffries' and Reynard's
classmates had just been announced; Brazil was breaking off diplomatic
relations with Germany, Japan and Italy.

Not all of the war news was far away: just the day before the 34th
arrived in Oregon, the Norwegian tanker, *Varanger*, had been sunk by a
German sub just 35 miles off the New Jersey coast, and the American
ore carrier, *Venore*, was sunk off North Carolina's Outer Banks.

In the dead of winter, sporting news was limited, but one game got every basketball fan's attention. The University of Oregon had just defeated Oregon State 45 to 37 to claim second place to the University of Washington in the Pacific Coast conference.

Philip Macomber could relate to Pendleton, Oregon, with its nearby forests, agricultural base, and mountains. As he arrived, farmers were concerned about grain and milk prices. The retail price of a quart of milk had just been set by the Pendleton Dairyman's Association at 14 cents a quart. Unatilla County farmers were also concerned about labor shortages and the availability of storage facilities, including burlap grain bags for what was anticipated to be a bumper crop year. As the 34th Bomb Group was moving into brand new barracks, Acting Price Administrator Leon Henderson in Washington had just been given power to ration commodities sold at retail. Nationwide, stores were starting rationing on their own due to shopper runs on sugar.

Although Pendleton in 1942 was much larger than Jay, Maine, it was not a large town. Pendleton had one radio station ("The 1000 watt voice of the Columbia Empire, 1420 on your dial"), one newspaper, and could not boast of a large entertainment district with as many theaters as had been available to Westover service men in Springfield, Massachusetts. Being intimately familiar with aircraft construction and identification, men of the 34th Bomb Group would have chuckled had they had time for the film which opened at the Rivolo on the day after they arrived. *International Squadron* featured several of the leading civilian sport planes superficially painted and modified to resemble the latest British interceptors. The film, based on the three American Eagle Squadrons in the Royal Air Force, featured a popular, young actor whose real future was in politics. His name was Ronald Reagan.

The 34th Bomb Group had no time for movies during its first week in Pendleton. Pendleton was very much an operational base, and the unit had to unpack, put new planes into service and start flying daily anti-submarine patrols. The Group's arrival went unpublicized in contrast to the coverage which frequently attended aviation cadet training classes. Also unpublicized was the Pendleton departure of several aircraft shortly after Philip arrived. Elements of the 17th Bomb Group took off in their B-25 Mitchells for Columbia, South Carolina.[4] These crews would subsequently undertake very specialized training in Florida and become widely known in April as Jimmy Doolittle's Tokyo Raiders.

Pendleton, like Westover, was a major, recently completed installation with good facilities. Here, the Group got new B-17s directly from the Boeing plant in Seattle, and Philip got his initial ride in one of them, a flight which convinced him that a job as flight engineer was the way to go because it combined this exciting flying game with what he knew best, mechanics. And, it was almost as much fun as riding his motorcycle. He found flying in the '17 to be exhilarating and intoxicating. It was flying in one of the "ultimate" aircraft of all time (it still is).

Strapped in, his reactions were those of anybody who has flown in a Fortress for the first time. He listened to an inertial starter's whine in what amounts to a mechanical groan, followed by cranking of the number three engine (right inner) and the "chur, chur, chir, chir" of turning blades. Then a cough, not quite a splutter, a brief "clattering" and an uneven, throaty roar as the engine comes to life while sending shudders throughout the ship. Blue-white smoke pours from the exhaust, just wisps at first, then followed by a cloud which quickly dissipates in the propwash as the engine sound starts to smooth out, but still doesn't lose its cyclical, repetitious quality at low rpm.

Some of the smoke seeps into the fuselage through the bomb bay doors to add another element to the experience. Tremors run through every sinew of the Fortress — vibration makes it come alive, eager to roll. The vibration and noise increase as each of the three remaining engines is started. Everything is quivering — the ammunition boxes and belts, waist guns, radio sets, oxygen tanks, control cables, fire extinguishers, and both of the little tables, the radio operator's and navigator's.

Suddenly, but briefly, there's a new sound — something between a whine and whir, almost like a little, muted horn screeching. Alarming when heard for the very first time, it is the sound of the auxiliary hydraulic pump coming on to maintain pressure for the system which supplies power to the brakes.

The left outer engine is revved up at the same time the right main gear brake squeals — the Fortress turns to the right. Brakes and engines steer the plane through the turns, and soon it's down at the end of the taxiway for the runup, and then a new crescendo rises from the engines as the '17 is rolling down the runway with throttles and prop controls all forward for maximum power. The sensation of power and acceleration is "awesome" in the fullest sense of that overworked word.

The noise and vibration are fused into one dimension which will shortly be joined by the third player in this multi-sensory adventure: momentum. Call it energy. It is everywhere in the Fortress.

The noise is very, very loud — almost deafening at full power. The radial engine sound is unique. A throbbing, rumbling roar — not the growling snarl of a liquid cooled V-12, like the Rolls Royce Merlin or Allison, but more like a bass chorus singing at the top of its lungs. It is felt as much as heard in what is a profoundly visceral experience.

The only thing that might be comparable is standing on a diesel locomotive as it is brought up to full power, but even that is tame and uni-dimensional in comparison. The sound is not just heard, it is experienced to the core of one's being. Heart, lungs, muscles, joints, bones, brain, and inner self are all subject to the pulsations which reverberate through every bulkhead, former, rib, stringer, longeron, rivet, cable, spar, tank, and aluminum sheet in this great craft. The event fuses man and machine into one creature.

National Archives

*The Boeing B-17 Flying Fortress, "Queen of the Skies."*

On takeoff, the '17 literally levitates — the nose is not really lowered as with nearly all other tailwheel aircraft — it just flies itself off with the pilot's hands only maintaining a firm grip on the control wheel. There is little sensation of becoming airborne since the change in sound and vibration remains almost constant during the transition to flight.

This majestic airplane is a "taildragger" as were most planes when it sprang from the drawing boards nearly 70 years ago. Only after the '17 becomes airborne and transitions to cruising configuration does one have the sense of being level. Indeed, being on the ground tends to insult one's sense of equilibrium and suggests that this great craft really wants to be in its natural element, that great wild, blue yonder. Feeling the changes in attitude, which are more pronounced in a tailwheel aircraft, does capture more of the "seat of the pants" orientation than in modern tricycle gear aircraft.

The Flying Fortress was not designed for creature comfort; hence the basic lack of sound and vibration dampening materials. Philip's getting from place to place in the '17 was an experience in itself — from the radio compartment "amidships" through a bulkhead into the bomb bay, onto the narrow catwalk and tip-toeing about ten feet to the back of the flight deck through another bulkhead (without concern that the only thing between Philip and *terra firma* 2000 feet below is the catwalk itself and the bomb bay doors).

Emerging from the bomb bay puts one adjacent to the top turret platform, and immediately beyond that is a gap, almost like a cubbyhole, between the pilot and copilot seats through which one crawls to arrive in the nose section. That is dominated by the navigator's station, bombardier's stool and bombsight just in back of the plexiglas nose which provides a stunning, panoramic view to the front.

There's equipment everywhere in this ship: fire extinguishers, oxygen tanks, portable oxygen bottles, oxygen regulators, machine guns, ammunition boxes with linked belts snaking their way to the guns, flare pouches, radio panels, restraint harness straps, piping, cables, first aid kits, and other items hidden from view in boxes and canvas bags. It is not a place for the claustrophobic, especially in a bygone era when the fuselage would also have carried 10 men with their parachutes, Mae Wests, radio headsets with cords, plugs and mikes, goggles, oxygen masks and hoses, steel helmets, and flak vests, not to mention leather flying suits, boots, and aviator's kit bags.

The sky invades the Fortress and vice versa. There is the sound of the slipstream "whooosshhing" past. The wind whistles in through slits in the turrets, open windows, and crevices in gunports. The air rushes by at 160 mph — best felt in the radio compartment where the gunner's hatch can be removed. Sunlight glints on some surfaces, is diffracted by windows, and reflections appear elsewhere. To the good earth below, the '17 casts a mighty shadow.

From all stations, it is an electrifying experience. Looking out from the radio compartment top hatch is a fabulous way of communing with the sky. Even better is standing tall to look out, and learning the full meaning of the word "slipstream." The top turret, which would have been Philip's secondary position, has an excellent view, maybe the best of all. The view from the bombardier's stool is breathtaking. Dominating all of it are those four Wright Cyclone engines — with oil smears here and there, and red hot gases escaping from the exhaust pipes which Philip cannot see beneath the engines.

A deep bank reveals that the turning radius is not as wide as might be expected for such a great ship. The '17 flies gracefully, borne on well-shaped wings and guided by the large ailerons, elevators and distinctive rudder which cleave the air so effectively that the Fortress' course and stability are easily assured.

To look out a window — sunlight glinting on propeller arcs, those great wings, with blue sky, fleecy clouds in an evening sky beginning to promise a silvery, rose-hued sapphire sunset, and the Oregon mountains below and beyond. That WAS flying.

Sadly, Philip's first flight cannot last forever. In keeping with its pedigree, the Fortress' approach and landing are graceful events — to be savored since the adventure is almost over. Those signs that betray the imminent return to earth, that is the sound of landing gear lowering and the flaps coming down, are muted against the engines' strong presence, but, soon, that too is a softer chant.

So quickly, the '17 is over the fence, flaring out over the end of the runway, holding off, and finally settling down into a smooth three point landing. Knowing precisely when it becomes reunited with earth is masked by the engines' sweet song and the vibrations which seem to say they savor their way of postponing assurance that man and ship have again become prisoners of gravity. The 17 is majestic — truly living up to its top billing as "Queen of the Skies."

Had Philip lived longer, he would have experienced the downside too, not just being shot at, but the reality of flights other than a lovely 45 minute excursion during an Oregon evening — the bone chilling cold at altitude, the monotonous, eternal drone of engines, instrument flights where visibility barely transcends the wingtips, gut-tumbling turbulence, aching joints from being cooped up in a cold, damp machine for hours on end, gnawing fear that he might not be able to fix something that went wrong in flight, and light-headed sweats induced by climbing into a heat-absorbing contrivance that's been sitting for so long on the midday, sunbaked macadam.

By the second week in February at Mather, it was clear that everybody still in the program would graduate, and, with that realization, McCurry Studios, Burt Hodson (in the Odd Fellows Building), Glen Fishback and the other portrait studios in Sacramento were about to do another round in the land office business from Mather cadets wanting pictures taken. Cadets bought new uniforms and insignia in anticipation of the big day using their graduation clothing allowance: $150 (two months full pay). Like many other cadets, Jeff bought a few extra items: a miniature set of

Photo courtesy of Mary Reynard MacArthur

*Aviation Cadet Charles O. Reynard, Jr. on the Mather flight line in front of an AT-6A.*

wings for Mary and the finest set of silver wings available for his mother. On those solid, sterling silver wing's reverse side were engraved the words, "Mother, from Roland. February 20, 1942." Her boy had indeed flown high and truly become the star of the Jeffries family.

The original graduation had been planned as a formal ceremony on Monday, February 23rd. However, the teletype clattered out new instructions which called for the graduation to be advanced to early on Friday the 20th. Thus, most families and guests were not part of the program which was hurriedly held in the base theater. As each name was called, a cadet marched forward, climbed the steps, walked to center stage, and received his certificate and wings.

There was one humorous glitch in the ceremony involving two roommates who, arriving back on base late, frantically put on new uniforms to get to the ceremony on time. They just barely made it, but unfortunately had grabbed the wrong uniforms. The first new officer marched across the stage amidst a few stifled snickers. His blouse was comically short and much too baggy. His trouser cuffs hung at nearly mid-calf. The occasional giggle erupted into guffaws when the tall, slender cadet's short, stocky roommate soon marched across the stage in a too-tight blouse that bottomed out nearly at his knees with pant legs all bunched up at his feet. Both cadets became bomber pilots in the Pacific, were decorated for valor, survived the war, and later retired as colonels.

At the conclusion of the ceremony, cadets pinned their wings on each other. Their services were urgently needed elsewhere, and by Monday, many of them were on their way to new stations.

To celebrate the wings and commissioning ceremony, a dinner dance was held at the Senator Hotel in Sacramento on the evening of the 20th. Fiancées and girlfriends arrived, and local dates were to join in the celebration. Mather cadets, who dined well on base, continued the tradition at the Senator that night, although the trappings were more elegant. Leading off the menu were California fruit cocktail, potage St. Germaine, and garden green salad with French dressing. The main course was Omaha corn-fed beef (U.S. Choice), string beans au poivre and potatoes au gratin. Dinner concluded with sherbet, cookies and coffee.

Three members of 42-B were remembered posthumously in the silver-inked souvenir program — they had been killed several weeks before in flying accidents. One perished on a night cross country, and although the wreckage was found, no precise cause could be established. Could it have been spatial disorientation that caused a classic stall/spin accident? There was no question about the other accident. Two cadets were out over Lake Tahoe on a T-6 buddy ride. Buzzing the summer home of a girlfriend's family, they failed to pull up in time, hit some trees on an island, and then cartwheeled into the lake. It was a case of irresponsibility, failure to allow for the Six's different performance at Tahoe's higher elevation, and target fixation exacerbated by the distortion in depth perception common to flying too low over calm water.

The wreckage was recovered, trucked back to Mather, put on display, and made the subject of an assembly at which the 139 cadets of 42-B were again reminded of the consequences of joyriding.

What was to be a festive, graduation day got off to a bad start when two twin-engine trainers from Mather's navigators' school collided during a formation flight and fell not far from the field. Three of the four occupants were able to bail out successfully, but one flier's parachute became tangled in the wreckage, and he was carried down to his death. It was not the only incident. A B-25 Mitchell crashed up in Washington state at McChord Field. Two were killed and three were injured. And closer, near Los Angeles, a Lockheed Hudson went in with both pilots killed. Those accidents were only in the West Coast air forces, not to mention the rest of the country.

Elsewhere, the news was almost exclusively bad as well. A Japanese fleet was reported off Burma, and Japanese planes were again over Darwin, Australia, and Mandalay, in Burma. One of the Kincheloes' favorite weekend getaway spots, the Island of Bali, had just been invaded by the Japanese. February 20th sinkings on the East Coast included a Brazilian freighter, the *Orinda*, whose cargo included castor and cocoa beans. Some precious cargos were getting through, eastbound too, including a human one. Due to the bravery of one Canadian destroyer which placed itself between an attacking German sub's torpedoes and a troopship, hundreds of recently trained Royal Canadian Air Force pilots were able to reach Scotland on February 20th. Only seven of the destroyer's crew of 100 survived.

And on this February 20th, a relatively obscure Army brigadier general best known for his former role as an aide to General Douglas MacArthur, was advanced from chief of staff of the Third Army in Texas to Chief of War Plans for the General Staff in Washington. His name was Dwight D. Eisenhower.

The graduation dance band played on and included a few Glen Miller tunes. Over that weekend, the real Glen Miller was riding high on the charts with the number one and two hits, *Moonlight Cocktail* and *A String of Pearls*. On the radio, Bing Crosby was singing *Deep in the Heart of Texas*, but Dinah Shore's soft Tennessee voice was moving two songs ever skyward, *Blues in the Night* and another wartime classic, *I Don't Want To Walk Without You*. Kate Smith was stirring American audiences with *The White Cliffs Of Dover*, a song that reminded America that its British ally was then into its third year of war.

At that stage of the program, cadets had to be single. The barrier came down with commissioning, and more than just a few cadets were married over the weekend. Although Elizabeth could not come out to California, Charlie's sister, Mary, drove up from Los Angeles for the weekend and Mary Casey came out from Kansas City. Jeff gave his Mary the beautiful pair of miniature silver wings, and they stood up with another couple who were married on Saturday.

The international news over the weekend did little to brighten post-party spirits even though the Allies had given the Axis a few lumps. The back and forth battle in North Africa resulted in the Germans withdrawing west of Tobruk. American and British fighter pilots in Burma were shooting down more than they lost, and the Russians were claiming victories in the Crimea, although paying a terrible price in manpower. German battleships were on the move; the *Tirpitz* was headed to Norway where it could menace Allied North Atlantic convoys. German submarines had a good weekend off the American east coast. The Norwegian tanker *Kongagaard*, the American tanker *Pan Massachusetts*, and another American tanker in the Caribbean were sunk.

# PART III

# RENDEZVOUS
# WITH
# TRAGEDY

# XVII

# THE ROAD TO KIRTLAND

> I've won the right to wear these silver wings
> And see the many awesome sights
> Of which the poet sings.
> I've earned a place among the gods of flight
> Under the sun and moon's eternal light...
>
> From *Silver Wings* by Marvin Peterson

"Hurry up and wait" best describes how Lts. Jeffries and Reynard graduated from pilot training. All of the 42-B advanced flying school programs had been accelerated in order to get more newly graduated pilots out into the Training and Combat Commands as quickly as possible. Many of the nine advanced flying schools operating in early 1942 were located in the Sunbelt and had no problem meeting the new deadlines since their flying schools enjoyed better weather than the two in California's central valley. California's Mather and Stockton were subject to ground fogs which seriously delayed daily flying schedules.

On February 20th, 35 of the brand new 2nd Lts. were ordered to report to the commanding officer of the Air Corps Basic Flying School at Lemoore, California, for duty as flight instructors in BT-13s. Another large group was sent to the Second Air Force for assignment to new heavy bomber groups or to other flying schools as flight instructors.

The Training Command also obtained the services of ten new pilots who were ordered to the Air Corps Flexible Gunnery School at McCarran Field, Reno, Nevada. Those men would start logging substantial time in AT-6s which had been modified with the addition of machine guns in the rear seats for training air gunners stationed in bomber waist and radio compartments.

Eleven pilots were ordered to the Air Corps Advanced Flying School at Albuquerque, New Mexico. Several of these men mistakenly assumed that they were being sent to the four-engine school there, but that was not the case. Rather, they were headed for Albuquerque and a checkout in the twin-engine Beech AT-11 employed by the Advanced School that trained bombardiers, not pilots. Most of these men, after gaining valuable hours flying bombardier trainees, would eventually go to the Pacific war as heavy bomber pilots.

Thirty-four pilots, including Jeffries and Reynard, were ordered on Friday, February 20th to remain at Mather Field "pending issuance of orders transferring them to other commands." Orders were considered secret. Thus, many of the cadets were not aware of where everybody was being sent. Indeed, decades could pass before a cadet might learn of the whereabouts or death of a close friend.

Elsewhere, General Ira Eaker arrived in the UK with six staff officers as one of the first steps which would initiate creation of the Eighth Army Air Force. There was no aerial action in the Pacific that day, but American light bombers were retreating from the Philippines as their ground crews remained behind. The 7th Bombardment Group (Heavy) arrived in Australia from Fiji as other American heavy bombardment squadrons left Australia for India. Among those leaving was the 11th Bombardment Squadron (Heavy) which flew B-17s. That was Hal Blackburn's old squadron. The 11th subsequently became a medium bomber squadron flying B-25 Mitchells and fought with great distinction in the China-Burma-India theater for the balance of the war.

Over the weekend, Major General George Brett, who was in command of all Allied Air Forces in the Southwest Pacific, announced the decision to withdraw the Fifth Air Force and American troops from Java. During the withdrawal, American heavy bombers flew numerous strikes against Japanese shipping and ground targets, but the effort failed to delay the enemy invasion of Java.

Howard Kincheloe and his wife had just arrived in the United States after catching the last ship out of Soerabaja, the *M.S. Noordam*, on New Year's Eve. Their journey was not without some peril from Nazi submarine attack. Indeed, German agents in Capetown, where the *Noordam* was taking on fuel and supplies, poisoned the ship's drinking water supply, thus delaying the Kincheloes' departure for the Atlantic. After nearly six weeks at sea, zig-zagging to avoid submarines, the *Noordam* sailed into New York harbor after having seen smoke from two allied ships torpedoed off Florida and Virginia. During the previous week, they sailed through the same waters where five Allied tankers and freighters had quite recently been sunk.

On February 28th, eight of the 34 pilots temporarily assigned to Mather received orders marked "Top Secret." They all had one thing in common in addition to about 75 hours of very recent AT-6 time: they all spoke fluent Spanish or Portuguese. They soon were on their way ferrying brand new AT-6s from North American Aviation's plant in Dallas, Texas, to the Brazilian Air Force in Rio de Janeiro.

The remaining 26, including Jeff and Charlie, also got their orders on the 28th.

RESTRICTED
HEADQUARTERS
AIR CORPS ADVANCED FLYING SCHOOL
ARMY AIR BASE, MATHER FIELD
Sacramento, California

February 28, 1942

SPECIAL ORDERS)

:

NO................51

EXTRACT

1. Pursuant to the instructions contained in Radiogram WD AGO Feb 27, 1942, the following named 2ND LTS are relieved from assignment and duty at this station and are assigned to the AIR FORCE COMBAT COMMAND, McCHORD FIELD, WASHINGTON. They will proceed thereto without delay reporting upon arrival to the CO for duty.

| | |
|---|---|
| Lyle M. Adams, 0438507 | Alvin L. Barker, 0438502 |
| John B. Brady, 0438497 | Gardiner Cornwell, 0438488 |
| Louis W. Cunningham, 0438486 | William W. Ely, 0438480 |
| Bradford A. Evans, 0438479 | Ernest J. Fauss, 0438469 |
| James H. Foster, Jr., 0438942 | Clay M. Isbell, 0438480 |
| Roland L. Jeffries, 0438522 | Cornelius A. Jenkins, 0438521 |
| Herbert R. Jenkins, 0438513 | Russell G. Kahl, 0438511 |
| Degland T. Kenealy, 0438456 | Melvin E. Neef, 0438441 |
| Harold P. O'Neill, 0438437 | Edwin F. Patterson, 0438566 |

Charles O. Reynard, Jr., 0438558     Russell E. Schleeh, 0438530
Zed S. Smith III, 0438548            Thomas W. Stein, 0438546
Earl C. Tunnell, 0438541             Vance W. Beckham, 0438501
Joe L. Rutan, 04389664               William E. Friend, 0385065

The travel directed is necessary in the military service. If travel is performed by privately owned conveyance 3 days DS is authorized. FD 1499 P 1-06 A 0410-2 and QM 1601 P 61-07 A 0525-2.

By the order of Colonel HEWITT:

OFFICIAL:   R.W. BOCKMON
            Capt. Air Corps
            Assistant Adjutant

Of those 26 men, enemy fire and flying accidents claimed the lives of 11 before the victory came three and one-half years later.

On the day Jeffries and Reynard received their orders, Secretary of War Stimson and Secretary of the Navy Knox announced that Major General Walter Short and Admiral Husband E. Kimmel, commanders in Hawaii at the time of the Japanese attack, would be tried by court martial for dereliction of duty.

In the several days before Jeffries and Reynard were ordered to McChord Field, General Ira Eaker was named commander of the fledgling Eighth Air Force. He had toured Royal Air Force headquarters and was being taken on a round of airfield inspections prior to establishing certain fields as bases when American forces would arrive later in the year.

In the Southwest Pacific, the air war was going from bad to worse, although new units were starting to arrive in Australia from the United States. These included one A-20 Havoc light bomber group, two B-26 Marauder groups, and a P-39 fighter group. It was to be several weeks before these groups could start operations. In the meantime, the Allies lost the Battle of Java Sea which was fought off Soerabaja. The carrier *U.S.S. Langley* was sunk and with it 32 P-40s in crates. An additional 27 P-40s recently delivered to the base at Tjilatjsap were destroyed to prevent their falling into the hands of the advancing Japanese.

McChord Field, located 40 miles southwest of Seattle and just a mile south of Tacoma, was a recently established base, and an active one in

National Archives

*McChord Field, Tacoma, Washington, in late 1940.*

March of 1942. The reason for its activity, anti-submarine warfare, was not widely reported in early 1942 nor was the "Battle of Los Angeles" which took place when 140 rounds of anti-aircraft artillery were fired at several unidentified aircraft approaching from the sea.

McChord, along with Pendleton Field in Oregon, was experiencing a major build-up in maritime patrol aircraft as a means of defending against the threat of invasion. The Seattle area was of prime importance to the war effort since it was home to Boeing Aircraft and numerous shipyards.

McChord Field, in operation for less than two years, was named for General William C. McChord, a WWI pilot who had been killed in the crash of an A-17 in Virginia in 1937. At the time of his death, General McChord was Chief of Training, Army Air Corps Headquarters. In 1942, McChord was a major facility with four large maintenance hangars and four runways.

The field was starting to suffer from a shortage of aircraft mechanics since the local aircraft industry had attracted many aviation tradesmen, and the Army Air Force had not begun to meet its aviation mechanic manpower requirements. Five thousand civilians were being actively recruited to train as aircraft mechanics at $75 per month during the six-month training period.[1] When hired as assistant mechanics, after six months, pay went to $150 per month. Physically fit, draft eligible young men were encouraged not to apply. The latter group were, however, being welcomed with open arms by the Washington State National Guard which was hurriedly trying to bring its brigade strength up to 143 officers and 4,016 enlisted men.

Charlie and several others took the train up to Tacoma on March 3rd. When the Mather 42-B contingent arrived, they learned that McChord was home to the four squadrons of the 42nd Bomb Group whose primary responsibility was anti-submarine patrol. Several flights of the resident units, the 75th, 76th, 390th, and 406th Bomb Squadrons, were actually detached to other fields in the area: Portland, Astoria and Seattle. For this task, they used the Lockheed A-29 Hudson, although most of these squadrons would later convert to the B-26 Marauder before shipping out to the Southwest Pacific Theater of operations in 1943.

McChord's commander, Colonel Armin F. Herold, had no idea why he had been sent so many young lieutenants which included 42-B graduates from several advanced flying schools. Very few of Jeffries' and Reynard's associates ever saw the inside of a Hudson. Their only daily responsibility was to report to the McChord operations office to see if any flying orders or mail had come in. After that, they were off duty. Charlie's view of their state of affairs was that it was the calm before the storm.

The lull was an opportunity to eat, sleep, and relax since their lives had been anything except slow-paced during the previous eight months. The novelty of leisure wore off quickly, and Charlie was not especially impressed with Tacoma. In a letter home, he indicated that he missed California which he viewed as being somewhere between captivating and fantastic.

It was increasingly difficult to stay in touch with former cadet classmates, but there was already news of another Mather 42-B graduate, and it was not good. Jack Pounds, of Tyler, Texas, had been among the newly commissioned pilots to go to Lemoore Army Air Base as a basic flying instructor. On March 2nd, his student spun out of a turn onto final and, although Pounds recovered from the spin, the BT-13 crashed. The student, who survived, had two broken legs and Pounds had a fractured skull with massive, fatal hemorrhaging. It was the first in a tragic list of flying accidents which would claim Jeffries, Reynard, and roughly as many 42-B'ers as those killed in combat.

At this time, hometown newspapers were starting to carry announcements of Mather cadets earning their wings and commissions, including a classmate and Tacoma native, Bill Gammon (about to ferry an AT-6 to Brazil from Texas). Another Puget Sound area flyer, Robert Neale, had also done well. A former Navy pilot, Neale was a Flying Tiger who had just shot down his twelfth Japanese plane. The downside of that news was that, with the British, the Flying Tigers had to evacuate their Rangoon base to onrushing Japanese.

There was another Japanese migration of immediate concern to Seattle area residents, and that was the local Japanese population. From a sociological viewpoint, it was of great interest to Reynard, but much more so to local defense contractors who feared sabotage.

To offset the ominous war news, and with time heavy on their hands, recent Mather graduates found no shortage of theaters which were offering such first run fare as *Pacific Blackout* with Robert Preston and Martha O'Driscoll ("From dark to dawn, they lived the world's most exciting adventure.") at the Rialto. Bogart was big in *All Through The Night*, and for a few laughs, W.C. Fields was playing in *Never Give a Sucker An Even Break* at the Riviera. Shortly after Jeffries and Reynard arrived at McChord, Hollywood awarded its Oscars for 1941; as a portent to the many war films to come, Gary Cooper earned the best actor award for his portrayal of World War One hero, Sergeant Alvin York.

With his ear for finer music, Charlie enjoyed another entertainment special when the Tacoma Philharmonic played a free concert at full strength for McChord airmen at one of the four large hangars. The piano soloist was Rudolph Ganz, conductor of the Young Peoples' concerts of the New York Philharmonic and the San Francisco Symphony.

Such distractions did not cover up an emerging darker side of civilian life in a wartime economy. Rubber was becoming scarce. The War Production Board in Washington had just banned the production of rubber heels for shoes. New tires were in tight supply; tire theft was on the rise. One local Tacoma garage was cashing in on the problem by "branding" customers' tires with their license plate numbers in order to discourage thieves.

The Price Administration Board in Washington had just taken steps to prevent profiteering and hysteria by placing ceilings on the producer and wholesale prices of fruits and vegetables. Many of the listed items, such as apples, apple sauce, pears, and cherries, were of direct interest to Washington state canners and wholesalers.

Retailing was in transition during this, the fourth month of the war

Photo courtesy of Mary Reynard MacArthur

*Newly-commissioned Second Lieutenant Charles Reynard on leave in Seattle, March 1942.*

for America. Fishers, "Tacoma's Own Store," was selling defense stamps and bonds on its second floor while offering the latest in feminine dresses on the first floor. The war had started to permeate marketing and advertising. Fishers encouraged its clientele to be "the woman he wants you to be" with "feminine dresses of gallant navy — white-capped with foamy frills. He wants you to look gay and cheerful — no olive drab for you. He wants you in flattering clothes ... young and feminine ... clothes in gallant navy, crisp as sea-washed air, and white capped with a touch of sparkling white lingerie at the throat." Prices ranged from $19.95 to $35.00.

Some hardgoods were still available, although most of their manufacturers were rapidly converting production lines to military items. A Hotpoint electric range with hi-speed calrods and flavor-seal oven could be purchased for $219.95. While young married pilots and their wives were not interested in purchasing furniture, a nice six-piece living room ensemble consisting of a sofa-bed, matching chair, lamp table, cocktail table, table lamp, and what-not shelf was on sale at Kegel's for only $88.00.

Ahead of its time, Payless Drug Store advertised a wide range of sale items including many brands that would still be popular decades later. A carton of cigarettes went for $1.55 — smoker's choice of Camels, Chesterfield, Old Gold, Raleigh, Philip Morris, Pall Mall, Luckies, Herbert Tareyton, or one brand that did not stand the test of time, Imperial Twenty Grand.

If the weeds proved too rough for the system, Bayer aspirin could be purchased for 59 cents, cigarette breath could be masked with Listerine at the same price per bottle, smoke-troubled eyes could be soothed with Murine for 49 cents, a queasy stomach might be settled with Sal Hepatica or Phillips Milk of Magnesia at 49 and 39 cents per bottle respectively, and smokers' cough soothed (possibly) by Vicks VapoRub at 27 cents a bottle. Charlie, not being a smoker, might have been attracted to a Univex camera on sale for $2.95, down from $4.95 (it was a close-out item).

Housing, however, was in short supply even with Tacoma's record increase in residential construction in January and February. The Seattle area, with its aircraft plants and shipyards, had attracted many new families. Married pilots had difficulty finding apartments for which rent was going sky high. The rental problem was about to be addressed by Washington which implemented maximum rates in key "defense rental areas" which included metropolitan areas where key armaments plants and/or military bases were located.

If it were not a good time to be renting in Seattle, it was a good time to be in Scouting. Enrollment was growing for both Boy Scouts and Girl Scouts in the Seattle area which was also a Sea Scouting stronghold. Troops were working on emergency service programs, and had started the first of their many paper and scrap metal drives of the war years.

When Jeffries and Reynard arrived in Tacoma, the general war news was very discouraging and highlighted by the Japanese invasion of Java. Only here and there were there bright spots, and those reported tended to be individual heroic incidents rather than major victories. The war on the eastern front was about to heat up again, and the Red Army with the help of its great ally, the Russian winter, was starting to inflict significant losses on the *Wermacht.*

With no flying to do, there was plenty of time for relaxation. Lts. Jeffries and Reynard each were given a three-day pass which was spent in Seattle. New orders were waiting when they returned on March 16th.

RESTRICTED

| | | |
|---|---|---|
| SO) | | HQ 4TH AF |
| : | | San Francisco, Calif. |
| NO 62 | EXTRACT | March 9, 1942 |

#  #  #  #

Pursuant to VO CG, AFCC, and auth fr CG, WDC & Fourth Army, the following-named 2 LTs AC:

| | | | |
|---|---|---|---|
| Lyle M. Adams | 0438507 | Melvin E. Neef | 0438441 |
| John S. Brady | 0438497 | Edwin F. Patterson | 0438566 |
| Louis W. Cunningham | 0438486 | Russell T. Schleeh | 0438530 |
| Bradford A. Evans | 0438479 | Thomas W. Stein | 0438546 |
| James H. Foster, Jr. | 0438942 | Vance W. Beckham | 0438501 |
| Roland L. Jeffries | 0438522 | William E. Friend | 0438065 |
| Herbert R. Jenkins | 0438513 | Floyd E. Love | 0438455 |
| Degland T. Kenealy | 0438456 | Ed. P. Maliszewski | 0437606 |
| Howard P. O'Neill | 0438437 | Lynn H. Mokler | 0437596 |
| Charles O. Reynard, Jr. | 0438558 | William E. O'Brien | 0437593 |

| | | | |
|---|---|---|---|
| Zed. S. Smith III | 0438548 | Martin E. Plocher | 0437586 |
| Earl C. Tunnell | 0438541 | Marlen E. Reber | 0437584 |
| Joe L. Rutan | 0438664 | Scott L. Regan | 0437650 |
| Alvin L. Barker | 0438502 | Harry A. Robey, Jr. | 0437650 |
| Gardner Cornwell, Jr. | 0438488 | Ellis J. Sanderson | 0437648 |
| William W. Ely | 0438480 | Frank A. Saunders | 0437647 |
| Ernest J. Fauss, Jr. | 0438469 | William D. Whitson | 0437626 |
| Clay M. Isbell | 0438523 | Robert C. Williams | 0437626 |
| Cornelius A. Jenkins | 0438521 | William A. Prentice | 0436534 |
| Russell G. Kahl | 0438511 | | |

are rel'd from assmnt. to AFCC, McChord Fld, Wash, are asgd to AFCC, Municipal Airport, Salt Lake City, Utah on a permanent c of sta and will proceed without delay to that sta.

Travel directed necessary in mil serv. FD 1459 P 1-06, 15-06 A 0410-2. This Hq will be furn a copy of the Pd vou. QM 1492 P 58-07 A 0525-2. A copy of the pd vou will be furn the CG, WDC & Fourth Army.

If travel performed by privately-owned automobile, Par 1 g, AR 605-180 applies.

#### ####
By comd of MAJ GEN FICKEL

Emil G. KIEL
COL, GSC
C of S

OFFICIAL
GEO A. MILLER
COL, AGD
AGD

DIST: 1-Ea 201 file.    2-CG, Com Zone, (CA
8-Ea O concerned    2-OCAC & CG AFCC
5 Ea Organ & Sta.    5-TAG, Wash, DC.
2-CG, WDC & 4th Army    2-QMG, Wash. DC.
1-Hq AAF (Attn: Air AG Per Div)

On the day that order was issued, the Japanese captured Rangoon and thereby cut off the Burma Road, a major supply pipeline to China. Although Washington decided that the defeat of Germany was the chief priority, some of the heavy bomber units retreating from the Dutch East Indies and Philippines were sent to India which was also starting to receive P-40s via the African ferry route.

While Lts. Jeffries and Reynard were in transit from Tacoma to Salt Lake, American forces were driven out of Java. American aircraft based in the Philippines were withdrawing and leaving ground support personnel to fight on as infantry.

Although American forces, along with the Royal Air Force and Royal Australian Air Force were in retreat throughout the Southwest Pacific theater of operations, the Army Air Force had already started a build-up as new fighter, medium and heavy bomber units began arriving in Australia and New Caledonia.

Salt Lake City was to become a major aircrew assignment center during the war — a place where bomber crews were formed up and then sent onto operational squadrons for "phase" training, i.e. combat tactics training. Later in the war, first pilots went through transition training on a specific aircraft type before being sent to Salt Lake. In early 1942, with the Air Force very much in transition, the process was reversed for Jeffries and Reynard.

Most of the men listed in Special Order # 62 were assigned to one of the two bomb groups then forming at Salt Lake Army Air Base located at the municipal airport. Those units were the 305th and 306th Bomb Groups (Heavy). The long arm of the Training Command, however, reached out and subsequently withdrew Barker, Evans, O'Brien, Fauss, Saunders, and Robey among others. Some of these men would go overseas later in the war, but an appalling number of both the early and later departures were killed in action in addition to several, including Robey, who died in stateside flying accidents.

There is a persistent legend that describes how assignments to the two groups were made. That was upon reporting to Salt Lake, new officers formed a line and were ordered to count off. Those calling an even number were sent to the 306th Bomb Group, and those with odd numbers became members of the 305th Bomb Group.

In the 306th Bomb Group's Special Order # 1 issued March 16, 1942,

Lt. Charles Reynard was the first new officer assigned to the Group's 367th Bomb Squadron and was followed by his Mather classmates William Ely, Earl Tunnell, and Edwin Patterson.[2] Of this group, only Earl Tunnell would survive the war after having been shot down in 1943 and spending two years as a POW. There was much work to do, and since Lt. Reynard and his fellow 42-B classmates were the first to arrive, they had to help their squadron commander, Capt. Harry J. Holt, organize the squadron until the remaining crews arrived.

Charlie was appointed squadron adjutant and S-1 (personnel officer), key jobs especially when starting a squadron from scratch. Bringing a squadron up to operating efficiency required wearing more than one hat, so these men had to carry the ball until new arrivals could assume some of the load for engineering, supply, maintenance, commu-

National Archives

*In the foreground, Salt Lake City Municipal Airport on which the Army Air Base was located. Jeffries and Reynard were respectively assigned to the 305th and 306th Bomb Groups (Heavy) which were activated in Salt Lake in early March 1942.*

nications, armament, ordnance, and intelligence. Later arrivals would also be responsible for managing navigation, bombardment, and medical functions.

Reynard was delighted with his assignment as a B-17 pilot. In his own words, he was "tickled pink, since I'd rather fly this ship than any other at all." He also found something special in Salt Lake: the Mormon Tabernacle Choir. He listened to the choir both Sundays he was there, and entertained thoughts of trying to audition with them in spite of his schedule and uncertain future. The Choir brought back fond memories of his Hiram College singing, and especially the exceptional '37-38 year choir.

The 305th Bomb Group's Special Order # 1 assigned 80 officers to the Group's headquarters, 364th, 365th, 366th, and 422nd squadrons. Jeffries was assigned to the 366th Bomb Squadron. All men remained at Salt Lake until their quarters assignment was terminated on March 27th. At this point, both bomb groups had little more than pilots. It would be another couple of months before they came up to operational strength and received their first B-17s.

There was little to encourage the Allies when Lts. Jeffries and Reynard arrived in Salt Lake City. The British were retreating from Burma, the German battleship *Tirpitz* had broken out into the North Atlantic, and, based on the massing of Japanese forces on New Guinea and on surrounding islands, there were fears of an invasion of Australia where the city of Broome had been bombed on March 3rd. On the plus side, the Russians were making some progress against the Germans in the north, and the Royal Air Force was pounding Germany hard at night. The Secretary of the Navy announced that the names and types of merchant ships sunk would not be announced: the Battle of the Atlantic was in doubt.

In relatively dry Utah, the season's first Bock beer was just going into retail distribution.[3] Ladies' spring coats were on sale from $19.75 to $29.75 at the Paris Company. At Sears, similar coats were selling for $16.98 and women's sport Oxfords were on sale at $1.98 a pair. Auerbach's, the department store, featured Duchess of Kent ladies' hats for $1.98, and ready-made draperies for $5.98 a pair. Western Auto was selling motor oil for $0.47 per gallon (gallon, not quart), but one had to bring his own can.

Utah Fuel was urging its customers to buy War Bonds and to plan ahead for their coal needs since the mines were not certain about their ability to meet future demand. The Solid Fuels Council had just met in Washington and recommended stockpiling coal. Tires and tubes, used that is, were advertised as "still available, but going fast."

The *Salt Lake Tribune* was carrying some other economic news, however. The Secretary of Agriculture was reported to be considering ceilings on the price of beef and mutton. Local sugar processors were urging Utah farmers to grow more sugar beets (sugar would be rationed shortly). Oil men convened in Washington and recommended gasoline rationing as a means of cutting consumption by 25 percent on the East Coast which was being hurt by tanker losses.

The tax outlook was blamed for declining stock prices. On the New York Stock Exchange, the Dow Jones 30 Industrials closed at 99.21, down 2.28. Blue chips led the decline with IBM, Westinghouse, DuPont, Kodak, AT&T, and GM down from one to four points. Utah farmers' incomes were up, but mining shares were weak on the Salt Lake Stock Exchange. Utah zinc production was up, and Phelps Dodge earnings showed an increase. Clairvoyant, quick-thinking GIs would have invested in nylon stockings: nylon hosiery production had just been halted. Americans had been buying war bonds, (or "defense bonds" as they had originally been called) heavily since they were first offered in May of 1941 — over $4 billion worth.

The big winner in Salt Lake on March 11th, however, was the U.S. Navy: 35 men enlisted in the USN to see the world. The Marines picked up five good men, but nobody knocked on the Army recruiter's door.

With a mixed economic picture and war developments almost exclusively negative, Americans increasingly turned to such diversions as movies and the radio. The young pilots who had just left the rainy Pacific Northwest for Salt Lake were faced with some less than Oscar-winning prospects at local theaters. Shirley Temple, in *Kathleen*, was playing at the Utah along with Rosalind Russell and Walter Pidgeon in *Design for Scandal*; Bette Davis, Ann Sheridan and Monte Woolley starred in *The Man Who Came To Dinner* at the Center Theater; and for 15 cents, *Suspicion* starring Cary Grant and Joan Fontaine could be seen at the Gem.

Western fans would not be disappointed with *20 Mule Team* starring Wallace Beery or *Wild Bill Hickok Rides* also playing in town. That the world had been at war for well over two years was obvious in other attractions including *Joan of Paris* with Michelle Morgan and Paul

Henried ("I am a flier, Joan, fighting with the RAF! — One day for life, one hour for love, and terror stalked each fleeting moment.") or *A Yank on the Burma Road* with Laraine Day and Barry Nelson ("Search all convoys, find the woman!").

News, including farm reports, dominated the radio airwaves which came alive at 6 a.m. Light comedy and music followed as typified by the "Don McNeill Breakfast Club" or Kate Smith. Midday was soap opera time with "Our Gal Sunday," "Helen Trent," "Ma Perkins," and "Young Dr. Malone" among others. Comedy series like "Lum and Abner" were popular evening fare as were serials such as "Death Valley Days," but most of the time, pilots of the 305th and 306th Bomb Groups listened to music including dance band shows, "Glenn Miller," or "Music Hall" with Bing Crosby.

At 6:55 p.m., CBS carried the "Edward R. Murrow News," as reported from London. The Germans were pounding the UK at night, but paying for it as the Royal Air Force developed an effective, airborne radar-guided night fighter force. Although RAF Bomber Command made deep penetrations well into Germany at night, much of its effort was directed at the German shipbuilding industry and submarine ports. It would be another year before Bomber Command had enough heavies, such as the four-engine Lancaster, to launch large-scale raids on the German heartland. Another year would pass before the tide turned in the Battle of the Atlantic.

Murrow had very little positive Allied news to report in the spring of 1942: Singapore had fallen, the British abandoned Burma, and the war in the Western Desert would not be favorably resolved until well into autumn. There was a glimmer of good news coming from a small, British island garrison in the Mediterranean Sea, though. Malta and its three airfields were a stubborn thorn in the Axis backside and could not be eliminated. *Luftwaffe* and *Regia Aeronautica* squadrons based on Sicily, despite vastly superior numbers, could not overcome the bulldog resolve of RAF pilots who kept Malta open to disrupt Axis supply and communication lines to North Africa.

Increasingly, more news was programmed into the daily schedules, and, although there would be a few rays of hope in the war news of the next few months such as Midway, it would be many months and tens of thousands of deaths before the big picture started looking better in late 1942 and early 1943.

Almost as soon as Lts. Jeffries and Reynard arrived in Salt Lake, they were introduced to one of their groups' few multi-engine aircraft, an aging B-18. Their checkout on the twin-engine B-18 was not thorough. Although it was a step up from an AT-6 and would facilitate their subsequent transition to the B-24, the B-18 flights quickly served the purpose of screening new arrivals into first pilot or copilot categories in addition to qualifying men for flight pay.

The Douglas B-18 "Bolo" was derived from the Douglas DC-2 transport which begat the workhorse DC-3 or, in Army Air Force service, the C-47. With the exception of the nose which carried the bombardier and gunner, the lines of the DC-2 and B-18 were quite similar. The B-18 had actually prevailed over the Boeing 299 design (early B-17) in 1935 as a replacement for aging Martin B-10 bombers. Although 350 Bolos were ordered, the Air Corps did take delivery of a handful of B-17s. When the war started, the obsolete and underpowered B-18 was relegated to training and antisubmarine roles, and the B-17 went on to write history.

National Archives

*Jeffries and Reynard qualified as first pilots on the obsolete Douglas B-18 Bolo in Salt Lake prior to the four-engine transition school assignment in Albuquerque.*

Having had only a minimal exposure to twin-engine aircraft, those pilots from the 305th and 306th rated as first pilots were subsequently scheduled for heavy bomber transition schools, principally the B-17 school at Davis-Monthan Field near Tucson, Arizona, or the Jack Frye Four-Engine School at Albuquerque.

Although Lts. Jeffries and Reynard did not live to go overseas with their squadrons, knowing what the future held for the 305th and 306th Bomb Groups is revealing in terms of the odds they would have faced. Although nobody then knew how costly American daylight bombing would prove to be, Jeffries and Reynard were quite aware that the Royal Air Force had tried it, found it too costly, and had concentrated on night bombing for which the odds were still unappealing to Bomber Command crews. Based on the mortality rate in those groups, it is quite likely that Lts. Jeffries and Reynard would not have lived beyond the spring of 1943.

In the late 1942 to mid-1943 time period, only about 35 percent of Eighth Air Force crews completed their quota of 25 missions and came home (including light and medium bomb groups). From mid-1943 to mid-1944, the averages improved to 65 percent. After long range P-51 escort fighters became available in large numbers, the final months of the air war in Europe saw 85 percent of aircrews surviving their tours.

But, in the very early days, a pioneer heavy bomber crew in the First Air Division, to which the 305th and 306th Bomb Groups were assigned, faced only a 20 percent chance of surviving 25 missions.

## 305th Bomb Group
## "Can Do"

The 305th, comprised of the 364th, 365th, 366th, and 422nd Bombardment Squadrons (Heavy), was activated on March 1, 1942.[4] After its first pilots returned from four-engine transition, the group moved to Geiger Field near Spokane, Washington, on June 11, 1942 under the command of Col. Curtis E. LeMay who had recently left the 34th Bomb Group. The 305th then moved to Muroc Lake Army Air Base (better known as Edwards AFB in later years) for phase training. In late August, the ground units entrained for the East Coast where they shipped out aboard the Queen Mary on which they arrived in Scotland after a seven-day crossing. Flight crews continued training with new B-17Fs and left for Prestwick, Scotland, via Syracuse, New York, Presque Isle, Maine, and Gander, Newfoundland.

Upon arrival in the UK, the group was initially based at Grafton Underwood, but moved to its permanent base at Chelveston in December. Its first mission was flown on November 17, 1942 and the last on April 25, 1945. As LeMay's group, it pioneered tactics that became standard procedures for the entire Eighth Air Force. In its 337 missions, the group lost 154 Flying Fortresses. It lost more aircraft than any other group on the October 1943 Schweinfurt raid, and was subsequently given the Nazi flag flying over the city when it was captured by U.S. troops in 1945.

## 306th Bomb Group
## "Reich Wreckers"

The group, consisting of the 367th, 368th, 369th, and 423rd Bombardment Squadrons (Heavy), was activated on March 1, 1942 at Salt Lake Army Air Base.[5] As soon as its pilots returned from Tucson and Albuquerque, the 306th moved to Wendover, Utah, for phase training. Ground crews crossed the Atlantic on the Queen Elizabeth and arrived on September 5, 1942. Flight crews with B-17Fs left Wendover and stopped at Westover Field in Massachusetts before taking the Gander-Prestwick ferry route and arriving in the UK on September 1st.

They flew their first mission a month later. Their last mission was flown on April 19, 1945. The 306th was the oldest operational bomb group in the Eighth Air Force, and lost 177 Flying Fortresses in the 342 missions it flew. The 306th also had the highest number of losses in the Eighth between October 1942 and August 1943. One of its members, T/Sgt. Harry Roscovitch, on April 5, 1943, became the first member of the Eighth Air Force to complete 25 missions. The group's 369th Bomb Squadron actually flew for six months in 1943 without a single loss (the bitter pill would come on the big mission to Schweinfurt later in 1943).

The highly acclaimed film, *12 O'Clock High*, starring Gregory Peck, Gary Merrill and Dean Jagger was based on the early history of the 306th Bomb Group and certainly captures the hard times associated with the above record.

Seven hundred, thirty-eight men of the 306th were killed in combat, and another 38 died in flying accidents after leaving the United States in 1942. Eight hundred, eighty-five became prisoners of war while another 69 were interned in Sweden and Switzerland. Forty-four evaded German patrols and escaped to Britain or Allied lines after being shot down, and one man successfully escaped from a POW camp.

Typical of most Air Force units, the squadrons of the 306th Bomb Group had their own logos and slogans which were designed to convey fighting spirit and offensive capability. The 423rd Squadron became the "Grim Reapers" while the 368th and 369th were, respectively, "Eager Beavers" and "Fightin' & Bitin'." Reflecting the grim realities of German AAA and intercepting Messerschmidt or Focke-Wulf cannon fire, Reynard's squadron, the 367th, would eventually call itself the "Clay Pigeons."

On March 27, 1942, men identified as first pilots in the 305th and 306th Bomb Groups, including Lts. Jeffries and Reynard, started leaving Salt Lake for heavy bomber transition schools in Albuquerque and Tucson.

# XVIII

# COMBAT CREW TRAINING SCHOOL

Jeffries and Reynard arrived in Albuquerque on Sunday, March 29, 1942. There were no quarters available at Kirtland for the entire contingent of 40 pilots from Salt Lake, so, like most of the others, Charlie and Jeff stayed at one of the many motels along Central Avenue, the old Route 66. Nearly all of the 40 pilots were from 42-B, but roughly half of them had graduated from Stockton, the other advanced flying school in California.

A second lieutenant's pay with flight time went far in Albuquerque. The Howland Hotel on West Central was advertising modern, steamheated rooms with private bath for $3 per week.[1] The much more upscale Albuquerque Hilton, where quite a few of the CCTS first officers stayed, cost $3 per day. A month at a good boarding house with homecooked meals came to $30. Even a modestly furnished house rented for an average of $55 per month. Hutch Thurston was married in Albuquerque, and rented a furnished two-bedroom home for $60 per month.

Although Charlie had abandoned plans to buy his brother George's car, for $925 he could have bought a 1941 Ford, four-door sedan at the Schick Motor Company lot on the corner of Third and Tijeras (or a '38 Buick sedan for $595). At the other extreme was a '32 Ford for $79.

The new arrivals missed one civic event held all weekend at Seventh and Gold Streets: a model victory garden put on by the Boy Scouts of Albuquerque. Supported by the U.S. Soil Conservation Service, the Scout display also featured eggplant, tomatoes, cabbage, peppers, celery, and okra in cold frames for later transplanting.

That several new classes of freshly minted second lieutenants had arrived in town was not newsworthy. Since a significant percentage of Army personnel in the Philippines was from New Mexico, most Albuquerqians were interested in the news from the beleaguered American garrisons there. Roughly 1,500 New Mexico national guardsmen had served on Bataan, primarily in an anti-aircraft regiment. Of that number, only 107 escaped to the island of Corregidor.

Some of the war news was good: General Joseph Stillwell had taken a Japanese airfield and battalion headquarters in Burma, and the Flying Tigers were scoring well. Before too long, however, Stillwell would be run out of Burma by the Japanese who were starting to threaten the India/Burma border.

Most of the war news, though, was indeed gloomy. Corregidor, among whose troops were the 107 New Mexicans, was taking a terrible pounding from Japanese artillery. The Battle of the Atlantic continued badly, and on April 1st, a large freighter loaded with American tanks for the Russians went down on the Murmansk run. In the Russian Donets Basin, the Red Army and the *Wermacht* were locked in a titanic struggle.

Even the popular media was not always an escape from world events. As the new pilots just down from Salt Lake found on the theater marquees, war movies were dominating Albuquerque's theater scene. While there were a few musicals, such as *The Chocolate Soldier* with Nelson Eddy and Risë Stevens, or *Smilin' Through* with Brian Aherne and Jeanette McDonald, tense war dramas attracted most Albuquerque moviegoers. *Torpedo Boat* with Richard Arlen and Jean Parker was playing at the Rio Theater. At the KiMo, Humphrey Bogart was starring in *All Through the Night* ("Killer Bogart takes the Gestapo for a ride, it's gangdom versus the Gestapo, a shooting battle royal."). Most of the music, as played on the radio back at the motel or from Wurlitzer juke boxes in restaurants, hadn't changed dramatically from what was playing during the last few weeks of advanced. Glen Miller's *Moonlight Cocktail* was number one, but two others were heard almost as frequently: *Jersey Bounce* with Benny Goodman and Jimmy Dorsey's *Tangerine*.

As the war deepened, the national economic news bleakened, although it never reached the depths to which that of the other major combatants plunged. In April, the Office of Price Administration froze prices for literally everything Americans ate, wore, or used at March 1942 levels. The same directive applied to services such as laundries and auto repair garages. Some items, especially seasonal produce, were exempted. The "War Board" also reduced auto battery production by 25 percent, eliminated taxis "cruising" for fares, curbed the activities of local and long distance delivery services, and minimized auto use by government employees. Rental properties in key defense centers were required to be registered as part of rental rate freezing.

The Albuquerque economy was growing, especially since Kirtland Field was expanding. Residential construction was increasing signifi-

Photo courtesy of Harry M. Davidson

*Kirtland Field, late May 1942. The Combat Crew Training School is in the center foreground.*

cantly in April 1942. As Jeffries and Reynard arrived in Albuquerque, the War Department announced plans to start construction on a $5 million project — a new Army flying school at Carlsbad in southeastern New Mexico. It wouldn't be the last. Other New Mexico communities would be getting major training fields in the near future. Most of these fields shared the same mission as Kirtland: bombardier training and transitioning newly-rated pilots to operational bombers. Among the new fields were those at Alamogordo, Hobbs, Fort Sumner, Deming, Roswell, Clovis, and Santa Fe.

There were some major changes going on to the northeast of Santa Fe. In the spring of 1942, Boy Scout officials arrived in Cimarron to arrange for the transfer of the balance of Philmont property from Waite Phillips. Moving out of Villa Philmonte, Phillips was in the process of purchasing "The Nairn Place." This was the home of Jack Nairn, heir to the Congoleum fortune. Nairn had retired to Colfax County, New Mexico, and built his lovely, Spanish-style residence on the eastern slope of Urraca Mesa and within easy view of the Tooth of Time and the Villa Philmonte. Nairn called the home "Casa del Gavilan" which, in Spanish, means "Home of the Hawk." It would remain, for many years, best known as Nairn Place. Phillips used Nairn Place as his New Mexico headquarters while completing other real estate transactions in the area before selling it and moving to the West Coast.

With Otis Bryan leaving Eagle Nest on January 22, 1942 to become TWA's V.P. War Projects, Blackburn became Superintendent at the Four-Engine School. Robert Redding then moved up to Director of Flight Operations after having been the instrument flying chief. In turn, Redding persuaded his old friend Jonas Ruff to apply for a job as a copilot instructor in January 1942.

Whereas the initial staff in the summer of 1941 was exclusively TWA, by early spring of 1942, all new pilot and copilot instructors were coming from outside the company, either as ex-military pilots and/or experienced commercial pilots.

The Jack Frye Four-Engine School (JFFES), known as the CCTS when Jeffries and Reynard arrived, was technically under the direction of a colonel whose permanent station was at the Air Corps Advanced Flying School at Stockton, California, although he did have an office at Kirtland Field which was commanded by another colonel, Frank J. Hackett. The colonel overseeing the CCTS was regular Army, cavalry, in fact, and it showed. He was usually seen in riding boots, occasionally spurs, and although an able administrator, tended to look at matters from a horse soldier's perspective. His first inspection of a B-24 prompted the observation that the airplane was big enough to haul half a dozen horses (as indeed it was).

If he knew what was good for a cavalryman after a bad spill, he also knew what was good for an aircrew whose confidence had been shaken. One of the B-24s got away from a crew on final and landed short and hard. It wasn't exactly a crash, but it did rearrange some real estate to say nothing of the crew's nerves. The colonel arrived in a car and a cloud of his own dust, and had the crew airborne again within half an hour in another '24 knowing that getting back into the blue as fast as possible was the best way to restore confidence.

The aircraft commander/instructor pilots who trained the 305th and 306th Bomb Group pilots were all very seasoned men who came to TWA with several thousand hours in multi-engine equipment and airline transport ratings (ATRs in those days) or the military equivalent in experience. Although the Royal Canadian Air Force contract was lost, there was a real need for instructor copilots which were also called "first officers." Jonas Ruff was hired in this category in early February 1942, but he and his other first officer peers were really being trained to become instructor pilots. Jonas was better qualified than many of the new hires since he had previously flown multi-engine, heavy equipment. In addition to orienting new Army Air Force pilots on the B-24, first officers were also involved in the ground school and setting up the flight schedules. Part of their ground school job was familiarizing trainees with the B-24 instrument panel by conducting blindfold checks to see if the new men could unerringly touch the right instruments or levers as they were called out. To facilitate his teaching the instrument panel, Jonas Ruff, who had draftsman's training, drew the instrument panel and control pedestal on the backs of expired sectional aeronautical charts until the dials and gauges were second nature to him.

Copilot instructors also familiarized students in the differences between the LB-30 and the B-24 which, beyond the differences in props and superchargers, were primarily a reflection of where the Royal Air Force preferred things. The navigator was not based in the nose, but occupied a position behind the pilot and just opposite the radio operator. The navigator's celestial sighting bubble was located where the top turret would have been on the '24. The top turret on the LB-30 was located half way back to the tail consistent with where the RAF placed turrets on its heavies, the Stirling, Halifax and promising new bomber, the Avro Lancaster.

There was a lot to learn since the B-24 was the most complex aircraft in the Army Air Force inventory, but there was not a lot of time to learn it. When the course began in 1941, each pilot was given nearly 30 hours of left seat time, although he might be aloft for longer than that since the Liberators often took off with several student crews aboard. When Lts. Jeffries and Reynard arrived as two of the 40 pilots in transition class number 42-4-E, the amount of left seat time had been reduced to just 12 hours. The Army Air Force was desperate for heavy bomber pilots. 42-4-E wasn't the only class going through in April, either. 42-4-F was on the same course with 25 pilots and 40 flight engineer and radio operator trainees from March Field in California along with 15 civilian ferry pilots from Transport Command bases in Long Beach, California, Baltimore, and Hensley Field in Texas.

It is fair to say that Jeffries and Reynard initially approached the B-24 with a blend of intimidation, enthusiasm, and one small part of resignation. The slight disappointment was based on the fact that given a choice (at least during basic flying school), they probably would rather have been flying something really zippy like a P-38 or A-20. And, they had been in the service long enough to hear that the B-17 Flying Fortress was a sweeter flying ship than this Fat Albert with which they were about to become acquainted.

There is no reason to believe that Jeffries and Reynard had been anything other than just passing acquaintances prior to their arrival at the B-24 school for transition training. They were brought together on the same crew by the simple clerical procedure of assigning 40 pilots, 20 flight engineers and 20 radio operators from half a dozen different bomb groups and air base service squadrons into one training class. Jeffries' name does not appear in Reynard's address book in which were jotted down the names of closest friends at the end of advanced. Jeffries and Reynard had gone to different primary flying schools (where most lasting friendships were formed). They were not in the same companies at basic flight and their names were alphabetically sufficiently separated to ensure they would not have been assigned to the same classes or duties where the first letter of one's last name was frequently the basis for list segmentation. Their educations and family situations were quite dissimilar. They weren't even in the same bomb groups, so their duties and quarters in Salt Lake were different.

Each did have friends in the Albuquerque contingent. Jeffries' Thunderbird roommate, Lt. Mel Neef, was on the course as was Lt. Lyle Adams, another Missourian, who was to go overseas in the autumn. Adams returned in the spring of 1943 decorated for heroism and was among the few pilots who survived 25 missions in 1942-43 with the 305th Bomb Group. Only one of Reynard's closer friends, a cadet leader, was in the class: Lt. Russell Schleeh who, like Adams, would successfully complete his combat tour with the 305th Bomb Group.

Yet it is quite likely that Jeffries and Reynard became friendly in Albuquerque. They did have a number of things in common. Both were engaged to be married. Each had a very well developed interest in singing. Both had good experiences in Scouting. Although Jeffries was not especially outgoing, Reynard was very much at ease with strangers. They both excelled at flying, and had been selected as first pilots in what amounted to competition among all of the new pilots when they had arrived in Salt Lake.

Ground school on the B-24 began the next day, March 30th, as did their first orientation flight. A normal instructional flight well into the course lasted two hours (and frequently four or five on a cross country leg), but within the roughly 24 hours in the air, each pair of pilots would get some night flying and instrument time. The introductory hop consisted of preflighting the bomber, sitting in the cockpit, going over the starting procedure, and observing the two instructors fly the plane.[2] Jeffries and Reynard each got a few minutes in the left seat just to get a feel for the controls, but the instructors landed the plane.

The second flight's takeoff and landing were performed by the instructors, but each student took turns in the right seat to operate the engines, props, turbochargers, carburetor heat, cowl flaps, wing flaps and landing gear. Several landings were simulated at altitude, but the instructors performed the real thing back at Kirtland.

As they started to log their first full hour on the plane, students were again flying in the right seat, but getting into airwork consisting of climbs, glides, spirals, and 45 degree turns — all at a minimum of 150 mph.

Lts. Jeffries and Reynard quickly learned not to increase loading by banking too steeply, and that the best steep turns were done the old

National Archives

*During the early stages of transition, the Combat Crew Training School usually took several training crews aloft in the same B-24 in order to minimize downtime.*

fashioned way: eyeballing the vertical speed indicator and laying a rivet or scratch on the nose to the horizon and holding it there. That done, there was a rewarding bump of turbulence as they rolled out 360 degrees later. Their first rollouts were not as polished as those they had done in AT-6s just a few weeks before because the B-24 required more muscle and initiating the rollout much earlier.

Next, they learned speeds where the ship stalled in steep banks and at various gross weights and flap settings. It was also impressed upon them that, although the B-24 appeared to be a sturdy machine, stresses in a high speed dive, especially an untrimmed dive, could buckle the fuselage, and that it was best to pull out of a dive manually and not trust trim tabs to do all the work (since they could easily compound the felony by inducing structural failure).

They got the basic feel for the controls which were discouragingly heavy compared to what they had been flying. Practicing approaches to stalls was done with plenty of altitude to spare, and with power on, power off, gear and flaps down and up. There were numerous cues that the big ship was getting ready to quit: mushy controls, an occasional shudder running through the plane, and a rising nose. When the break came, they were told, the nose would drop, but usually without a pronounced tendency to fall off on a wing. Recovery was to be normal, and done by moving the wheel sharply forward, using rudder to correct any roll, and gradually bringing power back in after airspeed had built up (taking care not to bang the throttles forward too soon which would induce more rolling). They were told never, but never, allow a '24 to spin since the airframe could not take the heavy loads quickly encountered in a spin. CCTS instructors never took the demonstration through an actual stall, but left that matter at the recommended procedure level.

Complicating instructors' lives was the fact that most cadets had practically no multi-engine time before arriving at Kirtland. Most pilots are slightly apprehensive when moving on to a substantially higher performance airplane, especially if it is quantum leap upward as this one was. Getting four or five hours in a B-18 was better than nothing, but even so, Lts. Jeffries and Reynard along with their 42-B associates were taking an intimidatingly major step up when they reported for B-24 training. Within a year, newly commissioned lieutenants going through B-24 transition would have around 75 hours in twin-engine planes, and would be able to spread out their Liberator transition over a couple months and nearly 50 hours of left seat time. But, no such luxuries were available in the early spring of 1942.

TWA had developed an instructors' syllabus, both flight and ground, for the B-24, and it was subsequently used by the Army Air Force and several of the plants which were starting to build Liberators under license to Consolidated in San Diego. One of the more noted users of the manual and checklists was Charles Lindbergh who visited Blackburn in Albuquerque in the spring of 1942. Lindbergh was serving as a consultant to Ford Motor Company which was starting to build the B-24 at its Willow Run plant in Michigan.

The ground school was devoted to a full familiarization with the Liberator's many systems and performance charts. The B-24 included equipment that Jeffries and Reynard had only read about such as superchargers and an autopilot. The superchargers were covered in detail during the flying sessions, but the autopilot got more attention in the ground school than it did in a Liberator aloft. Most of the other subjects were dispatched by simple rote learning and involved memorizing proper settings and indications for various stages of flight, i.e. manifold pressure, revs, cylinder head temperature limitations, capacities for hydraulic fluid, fuel, oil, anti-icer fluid, etc.

The syllabus was modular: some of the sessions were identical for pilots and flight engineers while others were devoted to one group or the other. Ground school session one, for pilots and engineers, was a two-hour, blackboard and printed handout general introduction to the B-24/LB-30's structural components, flight controls (including locks, cables, bellcranks, chains, sprockets, etc), powerplants, and crew stations.[3] Emergency exits were stressed with emphasis on bailout procedures (use the bomb bay if time is available).

Session two, for pilots, engineers and radio operators, was a "touch and feel" meeting out on the flight line in both the LB-30 and B-24D. In effect, it was a thorough pre-flight examination of the aircraft inside and out after which students were given printed preflight checklists.

In the next segment, a four-hour session for pilots only, one of the TWA instrument instructors reviewed instrument flying procedures in general and approaches into Albuquerque in particular. The session was timely since neither Jeffries nor Reynard had done any actual instrument flying in approximately six weeks and neither had substantial radio navigation experience to start with.

Philip Macomber joined Jeffries and Reynard for the fifth ground school session which was devoted solely to cockpit procedures and engine operation during all flight regimes from starting to shutdown. This session confirmed their impression that they were flying something more complicated than an AT-6. Key points: coordination and responsibilities of each member of the cockpit crew. Although Duane Peterson was not attending this session, it was impressed upon the pilots just what a radio operator's duties were, and that his supplemental tasks related to following through on aircraft commander requests for altimeter settings and time checks, obtaining clearances, and contacting ground stations for airway and weather information.

This session was strictly checklist-driven and was the basis for the detailed checklist cards contained in the airplanes. Students had to know the location of every instrument and control on the panel which, compared to the AT-6, had become extraordinarily complicated. All scenarios were reviewed: cold starts, hot starts, starting with engines warm, faulty primer, and with an inoperative electrical system. The instructor made it quite clear precisely how the first pilot and copilot divided the chores.

Session four for the pilots was combined with session three for the flight engineers and consisted of role playing in the airplane in which Peterson was a silent participant (radio operators were not responsible for any checklist items). In this play-acting, all key players alternated roles. Even though Lts. Jeffries and Reynard were becoming first pilots, each had to assume the role of a copilot for part of the training session. It was a valuable experience since even the slightest omission or faulty assumption could prove fatal. The session covered every last item in each checklist including Macomber's.

This session was from ground-zero and not just calling out a reading, but actually touching the indicator it was supposed to have come from. Where appropriate, controls were cycled even though the B-24 had not been cranked up. Thus, the students experienced traveling bomb bay doors, moving cowl flaps, brakes, wing flaps, etc.

Pilots and engineers shared the next session, too, which was devoted to an occasional source of trouble: the Hamilton-Standard propellers with constant speed control. Jeffries, Reynard, and Macomber were introduced to the props, their hydromatic governors, making rpm changes, proper settings for each stage of flight, synchronizing the props, and feathering and unfeathering sequences through blackboard diagrams and engineering cutaway handouts. Then they learned it all over again on the Curtiss Electric propellers which were employed on the LB-30s.

The next session, also two hours and for both groups, focused on the very reliable Pratt & Whitney R-1830 Twin Row Wasp engine. Again, this was a blackboard and mimeographed handout session, but the pilots and engineers also walked over to TWA's Technical School Building on one wall of which there was a huge cutaway poster of the engine. This was a highly technical session of great interest to Macomber, although Jeffries and Reynard were also responsible for knowing all the key specs including the operating limits, fuel and oil flow rates and consumption, and performance curves.

That type of data was not entirely new, but the next subject was: superchargers. It had only been touched upon in previous ground school

Photo courtesy of Carolyn Van Hoozer Fullerton

*The Van Hoozers enjoyed a family outing near Albuquerque on a warm spring day shortly before the fateful flight. George, infant daughter Carolyn Kay, and Ruth Van Hoozer.*

sessions for Jeffries and Reynard, although Macomber had first hand knowledge of supercharging as a result of working on the 18th Bomb Squadron's B-17s at Pendleton Field. When this two-hour module started, the pilots got a glimpse at some new words: "turbo," "wastegate," "nozzlebox," "turbine wheel," "impeller," and "intercooler." Once the system components had been reviewed, the lesson proceeded with operating the turbos during takeoff, climb, normal cruise, cruising at the rated altitude (25,000 feet), above rated altitude, and descent, including significant emphasis on troubleshooting.

Other key engine systems followed: magnetos, carburetors, and starters. This was familiar ground to all parties as was the next subject: carburetor ice. What ensued was a discussion of types of ice, how to remedy icing in the B-24A/LB-30 or the B-24D (the cures were different based on the B-24D's supercharger system). The B-24D did not use the traditional alcohol and carburetor heat remedies for carburetor ice as did the earlier Liberators. Rather, it had a much more effective means which was achieved by closing the turbo intercooler shutters.

Although conditions creating carburetor ice are not necessarily identical to those have an icing effect on an airframe, that which ices up an airframe usually has the same effect on carburetors and their air intakes. In that regard, the Liberator (D models and later), enjoyed a dubious distinction of employing relatively effective carburetor ice protection while having notoriously poor shielding from airframe icing.

At this point, Philip Macomber had to sharpen his pencil since flight engineers took the first written exam. It was just a 40 question quiz, but it thoroughly tested his ability to think and to use what he had been taught for both routine flight engineer duties as well as emergency situations. Macomber's ground school instruction was a 32-hour course at the end of which a particularly detailed final exam was given.

The subject that followed was guided from a classroom blackboard and really put Macomber in the starring role: the B-24's complex fuel system and crossfeed controls. The oil system was included in this module, but was quite elementary compared to the diagrams of the fuel bladders in the wings, pumps, sight gauges, pressure indicators, and valves.

The session on the B-24 electrical system was likewise complicated because so much more was controlled electrically compared to what Jeffries and Reynard had most recently been flying, the T-6 whose fuse box was quite rudimentary compared to the Liberator. On the pilot's side, the electrical panel was minimal (alarm bell, autopilot controls, formation, running, and landing lights, and the gear warning horn). The copilot's side had 21 different switches (principally for engine controls). The electrical system also contained a new wrinkle for Jeffries and Reynard: the "putt-putt" gasoline engine auxiliary power unit which provided electrical power until the generators were turned on.

They discovered that the bomber's flying habits really weren't that bad, and that its stalling characteristics were quite straightforward. Had they been getting shot at, carrying several thousand pounds more fuel and bombs than the book called for, and trying to stay in position on the outside of a formation turn, they would have found the plane somewhat more demanding.

As part of the third flying lesson, which consisted of basic airwork, students also learned how to taxi the Liberator. Neither Jeffries or Reynard had ever flown a tricycle-geared airplane. That type of landing gear was relatively new, although all of the frontline medium bombers had nosewheels as did the P-38 Lightning and P-39 Airacobra fighters. Most of what Lts. Jeffries and Reynard had been told about taxiing was a litany of "do nots."

"Do not turn with the brakes, do not turn the nosewheel more than 30 degrees, do not brake with the nosewheel turned, do not use excessive power, do not pivot — you've got to keep the inside wheel turning too, and don't forget to watch where you're going."

Through trial and error, they learned to be light on the brakes while advancing the throttle to the engine on the outside of the turn. Just how much throttle was learned through trial and error — after some ignominious see-sawing and correcting for overturning. Observing a green pilot learning to taxi a B-24 for the first time could easily be compared to watching a tubby man with a gouty toe trying to learn the waltz.

Beginning with the fourth flying lesson, students were responsible for all taxiing. Airwork, with students in the copilot's seat doing the flying, was dominated by simulated approaches and landings: gliding at 135 mph, half flaps, gear down, full flaps, and over the imaginary fence at 110.

Ground school continued since there was so much to learn before they could be considered the ship's true master in the air. The hydraulic system session was attended jointly by pilots and engineers who first learned just what type of fluid was used (Sperry mineral oil #3580) and that the Liberator's engine driven pump was located on number three engine, that the auxiliary hydraulic pump was bolted onto the front right side of the bomb bay, and that the emergency hand pump was located between the pilot and the flight engineer positions in the cockpit. This two-hour session was one of the more important since the hydraulic system operated the landing gear, bomb bay doors, wing flaps, power brakes, autopilot, and fuel transfer pumps.

The Liberator's hydraulic system was not perfect as Hal Blackburn and Bob Redding had learned first hand several months before. They had been up on a late afternoon checkride on November 19, 1941, when the hydraulically-controlled landing gear stopped in mid-travel during an approach to the field. Solving the problem had turned out not to be a simple matter of switching on the backup hydraulic pump. The emergency pump, which could not be used for extended periods, promptly failed as soon as it had been turned on. The flight engineer had to resort to their last backup system, the emergency hand pump. Inconceivably, that too couldn't get the job done, thus making an uneventful landing most unlikely.

Although the Liberator could be belly landed with minimal damage to most of the engines because of its high wing configuration, Blackburn was reluctant to do so. The West Coast Air Training Command headquarters in California was pleased with the quality of instruction being given by TWA, but was displeased about the three Hudsons which had been pranged during the summer of '41, not to mention the hard landing damage to several of the Liberators.

Blackburn and Redding concluded that the cable used to manually lower the gear had become fouled. Since the cable for the main gear and the nose gear was all part of the same closed-loop system, the cable had to be removed from its pulleys and, in effect, separate circuits had to be created for the mains and then the nose gear. It took two hours of droning around above Albuquerque before the improvisation could be tried, but it worked. The landing, with gear down and locked, was made quite uneventfully at dusk.

While Jeffries, Reynard and Macomber were in class, Peterson spent much of his time in the radio building practicing code. Peterson's ground school, beyond code practice, was taught in fourteen sessions totalling nearly 30 hours of instruction which included a 2-hour final exam. The majority of his instruction was devoted to the interphone, command, and liaison radio systems along with their components and troubleshooting. A surprising portion of his time was taken up with the radio compass. Peterson was also exposed to the rudiments of navigation and instrument approaches since he was considered, in effect, a backup navigator.

The next ground school session for the pilots and engineers was an introduction to subjects for which only Macomber had some detailed knowledge. This was the autopilot, the vacuum system, and anti-icer and deicer equipment. Although autopilots had been around for over a decade, the recently graduated cadets had no experience with them or the Norden Automatic Flight Control, the new, all-electric Honeywell autopilot used on the B-24D, or the Sperry system on the school's B-24A and LB-30s. In some cases, TWA passed along supplier literature relating to some of the Liberator's systems, but the autopilot wasn't one of them. The Norden unit was so new that information about it was highly restricted. One of the instructors was very familiar with the Honeywell unit, however. Before coming to Albuquerque, Hutch Thurston had been a junior engineer assigned to the group which designed it.

The two-hour autopilot session commenced with a blackboard discussion of concepts including rigidity and stabilization as well the system's key components, i.e. the vacuum pumps and gyros that drove the directional gyro (DG) and what was then called the "bank and climb unit" which later came to be better known as the "artificial horizon." The session quickly moved to the relays and servo-pistons which were connected to the B-24's control system.

After being shown how to engage, operate the unit and troubleshoot problems, pilots were given several warnings in this module with a frank reminder of what could happen if the DG's heading were not corrected at frequent intervals or what could happen if they did not follow proper caging and uncaging procedures for the gyro instruments. The "do's and don'ts" continued with predictions of distressing consequences for those who tried to takeoff, land or penetrate a storm with the autopilot on. The cautions continued: don't use it at low speed, be sure you have at least 1,000 feet of altitude and good airspeed before engaging it, make sure the B-24 is properly trimmed first, don't trust what the gyro instruments say unless the engines are turning at a fairly high rpm, and always make sure that the suction gauge confirms vacuum is in the proper range.

A review of the rubber deicer shoes on the leading edges followed, but it was a very brief session and contained no specific disclaimer about the B-24's notorious inability to carry anything but a very modest load of ice. More attention was paid to such precautions as making sure the system was off before landings or takeoffs. The session concluded with operation of alcohol spray deicer systems for the props and windshields.

Session thirteen was something of a catch all, and began with the environmental system which proved that it was best to be stationed on the flight deck or in the nose where all of the heater outlets were located. The gunners in the back could plug into outlets if they had electrically-heated flying suits (not available at the CCTS in early 1942). The Liberator had many fresh air ventilators which, to a crew climbing into a bomber which had been sitting in the sun for a while or cruising low over the desert midday, were of great interest.

Because it was a somewhat related subject, the basic air data instruments were discussed in the same session as environmental controls.

The altimeter, airspeed indicator, and vertical speed indicator were old hat for Jeffries and Reynard although they had never flown an airplane with so many sets of each instrument (the navigator and bombardier had theirs too). Here, the bulk of the attention was given to the location of static sources, drain tees, and the pitot heater switch.

The seemingly mundane topic of instrument and cockpit lighting, which was fluorescent in the B-24, followed. Since failure of the lighting would get immediate attention, if not a frenzy, Jeffries and Reynard had to know exactly and quickly how to change bulbs and fuses. TWA assumed that if the pilots weren't clever enough to carry a working flashlight, the flight engineers would be.

Because their previous training aircraft carried only one fire extinguisher, Jeffries and Reynard learned that they had a wealth of emergency equipment in the B-24 which was intended to be crewed by ten men. In addition to the engine fire extinguishers, there were handheld extinguishers liberally placed throughout the fuselage. The Liberator also carried two life rafts which were located in separate compartments aft of the top turret. When a release handle was pulled, the spring loaded doors popped open and ejected the rafts, each with a 1,000 pound carrying capacity.

Crew rations, dye markers, signal pistol with flares, and first aid kits completed the complement of emergency supplies. Although not considered part of the emergency equipment, there was a large metal water jug bolted onto the back bulkhead by the flight engineer's position.

After learning fuel, oil, armament, bomb load, and cargo capacities, pilots and engineers ran through a trial weight and balance exercise which rather incongruously concluded ground session thirteen.

The fifth and sixth flying lessons saw Jeffries and Reynard each taking turns in the left seat. In-flight emergencies were simulated during these lessons and included losing an engine, feathering, and transferring fuel. The first portion of these flights was a simple climbout to the practice area and reviewing simulated landings. When one was not in the left seat, he was getting some cross training by role playing at the flight engineer's station in back of the pilot's seat. They were taught how to feather props and fly with a simulated engine out. Then, the moment came. Each started to make landings. When three satisfactory landings had been made, they were signed off as competent in getting the beast back on the ground without breaking it.

They entered this stage with considerable trepidation since they had never before attempted anything that approached such an undertaking. After all, their only previous multi-engine experience was in the aging B-18. There were mitigating factors in landing the '24 at Kirtland. Although the approach speed was roughly half again that of an AT-6, the angle of descent was much flatter than that which they had been flying, the landing pattern itself was much larger, and, for the time being, they were landing on one of the widest, longest runways in the world. And, should things suddenly start going downhill, there was an experienced instructor pilot just across the control pedestal.

Although the B-24 was not difficult to fly, the first few landings were challenging to transitioning pilots since they were not used to an airplane with such momentum. With the Stearman, BT-13, and AT-6, Jeffries and Reynard were used to prompt response to control inputs. Pull the stick back, and the nose promptly came up. Such was not the case with the B-24. They were taught to make power approaches using a sink rate of 400 feet per minute, final approach airspeed not lower than 115 mph, and to start the flare out much earlier than with anything else

*Pilot's side, B-24D Liberator instrument panel.*

they had ever flown. Starting the flare five to ten feet off the deck as they had in basic or advanced would invite disaster with a Liberator, and the resulting hard landings were the most common problem CCTS instructors had to overcome.

The students also had to get used to the '24s tendency to pitch nose down as soon as the mains contacted the runway, unlike the T-6s they had been flying. Thus, the wheel had to be held firmly back until the nose settled as speed decayed.

Having been taught to initiate the flare out early, new pilots were reminded that a normal landing was with full flaps, done on the main gear alone, and that braking was to be done only after the nose gear had been lowered onto the runway. CCTS pilots were all leery of excessive braking to start with since early '24s had a bad reputation for brakes that locked up. Only in cases of dire emergency could a three-wheel landing with immediate braking be considered.

Once each student had demonstrated competence at landings, night orientation was introduced starting with a takeoff just before dusk. Each student pilot also got some simulated instrument time in the air through the simple expedient of draping him in a hood which obscured the view outside but allowed full vision of the instrument panel. Unfortunately, the budding bomber pilots got less than a couple hours of this type of instrument flying which included climbs, descents, turns to specified headings, and practice instrument approaches using the Albuquerque radio range.

Although pilots going through B-24 transition in 1942 had gotten BT-13 and AT-6 under-the-hood time and had about 12 hours in Link trainers, their instrument flying experience was not quite up to today's FAA instrument rating standards. To help students maintain their instrument edge, flying the Link trainer was a regular part of the program at the CCTS, especially since actual instrument air time was so limited. It was a necessary evil, and few pilots ever really enjoyed their sessions in the simulator, although it taught the proper instrument approaches into Albuquerque which, because of the mountains to the east, could be unforgiving of a serious lapse in judgement.

The Link module of the CCTS course consisted of five hours which commenced with the basics and ended with something quite new: QDM approaches. Those approaches were the forerunner of the localizer portion of today's instrument landing systems, and provided landing aircraft with left/right directional guidance to a runway centerline while still several miles out on the approach. The system was essentially a modified range station with two beacons instead of four. With the QDM system and radio compass, the CCTS had taken Jeffries and Reynard right up to what was then state-of-the art in operational radio navigation systems.

If student pilots were lucky, they might get a session on formation flying through the generosity of the instructors who had to bend the rules to do so since it was not part of the curriculum. What little Jeffries and Reynard got of flying a vee or an echelon was very loose, and paled in comparison with that which they would have learned in phase training had they lived to rejoin their bomb groups.

The next ground session relieved the tedium of classroom sessions and was devoted to the radio equipment. The introduction started in the classroom, but the learning was promptly applied out in the aircraft. Jeffries and Reynard already had some familiarity with radio equipment and procedures, but the radio compass was still relatively new to them, and entirely new to Peterson who also had to be familiar with its operation. Much of this session was devoted to very quickly learning where all of the equipment, call boxes, and antennas were located along with how to change fuses and troubleshoot such common problems as sticky relays and solenoids, broken filaments in tubes, and noisy or weak reception.

Part of the radio session was devoted to proper radio procedures and phraseology as it related to carrying on a conversation with tower controllers and radio voice ranges. Jeffries and Reynard had been using such buzzwords as "roger," "wilco," and "over," but it was all new for Peterson whose previous duties had been ground-based. Crews were exposed to the use of throat microphones, but used handheld mikes in the aircraft since nearly everybody objected to the chafing and irritation caused by the throat units.

The radiotelephone procedures section ended with some sound advice, "Never argue with the control tower operator, and never proceed contrary to the methods prescribed by the control tower."

Although Mather had the capability to train cadets in oxygen systems, it had not been integrated into the single-engine curriculum when Jeffries and Reynard went through. It was, however, an important part of ground school at the CCTS, although the practical demonstration in flight was limited to the supercharger familiarization and cross country portions of the curriculum. The oxygen orientation began with a medical discussion on hyperventilation, aeroembolism, hypoxia, how to recognize their symptoms, and then moved to the B-24's oxygen systems. The ground school provided crews with a review of the B-24's high and low pressure oxygen systems, the regulators located at crew stations, and the types of oxygen masks then in use. There was another aspect of oxygen usage not mentioned in most training curricula, and that was its remarkably curative qualities when introduced to subjects suffering from particularly annoying hangovers.

Considerable ground school emphasis was placed on takeoff emergencies. What might Lt. Roland Jeffries do should he lose the number three engine on takeoff and how would his response differ had he lost one, two or four? In the case of one, two, or four, he would quickly be sure to maintain 135 mph, make certain which engine he had in fact lost, retrim the ship to maintain straight and level flight, retract the gear, promptly feather the prop, and follow that by shutting down the engine (shoving mixture into cutoff, turn off the fuel boost pump, cutting the ignition, and closing the cowl flaps). He would also make sure that a good engine was driving the vacuum pumps (most certainly if it were an instrument takeoff). Finally, he would confirm that the automatic pilot had not somehow been turned on. All of that would be done in less time than it took to read the above procedure. Jeffries would have raised the wing flaps in small increments at a time, but probably kept five or ten degrees while at low speed. He would have avoided any steep turns while calling the tower for an emergency landing clearance. And, he would have asked the flight engineer to see if the cause could be determined. Just as a precaution, the flight engineer would have closed the fuel valve to the dead engine in case the problem had been a broken fuel line.

Losing number three meant to lose hydraulic pressure which is why Jeffries would make sure the auxiliary hydraulic pump was running. Losing two engines was rare, but the B-24 would still fly after a fashion, even with two fans gone on the same side. There weren't too many consoling factors to be discussed about losing two engines on takeoff, other than hoping that Jeffries and his crew had taken off on runway one-seven which faced relatively flat, uninhabited land through which the Rio Grande flowed.

Then came the final exam — a 150-question test that required knowledge of all data and parameters in the pilot's operating manuals for the

National Archives

*CCTS Liberators over Albuquerque, spring 1942.*

B-24D and LB-30B, but more importantly required quick thinking since most of the questions were devoted to "what if" emergencies.

What if, for example, you notice a momentary lack of longitudinal stability immediately after takeoff? Charlie Reynard would have been correct by observing that the cowl flaps had not been trailed (closed partially). What would he do if flying on instruments and it suddenly became necessary to shut down the number two engine? He would be sure to move the vacuum control selector to the number one engine before shutting two down.

We're cruising in an LB-30 with the autopilot on, and to make things interesting, we suddenly have to feather number three for one reason or another. State in great detail what you must do relative to the hydraulic system. Then, you've lost the electric hydraulic pump, just before landing. The complete B-24 pilot would turn on the electric hydraulic pump switch, open the red star valve on the back of the electric pump, and turn off the autopilot. Then, hand crank the gear down, reverse the hand pump valves and pump the flaps down. Be sure the accumulators are up in pressure. Finally, check the lock indicators on all landing gears. The problem-solution questions ran the full range of potential trouble. Number four cylinder head temperature has started to climb, then dropped, and the engine started running rough. Its manifold pressure began to drop. Nobody has touched the engine controls and ignition is normal. What's the problem and what are you going to do about? It's carburetor ice which is best prevented by closing the intercooler shutters to bring heat to the carburetor.

Some of the questions were designed to keep students from doing stupid things. "The gear is coming down and you select 20 degrees of flaps, but they won't stay down. What's the problem?" Answer: "They work best when dropped at speeds below 155 mph." Other series of questions made sure students knew proper locations of emergency equipment, fuel sight gauges, prop anti-icer fluid reservoirs, landing gear emergency hand crank, battery connect/disconnect solenoids, de-icer boot controls, and on and on until the young pilots were seeing the B-24 interior, instrument panel, and controls in their dreams.

A total of 24 hours airborne in a Liberator including 12 hours in the left seat, enough takeoffs and landings to prove that they wouldn't damage the airplane, a solid ground school introduction to the machine, and a familiarization with emergency procedures cannot be described as a thorough orientation. But, it was all that was available, and based on how its students in the 305th and 306th Bomb Groups progressed, TWA's CCTS had done as much as humanly could be done given the limitations of time.

Toward the end of their month at B-24 transition, a significant cross country was flown, with one student taking the outbound leg, and the other the return flight. Occasionally, the "long" cross country was shortened to a quick roundtrip between closer points, such as Salt Lake City or Phoenix, in order to maximize aircraft availability. The longer cross country was regarded as the "graduation" exercise, and occasionally flown to a student's hometown if it happened to conveniently fall within a 700 to 1200 mile radius of Albuquerque. Thus, there were trips, usually overnight, to such cities as Minneapolis, St. Louis, Kansas City, San Francisco, and, less frequently, New York, Washington or Miami. Jonas Ruff had made his first cross country training flight to Moffett Field, just outside San Francisco in mid-February, so it was possible to see family and friends even with the busy schedule.

Charlie was hoping to be able to fly his cross country to Los Angeles to see his sister, Mary, and college friends there. The sojourn in Albuquerque was pleasant for him. He enjoyed flying the B-24, had enough time to get in some singing with the choir of the local Christian Church, and made some new friends in the academic community. He also had driven up to Santa Fe to see his fiancée's eldest sister, Ruth, who worked for the New Mexico Health Commission.

The cross country to Los Angeles, however, had not worked out. It was going to be Kansas City instead.

# XIX

# THE CRUEL SKY

Some evening, when I'm sitting out alone
Watching, perhaps, a cloud across the sky,
I'll feel as if a strange cool wind has blown
And suddenly I'll know that I'm to die.

From *Prayer* by John Gillespie Magee[1]

The takeoff was scheduled for 5 p.m. local time (4 p.m. MWT). The preflight was a carbon copy of the one performed that morning in Albuquerque with two exceptions. First, Jeffries' family and fiancée, Mary, walked through the preflight with him and were briefly taken on a tour inside the bomber. Second, there was no Army ground crew readying the ship for flight. The men of 41-1133 pulled the props through, served as their own fire guard, and prepared to start the Liberator with its own power using the onboard auxiliary power unit.

In his flight plan, Charlie calculated block flying time at exactly four hours. The actual straight line time was closer to three hours and 45 minutes, but he had to allow for takeoff, climb to altitude, and the strong possibility of an instrument approach into Kirtland which would add a few minutes to their flight.

The Liberator was clocked out of Kansas City at 4:02 p.m. MWT. They were flying direct, and Jeff made a position report 50 minutes after takeoff indicating they were 25 miles northwest of Newton, Kansas.

They had not flown into the strongest headwinds at that point since their first position report, transmitted roughly 165 miles out of Kansas City, indicated a ground speed of approximately 200 mph. The headwind picked up when they had covered another 100 miles. An oil-soaked map was later found in the wreckage; on it there was a notation indicating a groundspeed of 190 mph at a position ten miles north of Kinsley in south-central Kansas.

At 8:45 PM, not having arrived within 45 minutes of its ETA, the Liberator was declared overdue. At midnight, when fuel exhaustion would have occurred, the ship's status was moved to "missing." State police and civilian volunteers started searching the countryside near Las Vegas the next morning. Telegrams were sent to families on the morning of the 23rd. News of the plane's missing status had been released by Col. A.D. Smith, Kirtland's operations officer and was picked up on the Associated Press wire. Newspapers from coast to coast on April 24th carried articles on the "giant bomber" being overdue and many followed the story through to its conclusion. Colonel Frank Hackett, Kirtland Field's base commander, was usually quoted in the reports, and he painted a very realistic picture of what was expected to be a difficult search hampered by the Liberator's dark olive green camouflage and the strong possibility of snow covering the plane.

CCTS crews were to search by air in 100 mile square grids beginning Friday, April 24th. Although the weather was bad on Thursday, five Army planes searched briefly late in the day in the Las Vegas area. Police, forest rangers, Army personnel, and Boy Scout troops continued the ground search. In spite of the crew's last radio message noting their position well north of Las Vegas, the search on Friday was concentrated in a quadrant formed by the Rio Grande River, Route 64, and Las Vegas. Unfortunately, the weather remained sour, and the Friday search mission, scheduled for a dawn takeoff, was postponed until midday.

With clearing weather on Saturday, April 25th, flights of 11 to 15 CCTS Liberators resumed their aerial grid search until the bomber was located — not an easy feat considering the ship's olive drab/gray camouflage and the heavily forested terrain where the Liberator went in. Complicating matters was the snow. The Sandia Mountains northeast of Albuquerque were covered with it, and, north of Albuquerque, elevations above 8,000 feet had received considerable snow too.

Since training could not be suspended, flight instruction was combined with searching. The lucky Hal Blackburn, who had remained behind in Kansas City on the 22nd, joined the search on April 25th, and logged nearly 22 hours in the five search missions he flew through April 30th. Some of the search flights were long; Hutch Thurston logged over eight hours on his April 25th search mission.

On Sunday the 26th, good flying weather prevailed, and 16 planes from Kirtland searched in an inverted triangle with Albuquerque as its apex and the Colorado line as its base. Eleven of the planes were CCTS B-24s which collectively logged 95 hours in that day's search. They came home empty-handed. Over the next several days, CCTS crews searched along the east slope of the Sangre de Cristos and in an area extending from Las Vegas to Eagle Nest Lake (the latter about 25 miles west of Cimarron). The apprehensive families of the missing crew members got a very cold splash of water in their faces on the morning of the 27th. It came in the form of telegrams from Col. Smith and Frank Busch, the CCTS assistant operations manager. Although the families continued to hope for the best, Kirtland authorities had concluded that none of the crew would be found alive. The telegrams advised that the extensive aerial search was continuing, but ominously asked the families what should be done with their sons' personal effects (including Jonas' automobile).

On Friday, May 1st, at 10 a.m. one of the '24s searching over the Cimarron Mountains observed something unusual. There appeared to be a disruptive pattern on one of the forested mountainsides below. The aircraft commander/instructor pilot took his '24 lower where he observed several parallel, dark, greasy tracks leading up almost to the crest of a mountain nearly ten miles west of the village of Cimarron.

The instructor pilot was Howard Kincheloe. After returning to the United States, he had contacted TWA upon the advice of a friend in Wichita. He was hired and quickly became a highly respected instructor. With him as first officer was Hutch Thurston. Howard took the '24 down below 11,000 feet, started circling counterclockwise, called other '24s, and soon there were several Liberators circling Trail Peak.

When radioed the grim news, Col. Frank Hackett called police and arranged to conduct a ground search on Saturday, May 2nd. The party's guide was a young man who was intimately familiar with the territory around Trail Peak. He was Elliott "Chope" Phillips, son of Philmont's donors, and before the war ended, he too would become an Army Air Force officer. One of the search party leaders was Hal Blackburn who, with Kirtland Field's executive officer, Colonel William C. Lewis, and two other officers had flown a pair of BT-13s up from Albuquerque and landed at Philmont.

Lewis and Blackburn were a study in contrasts. One was a "full bull" colonel and the other a lieutenant in the reserves. Lewis, an Oklahoman by birth and lawyer by training, had just been promoted to full colonel. He was about ten years older than Blackburn, a WWI veteran, a gradu-

Photo courtesy of Howard M. Kincheloe

*Upon his return to the United States, Howard Kincheloe joined the CCTS as an instructor pilot. While on a combination training and search flight, he discovered the wreckage of Liberator 41-1133 on May 1, 1942.*

ate of the Army Command and General Staff School, and was particularly well-educated. His A.B. and LL.B. degrees were from the University of Michigan, and his doctor of jurisprudence was from Columbia. He had been a reserve officer in the Judge Advocate General's Department, but switched to the Air Corps in 1931 when he obtained his pilot's rating. Prior to going back on active duty in 1941, he had practiced law and been an assistant attorney general in Oklahoma City.

The second half of the route up to Philmont roughly paralleled the instrument airway between Albuquerque and Denver. They did not fly directly since the BT-13 was not designed for high altitude flight; to avoid flying at altitudes nearing 14,000 for terrain clearance, Blackburn led the flight north immediately out of Kirtland, turned east halfway to

Santa Fe, and then overflew Las Vegas which, like many other New Mexico communities, would shortly be home to another of New Mexico's growing list of Army airfields.

Today, what was once a busy Adcock radio range station with nearby army airfield is a relatively quiet airport on the high plain north of town. The old low frequency range station has been replaced by a modern VHF omnidirectional beacon. The field that served military and civil flights alike now basks in the New Mexico sun, visited primarily by gusts of wind and the shadows of high cumulus aloft.

From Las Vegas, Blackburn took up a north-northwest heading. After roughly 30 minutes of flying, Philmont's most memorable landmark was in full view as it had been for Santa Fe Trail travelers a century before — the Tooth of Time. This remarkable, massive stone formation emerges tooth-like from a steep ridge just west of Philmont ranch headquarters. The flight's landing was made in what is today's buffalo pasture, a large, level 10,000-acre tract between Tooth of Time Ridge and the village of Cimarron several miles to the east.

Almost seven years before, Will Rogers and Wiley Post had landed at the same grass field as guests of Waite Phillips. Several weeks after their Philmont visit, Rogers and Post perished on their ill-fated takeoff from Point Barrow, Alaska.

There were no trails up Trail Peak when the Blackburn and Lewis search party arrived; several decades were to pass before any paths would be cut into the mountain. The "Trail" in Trail Peak is derived from its being the dominant peak along the "trail" from Crater Lake Lodge to Rayado Lodge at Fish Camp (by way of Fowler Pass and then Webster Pass).

It was tough going because the spring of 1942 was wet. The storms on the 22nd and subsequent days had shut down Raton Pass. Hundreds of workers were required to restore the rail line over the pass, and even when it did re-open on the 29th, it ran only on a limited basis.[2] Water mains were washed out in the town of Raton, and residents had to rely on water from springs and wells. Slides and washouts, caused by rain, snow melt, and rampaging creeks and rivers, closed roads to many northern New Mexico communities. It was not until late on April 24th that traffic on major highways between Santa Fe and the Colorado line could be resumed.

Since the dirt road approaching Crater Lake Camp was impassable, the search party rode horses from headquarters to Trail Peak via Fowler

Pass whose vistas looking back at the Tooth of Time Ridge and sweeping prairie were one of Waite Phillips' favorite views at Philmont. Crater Lake was a "half-way house" camp on the way to Philmont's prime trout fishing streams and a natural jump-off point for the search. The Trail Peak ascent was very difficult, particularly on the mountain's lower flanks where the snow was deepest. The snow at the crest was actually quite patchy, but further down in the taller, heavier timber and within the shadows of the nearby mountains, it was very deep. In fact, the snow was waist high on the men and, in some places, belly deep for the horses.

There were two parties converging on Trail Peak. Bruce Bull, a rancher from Black Lake (near Angel Fire, just south of Eagle Nest), had seen Army planes circling Trail Peak and decided to make the long ride over to investigate. Bull could accurately be described as part cowboy and part mountain man. He managed a ranch for another cattleman, operated his own small spread, and was a skilled hunter of bears and mountain lions.

Bull reached the crash site shortly before the Chope Phillips search party did at 3 p.m. Although they quickly located the bodies, bringing them out that day was impossible due to the late hour and deep snow. The searchers left the mountain and arrived back at ranch headquarters hours later. Most were exhausted, and in several cases, quite saddle sore, but cheered by the prospect of supper at Chope Phillips' home where they arrived well after dark. Home for Phillips was the "Webster Place," now the current residence of Philmont's general manager (located just below Villa Philmonte and diagonally across the road from the Ranch administration complex).

The discovery prompted all sorts of reports. The bomber had been heard droning over the Estancia Valley. It had been sighted flying low over the village of Miami, near Philmont, making popping noises. Other accounts had the plane crashing at Questa, north of Eagle Nest. Still another witness from the now abandoned coal mining village of Brilliant (north of Cimarron) said the plane had "faltered" and then headed north. A ranch hand near Rowe (about 25 miles southeast of Santa Fe) had seen "something fall out of the sky Wednesday night."

The search party, aided by more Philmont Ranch personnel, medical and technical crews from Kirtland, and state and local police returned to the mountain very early the next day, May 3rd, with seven pack horses to bring the bodies out. The Army men had spent the night at Cimarron's

St. James Hotel which was then trading as the Don Diego Hotel. For Blackburn, a man used to nice accommodations as an airline pilot, the St. James was a throwback to the western frontier. Still standing as a charming, AAA rated "historic hotel," the St. James does a lively business in the summer during the peak of Philmont's camping season. It dates back to post-Civil War days where many patrons passed in through the front doors, others passed out once therein after spending too much time at the bar, and a few were carried out (dead). The latter were hit by bullets other than those whose holes are still visible in the pressed tin ceiling of what is now the "formal" dining room.

The St. James guest register reads like a "Who's Who" of the Old West and encompasses everything from Army generals, outlaws, including Billy the Kid, Clay Allison and other lawmen, snake oil salesmen, frontier preachers, and hopeful prospectors. For the saddlesore searchers, the Don Diego, with its spacious rooms and comfortable beds, was as good as it got in downtown Cimarron.

A shortage of horses actually limited the size of the recovery party. Most of Philmont's horses had not been reshod after spending the winter in pasture. A number of Cimarron residents tried to reach Trail Peak by foot, but turned back, exhausted and bedraggled. Others, including local cowboys, were deflected by Colonel Lewis.

Late on Sunday, May 3rd, the bodies were taken in three ambulances back to Albuquerque and identified at the Strong Thorne Mortuary Service where the death certificates were completed. An inquest was held; there was no need for autopsies. The immediate causes of death were listed simply by coroner's jury as "Airplane Crash - U.S. Army Plane, April 22, 1942." Other than a terse notation of injuries suffered by the two pilots and flight engineer trainee (each of whom had been catapulted directly through the cockpit canopy on impact), there was no mention of specifics as to the causes of death among the other four flyers.

The personal effects of Army personnel were collected by Col. Lewis who subsequently turned them over to Col. McAllister, the West Coast Air Training Command liaison, while Hal Blackburn took charge of the TWA fliers' possessions. Blackburn arrived back in Albuquerque well ahead of the ambulances since he flew back in the BT-13 in an hour and a half with Col. Lewis. An Army maintenance crew completed recovery of what few instruments and components were worth salvaging. The engines and remaining intact airframe structures were subsequently dynamited.

Before initiating the technical investigation at the crash site, several facts could be deduced by looking at the damaged trees.[3] The '24 was in nearly level flight when it flew into the mountain on a true heading of 80 degrees (70 magnetic) with the left wing slightly low. The search party deduced that the number four (right outer) engine was dead before impact since its propeller showed no sign whatsoever of revolving contact with trees as did the other props. Sixty feet after hitting the first tree, the bomber slammed into the upslope which has a grade of approximately 35 percent. Five indentations were made in the mountain — one for each engine and one for the 24's nose which was demolished to the rear of the flight deck. In fact, the nose was broken into smithereens — totally gone all the way back to the leading edges of the wings. Then, the ship careened on for another 250 feet before coming to a stop.

The initial impact site is dense woods. The location where the bomber came to rest is still wooded, but there are a few small open patches which support grasses and wildflowers. Although the timberline in that part of the Rockies is above Trail Peak's crest, the mountain top and its northwestern ridge are dominated by smaller trees with occasional outcroppings of rock with attending small, boulder fields. What little topsoil exists is very thin. The circumstances cannot be described as those supporting a soft landing.[4]

The impact was of such force that the bomber's strongest structure, the wing center box section, was broken in two.[5] The left wing was sheared off at the root, and most of the upper portion of the fuselage center back to the wing trailing edges remained attached to the right wing. Both emergency compartments aft of the top turret had popped open exposing the life raft cradles. The bottom portion of the fuselage containing the bomb bay, below the wings, was completely stripped away. The fuselage was broken off just in back of the wings (very typical of B-24 crashes) with the aft section rolling inverted. The remains of the fuselage mid-section came to rest pointing approximately north while the engines, with their momentum, tore free of their mounts and were hurled another 100 feet ahead of the wreckage. One engine disintegrated and scattered parts down the mountain's north slope. The tail section remained surprisingly intact with relatively little damage to the rudders.

Ironically, the breakup of 41-1133 into its major components, except the nose (which was basically shredded) almost exactly duplicated the subassemblies from which Liberators were built: tail unit, aft-fuselage,

*A snow-covered Trail Peak from the east as seen in mid-April from the lower, northeastern flank of Urraca Mesa near Philmont's camping headquarters. The wreckage is on the mountain's western side, not visible in this view.*

wing box with fuselage top center section, outer wing panels, flaps, nacelles, leading edges, and bomb bay.

Death came instantly. Lt. Jeffries had been in the pilot's seat and was found 60 feet ahead of and to the left of the wreckage. Captain Redding was located 70 feet in front and to the right of the crumpled fuselage. Corporal Macomber had probably been sitting on the little jump seat behind Jeffries, was also thrown clear, and found about 25 feet in front of the wreckage. George Van Hoozer was located outside the fuselage under the leading edge of the left wing. He had been at the rear of the flight deck next to the bomb bay bulkhead. Peterson was pinned to the remaining left side of the fuselage near the trailing edge of the left wing, i.e. at the back of the bomb bay and far removed from his normal position immediately behind the copilot on the right side of the flight deck. Jonas Ruff was found on the ground just outside the left waist gunner's hatch. Lt. Reynard, whose body was the least disturbed of all, was found still strapped in on the right side of the waist compartment. In all likelihood, Ruff was occupying the waist compartment at the time of the crash and had been joined by Reynard who moved aft from the navigator's station at some point during the last half hour of the flight.

Thanks to the bad weather, snow, and cold at nearly 10,000 feet, the crew's broken bodies had not really started to decompose, although much of the snow on the mountain's crest was receding. There was not that unforgettable smell of human death at the crash site. The prevailing odor was that of a dead airplane whose life fluids had spilled out onto snow and dripped down to pool amidst the iced rocks and frozen earth. The scent of aviation gasoline, oil, and hydraulic fluid would not have attracted wildlife had any been in the area at the time. Although spring is starting to arrive in late April at Philmont, the mountain crests are only beginning to emerge from winter's firm grip. The bears continued in hibernation. The deer and elk were still in winter pasture in the open country of the foothills far below. Philmont's predators, the mountain lions, bobcats, and coyotes, were lower, closer to their traditional prey. It would take several more weeks before the ridges would echo the raven's rasp or the golden eagle's shrill cry. The men of 41-1133 had remained alone with their shattered airplane, more snow and rain, the penetrating cold of night, and for a few days, a bright, but not especially warming sun.

The only sounds of the previous ten days had been those of the moaning wind, creaking branches swaying in the breeze, and, until May 1st, the distant drone of Liberators too far away to discover Trail Peak's terrible secret.

Examination of the aircraft when finally found established a few facts, but raised even more questions. Corporal Macomber's was the only watch found on a body; it was not damaged and had stopped at 10:27. Several other watches, all damaged, indicating times from 8:22 to 8:27 were also found. The instrument panel clock could not be found, but the radio panel clock was located and ran perfectly after winding. However, a wrist watch with its hands firmly intact and indicating 8:29 p.m. was found among the flight deck debris. The back of the watch was missing, so it was accepted as the best evidence of the time of the crash.

All of the crew had been on oxygen as confirmed by settings on the oxygen regulator controls and locations of the masks relative to where the bodies were found.

The crew had been expecting the worst. Parachutes were attached and adjusted. Normally, 'chutes were stowed near one's station and grabbed only in an emergency. The bomb bay doors had been retracted since the door piston rods were found fully extended. Although the '24 had a number of emergency exits, standard procedure was to set the ship on autopilot, and bail everybody out from the bomb bay. A cautious Liberator skipper usually flew with doors at least slightly open to clear out gasoline fumes. Wide open doors usually meant a lot of fumes had to be cleared in a hurry. Although the bomb bay doors roll up and down their tracks quickly, the retraction was not likely actuated by the impact since it was too sudden for the doors to go full travel.

Not all of the flight instruments could be found. One of the altimeters suggested they had been flying at 12,500 feet, but since its pointers were loose, it was not accepted as good evidence. The altimeter on the pilot's side was found; although the mechanism was broken, the pointers were tight, and indicated 10,050 feet — about 200 feet too low to miss Trail Peak's crest. What remained of the engine controls (throttles, turbo-supercharger levers, mixture controls, friction locks, and prop and feathering switches) also suggested that the number four engine had indeed been shut down. The throttles and turbo controls for engines one through three were wide open, not something that would be expected in cruise — even with one engine dead. The mixture control for number four was found in idle cutoff, and the other three mixture controls were in auto lean (about mid-travel). Whether or not the friction locks could have held the controls in position through the terrific g-forces of the impact is not known. Thus, the position of the power controls of the operating engines at impact cannot necessarily be assumed to have been the same as those in flight with absolute, airtight certainty. The engine instruments, which would have told a more complete story, were hopelessly damaged (not all were found), thus masking clues as to the cause of engine failure and the final word on power settings.

The aileron trim wheel was found, and it indicated that the left wing had been set one degree low (the proper procedure for losing an engine on the opposite wing). What remained of the deicer and anti-icer controls appeared to be in the off position. The landing lights were partially extended and had presumably been pushed into a semi-retracted position by the impact. Turning landing lights on, except during approaches, almost certainly suggests that the pilots were looking for snow or examining the wings and intakes for the presence or extent of ice accumulation.

Based on the assumed power settings and familiarity with similar crashes, the investigators suggested that the ship had been doing close to 200 mph at the time of impact, or probably 50 mph faster than operating procedures would have called for during the stresses encountered in the average thunderstorm. The B-24's wings were not at all well regarded for their ability to tolerate ice, and a Liberator carrying even the lightest load of structural ice, especially on three engines, could not maintain 200 mph in level flight, so we have to assume that icing was not the primary cause of the accident (although staying below the freezing level robbed the crew of a safety margin considering the mountainous terrain over which they were flying).

Considering the airspeed, carburetor ice was probably not a factor. The intercooler controls, which would have pointed to the possibility of carburetor ice, were damaged beyond recognition anyway.

Scuttlebutt back at Kirtland when the crew was posted as missing focused on '1133 icing up and going in. The actual impact configuration refutes that conclusion. Had they been carrying a load of ice, but still flying, they would have impacted nose high and at an airspeed much, much lower than 200 mph. As such, hanging on its props, the bomber would have mushed into the tree and snow-covered upslope with a much greater chance that some of the crew could have survived. The darker scenario would have produced one of two types of spins. Had they spun out of an ice-induced stall, they probably would have gone in closer to the vertical, i.e. the devastation would have been much more substantial with nobody having been thrown clear. They weren't flying high enough for a potential spin to cause an in-flight breakup before hitting the ground. The other, much less likely, possibility would have been a flat spin in which case the impact would have been primarily from the bottom.

The fuel controls could not be found. Had they been available, they might have shed more light on the ship's fuel state, and if there had been a crisis in which Van Hoozer would have been very busy at the crossfeed controls. They might also have indicated why the bomb bay doors were retracted. Fuel starvation was unlikely since three engines were developing full power when the bomber hit Trail Peak.

There was no evidence of explosion and fire upon impact. That was quite atypical of such crashes — even with a minimum of fuel on board. Perhaps the 35 percent grade, a very modest cushioning effect of snow and trees, torrents of rain, and possibility of the fire extinguishers having been actuated at impact eliminated the fire potential.

The navigational equipment raised more questions. The artificial horizon indicated level flight while the directional gyro, although not in perfect condition, suggested a magnetic heading in the vicinity of 70 degrees, i.e. to the east. The radio compass dial (the rotatable azimuth card, not the needle pointer) indicated 250 degrees or roughly the heading that would take them to Kirtland from the original contact course, although the frequency as reported was set on 218 kc, a frequency that was not used for navigation anywhere in the United States in 1942. The 218 kc was probably a typo on the report which should have read 278 kc which was the frequency for the Anton Chico radio range. The latter station was down on the airway leading into Albuquerque from Amarillo, and would not have been used for airway navigation from Las Vegas southbound other than a position check. It is quite possible, considering the static from the storm, that the crew was trying to take bearings on any station they could receive, not necessarily the closest one. Or, more likely, the impact could have very easily jarred the frequency selector into a different position.

Still, the question has to be asked why they were off the airways, well north of their intended course, and heading east-northeast when their objective was to the southwest? Fly into a thunderstorm to give the trainees some realistic practice? Doubtful. Purposefully fly below the minimum enroute altitude and off the airways in instrument conditions? Captain Redding, the veteran pilot, had too much experience for that.

Fortunately, a record, or at least a fragmentary one, of 41-1133's last hour is available since they were in radio contact with the range station at Las Vegas. At 7:35 p.m., the ship reported its position as 25 miles east of Las Vegas, and, knowing about the weather ahead, requested an instrument clearance. The next contact, at 7:53, was quite garbled, but they reported their position as 75 miles northwest (or northeast) of Las Vegas, going on instruments and climbing to 14,000. The crash occurred roughly 35 minutes later.

What went wrong? Lapse in airmanship? Mechanical problems? The weather complicated matters, especially the way it interfered with that era's radio navigation and communication equipment which became practically useless in the vicinity of thunderstorms. Range stations also became nearly worthless, and their effective reception distance diminished sharply in electrical storms. The radios just crackled with static and the radio compass needle spun round and round senselessly. With enough turbulence, the directional gyro and artificial horizon would tumble, thus driving the pilots back to the basics — needle, ball, airspeed, the magnetic compass (with all of its foibles), and the seats of their pants.

To this day, the Air Force Aerospace Safety Directorate censors accident reports regarding airmanship errors (as they should, considering how painful complete disclosure might be to some surviving family members). The official accident report, in this case, lists weather and the loss of an engine as contributory factors, and implies that pilot error was another reason for the "collision in full flight with objects other than aircraft."

Since Captain Redding and his crew were unable to testify before the board of inquiry, the precise cause of the accident can never be known. Indeed, over three decades were to pass before aviation science would acquaint accident investigators with such hazards as downburst, microburst, and windshear, thus reducing some of the kneejerk tendency to immediately write many weather-related accidents off to "pilot error."

Therefore, it is pretty much an educated guess as to what actually caused Liberator 41-1133 to crash into Trail Peak. There are a number of scenarios which involve structural icing, the dead engine and crosswind moving them off course, poor reception of their radio direction finder, and the distraction of a potential fuel crisis. Those problems may actually have contributed to the crash, but, even collectively, they were situations that a highly experienced, multi-engine instructor crew could have managed.

What really happened? Nobody will ever know for sure, but the loss of nearly 4000 feet, the aircraft's attitude and speed at impact, and the probability that icing was not a direct factor point to only one cause back in those days when radar technology and ground control were in their infancy and not available to Redding and his crew. The real cause of the crash may well have played out along the following, speculative scenario's lines.

It is a long, boring flight back to Albuquerque. The newness of the day's flight is lost, a situation not helped by the featureless prairies of Kansas. The Rockies to the west are obscured in what is obviously going to be some worsening weather. The crew has been subjected to the roar of 4,800 horses for hours. There's the constant aggravation of their ever-vibrating environment which hasn't exactly been set for room temperature. For Jeffries, there's the added tension of being evaluated. Could every call Reynard makes for a course correction be an indictment of their flying ability? Sky conditions are starting to deteriorate. Whereas they have been flying with a clear sky, the horizon to the west is not encouraging. It is, in a word, discouraging. They are headed for some heavy weather because storms are occurring throughout central and northern New Mexico. Within a fat crescent running from El Paso to the Four Corners, and including Albuquerque and Santa Fe, flying conditions are quite simply miserable. And getting worse.

Structural ice is not a problem at this point, as they enter New Mexican airspace, since they are not flying in cloud. There is some static which is making use of their navigational equipment difficult — a sure sign of thunderstorms ahead. Although they are not flying on the instrument airways, they use the radio compass to periodically confirm their position. There are forecasts of storms around Tucumcari, New Mexico, and the weather at Las Vegas is definitely deteriorating.

Captain Redding occasionally puts his hand over the throttles where he can almost feel the heartbeats of the engines. His pilot's sense tells him something is amiss which is confirmed on his next scan of the instrument panel. Number four's oil pressure is falling fast, and oil temperature is starting to climb. Had it been something simple, like carburetor ice or a broken fuel pump, simply closing the intercooler shutters or starting the electric booster pump would have quickly set matters right. Unfortunately, this time, it is not that simple.

Was it a cracked oil line whose consequences would have been as just described? For whatever reason, a stuck valve, seized piston, or broken main bearing, the bomber has lost number four whose prop is promptly feathered. It is not a disaster since the '24 can still maintain flight on three fans.

Nearly all pilots and mechanics, however, had nothing but praise for the Pratt & Whitney Twin Row Wasp engine, although stoppages and failures were not unheard of. Most verbal abuse was heaped upon the Liberator's hydraulic and electrical systems, especially the electrically-controlled propeller governors which were subject to frequent malfunctions.

At 7:35, Redding calls Las Vegas radio, reports their position as 25 miles east of the station, and requests an instrument clearance. He would have been made aware of the latest weather at various stations around New Mexico as reported twice an hour by Las Vegas radio — assuming that reception was satisfactory (not a certainty by any means).

At 1930 hours, or 7:30, Las Vegas is ugly with a 300 foot ceiling, rain, and the wind at 27 knots from the southwest.

The crew is being jostled about as they encounter rain and increasing turbulence. Jeffries cranks the aileron trim wheel to lower the left wing slightly, thus reducing the bomber's natural tendency to turn toward the dead engine, and quickly scans the autopilot selector panel to make sure it is disengaged. Still, he has to maintain pressure on the left rudder pedal to the extent that it will eventually become a tiresome task even with the rudders retrimmed. Now that the power crisis is stabilized, the weather is their real problem. There's a major thunderstorm right in front of them, and they are technically on the borderline between visual and instrument flying. As aircraft commander, Redding is well aware of the options as dictated by the type of thunderstorm they are encountering.

Army Air Force policy was blunt, "Fly over or around, never through or under." There were exceptions, such as flying under a warm front-induced storm system, but for orographic and convective thunderstorms, the law was over or around, and, informally, between cells, but only for the most compelling of reasons. The generally accepted minimum for overflying mountains is a clearance of 3,000 feet — any more, so much the better.

Redding's choices are to hunker down and chug right on through (not advisable), divert either north or south and pick a route around the storm, or make a 180 in order to find some alternate field to land and wait the storm out. The latter approach would have saved them, but was out of character. Only a pantywaist amateur in some puddlejumper would cut and run; '1133 was a B-24 and not about to be frightened by a few drops of rain on the windscreen.

The storm was of the type and intensity that the first option was readily dismissed. In fact, the current ceiling in Albuquerque was relayed to Las Vegas at 8:05 for onward transmission to '1133 although its receipt by the bomber can never be confirmed due to the static that night. Had they received it, they would have been encouraged because Albuquerque was reporting an estimated ceiling of 5,000 with eight miles visibility in rain and winds only nine knots from the south. It is possible, and indeed likely, that Redding could have gotten the 7:30 p.m. weather to the south from Las Vegas radio. Had that been the case, 41-1133 would have been advised that there were thunderstorms at Otto and Las Vegas with ceilings down to 600 feet. At 8 p.m., the ceiling at Trinidad, Colorado, was reported as 5,000 feet, and thunderstorms were widespread around Tucumcari to the south. With storms and ceilings ranging from 300 to 600 feet ahead and to the south while better ceilings were reported to the north, a northerly detour was logical even though it was an area of rising terrain unlike that to the south. After all, Santa Fe was reporting a broken ceiling of 6,000 feet. On the other hand, the 7:30 p.m. weather at Raton was a different matter: an overcast ceiling at 1000 feet, rain, and surface winds from the south at 23 knots.

Still, conventional aeronautical wisdom dictates choosing lower, flatlands instead of mountains if heavy weather must be flown through. On balance, the reported weather at 7:30 p.m. looked worse over the more inviting topography to the south.

After years of dodging thunderstorms, Redding knows better than to penetrate one of those big storm cells especially after losing an engine. Hoping for some good luck, they turn north assuming they'll find a less turbulent path around or between the cells with plans to turn west at some point, and maybe break out north of Santa Fe for an easy flight down to Albuquerque. Heretofore, they have been flying in and out of instrument conditions. Soon, they will go solidly "on the gauges."

Waiting for an instrument clearance on an airway that was blocked by a towering storm, not to mention their already being on the storm's edges, was quite simply unrealistic. Furthermore, there is no indication from the radio records at Las Vegas that the clearance, if indeed it was issued, was ever received by the crew. Better to muscle their way north even if they have to fly through the storm's fringe was clearly the path they chose.

There was one additional element of logic in the decision to turn north. As a thunderstorm grows to maturity, the winds feeding the updrafts in the core tend to blow counterclockwise. Thus, passing to the south would result in headwinds. Given a choice, pilots familiar with thunderstorms, as Redding was, will pass a storm on the right.

Just as the crew becomes accustomed to the storm's roar, Mother Nature slings another nasty surprise at the Liberator: hail. It is as though the bomber flies head-on into a barrage fired by 10,000 malevolent BB gunners. The metallic staccato goes on for about 45 seconds and then gives way to more rain. The bomber emerges from the hail with no more damage than some peeled paint, but the crew's nerves are starting to fray. At this point, 41-1133 is flying in and out of cloud (mostly the latter).

Today, with ground-based controllers and airborne weather radar, picking the least dangerous way through a squall line, especially in daylight, is commonplace. Redding had to find his way through those angry battlements and seething vapors in the dark, off the airways and light lines, with radio navigation rendered nearly useless by the storms, with one engine dead, and quite likely with the distraction of icing and/or fuel problems.

At this point, the storm is pummeling them severely, and the lightning is blinding, so Captain Redding turns the cockpit lighting up to full bright as he and Jeffries crank their seats down to the lowest settings. Now, there's another irksome task — there's the fuel imbalance due to number four's having been shut down, so Van Hoozer has to work the crossfeed controls. Van Hoozer calls on the intercom with more bad news. The crew can already smell the problem — there's a leak somewhere in the '24's notoriously balky fuel system, and it's serious.

Captain Redding orders the crew to fasten and adjust their 'chutes just to be on the safe side, and asks Lt. Reynard, who is handling the navigation on this leg, to plot their position immediately. Redding now looks at an instrument to which he has paid little attention all day. It is the outside air temperature gauge; from its reading, and knowing the lapse rate, he quickly calculates that they might just be able to climb as high as 14,000 before running the risk of icing up.

In spite of the static, Reynard manages to plot their position; it's about 70 miles northwest of Las Vegas, but they still haven't found a safe way past this storm. Their position report was relayed to Las Vegas radio at 7:53 p.m. along with advice of their going on instruments and climbing 14,000. There is great significance and not a lack of coincidence in the altitude to which they reported climbing. It was the minimum enroute altitude (MEA) for flights heading south and/or west on the Amber Three airway, the instrument route from Denver that intersects Green Four airway just east of Albuquerque for the approach into Kirtland. 14,000 is the least altitude with which they could maintain the barest margin of safety from ground contact.

Had Redding indicated a climb to 15,000, that would have signified his intention to head north to Denver, but then he would have subsequently iced up quickly and certainly. Clearly, he had made the decision to tough it out on the airway southbound since the storm was proving to be worse than anticipated to the west, and he was already well into instrument conditions. To complicate matters, the radio compass was all but useless considering the weather. They were flying strictly by reference to their basic air data instruments, plus the directional gyro and artificial horizon. Jeffries hadn't even touched the dial on his radio compass indicator in over a half hour.

Fourteen thousand was an altitude which '1133 could not have maintained, at least not for an extended period of time. Today, knowing exactly what the falling surface temperatures were at Raton that evening, we can conclusively be assured that the bomber would have been lucky to maintain 13,000 which was approximately the freezing level's location at 8 p.m.

Redding was familiar with the mountains surrounding Philmont, and had flown over them recently. Only two weeks previously, he had taken a Liberator and training crew to Scottsbluff, Nebraska, to be present while minor surgery was performed on his 14-month old son, Michael. He returned to Kirtland the same day, and would have seen all of Philmont's great peaks beyond his left wing if the flight had been direct under contact (visual) rules. Had he flown on instruments, he would have passed only 20 miles east of the Philmont Ranch since the airway was based on radio ranges at Cheyenne, Denver, Pueblo, Trinidad, a little dogleg at Maxwell just northeast of Cimarron, Las Vegas, and then down to Otto for a right turn onto Green Four which leads to Albuquerque. Today's Victor 19 Airway follows a similar path: Denver, Colorado Springs, Pueblo, Cimarron, Las Vegas, and then on Victors 60 and 12 to Albuquerque.

Meanwhile, the '24 is no longer between cells; they are now flying into the heart of a cell — one of those towering New Mexico thunderboomers that reaches up to 30,000 or 40,000 feet, which, from their situation, is impossible to climb over. Worse yet, they are going to encounter a downburst.

Downbursts and the more severe, localized microburst were not described by aviation science until 1975. Downbursts and their related windshears are usually associated with thunderstorms and involve a column of rain-chilled, cold air rushing earthward at thousands of feet per minute. The gusts fan out at the bottom of the column and form "increasing" and "decreasing" performance windshears of 60 to 80 knots. The winds in a decreasing performance windshear, essentially a massive tailwind, are quite enough to quickly reduce indicated airspeed in a B-24 from 150 mph to 90 or below stalling speed.

An aircraft's heading emerging from a downburst (assuming it does emerge) may or may not be the same as that entering, depending on what the downburst penetration angle was. That phenomenon and the near certainty that Redding had given up trying to fly northwest around the storm account for the Liberator's easterly heading at impact.

In most instances, aircraft (the lucky ones) don't enter the descending air column head-on, but hit it obliquely or experience only the windshear from an angle closer to the ground. The truly unfortunate are those who fly directly into a microburst during takeoff or landing. The best known instance of the latter misfortune was the case of the Delta Airlines L-1011 which crashed on approach to Dallas-Fort Worth in 1985. That catastrophe and the loss of life associated with other wind shear-related accidents prompted the FAA's installation of Doppler radars at major aerodromes to more accurately pinpoint windshears whose previous presence was largely reported by word of mouth, i.e. pilot reports.

Conditions on April 22, 1942 were ideal for the microburst/downburst phenomenon: virga (rain falling from convective cloud and evaporating before reaching the ground) was observed east of Albuquerque, and there were scattered, heavy thunderstorms throughout northern New Mexico. Indeed, the eastern flanks of the Rockies are well known for their high incidence of downburst and windshear activity.

'1133 would not be the last bomber to be claimed by night storms in the Cimarron Mountains or Sangre de Cristos. Almost six months later to the day, the next accident occurred when another Kirtland-bound '24 crashed on Little Baldy Peak in the Costilla cluster not far from Philmont (near Vermejo Park).

The vertical winds in the core of a downburst can push a 27-ton bomber earthward as though it were a toy. The crew is terrified since they know that the sky below is filled with "cumulo-granite" especially to the north and west.

The lightning's flash and thunder's booming crash come simultaneously. The bomber reeks of gasoline which needs only the slightest electrical spark to turn the '24 into a fireball. The wingtips are flapping up and down alarmingly in the turbulence which is shoving the crew around like rag dolls. The crew, however, can't see the wingtips moving since their windows look like oozing, charcoal smudges so intense is the rain. The storm even mutes the sound of their engines. Anything that's not tied down, flies around: a B-4 bag or two, aviator's kit bags, flashlights, that department store package from Kansas City, a thermos bottle, and Reynard's E-6B.

The tension is tremendous. Redding is afraid of structural failure, and takes the added precaution of fully retracting the bomb bay doors for the bailout that he feels might soon be inevitable — besides, it clears out all of the gasoline fumes in a hurry. He's pulled the power back until they are indicating about 150, the recommended maneuvering speed for storm conditions.

The turbulence digs restraint straps into shoulders and waists, and on top of that, it's very difficult to handle the controls with a chest parachute on. Pushed up one minute, and down a few minutes later as they career in and around the mighty cells. They all vow never, but never, to be caught in anything like this again, ever. That's exactly what Redding and Ruff had said the last time. And the time before that. It's hard to say who is more frightened, the veterans who've been there before and have lost friends in storms, or the rest of them for which this is one intimidating introduction.

They're all on oxygen, and their continuous flow masks, with their external rebreather bladders, are cumbersome and uncomfortable. It's a hellish place in this thunderstorm, the sky's own dungeon. There's nothing else they can do except take the thrashing for a little bit longer. Visions of planes with wings folding under the heavy loads of storm turbulence pass through the pilots' minds. The training lessons come back, "You can wrinkle a Liberator pulling out of a dive if you aren't trimmed up right."

More lightning. It's terrifying, yet wickedly beautiful the way it lights up the sky and turns those nearby black masses into big, white fluffy cotton balls — for a second or so, before pitch blackness returns. The lightning comes and goes, some close, and some far away, but powerful enough to make clouds look like they have red-hot volcanoes in their bellies. There's no help anywhere, no contact with the outside world because their radio is, for all practical purposes, dead useless.

Suddenly, the cockpit and instrument panel lighting fail, plunging the pilots into darkness. To lose touch with the primary air data instruments is to lose control of the ship. Furious pounding on the glareshield and cycling the lighting switches bring illumination back moments before a flashlight can be located to find a new fuse.

For readers unfamiliar with what it is like to fly an older generation, piston-engined aircraft through the angry cauldron of a monstrous thunderstorm, just pretend that you are within the engine compartment of a Mack Truck 18-wheeler climbing and descending on a switchback-laced mountain road blended with a ride through Disney World's Space Mountain as it is being zapped with sporadic laser-light show bursts while shotguns simultaneously go off next to your ears. This twisting, torturous up-and-down route you are on is littered with deep potholes, and you hit them all. Imagine that there is absolutely no guarantee when this rollercoaster ride will end (or if you will even survive it), and then you will have a good idea of what Captain Redding's crew is going through.

Now add to all of that, the insidious fear that perhaps some of this turbulence is terrain-induced. Just how close are they to *terra firma?* And how terribly haunting have all of those warnings about flying beneath mountain storms just become?

Captain Redding, now around 13,000 and hard-pressed even to hold any heading in the severe turbulence, struggles to maintain an easterly course away from the mountains and out to the airway. He knows there is sanctuary above the prairie which he had overflown in comparative safety just an hour ago. He is roughly level with Wheeler Peak and approximately 3000 feet above Trail Peak. Immediately below them, the landscape is studded with peaks in the 10,000 to 13,000 foot range. "Skip Kirtland, enough of this beating," he may have thought as the possibility of landing at an alternate field somewhere to the east in Texas or Kansas became very appealing. After all, he had enough fuel to fly back to Kansas City if he wanted to.

The heavy bomber is now just several miles outside of Philmont's southwestern boundary. The Liberator's groundtrack in Philmont airspace will take it just north of Bear Canyon Camp and across the Rayado Creek almost exactly halfway between Phillips Junction and Fish Camp. The heavy rain reduces visibility to zero and obscures the western ridge of Burn Peak which is dead ahead. Beyond the ridge, Trail Peak rises even higher in the darkness.

Liberator 41-1133 is suddenly caught in the downburst, the VSI shows how bad it is, and the pointer moves inexorably counterclockwise toward the maximum descent on the scale, 6000 fpm. Ominously, their indicated airspeed starts declining. The horror of watching the VSI and airspeed indicator immediately produces dry mouths, cold sweat, turning stomachs, and pounding hearts. Their situation is terrifyingly perplexing; they are plummeting earthward, but why isn't their airspeed increasing correspondingly? Then, they break out of the downburst's deathly grip and run directly into even more trouble: a decreasing-performance windshear.

The bomber has lost nearly 3000 feet of precious altitude as the

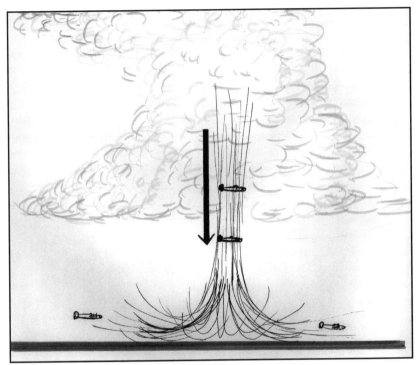

*The anatomy of a downburst (not to scale). Cold air rushes earthward from a thunderstorm in a column at a rate of thousands of feet per minute. An aircraft caught in the core of the column loses altitude dramatically while airspeed starts to decay. The descending column fans out over 360 degrees after hitting the earth's surface and forms gale-force windshears. The aircraft on the left side of the diagram will enter an increasing performance wind shear (massive headwind) which substantially increases the indicated airspeed. The aircraft on the right side is caught in a decreasing performance wind shear which can degrade an aircraft's airspeed to the point of stalling.*

*While the actual cause of Liberator 41-1133's accident can never be known for sure, the only logical explanation is the downburst/microburst phenomenon.*

windshear comes in the form of a tremendous tailwind which puts the brakes on the descent and dramatically decreases the B-24's airspeed even more. Other than having had more altitude to start with, the best piloting skill in the world is not likely to get them out of this evil trap. They are now truly between the proverbial rock and a hard place: on instruments and facing an imminent stall right at the minimum altitude which will guarantee safety from a ground collision.

The pilots react with a well-conditioned response for the declining airspeed: shove the nose down immediately and go to full war emergency power (but not for the engine they lost and really could use now).[6]

Moments after Robert Redding and Roland Jeffries leveled off with airspeed at nearly 200 mph over the Bonito Valley, the big ship shuddered as the first trees on Trail Peak were hit. One-fifth of a second later, the final impact occurred.

# XX

# AFTERMATH

Oh, give me something to remember you by
When you are far away from me,
Some little something meaning love cannot die
No matter where you chance to be.

From Dietz and Schwartz's *Something to
Remember You By* as popularized during the
war years by the Gordon Jenkins Orchestra

Jeffries' 3:30 p.m. funeral service on May 7th was conducted where
he had risen to prominence as an Eagle Scout — St. Paul's Episcopal
Church which was the sponsor of Kansas City Scout Troop One. Jeffries'
closest friends were the honorary pallbearers. Those serving as pallbearers were lieutenants from the Kansas City military district. Jeffries
was then laid to rest in Mount Moriah Cemetery South. On the evening
prior to Jeffries' funeral in Kansas City, Chief Roe Bartle led a special
memorial service at the Newcomer Funeral Chapel which was attended
by Mic-O-Say tribesmen. Based on a review of Mic-O-Say records, it is
almost certain that Jeffries was the first Mic-O-Say to die in military
service during WWII. Although there is a standard Mic-O-Say memorial
service today, the Jeffries service could be considered a forerunner and
contained Mic-O-Say music and poetry, preceded by soft organ music
including *On My Honor*.

Redding's funeral service was held in the house on his farm north of
Minatare, on Saturday, May 9th. An earlier, crematory service had been
held in Albuquerque at the Fairview Park Crematory on May 4th. There
was no interment at the Minatare service. As the funeral concluded,
mourners heard a low-flying aircraft. At the controls was Hal Blackburn.
Earlier he had flown a B-24 into Scottsbluff (and briefly got stuck since

it was an unpaved field and muddy at the time). The plane then dropped Redding's ashes into the sky over the family farm. For years afterward, on the anniversary of Redding's memorial service, roses fell from the sky into the field where the ashes had been scattered.

Blackburn and Redding had been very close friends, and although Blackburn had lost friends in crashes, he was shaken by Redding's death. He would always wonder what might have happened if he had returned to 41-1133 for the flight back to Albuquerque from Kansas City and taken charge when the going got tough. In time, though, after seeing so many more pilots perish, he would become hardened to his friends folding their wings. He would comment years later as a transatlantic captain on the passing of his peers:[1]

> In our business, the really mature folks don't talk much about them. They talk some. I might be sitting here or at a hotel table in Paris or Frankfurt, and a crew will come in and say, "Did you hear that such-and-such an airline flopped one this morning?" You say, "No. What happened?" They may say, "Well, he took off. The weather was clear, and he was just starting his turn. Maybe eight hundred or a thousand feet. He was making a left-hand turn. The left wing continued to go down. The nose dropped, and he continued straight in."
>
> Inevitably, you say, "Who was the crew?" Maybe you also ask, "Got any idea why?" That's about it. A few months after I came to T.W.A., another copilot, who was an old Air Corps classmate of mine and the best man at my wedding, was killed at the field in Kirksville, Missouri. The weather closed in, and they had to come in when it was zero-zero. I was at our Kansas City base right afterward, and the way the older pilots reacted to it kind of shocked me. They listened to what happened, made some noncommittal remark, and then went on planning their next flight. Over the years, I've become that way myself. Of course you're affected when a good friend gets killed. Regret it? My goodness, yes! But you don't get maudlin about it. You know that he knew the risk he took, and you know you're going out the next day. It rains on the just and it rains on the unjust.
>
> I've always said that if anybody has to get killed in an airplane accident, I hope it's the captain. After all, he's the one who gets the most pay, the one who makes the decisions, and the one who can do the most about

it. Then, in descending order of rank, the first officer
and on down to the fellow who can't get at the controls.
This is our business. We accept the money. We
accept the working conditions. We accept the fun of it.
We should also accept the liabilities — the possibility
that something will happen.

There was a move to rename Scottsbluff Airport after Redding who
was a very popular figure in that city, but most of the aviation activity
there focused on the new Scottsbluff Army Air Field whose C-47s and B-
24s literally darkened the skies. The old municipal airport would soon
close and move to the Army field as the war wound down.

Following the memorial service in Albuquerque, Mary Reynard
accompanied her brother's body home by train to Ohio. The Reynard
family had been led to believe that Charlie was the navigator on the
return leg, which indeed he was, although he was not commanding the
aircraft or determining headings after the decision to turn north.
Reynard's mother mistakenly assumed that her son's faulty navigation
was the reason for the crash, and wrote letters of apology to each of the
other families.

Reynard's funeral service was held at the Hiram Christian Church on
Thursday, May 7th, and the eulogy was given by Dr. Kenneth Brown who
had been President of Hiram College when Reynard was a student there.
Burial, with full military honors, was in the Hiram Cemetery with the
salute fired by American Legionnaires from the nearby town of
Garretsville. Reynard's death was widely reported; there was a moving
tribute which appeared in the *Cleveland Plain Dealer*.[2]

In our more pessimistic moments, we sometimes
question what it is we are fighting for. At such times, let
us think about Lt. Charles Reynard. He died to preserve
things which outsiders recognized in him: a free mind,
a pure heart, and a positive faith. Could we be fighting
for more? We must not fight for less!

Jonas Ruff's parents and sister came to Albuquerque to take his ashes
and possessions home by train and drive his car back to California. Ruff's
death left several ladies with broken hearts on both coasts of the United
States and in Panama. His funeral service was held in the beautiful
Chapel of Roses at San Jose's historic Oak Hill Cemetery, the final resting place of so many of California's pioneering families. Soon after his

ashes were buried, the plot was marked with a dark gray stone on which was emblazoned a winged disk. Within the disk were the continents of North and South America, symbolic of Jonas' two flying worlds.

The Ruff family was particularly devastated since Jonas was their only son to live to adulthood; their other boy had died in childhood. Soon after Jonas' death, the arrival of a grandson, Helen Ruff Crawford's firstborn, and then a daughter, helped reduce some of the pain.

A Baptist funeral service was held at the Strong Thorne Funeral Chapel in Albuquerque for Van Hoozer on Tuesday, May 5th. Van Hoozer had been a member of the Masons, originally in Panama and then in Kansas City. Part of his funeral included Masonic rituals, and the service concluded with one of his favorite hymns, *The Old Rugged Cross*. A graveside, Baptist service was subsequently held for Van Hoozer at the Laurel Oak Cemetery in his hometown of Windsor, Missouri, on Sunday, May 10th.

On May 12th, Philip Macomber was buried in the Jay Hill Cemetery in Jay, Maine, following a Methodist service at the L.P. Brown Funeral Parlor in Livermore Falls. Every member of the North Jay Fire Department attended the funeral whose color guard and rifle squad were provided by the American Legion post in nearby Wilton. Philip's was the first war death in the area, and with his being such a popular young man, there was a significant outpouring of sympathy at the widely attended funeral. Although no immediate family members remain in the Jay area, the Macomber family plot is still exceptionally well cared for today, and has a commanding view of the mountains to the south and east.

Cpl. Peterson's body was sent home by train for the funeral in St. James. Presiding at the service was his pastor from the First Baptist Church in his real hometown, Worthington. Peterson was buried in the family plot at St. James' Mount Hope Cemetery on May 8th.

Nearly 60 years later, surviving relatives who were in Albuquerque when their loved ones were brought off the mountain recall how wonderful and comforting Blackburn had been during those terrible days. On July 1, 1942, Blackburn was posted to Washington as Superintendent of Flight Operations for TWA's Intercontinental Division (ICD), a unit of the AAF's Air Transport Command.

On that day, one B-24 departed Kirtland for the new Army Air Base at Smyrna, Tennessee, where the Air Force had just completed work on the first of several B-24 transition schools.[3] The Liberator paused briefly in Smyrna to take aboard 16 more pilots qualified in the B-24 for a return flight to Kirtland. On July 2, 1942, those pilots flew seven of the Kirtland CCTS B-24s back to Tennessee where they would serve as the nucleus for Smyrna's Liberator transition school. With its modest origins at Kirtland, the Smyrna operation would eventually train nearly 6,500 Liberator pilots by 1945, a time when it had over 100 Liberators on the field for the job.

Blackburn moved to Washington and was, in effect, running an international airline which flew cargo and passengers all over the world. ICD's most noteworthy "cargo" was VIPs. Every major Allied leader flew with TWA including Roosevelt, General DeGaulle, General Marshall, Admiral King, Chiang Kai-Shek, kings, queens, princes, and princesses.

ICD had been formed shortly after Pearl Harbor with Otis Bryan in charge. Blackburn would become Assistant Manager in early 1943 and then, on New Year's Day 1945, Manager of ICD. 1942 was a time of massive expansion for TWA and the other airlines which flew for Air Transport Command.[4]

Pan American and TWA both saw their entire fleet of four-engine aircraft commandeered by Uncle Sam. The larger portion of the industry's fleet of DC-3s suddenly became C-47s and acquired new paint schemes: olive drab and aircraft gray.

For TWA, those tumultuous times were also the foundation for its future as an American flag carrier since it put the "World" in TWA. For Blackburn, the transition meant an office in the TWA hangar at Washington National Airport, which had only been open since mid-1941. In several ways, this was a frustrating period for Blackburn. It was not strictly a flying job although he managed to fly quite a few transatlantic trips. Some of the non-flying staff initially resented Blackburn's running the show, but his forthrightness quickly prevailed.

Blackie would have made a good management consultant. The story circulates about his assembling the staff when he became ICD chief and announcing, "Anybody can call anybody else an S.O.B., provided the guy you're talking about is present. I don't want anybody coming to me with stories about somebody else. There's only one real problem in the world, and if you can solve it, you've got it made. There are no technical problems or political problems — just human relations problems."[5]

Blackburn was not the type to ask another pilot to do something that he himself would not undertake. He did his best to get back onto active service with the Army Air Force, but both senior military commanders

Photo courtesy of Harold Thurston

*Hutch Thurston, copilot on the flight
which discovered the wreckage, went
directly to TWA after the CCTS closed, and
retired years later as a captain flying 747s
on the San Francisco to London route.*

and his bosses at TWA all insisted he was already making a major contribution to the war effort. Still, it did not deter him from flying.

On one occasion, a C-87 had to be ferried from Washington to Miami.
The C-87 was the poor relation, cargo version of the Liberator bomber
with a de-rated turbocharger system. Its regular crew failed to show up,
so Blackburn soloed the ship to Miami, an accomplishment somewhat
similar to that of the proverbially successful one-armed paperhanger. He
also flew the Atlantic 44 times during the war and, on some post-D-Day
routes, involved TWA directly in the war effort. He authorized high
flights over the German rocket test center, Peenemünde, which was
photographed by his cargo-carrying C-54s.

On another occasion, Blackburn was obliged to fly so low to avoid
German radar that his C-54 had to be thoroughly washed after landing
— he had picked up salt spray from the ocean.

Photo courtesy of Howard M. Kincheloe

*After the TWA lost the Army contract, Howard Kincheloe moved to Consolidated as a B-24 test pilot. He ended the war as a test pilot for Chance-Vought flying F-4U Corsairs as pictured above.*

With the passage of another two months after the accident, the TWA-operated CCTS passed out of existence, and several months later, the Army Air Force established its own B-24 transition course as part of the Advanced Flying School at Kirtland. Harry Campbell, one of the TWA pilots from CCTS days, was commissioned into the Army Air Force and became commanding officer of the new B-24 school.

Some of the TWA pilots also accepted Army commissions and went into the Training Command including several who were ordered directly to the new B-24 transition school at Smyrna, Tennessee. Some of those men, including Richard Ruble and Larry DeCelles, returned to TWA in flying positions after the war. Others, including Howard Kincheloe, became test pilots for aircraft manufacturers such as Consolidated or Martin. A few of the first officers, including Hutch Thurston, Lyman Keele and Tom Morris, went into TWA's domestic operation as copilots on DC-3s and soon moved into the left seat as captains.

The majority, however, followed Hal Blackburn, Frank Busch and Joe Carr into TWA's Intercontinental Division. These men included Don Brown, Harlin Stewart, Nick Wasil, Virgil Elliott, Cliff Dombrowski, J.T. Miller, Merrill Shirtleff, Fred Sigman, Bill Dugan, Tom Ward, Robert Hunton, and Fred Ward. The vast majority of the flight engineers also went directly into ICD. Although not considered combat duty, flying for ICD was not without hazard. Several of the pilots and engineers were to die in flying accidents and one was killed in a tragic case of mistaken identity.

Nick Wasil had progressed quickly from first officer to captain and in 1943 perished as the aircraft commander of a C-87 on the South Atlantic route. The cause was no mystery: all signs pointed to a fuel vapor explosion. The C-87, being a cargo version of the B-24, was not equipped with the bomb doors which were so often used to suck away gasoline fumes.

Royce Welliver, the engineer who had co-authored the Eagle Nest B-24 training syllabus, was lost in 1944 when the C-54 on which he was the flight engineer crashed during a tropical storm in the Caribbean while on the way to South America.

The mechanic who had identified Van Hoozer's body when it was returned to Albuquerque was killed in 1944 when the four-engine C-54 on which he was the flight engineer was shot down by accident over the North Atlantic by a Royal Navy fighter who mistook the C-54 for the four-engine German long range patrol bomber, the FW 200 Condor.

At least one other ICD C-54 was hit by naval anti-aircraft artillery on the North Atlantic route. Another C-54 on the South Atlantic route went missing. Days later, several bodies were found in life rafts, but there were no clues as to the cause of their plane's loss.

All of these men, those of 41-1133, those of TWA, and thousands of others in the Air Transport Command, died without having directly engaged an enemy, but their value to the war effort was immense, and well summarized by a letter Harold Blackburn received the day after 41-1133 was reached. The letter came from Major General Ralph P. Cousins, Commander of the West Coast Air Force Training Center, who was aware of the deep friendship between Blackburn and Redding.

Please accept my sincerest sympathy for yourself and the other men in your school there on the tragic death of Mr. Redding. I sincerely feel that you fellows are making a great contribution to our war effort, that your devotion to duty is, and has been, of the highest quality, and that Mr. Redding gave his life for his country just as clearly and just as gloriously as did Captain Colin Kelly, Don Gibbs, and our other fine fellows who are sacrificing themselves in the defense of our country.

All of you have my every wish for your continued success.

The Redding, Ruff, and Van Hoozer families each received letters with a similar message about their loved ones' service to the war effort from Colonel Frank Hackett, the Kirtland base commander, and his executive officer, Col. Lewis.

Although technically in company management, Blackburn managed to fly quite frequently, especially on the North Atlantic run. Like Otis Bryan, who was then Vice President-War Projects, Blackburn flew his share of VIPs, including General George Marshall and Admiral Ernest King. Other passengers included American GIs wounded at Normandy and enemy VIPs, the first high-ranking German officers captured after D-Day.

Blackburn himself had flown on D-Day — over the invasion front in an F-5 Lightning (photo-reconnaissance version of the P-38 Lightning). That was not publicized at the time since it was officially unauthorized. One of Blackburn's classmates from March Field, Col. Clarence Shoop, was then commanding the Seventh Photographic Reconnaissance Group (P.R.G.) at Mount Farm, near the University town of Oxford, northwest of London. Shoop OK'd Blackburn's quick check out on the F-5 and Spitfire P.R. Mark XI (the long range, photo version of the legendary British interceptor which was supplied to the Army Air Force in a reverse Lend-Lease program).[6] Col. Shoop's superior, with whom Blackburn enjoyed a good relationship, was the Eighth Air Force's photographic reconnaissance wing commander, Col. Elliott Roosevelt, son of President Roosevelt.

With the Seventh P.R.G., Blackburn flew six "guest" missions over Germany, Italy, and France. Several of these were long range "shuttle" missions with landings in Crete or Sardinia after overflying enemy territory. These were hardly walks in the park, and Seventh Group pilots

Photo courtesy of Dr. Robert Blackburn,
aircraft photos courtesy of Patricia Russell Keen,
Seventh Photographic Reconnaissance Group historian.

*Hal Blackburn emerging from an F-5 Lightning after a sortie over Occupied Europe in 1944. The F-5 was the photo version of the P-38 Lightning twin-engine fighter. Blackburn also flew several missions in the Spitfire Mark XI, the photo variant of the legendary British interceptor.*

faced a number of hazards other than the German kind. Hypoxia from oxygen equipment failure claimed a few pilots, and mechanical difficulties, especially with the Lightnings, could be severe. Some of the Seventh Group F-5s shed their tails in high speed, evasive pull-outs or under the stresses encountered in thunderstorms. When an overboosted turbocharger blew up on a fighter like the P-47 Thunderbolt, the effect was not quite as serious as that on a Lightning whose cockpit location, in the central gondola just a few feet from the superchargers, ensured the pilot being hit by the resulting shrapnel. Seventh P.R.G. pilot losses, particularly in 1944, began to climb as the Lightning and Spitfire pilots increasingly were opposed by the new German jet fighters. Pilot losses in the summer of 1944 were running at the rate of 33 percent.

The deaths of the men of 41-1133 and the Seventh P.R.G. pilots alike, along with hundreds of thousands of others, generated considerable music, art and literature relating to the loss of friends and loved ones.

Those deaths revived a subset of essays, poetry, and books such as *Your Daddy Did Not Die*, which was designed to alleviate the personal anguish, although some of it was so poignant that it had quite the opposite effect.[6] Of the poems about death, one of the most frequent to find its way to homes where a loved one had been lost in military service during the war years was *Remembrance* by Edgar A. Guest.

### Remembrance
Shed not too many tears when I shall leave;
Be brave enough to smile.
It will not shorten, howsoever you grieve,
Your loneliness, the while.

I would not have you sorrowful and sad.
But joyously recall
The glorious companionship we've had.
And thank God for it all.
Don't let your face grow tearstreaked, pale and wan;
Have heart for mirth and song;
Rejoice, though for the little time I've gone,
That I was here so long.

For if I thought your faith would fail you so
And leave you so distressed,
That sobbing to my body's grave you'd go,
My spirit could not rest.

# XXI

# AFTER THE WAR
## (EPILOGUE)

> Those who have long enjoyed
> such privileges as we enjoy
> forget in time that men have
> died to win them.
>
> Franklin D. Roosevelt

The daisies and dandelions no longer dance in the propwash and jet exhaust beside most of the taxiways and runways where the crew of 41-1133 crew exhilarated in takeoffs and landings. A few of their bases still serve, though.

Kirtland Field in Albuquerque is very much a major installation, and is one of the Air Force Material Command's largest operations. Today, it occupies 52,000 acres and, with an employment of nearly 20,000 people, is one of Albuquerque's largest employers. Among the principal organizations based at Kirtland are the Air Force Phillips Laboratory, New Mexico Air National Guard, Defense Nuclear Agency Field Command, Department of Energy, and Sandia National Laboratories.

McChord Air Force Base, located just south of Tacoma, Washington, is an active field within the Military Airlift Command. The C-141 Starlifters of the 62nd Airlift Wing now fly global missions from the runways where the Doolittle Raiders were once based and the first Royal Air Force crews trained on Lend Lease B-17s.

Westover in Massachusetts, where Philip Macomber first paused to look at the majestic Flying Fortresses, is a reserve base where weekend warriors hone their skills.

Salt Lake Army Air Base, which started as and reverted to the municipal airport, now serves skiers, tourists and businessmen, although nearby Hill AFB in Ogden continues as a key installation in the Air Force Logistics Command.

Pendleton Field, Philip's springboard to the CCTS and Liberators, closed shortly after the war. Mather Air Force Base, from which Charlie and Jeff checked out in AT-6As and learned to fly radio ranges, was closed in 1993. After training thousands of pilots and navigators, Mather is now an industrial park.

There is an airport in Oxnard, but it is not the same Ventura County Airport where Charlie learned to fly. Mira Loma is long gone, and closed down in the summer of 1944 as many of the primary schools ceased operations when it became clear that the war was going to be won. The lovely cottages with their knotty pine cabinetry became a decaying, county housing complex.

Thunderbird, where Jeff realized his dreams of learning to fly, graduated its last class on June 30, 1945 after training over 10,000 American, British and Chinese pilots.[1] In 1946, Thunderbird Field, with its classrooms and barracks, became the American Institute for Foreign Trade. Its first president, and one of three co-founders, was none other than Lt. General Barton K. Yount, the recently retired general in charge of the Army Air Force Training Command. Soon, the school became known as the Thunderbird American Graduate School of International Management, and today it enjoys a reputation as one of the finest graduate business schools in the world.

Two of the original four hangars are parking lots, but the remaining two are still standing and much modernized. The control tower, now a student center, remains with its original field name and elevation signs, although it is surrounded today by attractive landscaping, modern buildings and dormitories. The farming fields and road intersections over which Jeff used to practice S turns, elementary eights, and eights on pylons are now residential developments.

Thunderbird II, the expansion field, was completed in mid-1942, graduated 5,500 cadets during the war, and now comprises part of present-day Scottsdale Airport.

Minter Field went on standby status in 1946, and in 1947 the property was turned over to Kern County. In its heyday, the field was like a small city, and its many BT-13 aircraft were later joined by AT-6s, UC-78s (twin trainers), and B-25 Mitchell bombers. Today, the base is an industrial complex where, once a year, the Minter Field Air Museum hosts "Warbirds in Action." That airshow attracts thousands of enthusiasts to see several dozen WWII era trainers, fighters and bombers fly in for the event. Many of the surviving members of 42-B remained in the Air Force after the war, retired as colonels in the 1970s, and took up second careers before finally retiring in the mid-1980s. Of those who did not remain in the military, many finished their college training and went on to careers in education, sales, engineering, entrepreneurialism, business management, government service, and a broad spectrum of other occupations.

Of the roughly eleven hundred members of cadet class 42-B, one in four did not survive the war, however.[2] Fortune was somewhat kinder to the Mather members of 42-B since their loss rate was one in five. That is due largely to a high percentage of Mather graduates being initially assigned as instructors. The class produced relatively few fighter or transport pilots, but, reflecting the needs of early 1942, training and bombardment squadrons had the highest priority.

A small handful of 42-B fliers became test pilots; among them was Glen Edwards for whom Edwards Air Force Base is named.

Two members won the Medal of Honor: John Jerstad on the August 1, 1943, low level bombing mission to Ploesti and high-scoring ace, Thomas McGuire (both posthumously). Ten 42-B'ers became generals. During the course of the war, 42-B also won six Distinguished Service Crosses, 41 Silver Stars, 187 Distinguished Flying Crosses, and 291 Air Medals.

Today, the Aviation Cadet Class 42-B Association has a reputation of being one of the strongest and most cohesive among the many aviation cadet associations. Now, these men are in the autumn of their years. Many are great grandfathers. A few still pilot planes, but nearly all rely on the airlines for their flying nowadays. Like most cadet associations, they have a newsletter and an annual meeting. They do a wonderful job of remembering their comrades who could not share in the Allied victory in that distant summer of 1945.

In 1997, under the leadership of Trent Wells, Ralph Monroe, and Ed Radtke, the 42-B Association published an extraordinary book containing a class history which includes the pictures and biographies of <u>every</u> known member of 42-B. That remarkable effort again brings life to so many pilots whose existence heretofore has been consigned to darkened desk drawers, steamer trunks, and old cardboard boxes in the backs of closets or weathered inscriptions on cemetery monuments.

How easy it is to let one's thoughts drift into wondering what might have happened if the crew of 41-1133 had not hit Trail Peak. What if they had taken off from Kansas City a few seconds later, or earlier? What if their heading back to Albuquerque had been one degree less, or more? What if the winds aloft had been one knot weaker, or stronger? What if they had used a different runway at Kansas City? What if the air temperature had been a few degrees colder, or warmer? What if they had lost number one instead of number four? What if they had lost number four sooner, or later? What if ... what if? Given another couple hundred feet of altitude or several hundred yards to the left, they would have just missed the peak.

What if Captain Redding had survived? He had his call-up orders, but TWA could easily have intervened and had him deferred (although Redding probably would have had none of it). Blackburn would dearly liked to have had Redding in ICD. His talents would have been very much in demand with the Training Command which was desperate for heavy bomber transition unit commanders. Any Liberator or B-17 group commander would have grabbed him in a moment as a group exec or squadron commander. Had he survived the war, with his connections (Otis Bryan and Hal Blackburn), he probably would have flown with TWA. With an airline pilot's schedule, he would still have had time for ranching in Nebraska and Wyoming.

If he had flown for TWA, his age would have placed him in that small circle of men who started on Trimotors and finished on 747s. And then, he could have pursued ranching on a full time basis.

His widow, Helenjane, happily remarried and lives in Texas with her husband, a highly decorated B-24 combat pilot who retired as an Air Force general. Redding's son Michael grew even taller than his father and became a prosperous retail businessman in Denver.

Redding's brother-in-law, Fred Gray, became an aviation cadet in 1944, did primary on Stearmans at El Reno, Oklahoma, before going to basic at Waco, Texas. Flight training had changed by then, and instead of BT-13s, he flew the Six in basic. Selected for the fighter track, Fred flew AT-6s and P-40 Warhawks in advanced before finishing the war as a Mustang fighter pilot. Prior to going into the Air Force, and with the

Photo courtesy of Fred Gray

*Robert Redding's brother-in-law, Fred Gray, helped run the family farm early in the war. He later completed aviation cadet training and ended the war as a P-51 Mustang pilot.*

help of the Jurgens and Redding families, he helped keep the Redding farm going by working long hours even during the school year. Many of the farms around Minatare did not actually suffer labor shortages since there was a prisoner of war camp in the area, and one of Fred's jobs was to drive a truck taking German POWs to work in the fields.

However, after the war when the Redding farm had been sold, Fred moved to Illinois and enjoyed two successful careers, the first in clothing and the second in printing, before retiring in 1991.

Charles Reynard most likely would not have made a career of flying since it could not have fulfilled his inclination for some sort of public service. In truth, he probably would not have survived 25 missions with the 306th Bomb Group. Practically none of his peers did. Many options would have been open to him had he been among the lucky few who returned from the ETO: law school, Ohio politics, or writing. Had he survived, he would more likely have gone into some form of public administration, possibly in the diplomatic corps. He would have been a superb leader in the Peace Corps too. It is very easy to picture him completing a Ph.D., teaching, becoming a college administrator, and returning to Hiram as its president. Had he survived to write more about flying, the resulting work quite likely would have been some of the best aviation literature to come out of the war years.

Roland Jeffries might have survived 25 missions over Europe with the 366th Squadron of the 305th Bomb Group, but the statistics suggest not. If he had been fortunate, though, and a handful were, he would have returned to America in late spring of 1943 with a Distinguished Flying Cross and several Air Medals, and probably been assigned to the Central Instructors' School with subsequent posting to a heavy bomber transition unit as an instructor. Having been shot at by the best in the business, it is somewhat unlikely that he would have volunteered for B-29 training and a subsequent combat tour in the Pacific.

He and Mary Casey would have been married upon his return if they had not been married before his departure, and possibly would have remained in the military, retiring as a colonel in the 1970s (as did many of his 42-B classmates). As a bright young man who was quite conscious of his lack of college training, he might have taken advantage of the G.I. bill and pursued a degree in the sciences. But, having been a "Sky Scout" in Kansas City, and having a strong pre-war interest in flying, he probably would have worked his connections and retired from TWA in 1980 after having flown DC-3s, Constellations, 707s, and 747s.

Had he been more fortunate, it is no stretch to say that if he and Mary had sons, he would have taken them to Philmont, probably in the early 1960s, where Trail Peak would have been one of the less interesting mountains on the South Country landscape.

The Casey family moved back to Chicago later in 1942 where Mary met a young army officer, William Homiller. They were married in 1943 and raised their family in several locations in America and Europe. In 1993, Mary Casey Homiller died in Atlanta after a long and very happy marriage.

Jonas Ruff probably would not have been offered a commission in the Air Force due to his color blindness unless a waiver could have been secured. Quite a few of the other first officers accepted commissions as first lieutenants and immediately became B-24 instructors. The color blindness would not have been a problem for TWA which could have gotten a medical waiver. Jonas would have opted for ICD, due to the foreign travel and adventure, flown right seat for a while, and would have ended the war as skipper of a C-54. Barring any new objection to his color blindness, he probably would have been employed by TWA, flown as a copilot on domestic routes, and eventually moved to the left seat. Had the color vision problem become an issue, it is possible that he would have signed on as a flight engineer after quickly acquiring an airframe and powerplant (A&P) mechanic's rating which was the common denominator of most flight engineers. Considering Ruff's mechanical talents, picking up an A&P rating would have been a very simple matter indeed. Jonas Ruff might have closed out his TWA career in the late 1960s as captain of a Lockheed Constellation; he would have hit the mandatory retirement age of 60 before TWA put the 707 into widespread service. Considering his lifelong love of mechanics and flying, it would be easy to picture him retired in California, perhaps as a partner in a flying service where he could do a little instructing, possibly in gliders, and still work on planes, engines, and instruments.

In 1991, Helen Ruff Crawford, Jonas' sister, and her husband, Herb, followed through on the wishes of her father to have his ashes scattered over the land the Ruff family had homesteaded. The elder Ruff, who died in 1947, owned 1,000 acres on the side of Mount Hamilton, the 4,209 foot peak east of San Jose which is also the site of Lick Observatory. It was from this mountain that Jonas frequently soared as a glider pilot and it was the home of the Ruff' family's "**4R** Ranch." Helen had Jonas' and her father's ashes disinterred and then scattered them over the land that was so treasured by her family.

So little is known about Duane Peterson that any speculation about what might have been has to be vague at best. In fact, he probably would not have survived the war unless he were to have been reassigned to ground-based radio duties. Most of the radio operators in Class 42-4-E were subsequently assigned to the 305th or 306th Bomb Groups whose losses in 1942 and 1943 were exceptionally high. As an indifferent student, had he survived, attending college under the G.I. bill probably would have been unlikely. He might have made a career in the Army, but returning to Minnesota and starting a business in radio and television repair, a track that many a former radio operator followed, would have been a possibility.

Philip Macomber would have been very lucky to survive the war since many of the 1941 recruits into the 34th Bomb Group were subsequently assigned to the 306th Bomb Group whose losses as a pioneer group in the Eighth Air Force were staggering. Still, if his luck had held, it is easy to picture him returning to North Jay, keeping the farm, marrying his sweetheart, and probably starting an automotive repair business in nearby Jay or Livermore Falls. The Grange and Volunteer Fire Company in North Jay would have dearly loved to have seen him come home. A year after Philip's death, his mother sold the farm and moved up the valley to Wilton.

During the war, there was substantial aviation activity in the Jay region since it was overflown constantly by aircraft on the North Atlantic ferry route, particularly those flying from Westover Field in Massachusetts and other fields in the mid-Atlantic States. North Jay was the site of a key Ground Observer Corps post. The "GOC" was an important part of the war effort and filled a gap that only widespread use of radar would overcome over a decade later. The North Jay post was renamed in honor of Philip in 1943. His sister, Eloise, became one of the first observers. She graduated from the University of Maine at Farmington, became a home economics teacher, married, and later was with the University of Maine extension service. She and her husband subsequently moved to Florida where she now lives in retirement. Her enduring and beautiful Maine accent is a marvelous reminder of how Philip must have spoken.

George Van Hoozer would have gone into ICD at TWA, had he not followed through with an offer of a direct commission in the Army. Had he gone the TWA route on C-87s and C-54s, he would have been able to realize his desire for international travel. His timing would have been just right for post-war aircrew employment because TWA started using flight engineers on transports such as the Constellation which replaced the DC-3. Whether or not he would have returned to Missouri is unclear; he would have had the opportunity to live abroad at some point. Or, he might have returned to Kansas City, after serving as an Army engineering instructor, and moved into engineering or maintenance management as TWA's fleet grew.

Van Hoozer's widow, Ruth, left Kansas City, moved to California in 1942 and stayed briefly with her brother in Los Angeles where she became a Ground Observer Corps volunteer. She remarried in 1945 and today lives in Santa Ana, near her daughter Carolyn Kay Fullerton and several grandchildren and great grandchildren.

There was an "after the war" for several of the central personalities in this story. Captain Harold F. Blackburn went on to a distinguished postwar flying career. He turned down a TWA vice presidency after the war because he loved flying too much to be deskbound, and he didn't care much for corporate politics. Although Blackburn's circle of friends was a wide one, he had a few detractors. The principal point of contention was a labor relations issue relating to the significantly higher pay scales earned by ICD pilots during the war and seniority relative to TWA pilots flying domestic routes. About one point, both parties agreed, Blackburn was a class act and a pilot's pilot.

On February 5, 1946, Blackburn made the first commercial flight from New York to Paris in one of TWA's new Lockheed Constellations. He would go on to more special assignments, opening new foreign routes and, particularly, training foreign airline crews such as Germany's

Photo courtesy of Lockheed Martin

*Hal Blackburn flew TWA's Lockheed Constellations on the New York to Paris run during most of his postwar career. He flew the Atlantic 750 times and later retired to farming in Pennsylvania.*

Lufthansa. His unique ability as a flight instructor, especially with overseas carriers, would eventually qualify him for nearly a dozen sets of airline wings. There were two noteworthy coincidences associated with
his transatlantic flying days from 1946 through 1961. First, in 1956, he
became the subject of an article in *New Yorker* magazine. The article
essentially took readers along for a few days in the life of an international pilot.

The plane involved was a Lockheed Constellation, then the backbone of TWA's international fleet (until the first Boeing 707s arrived several years later). All of TWA's planes were named individually, and this
beautiful four-engine, tri-tailed classic airliner that Blackburn flew to
Paris and back in that article harkened back to an important era in his
life. That particular Connie was named "The Spirit of New Mexico."

Among the passages in the article were several which revealed a very
reflective and introspective Blackburn as he guided the Connie into a
North Atlantic dawn:

> Now that Blackburn had a little weather to deal
> with, he seemed to be enjoying himself. Scanning the
> clouds, which then stood scattered about in a slowly
> brightening sky, he pointed out their resemblance to
> things and people. Off to one side, a cloud reminded
> him of a hunting dog on point, off to the other was the
> figure of a bearded man, while up ahead stood a church
> with a steeple rising almost out of sight.
>
> As the plane neared the church-shaped cloud,
> Blackburn said, "You've got to be religious if you fly.
> You can't help it. You know what they said in the war —
> there are no atheists in foxholes. Well, it's an extension
> of that. I remember reading what Sir James Jeans said
> about the business of scientists being atheists. He said
> nobody — a scientist or anybody else — could study
> the heavens and not realize that there's a power so
> great that our poor little minds can't encompass it."
>
> Blackburn was silent for a while, and then contin-
> ued, "I never flew solo at night until I was in the Air
> Corps. I remember how it was when you got up there at
> night for the first time, and you lost the horizon and you
> saw the exhaust kicking out the sparks; of course, it
> had always been doing that, but you'd never noticed it
> before. You'd be up there, and it would be black, and
> you'd have to bring that plane down. No lights to land

by, as we have now. Just one searchlight on the ground. You realize when you're up there how small you are, how insignificant and powerless. It's the feeling that comes over a man who camps out in the mountains, or a shepherd in the hills. The powers of nature overwhelm you.

The same thing happens when you're cruising the Atlantic. Of course, it was more fun during the war. You carried less gas, you had no guns, and you knew they were looking for you. You were keyed up. You got up there and made it over, and coming back, you couldn't help having a sense of relief and thankfulness.

I'm not a formally religious man, but there must be some design, some justice. We couldn't raise kids unless we believed there's something after this, could we? Otherwise, the whole thing wouldn't be worth it.

Secondly, Blackburn was on foreign training missions when the first Boeing 707s went into revenue service, and at first he thought he would finish out his career on Connies, but immediately upon his first visit to a 707 flight deck, it was love at first sight. He would say that the magic he felt on that occasion was the same as that produced by his first experience with a Jenny roughly 40 years before. At nearly 59 years of age, he was top man in his Boeing 707 transition class (being oldest _and_ best was a source of great pride). Subsequently, he was invariably assigned to TWA's early evening flight to Paris from New York. The flight number of that trip, from Idlewild (now Kennedy) to Orly in Paris, remained the same over the years. It was the same TWA flight number 800 which exploded from unknown causes just off Long Island's south shore on July 17, 1996.

Blackburn made his last Atlantic crossing as skipper of a Boeing 707 on his 60th birthday in 1961 when he reached the mandatory retirement age — 15 years after the maiden voyage in 1946. He was the oldest flying TWA pilot and could still pass the semi-annual vision test without eyeglasses. He had by then moved from the New York City area to "Hidden Brook Farm," a working, 90-acre farm which he had purchased in Mertztown, Pennsylvania, between Reading and Allentown.

Blackburn did not immediately retire from transatlantic jet transport flying, however, since he did fly a few non-airline ferry flights after turning 60. One of these flights was flown for the CIA which had "borrowed" a large Russian jet from a friendly country in the Middle East. The plane had to be returned by a civilian, and Hal Blackburn took the job on during the height of the Cold War. There were certain frustrations since the agreement stipulated that the plane had to be returned with its original Russian instrumentation unmodified, i.e. Blackburn had to be comfortable reading Russian and metric data. His travel allowance was exceptionally generous, but at several locations, the currency was useless since most airports in NATO countries wanted nothing to do with the flying pariah even if the pilots wanted to pay hard cash money for fuel and landing fees. The job was completed, though, and served as a memorable counterpoint to Blackburn's early days of flying FBI agents on DC-3s in the late 30s.

For several years, he remained in TWA's employment as a consultant and speaker before really retiring in 1966. He was gone from TWA, but not forgotten since the company made him their guest of honor on a February 5, 1981 transatlantic flight commemorating his groundbreaking flight to Paris 35 years before. In later retirement, five years after Martha's death in 1975, he moved from his beloved "pore farm" to Sun City, Arizona, and, in 1989, after a long, rich, exciting, and very productive life, passed away quietly in the home of his son Robert, an Oakland, California, university professor.

Howard Kincheloe declined the offer of a major's commission in the Air Force in 1942, and became a test pilot. First, he flew B-24s with Consolidated, and after their merger with Vultee, he moved to Tennessee, and test flew the Vultee Vengeance light attack bomber. Then an opportunity with Chance Vought surfaced, and Howard moved to Stratford, Connecticut, and test flew F-4U Corsairs, the "bent-winged bird" ("Whistling Death" to the Japanese) until the war ended. After the war, he flew as a corporate pilot, but returned to flight training as an instructor pilot with the U.S. Air Force in Arizona where he taught aviation cadets on T-6s and T-28s. He is one of few pilots to wear both the gold wings of a naval aviator and the silver wings of an Air Force military pilot.

After his instructing days with the Air Force, Howard went into industry as a corporate planner with Grand Central Aircraft which had Air Force maintenance and modification contracts on the B-47 Stratojet aircraft. He retired after 16 years with Hughes Aircraft in Tucson in the late 1970s. He later moved to Las Cruces, New Mexico, and, with his wife Edna, was a guest of the Philmont Staff Association annual rendezvous in 1997.

*Old-time Philmont rangers from the late 50s through early 70s at the crash site during a Philmont Staff Association annual Rendezvous Weekend. From left, Jim Place (the author's training ranger), Albuquerque, New Mexico; Steve Harmony, Los Alamos, New Mexico; the author; and Ned Gold (Philmont Staff Association founder), Warren, Ohio.*

At that gathering, which also commemorated the 40th anniversary of the founding of Philmont Rangers, Howard unveiled one of a series of paintings on the Trail Peak tragedy. The painting, *Discovery on Trail Peak*, depicts Howard's B-24 in a climbing left turn between Rayado Peak and Trail Peak. In the foreground, a snowscape with broken pine and aspen branches, there is a relatively intact, but upside down, olive drab rudder with the numbers "11133" in yellow.

Howard's eyes are still the bright, steely-blue eagle's eyes that twinkle with the thought of flights past, present and future.

Joe Carr, who was with the TWA operation in Albuquerque from its inception to the last days, went directly into TWA's ICD. With his background in four-engine flight training and rating from the Navy as a celestial navigator, he trained many ICD crews in addition to flying the North and South Atlantic routes during the war. The immediate post-war years saw him writing the DC-4 pilot manual for TWA and flying out of Paris as TWA's staff check pilot for Europe. Also involved in route development, he pioneered many of TWA's postwar routes. He hung up his airline pilot's wings in 1971 after flying Boeing 707s and 747s between Europe and New York. In semi-retirement, he became an aviation consultant and kept on flying. Later, he fully retired to Florida but still spent many summers in New Jersey. Hangar flying with Joe Carr was a spectacularly enriching experience. He had the remarkable ability to put younger pilots at ease and make them think they were talking to a peer. Not only that, he was a very incisive writer, and fortunately, for aviation history, his insights were published. Joe Carr died in Florida on Easter Sunday, 1998.

Hutch Thurston, first officer on the flight that found the wreckage of 41-1133, went into the right seat of a TWA DC-3 on domestic routes and became a captain soon thereafter. In the immediate postwar years, he was qualified on the DC-4, Martin 404 and Connie before settling down to flying international routes out of New York. When he retired in 1978, he was a 747 captain flying the San Francisco to London route. He now lives a very active retirement in California, and still has the commanding voice of an in-charge airline pilot.

The three major Scouting institutions in this narrative have flourished over the years. Roland Jeffries became a Mic-O-Say tribesman in that organization's youth. The Tribe's cumulative membership nears 60,000 at this writing. The Heart of America Council's current youth membership numbers roughly 50,000, thus making it one of the strongest of the BSA's roughly 330 councils nationwide. Roland Jeffries would probably not recognize Camp Osceola today. Much expanded, it is now known as the H. Roe Bartle Scout Reservation. Including figures from the council's High Adventure operation, Theodore Naish Scout Reservation, Heart Of America Council annually provides over 9,000 Boy Scouts with a long term camping experience which makes the council a national leader in the BSA outdoor program.

Chief Bartle's shadow lingers over the Kansas City skyline. He declined an opportunity to become Chief Scout Executive of the BSA, and remained in Kansas City after two terms as mayor, serving on many boards, speaking nationwide, and maintaining his close ties with Scouting and Mic-O-Say. He died on May 9, 1974.

Waite Phillips retired to California and passed away there on January 27, 1964, after a lifetime marked by success in business and generous phi-

Photo courtesy of Jimmy Bartle Taylor

*The Chief, H. Roe Bartle, served as Heart of America, BSA, Council Executive until 1953 when he became the mayor of Kansas City.*

lanthropy. He occasionally visited Philmont and would mingle incognito with campers and their leaders. Thus, he was well aware of the magnitude of his gift, and how it had such an impact on generations of campers and, particularly, the staff. Today, his New Mexico home, the beautiful Villa Philmonte, remains as it was in his day and is the subject of guided tours.

After the second gift to the Boy Scouts of America, Waite Phillips vacated the Villa, but did not leave Cimarron or Nairn Place immediately. Phillips later sold Nairn Place which was successively owned by several ranching families; the last group operated it as a bed and breakfast when they were not in residence. In the mid-1990s, Nairn Place, which had then been operating as Casa Del Gavilan (its original name), was acquired by a group of investors who were also members of the Philmont Staff Association. Today, it continues as a bed and breakfast whose vistas of the New Mexico prairie, Urraca Mesa, the Tooth of Time, and Trail Peak make it one of the most spectacular bed and breakfasts in the United States.

Chope Phillips became a rancher after the war. His ranch is located not far from Las Vegas, New Mexico, whose radio range facility was so well known to TWA and Army Air Force crews. He retired from active ranching in 1996, moved to Texas, and still maintains close ties to Philmont. In 1998, the BSA National Council recognized Chope Phillips' service to Scouting and American youth by bestowing on him its highest honor, the Silver Buffalo award.

At Philmont, the National Executive Staff intentionally limited attendance during the war in compliance with the gasoline and rubber rationing restrictions then in effect. Thus, those who did attend had not far to travel. Many of those who were able to reach Philmont in the war years joined the Service Corps which built trails and helped in such ranch activities as haying, gathering apples in the orchards, and working

Philmont Museum, Cimarron, New Mexico

*Chope Phillips, from the 1969 painting by Santa Fe artist, Bettina Steinke Blair.*

in gardens or the dairy. Several of today's gateway camps, Carson-Maxwell (later renamed "Rayado"), Abreu, Cimarroncito, and Ponil (called "Five Points" at first) were initially developed with the construction of fireplaces and camping shelters during the immediate post-war years.

The first visitors to Trail Peak's summit started arriving as camping attendance picked up in the immediate post-war years. The climb was usually made as a sidehike from the Webster Pass trail between Crater Lake and Fish Camp. Years of pilfering by souvenir hunters and the effects of weather have taken their toll. With the passage of time, pieces of the wreckage have been carted off and others dispersed into the woods to reduce the number of pilot reports of a "new crash." One of the Philmont Staff Association's first service projects was to paint a large yellow "X" on each wing to prevent pilot reports of a downed aircraft, but now that paint has virtually disappeared.

In the late '40s, Philmont's program started to expand. Although beginning with only a fraction of the trails now available, campers then could pack with burros for their trek, ride horses on a cavalcade, or backpack for their entire expedition as most crews do today. By the early 50s, camping attendance swelled past 10,000 and many of today's best known camps, Beaubien, Black Mountain, Harlan, and Dean (the first of many "Dean" camps to come) were established. And a few "new camps" from those early days, including Stockade, Porcupine, and Olympia, have, quite literally, been put out to pasture.

Philmont hit its stride, in terms of attendance, in the 1960s. In the late 1960s and early 70s, the modern interpretive history program was initiated. In the mid- to late 90s, Philmont's general and program managements made significant, new improvements to the headquarters physical plant and backcountry cabins, brought staff enthusiasm to even higher levels, and built a solid foundation for Philmont's entry into the new millennium as the world's premier youth camping and character development facility. Today, the annual camping attendance reaches 20,000 of which roughly two thousand make the trek up Trail Peak.

The crash site on Trail Peak now has much less traffic than it used to. The arrival of pre-planned expedition itineraries evened out the camper loads, and took some of the pressure off Crater Lake and Beaubien camps from which the peak is usually side-hiked nowadays.

Mic-O-Say tribesmen first visited the crash site in 1947, and were led by Ernest Modlin, age 47, a professional Scouter and highly respected Mic-O-Say leader from Kansas City. Modlin, tribal "Medicine Man Curly Hawk," returned with a council expedition in 1948 and was climbing Trail Peak again when he was stricken with a massive, fatal heart attack not far from where Jeffries was killed. Now, their graves are within sight of each other in Kansas City's Mount Moriah South Cemetery. Modlin was posthumously elevated to Chieftain status at the tribal memorial service led by Chief Roe Bartle.

Mic-O-Say tribesmen placed a memorial marker on the site to honor Jeffries in the 1970s, but the old canister, subsequently moved to the crest of Trail Peak itself, now contains only little scraps of paper on which expedition numbers and dates have been scrawled. By 1991, the memorial site had started to deteriorate and become somewhat tacky looking. Philmont's new general and program management which arrived in the mid-1990s quickly responded to the suggestion that the

Photo courtesy of the Tribe of Mic-O-Say via F. Gail Hixson, Historian

*Members of the ill-fated 1948 Kansas City expedition to Philmont. Ernest Modlin, a Mic-O-Say and Camp Osceola leader, second row far left, suffered a fatal heart attack while climbing Trail Peak. He is buried not far from Lt. Roland Jeffries in the Mount Moriah South Cemetery in Kansas City.*

crash site should be cleaned up. Today, the scene, located on Trail Peak's western ridge, projects a proper image.

In late 1997, the Philmont Ranch Committee (a board of directors) denied a formal petition to place a small, donated bronze plaque, listing all members of the crew, at the crash site on the basis that such signage would detract from campers' wilderness experience at Philmont. Thus, Jeffries alone is the only member of the crew to be memorialized on Trail Peak.

It is impossible for the average aviation archeologist or historian to visit the crash site. Passage to Philmont's backcountry is firmly restricted to registered members of the BSA who are attending Philmont on a properly qualified council or unit expedition or other formal program. No exceptions are made; the climb is demanding and best left to the physically very fit.

Several myths surrounding the crash have persisted over the years. The first is that some of the crew did survive, and built a fire to stay warm, but perished nonetheless due to injuries and exposure. Although the search party did build a fire to warm up on the afternoon of May 2nd, Chope Phillips confirms that there was no sign of explosion or fire from April 22/23 at the site when he arrived. And, he also verifies that the crew had been killed instantly on impact and therefore hardly able to build a fire.

The second myth suggests that the bomber crashed while testing a new, top secret radar. It would be months before the Army Air Force was testing its own, homegrown radar — all airborne radar sets in service with Army aircraft, such as the LB-30s in Panama, in the spring of 1942 were British units. 41-1133 was not even equipped with what was then secret equipment, a Norden bombsight.

A more fundamental reason for the radar myth's being false is that nobody on board 41-1133 would have had the foggiest idea of how to operate radar. Nor would the Army Air Force have placed an experimental radar in a Western Training Command airplane with civilians on board. Radar testing early in the war was conducted by personnel from M.I.T., Wright Field in Ohio, and Scott Field in Illinois, each of which had no involvement with 41-1133. Finally, and most conclusively, 41-1133's Army Air Force aircraft record card (used to log significant repairs, modifications, or installation of new equipment) shows that it was shipped as a stock B-24D and that no radar (or any other equipment) was ever subsequently installed.

Another story concerns the Army's bringing a bulldozer in to carve a trail up the mountain so the "secret" equipment could be removed from the wreckage. How the Army could have gotten a 'dozer up Fowler Pass, let alone the mountain, in the very wet, muddy spring of 1942 is beyond speculation (not to mention the very heavy timber which the machine would have had to negotiate).

No Philmont staff veterans from the immediate post-war years recall any such earthmoving activities or remains of a bulldozed road. Any vestiges of a such a road would have immediately been seized upon as the best trail up the mountain. Well over 25 years passed after the crash before any semblance of a trail was first formalized on Philmont maps, and that was only a narrow footpath created by successive summers of sidehiking the shortest route from the mountain's base up to the wreckage.

The originators of this tale were not aware that Norden bombsights were never installed as an integral component in any bomber. Rather, the sight was taken from secured storage, carried in its own special pouch to a plane and locked into position before actual bombing or training missions by the bombardier who also removed it after landing. The sight was never installed for any other mission profile, i.e. roundtrip navigation training. Of course, nobody on 41-1133 was rated as a bombardier or even remotely qualified to operate a gyro bombsight. The only bombsights flown out of Kirtland on April 22, 1942, were those aboard the AT-11 trainers attached to the bombardier school.

The most amusing myth circulating is that the Army used the bulldozer to reach the bomber which was carrying radioactive materials back to New Mexico. "Los Alamos," "Oak Ridge," and "Manhattan Project" weren't in the "top secret" lexicon until later in the war.

Today, only the wings are in plain view in a clearing just below the western ridge. The woods beneath the clearing holds most of the remains: a wingtip, a propeller, hatches, one of the oil coolers, a flap track, an engine mount, tangled electrical cables, bellcranks, twisted fuel lines, mangled sections of fuselage skinning, crumpled bulkheads, bent bomb bay supports, dented wheels, still shiny oleo legs, corroded control surface skeletons, wrinkled cowl flaps, and control cables snaking in and out of the rocks. Here and there below the crest on the north slope are a few parts, especially engine-related items.

Most of the wreckage is bare metal now — sunlight-silvered. Only in the deep woods can olive drab debris be found. The bold red and blue

Photo courtesy of Philmont News & Information Service

*Over the years, the remaining wreckage has become sunlight-silvered. The great wings remain in a rocky clearing; most of the other wreckage is located in the woods below. The view is exactly that from which the bomber approached the mountain.*

of the national insignia on the outer wing panels have faded almost to the point of invisibility and survive only as little flecks of pastel pink and pale sky blue. The white of the stars is completely gone.

Souvenir hunters have scavenged even the shards of plexiglas. There is evidence of lightning strikes: parts of the wing spars now have a molten appearance. The thoughtless have seen it important to scratch their initials onto the wings.

If the spirits of 41-1133's crew still occasionally linger around Trail Peak or its immediate surroundings, such as the North Fork of the Urraca or the lovely, alpine Bonito Valley, they must be enchanted by what they can see and hear. Cattle pass this way in the spring when Philmont's cowboys drive the herd to pasture in the high South Country and again in the autumn when they return past Trail Peak on the way down to winter pasture. Captain Redding would have found some prime stock in the cattle and kindred souls in Philmont's cowboys.

For Roland Jeffries, the Eagle Scout, Philmont would be as it has been for hundreds of thousands of campers and staffers, the summit of Scouting. How easy it is to picture Jeffries and a 15-year old son saying goodbye to Mary as they head to Philmont in 1962 as members of a Heart of America Council expedition.

Charlie Reynard's vision of a better world would be encouraged by what he could see happening at Philmont — young people getting a good start on life by learning teamwork and traditional values in a mountain-top, character-building outdoor experience.

That glider pilot, Jonas Ruff, could sense the ridge currents, thermals rising from the prairie, and plenty of towering cumulus clouds from whose origins he could reach those heights treasured by all pilots.

Philip Macomber would be at home here, with fast, rushing cold streams, deep forests, horizons broken by mountains, and by legions of young people who shared his "... loyal, helpful, friendly, courteous ..." ethos.

Duane Peterson would have found friendships in the Scouting precepts which prevail, and probably been intrigued by the modern VHF radios used for inter-camp and headquarters communications in the summer.

For George Van Hoozer, there would have been plenty of adventure in Philmont's wild mountains and canyons to at least temporarily satisfy some of his wanderlust. The nightly campfire up the valley by Beaubien Camp's Trappers' Lodge would certainly have welcomed his singing and guitar playing.

And fliers all, they would be reassured to see jet transport vapor trails aloft in Philmont's airspace or be fascinated by the golden eagles which soar above Philmont's "magic mountains."

The eternal sky, though, temptress to all airmen, joined with wartime fate, guardian of the lucky and betrayer of the less favored, and turned her back on Liberator 41-1133. First deserted by fortune, the crew has been largely abandoned by time with the exception of a few, such as Mic-O-Say tribesmen, who are still pledged to sustain the memory of those who gave all they had for their ideals and their country.

So long ago it happened. Yet, for some the memory is so fresh it could have been yesterday.

Around Memorial Day, the Jeffries, Reynard, Macomber and Peterson families received a letter which applied in spirit as well to the Redding, Ruff and Van Hoozer families. The letter was posted from the Headquarters, Army Air Forces, Office of the Commanding General, Washington, DC. Its poignant message read,

> We are again mindful on this Memorial Day of our debt to those of the Army Air Forces who have given their lives for our Country. Their memory is always with us.

> Very sincerely,

H.H. ARNOLD
Commanding General, Army Air Forces

# Chapter Notes

## Part One: Outbound

### Chapter I    To The Heart Of America

1. Mrs. Helen Ruff Crawford generously and enthusiastically provided the author with all of her brother's correspondence, among which was one of this project's several rosetta stones: the roster listing each of the 20 crews comprising class 42-4-E. This resource, combined with the Internet, led to several other surviving participants of that class.

2. The weather, as reported in this and all chapters for April 22, 1942, was obtained from the Airway Weather Reports archives of the National Climactic Data Center (U.S. Department of Commerce, National Oceanic and Atmospheric Administration), Asheville, North Carolina.

### Chapter II    Charlie

1. "War Scare" From the *Hiram Broadcaster*, September 30, 1938

> The events of the last few weeks abroad have tended to make many of us college students stop and reflect what the actualities of the situation are.
>
> Here in Hiram, in our picturesque, rustic setting, we are apt, as are students in many other colleges and universities, to take very little active interest outside our personal ones.
>
> The greatness, the stark drama, the sheer excitement of the present European situation has awakened capabilities of thought among us. We find ourselves asking these questions. Will Germany plunge Europe into another world war? Will France and Great Britain be able to force Hitler to give ground? Can the United States keep out of war if it does come?

But still there are many that concern themselves with questions like those above, but who rather say thusly, "Let's leave Europe to work out her own problems."

You know as well as I do that if war comes in this world of narrow boundaries, where the airplane, ocean liners, and other forms of communication and transportation which have tended to bring us closer and closer together with one another, that we will be brought into the fighting sooner or later.

So, let's keep abreast of the times. Let's know what's going on in the world outside of Hiram so that we may better serve ourselves and our country.

2. Elizabeth Fellowes is not the real name of Lt. Charles Reynard's fiancée. When contacted by the author, her family requested anonymity for her, and regretfully (although understandably) declined to release any information based on how reviving sad memories would negatively impact her already frail health. From the Radcliffe College Alumnae Department, it is known that she did, however, subsequently marry, have children, and move to southern California.

3. Dingle Dell, a township park in Hiram, is popular with college students.

4. Logbook Number Five, entry on 4/22/42 for Harold F. Blackburn, Airline Transport Rating Certificate # 10472.

## Chapter III    Blackie

1. Serling, Robert, *Howard Hughes' Airline*, New York, St. Martins/ Marek, 1964, pp. 242-7.

## Chapter IV    From the Eagle Nest

1. From the manuscript "The Year 1941" by Ed Betts, retired TWA pilot and noted aviation historian. The manuscript later appeared as an article in *TARPA*, the *Journal of The Active and Retired Pilots Association of TWA*.

2. *Ibid.*

3. From the manuscript "Eagle Nest Flight Center" by Joe Carr. This manuscript, the source of much Chapter IV's anecdotal information, also appeared in *TARPA*.

## Chapter V    The Rancher

1. "Philturn Rockymountain Scoutcamp" is not a typo. The National Council of the Boy Scouts of America originally combined part of "Philmont" with the "turn" from the Scouting slogan, "Do a good

turn daily," and for brevity's sake integrated the words "Rocky," "Mountain," "Scout," and "Camp" into just two words. Fortunately, the name never stuck, and since the mid to late 1940s, Philmont Scout Ranch has simply been called "Philmont," or more commonly by the past and present staff simply as "the Ranch."

## Chapter VI    Jonas Ruff

1.  The same Vultee V1-AD that Jonas Ruff flew survives and, of the roughly three dozen V1s that were built, is the only remaining V1 left in the world. After being abandoned in the United States in the 1950s, it was restored in 1971 and can be seen at the Virginia Aviation Museum in Richmond, Virginia. Visitors to the museum will also be able to see several aircraft types with which Ruff was very familiar including the Curtiss Robin, Piper J-3 Cub, and several Stinsons and Fairchilds.

## Chapter VII    The B-24 Liberator

1.  LLoyd, Alwyn T., *Liberator, America's Global Bomber*, Missoula, Montana, Pictorial Histories Publishing Co. 1993, p. 485. (one of the more definitive works on the B-24).
2.  Pearcy, Arthur, *Lend-Lease Aircraft in WWII*, Osceola, Wisconsin, Motorbooks International, 1993, p.51.
3.  Aircraft Record Card for Consolidated Aircraft B-24D Serial Number 41-1133, Air Force Historical Research Agency, Maxwell Air Force Base, Alabama.
4.  "Airplane Accidents in Continental US by Principal Model of Airplane - Number and Rate: 1942-1945," Headquarters United States Air Force, History Support Office, Bolling Air Force Base, Washington, DC.

## Chapter VIII    Keep'em Flying

1.  Craven, W.F. and Cate, J.L., *The Army Air Forces in World War II*, Chicago, University of Chicago Press, 1955, Volume VI, p. 461.
2.  McAllister, Walter L., *et al, 34th Bombardment Group (H) 1941-1945*, Turner Publishing Company, Paducah, Kentucky, 1988. A good reprise is also available on the web at www.excel-tech.com/34th

## Chapter IX    Kansas City

1.  From the manuscript, "The ICD Story" by Ed Betts.
2.  *Kansas City Times* for April 22 - May 8, 1942.
3.  Lutgens, Frederick and Tarbuck, Edward, *The Atmosphere*, Englewood Cliffs, New Jersey, 1998, p. 145.

# Part Two:   The Aeries

## Chapter X   Jeff, the Eagle Scout

1. Tribe of Mic-O-Say, *The Inner Circle*, Vol. I, 1974, p. 2.

### MIC-O-SAY

My work is done;
Though brief has been life's span
I have known brotherhood,
And man to man,
Have felt the stirring kinship of the tried,
The nobleness of sacrifice, the pride
That causes man to taste the bitter with the sweet
And, tasting, lift his head above defeat
And strongly brave his tasks;
For serving thus, he gives to life and eternity
That spark bequeathed to him
By her who gave him life,
Who faced the grim dark valley of ordeal,
That he might live,
And he might guide mankind to freely give.
And I have stood beside a sacred place
And there with my fellow tribesmen made my vows,
Have searched myself, and sought my inner strength,
Have goaded mine own spirit
To enshrine
Within my heart a long-enduring goal
That on the morrow might have more avail
Than just the mem'ry of a totem pole
Or white-washed rock.
Yes, these things I have known in mine own heart,
And they are good.
And this I know when my race is run,
When starlight falls o'er oak-clad hills,
And the setting sun bespeaks the end of my life span -
I have been challenged to the best in me,
I have been strengthened by an Eagle's Claw.
I go, Great Spirit, answering Thy call
For it is well - my brothers carry on.

Chief Lone Bear

2. "Kansas City Scouting Troop History," monograph provided by Mic-O-Say Historian, F. Gail Hixson.

## Chapter XI    The Training of Aviation Cadets

1. Severe, Errol D., *The Last of a Breed*, Lighthouse Productions, Eureka Springs, Arkansas, 1997, p. 140.
2. Craven and Cate, *op. cit.*, p. 455.
3. "Thunderbird Training Program," Army Air Force Training Command, 1946, Appendix C.
4. Craven and Cate, *op. cit.*, p. 577.
5. Watry, Charles A., *Washout!*, California Aero Press, Carlsbad, California, p. 96.
6. *Ibid*, p. 97.
7. Kroesen, Paul, editor, *et al*, *The Thunderbird*, Glendale, Arizona, 1941, p. 17.
8. *Ibid*, p. 36.
9. "Reflections on the Origin of Thunderbird Field," archived monograph from the Thunderbird American School of International Management.
10. "Thunderbird Training Program," *op cit.*
11. "History of the 7th AAFTD," June 1941-December 1941, Army Air Force Training Command.
12. *Ibid.*
13. Zimmer, Stephen and Walker, Larry, *Philmont, An Illustrated History*, Boy Scouts of America, Irving, Texas, 1988. p. 53.

## Chapter XII    Primary

1. Contemporary local, national and international news during the summer of 1941 derived from the now defunct *Oxnard Press Courier*, Oxnard, California.
2. Davis, Howard, editor, *Crosswinds*, Oxnard, California, 1941, p. 22 (also the source of anecdotal information on Mira Loma Flight Academy).

## Chapter XIII    Get On The Ball, Mister!

1. *Arizona Republic*, Phoenix, Arizona, period from July 15 through September 30, 1941 for local, national, and international news.
2. "Thunderbird Training Program," *op. cit.*, Appendix C.

## Chapter XIV    Basic Flight

1. The entire poem is reproduced below primarily for the benefit of non-aviation oriented readers. *High Flight* appears in so many books about flying that its presentation here borders on the hackneyed. The reason that *High Flight* adorns so many posters, plaques, and book pages is that better poetry about flight probably has yet to be written.

   At age 19, John Gillespie Magee was killed in his Spitfire near Digby Aerodrome on December 11, 1941, in a mid-air collision. He had quite recently been assigned to 412 Squadron, R.C.A.F., and had flown several missions over the continent in the previous month. Educated in England, America and China, he was the son of an English mother and a missionary American father of Scotch-Irish descent. Magee's life is well-documented in the 1942 book, *Sunward I've Climbed*, by Hermann Hagedorn.

### *High Flight*

Oh! I have slipped the surly bonds of earth
And danced the skies on laughter silvered wings;
Sunward I've climbed, and joined the tumbling mirth
Of sun-split clouds - and done a hundred things
You have not dreamed of - wheeled and soared and swung
High in the sunlit silence. Hov'ring there,
I've chased the shouting wind along, and flung
My eager craft through footless halls of air.

Up, up the long delirious, burning blue
I've topped the wind-swept heights with easy grace,
Where never lark, or even eagle flew -
And, while with silent, lifting mind I've trod
The high untrespassed sanctity of space,
Put out my hand and touched the face of God.

2. *The Californian*, Bakersfield, California, is the source of Minter Field, local, national, and international news for the period September 30 - December 10, 1941.
3. Zimmer and Walker, *op. cit.*, p. 59.
4. Thompson, Jonathan, *Vultee Aircraft*, Narkiewicz/Thompson, Santa Ana, California, 1992, p. 78. Also contains a good discussion of the Vultee V1 series.

## Chapter XV    Advanced

1. Kempner, Seymour, Lefevre, Ivan, and Stinson, Roland, *The History of Mather Field*, California, Installment I, 1943, p.3.
2. *Sacramento Bee*, Sacramento, California, is the source of Mather Field, local, national, and international news for the period December 9, 1941 to March 1, 1942.

## Chapter XVI    Silver Wings

1. *Air Navigation Radio Aids*, Department of Commerce, Civil Aeronautics Administration, Washington, DC, July 1941.
2. *Op. cit.*, *Sacramento Bee*. Also cited as standard reference for music popularity throughout this book was the weekly section, "Music Popularity Chart" in *Billboard Magazine* for the period June 1941 through April 1942.
3. *East Oregonian*, Pendleton, Oregon, January 26-28, 1942.
4. All Army Air Force personnel and aircraft deployments and actions in this and succeeding chapters are derived from a remarkable website prepared by North Jersey aviation historian Jack McKillop. http://www.lts.aetc.af.mil/ho_www/combat.html is a compilation derived from the *Air Force Combat Units of World War II*, *Combat Squadrons of the Air Force World War II*, and *The Army Air Forces in World War II: Combat Chronology*.

# Part Three: Rendezvous With Tragedy

## Chapter XVII   The Road To Kirtland

1. *Tacoma News Herald*, Tacoma, Washington, for base, local, national, and international news for the period March 1 to March 12, 1942.
2. Strong, Russell A., *First Over Germany*, Hunter Printing, Charlotte, North Carolina, 1990, p. 10.
3. *Salt Lake Tribune*, Salt Lake City, Utah, for local, national, and international news in mid-March 1942.
4. In addition to the *305th Bomb Group*, (Collins, John D. *et al*, Turner Publishing Co., 1997), the website http://collectorsnet.com/milhist/305bg.HTM is a good source of concise information.
5. *Op. cit.*, Strong. The website http://collectorsnet.com/milhist/306bg.HTM provides a thorough summary.

## Chapter XVIII Combat Crew Training School

1. *Albuquerque Journal*, Albuquerque, New Mexico, referenced for all local, state, national, and international news from March 29 through May 12, 1942.

2. *Outline of Instruction, Four Engine Transition School, Instructor's Manual for B-24A, LB-30 & B-24D Airplanes,* Combat Crew Training School (4 Eng.), Division of Transcontinental & Western Air Inc.
3. Welliver, Royce and Carr, J.P., *Technical School Instructor's Manual,* Combat Crew Training School (4 Eng.) Division of Transcontinental & Western Air Inc.

## Chapter XIX   The Cruel Sky

1. Unfortunately, the universal popularity of *High Flight* overshadows the rest of Magee's poetry.

### *Prayer*

Some evening, when I'm sitting out alone
Watching, perhaps a cloud across the sky,
I'll feel as if a strange cool wind has blown -
And suddenly I'll know that I am to die;

Then I'll remember how we stood together,
And laughed and kissed the lovely sun to bed;
And how we talked of death among the heather;
And wondered gaily at the ancient dead.

When breath comes short, and tears come all in vain,
And in the silence I must realize
That I shall never laugh, nor love again,
May I find, leaning over me, your eyes.

2. Conversation with Chope Phillips who well recalls the severity of the thunderstorm and adverse weather subsequently persisted (also reported in the *Albuquerque Journal*).
3. Form 14, Army Air Force B-24D liberator, serial number 41-1133. Attachments included unintelligible xeroxes of original photo negatives, weather reports, and news clips from the *Raton Range*.
4. It is only the rarest of geologists and naturalists who cannot have a field day at Philmont due to the extraordinary diversity of the rocks, minerals, flora, and fauna there contained. In fact, the Gemini astronauts, including Eagle Scouts James Lovell and Neil Armstrong, did their geology training at Philmont. Mining, particularly for gold, is an important aspect of Philmont's heritage.

Nearly all of the earth's rock types appear at Philmont as

do fossilized shark's teeth. The Cimarron Mountains, still rising, have been shaped by a variety of forces. What is now Philmont was once ocean floor. Volcanoes later erupted in the same area. Trail Peak is one of the three or four most striking features visible from Philmont's Camping Headquarters. Although mountains are the dominant aspect of the landscape, there are numerous examples of western land forms including canyons, gulches, mesas, benches, and prairies.

Trail Peak's geology is dominated by metamorphic rocks of the Precambrian Age, principally gneiss and schist. Imposing as it is, Trail Peak (elev. 10,242 feet above mean sea level), is one of Philmont's lesser peaks, ranking tenth in Philmont's list of ten mountains over 10,000 feet. Technically, it is not a difficult climb, and does not require ropes or artificial aids since it really is an uphill hike, albeit a breathless one. The crest is served by two trails whose easier sections are in the 30-40 percent grade category, and the vertical gain is roughly 1,000 feet from the less taxing starting point. The easier trail is from the top of Fowler Pass on the Crater Lake (southeast) side, and the shorter, more difficult trail (from the southwest) is out of the Bonito Valley in the vicinity of Bonito Cow Camp. The mountain is never climbed from the north or east, which involve substantially more vertical gain and grade. However, on the most infrequent of occasions, off-duty Philmont rangers have been known to descend to the north by bushwhacking down to the South Fork, Urraca Creek trail (off-trail hiking is officially prohibited).

The mountain's crest is below timberline (in that latitude) by roughly 1,500 feet. Trail Peak's base is heavily forested with Ponderosa pine and, to a lesser extent, by aspen. The top of Trail Peak is wooded, but not by the tall Ponderosa pines which are the dominant feature of most Philmont forests. At 10,000 feet they have given way to smaller aspens, limber pines, and firs.

Unlike Philmont's two greatest peaks (Mount Phillips, 11,711 feet, and Baldy Mountain, 12,444 feet), Trail Peak does not offer a particularly scenic view from its summit. The best panorama is from one of the rock falls, a great boulder field just below the northwest ridge which affords good views of Baldy Mountain in the north, Philmont's midlands, and the rest of the Ranch's high South Country, including the Mount Phillips massif. Another rockfall, on the east side of the mountain, presents a superb view of Tooth of Time Ridge, Urraca Mesa, and Camping Headquarters.

The bomber's great wings are in a small boulder field located just below the peak's northwest ridge, on the south side. The view from this vantage point provides a good vista of the bomber's tragic, final route and includes the Bonito Valley, Rayado Peak, Burn Peak, and more mountains beyond Philmont's southwestern boundary.

5. The Army Air Force crash report includes only a primitive diagram of how the bomber broke up. One of the victim's family members made state police photographs available to the author, and those photos clearly showed the bomber's final configuration.

## Chapter XX    Aftermath

1. Bainbridge, John, *Like A Homesick Angel*, Houghton Mifflin, Boston, 1964, pp. 106-107.
2. "A Tribute" by Stephen K. Bailey from the *Cleveland Plain Dealer*.

Lieut. Charles O. Reynard., 23, of Hiram, has made the supreme sacrifice. Not until a blow like this strikes home do we understand the full meaning of this war. For Charlie Reynard was not just an ordinary citizen. When he entered the Army Air Corps ten months ago, he had behind him a distinguished honor record in college and a graduate degree in sociology from Harvard University. All those who knew him well predicted a brilliant career for him in the field of social leadership. His death is a tragedy in more than one sense — for added to the bereavement of his family and friends is an unfathomable loss to the future of our country. The postwar world will have real need of all the "Charlie Reynards" it can find.

But in the face of the inscrutable mystery of death, it may be well to put Lieut. Reynard's life in another perspective. I write from personal observation when I say that Lieut. Reynard symbolized the very fundamentals for which we are fighting — fundamentals which our enemies do not and can never understand.

In the first place, he was a student. He had an open, scientific mind which was never dogmatic, never closed to new ideas. His enthusiasm for new ideas was one of his most distinguishable characteristics. He understood the issues of the war better than most, and fought because of his understanding. A Nazi's blind acceptance of a race-Fuhrer, a Jap's pathetic allegiance to a god-emperor, a totalitarian mind closed to truth — these things were to Charlie an anathema, for they meant the perpetuation of fear and ignorance, and limited personality.

In the second place, Charlie had a deep-rooted, ethical motivation. Whether in committee, or club, or classroom, or work, his first consideration always seemed to be, "Is this right. Will it make for a better situation?" In contrast to Goebbels' notorious statement, "Important is not who is right, but who wins." Charlie Reynard never wanted to win if winning meant hitting below the belt.

Finally, Charlie's ethics were based on a deep and abiding religious faith. For two years at college, he was president of the Y.M.C.A., and a member of the college class program committee. One of the last reports which his family had about him concerned the fact that Sundays he took time out from his Army flying to sing in a local church choir. His faith was in a man who, 2000 years ago, preached goodwill and sacrifice that others might live more abundantly.

In our more pessimistic moments, we sometimes question what it is we are fighting for. At such times, let us think about Lt. Charles Reynard. He died to preserve things which outsiders recognized in him: a free mind, a pure heart, and a positive faith. Could we be fighting for more? We must not fight for less!"

3. Thole, Lou, *Forgotten Fields*, Pictorial Histories Publishing Co., Missoula, Montana, 1996, pp. 107-121.

4. Serling, *op. cit.*, pp. 93-94. Serling's discussion of TWA's role in WWII (summarized below and supplemented with figures from TARPA) revives an aspect of American aviation history that has all but been forgotten: how the airlines of America essentially became the backbone of the Army Air Force's Air Transport Command early in the war.

Jack Frye, TWA's CEO, and Edgar S. Gorrell, president of the Air Transport Association (ATA), had prepared a war mobilization emergency plan as early as 1936 although it was not met with enthusiasm by official Washington. Gorrell was no lightweight; he had been a colonel in the Air Corps and Chief of the Air Staff during WWI. The ATA was the airline industry's trade association, and one of its charters was liaison with the military. Summer's end in 1939 found Gorrell on a fishing trip to Canada. He was surprised to have a Canadian bush pilot circle, alight on the lake, and inquire if he were a Mr. Gorrell. After being informed by the floatplane pilot that Germany had invaded Poland that morning, Col. Gorrell was on his way that day to Hap Arnold's office.

Just as President Roosevelt was poised to nationalize the airline industry immediately after Pearl Harbor, the Air Transport Association had its revised plan ready to go. In effect, the airlines became a civilian auxiliary, a reserve force which supplied planes, aircrews, and ground crews. Gorrell met with Roosevelt who cancelled his planned executive order nationalizing the airlines.

The airline industry as we know it today was in its infancy. There were only 434 aircraft involved, and the majority (358) were employed on domestic routes. Of the remainder, 53 were flown on Latin American routes, seven to Alaska, six to Hawaii, and ten on transatlantic flights. The most common plane, by far, was the DC-3, but the most coveted were the four-engine Boeing 307s of TWA and Pan Am's Boeing Model 314 Clippers.

Although the air carriers had Gorrell's plans in hand — plans which were constantly updated through 1941 — the mobilization posed major challenges. There were personnel and training problems since many of the airlines' pilots were reservists who were going on active duty. This problem was partially alleviated by finding, hiring, and training men like Jonas Ruff and Hutch Thurston, but TWA struggled to find the 70 to 80 qualified pilots it would be hiring each month during the peak years of 1944 and 1945.

5. There is an interesting, Colfax County, New Mexico, connection relating to Blackburn's service with the Seventh P.R.G. The Group's squadrons formed at Peterson Field, Colorado Springs, in late 1942 and early 1943. Among their bivouac training sites was one of the Army Air Force's smaller bases in New Mexico: Crews Army Air Field which is located just south of Raton. Thus, many of the photo-reconnaissance pilots Blackburn flew with in mid-1944 were very familiar with the Philmont landscape which appears only 30 miles south-southwest of Crews Field.

Blackburn's flying with the Seventh P.R.G. placed him very much in harm's way. During the Group's operations in the ETO, its losses were comparable to the average Eighth Air Force fighter group. From July of 1943 through May of 1945, the Seventh P.R.G. lost 62 pilots who were killed in action or in flying accidents. Twenty-three pilots became POWs and eight others were shot down, but returned to England after evading Germans on the continent.

During most of this period, a standard tour with the Group was

25 missions whereas a tour in a fighter group was 200 hours or, very roughly, a hundred missions in 1943 and significantly fewer sorties in 1944-45 when the long range Mustang fighter equipped most groups. By late 1944, after Blackburn's flying with the Seventh had come to an end, the group's increasing loss rate resulted in the photo ships being escorted by a flight of Mustangs when flying to particularly sensitive targets.

Among the other "guest" pilots with Seventh P.R.G. was the RAF's leading PR "ace," Wing Commander Adrian Warburton, D.S.O. and bar, D.F.C. and two bars. Warburton was killed on April 12, 1944 in a Seventh Group Lightning while on a mission to photograph the ball-bearing works at Schweinfurt, Germany. He never made his planned landing at Sardinia, and his remains have never been found.

Nearly four months later, another well known F-5 Lightning photo-reconnaissance pilot failed to show up after flying a mission to southern France. Like Warburton, no traces of the French writer, Antoine de Saint-Exupery, were ever found after his takeoff from Corsica in an F-5.

The impeccably researched, lavishly illustrated book by Patricia Keen, *The Eyes of the Eighth*, is the definitive work on the Seventh P.R.G. and the source of statistics noted above.

6. Although not devoted to an Air Force death, *Your Daddy Did Not Die* was written in 1944 by Protestant clergyman Dr. Daniel A. Poling for his grandchildren about his son, Army Lt. Clark Poling. The book's purpose was to acquaint the little boy and girl with the father they would never get to know. Lt. Poling was a chaplain, one of The Four Chaplains, who gave up his life jacket and perished after saving others following the February, 1943, torpedoing of his ship, the *USAT Dorchester*, in the North Atlantic. The book was received by 1944 audiences as one of hope and inspiration in addition to serving as Lt. Clark Poling's biography.

## Chapter XXI   After The War (Epilogue)

1. In addition to the Army Air Force history on Thunderbird, the other definitive source on Thunderbird Field is the article by Charles R. Hyer, "Thunderbirds in the Southwest Desert," *Journal of the American Aviation History Society*, Volume 30, Number 3, Fall 1985, pp. 162-181.

2. Wells, Trent, editor, *et al*, *The History of Aviation Cadet Class 42-B*, Coulterville, California, 1997.

The United States Army Air Force is referred to in the singular throughout this book since that was the more accepted colloquial version. The proper usage, however, is plural: "United States Army Air Forces." Readers will note that the term "Air Corps" appears frequently in early chapters. The name United States Army Air Corps was terminated in mid-1941, and replaced with United States Army Air Forces, although many Army flying schools continued to use the older terminology in names such as "Air Corps Advanced Flying School, Mather Field" well past 42-B's graduation.

# Bibliography

**Books (Aviation, WWII, Training, Meteorology)**

Allen, Lois T., and Bonnewitz, Roberta L., *Airway Pioneers*, Raytown, Missouri, Pilot News Press, 1979.

Astor, Gerald, *The Mighty Eighth*, New York, Penguin Books, 1997.

Bainbridge, John, *Like A Homesick Angel*, Boston, Houghton Mifflin, 1964.

deBusk, Robert H., editor, *Thunderbird Annual 1941-1942*, Glendale, Arizona, Thunderbird Training Detachment, 1942.

Carigan, William, *Ad Lib*, Manhattan, Kansas, Sunflower University Press, 1988.

Cassagneres, Ev, *The New Ryan*, Eagan, Minnesota, Flying Books International, 1995.

Cave, Hugh B., *Wings Across the World*, New York, Dodd, Mead & Company, 1945.

Collins, John D. *et al*, *305th Bombardment Group* (H), Paducah, Turner Publishing Co. 1997.

Craven, W.F., and Cate, J. L., *The Army Air Forces in World II*, vol. VI., Chicago, University of Chicago Press, 1955.

Davis, Howard, editor, *Crosswind*, Oxnard, California, Oxnard Training Detachment, 1941.

Day, Karl S., *Instrument and Radio Flying*, Newark, Air Associates, 1940.

Dmitri, Ivan, *Flight to Everywhere*, New York, McGraw-Hill, 1944.

Faulkner, Frank, *Westover*, Springfield, Massachusetts, Hungry Hill Press, 1990.

Fletcher, Eugene, *Mister*, Seattle, University of Washington Press, 1992.

Gunn, Walter, *A Life Aloft*, Mission, Kansas, Wings Publications, 1998.

Hagedorn, Hermann, *Sunward I've Climbed*, New York, Macmillan Company, 1942.

Harbord, James G. *et al*, *The Officer's Guide*, Harrisburg, Pennsylvania, Military Service Publishing Co., 1942.

Hibbits, John J., *Take 'er Up Alone Mister*, New York, McGraw- Hill, 1943.

Johnsen, Frederick, A., *B-24 Liberator*, Osceola, Wisconsin, Motorbooks International, 1993.

Johnston, Lew, *Look Proud, Mister*, (to be published).

Juptner, Joseph, *U.S. Civil Aircraft Series*, Blue Ridge Summit, Pennsylvania, TAB/Aero, 1993.

Kahn, Leo J., *The Story of the Texan*, Appleton, Wisconsin, Aviation Publications, 1975.

Keen, Patricia F., *Eyes of the Eighth*, Sun City, Arizona, Cavu Publishing, 1996.

Kingsley, Ruth R., editor, *Recollections and Collections of Charlie*, privately published booklet in memory of Second Lieutenant Charles O. Reynard, Jr., Willoughby, Ohio, 1985.

Kroesen, Paul, Ed., *et al, Echelon*, Bakersfield, California, Merchants Printing, 1942.

Kroesen, Paul, Ed., *et al, The Thunderbird*, Glendale, Arizona,, 1941.

Lloyd, Alwyn T., *Liberator*, Missoula, Montana, Pictorial Histories, 1993.

Lutgens, Frederick, and Tarbuck, Edward, *The Atmosphere*, Englewood Cliffs, New Jersey, Prentice-Hall, 1998.

Maurer, M., Ed., *Combat Squadrons of the Air Force in WWII*, Washington, Zenger Publishing Co., 1969.

Mayborn, Mitch, and Bowers, Peter, M., *Stearman Guidebook*, Dallas, Flying Enterprise Publications, 1973.

McAllister, Walter L. *et al, 34th Bombardment Group (H) 1941-45*, Paducah, Turner Publishing Co., 1988.

Mueller, Robert, *Air Force Bases*, Washington, DC., Office of Air Force History, United States Air Force. 1982.

Ohlrich, Walt and Ethell, Jeff, *Pilot Maker*, Osceloa, Wisconsin, Specialty Press, 1983.

Orriss, Bruce W., *When Hollywood Ruled the Skies*, Hawthorne, California, Aero Associates, 1984.

Pearcy, Arthur, *Lend-Lease Aircraft in World War II*, Osceola, Wisconsin, Motorbooks International, 1996.

Phillips, Edward, *Travel Air*, Eagan, Minnesota, Flying Books International, 1982.

Richards, Denis and Saunders, Hilary St. G., *Royal Air Force 1939-1945* vol. II, Norwich, U.K., Jarrolds & Sons, Ltd. 1954.

Serling, Robert, *Howard Hughes' Airline*, New York, St. Martin's, 1983.

Severe, Errol, *The Last of a Breed*, Eureka Springs, Arkansas, Lighthouse Productions, 1997.

Strong, Russell A., *First Over Germany*, Charlotte, North Carolina, Hunter Printing, 1990.

Thole, Lew, *Forgotten Fields*, Missoula, Montana, Pictorial Histories Publishing Co., 1996.

Thompson, Jonathan, *Vultee Aircraft*, Santa Ana, California, Narkiewicz/Thompson, 1992.

Watry, Charles A., *Washout!*, Carlsbad, California, California Aero Press, 1983.

Wells, Trent, *et al*, *The History of Aviation Cadet Class 42-B*, Coulterville, Calif., Cadet Class 42-B Association, 1997.

### Books (Philmont, Scouting)

Huffman, Minor, *Magic Mountains*, Allendale, New Jersey, TBS Inc., 1988.

Robinson, G.D., Wanek, A.A., Hays, W.H., McCallum, M.E., and Stacy J.R., *Philmont Country*, Washington, U.S. Geological Survey, 1964.

Steuver, Mary and Shaw, Daniel, *Philmont Fieldguide*, Cimarron, New Mexico, Philmont Scout Ranch, 1985.

Taylor, Jimmy Bartle, *Down Home With The Chief And Miss Maggie*, Prairie Village, Kansas, Leathers Publishing Co., 1995.

Wallis, Michael, *Beyond the Hills*, Oklahoma City, Oklahoma Heritage Association, 1995.

Willens, Sidney, *The Life of H. Roe Bartle*, Kansas City, Memorial Exhibit Committee.

Zimmer, Stephen and Walker, Larry, *Philmont, An Illustrated History*, Irving, Texas, Boy Scouts of America, 1988.

Tribe of Mic-O-Say, *The Inner Circle*, Kansas City, 1974.

### Documents

Aircraft Record Card, Consolidated B-24D Liberator Heavy Bomber, Army Air Force Serial Number 41-1133, United States Air Force Historical Branch, Maxwell Air Force Base, Alabama.

"Airplane Accidents in the Continental United States by Principal Model of Airplane - Number and Rate: 1942 to 1945," Office of History, Bolling Air Force Base, Washington D.C.

*Air Navigation Radio Aids*, for April 1942, Civil Aeronautics Administration, Department of Commerce, August 1941.

Airway Weather Reports, United States Department of Commerce, National Climatic Data Center, Asheville, N.C. (For Albuquerque, Kansas City, Las Vegas, Raton, and Santa Fe, on April 22/23, 1942).

*Combat Chronology of the U.S. Army Air Forces - December 1941-May 1942, Air Force Combat Units of WWII, Combat Squadrons of the Air Force World War II, The Army Air Forces in WWII*, and *The Mighty Eighth War Diary* as compiled and edited online by Jack McKillop (www.lts.aetc.af.mil/ho_www/combat.html).

"Certificate of Proficiency, Sacramento," Air Corps Advanced Flying School, Mather Field, February 20, 1942 (copies of certificates awarded to Class 42-B pilots).

*Directory of Airfields*, Washington, D.C., Headquarters Aeronautical Chart Service, Army Air Forces, 1944.

*Digest of Civil Air Regulations for Pilots*, Civil Aeronautics Bulletin No. 22, Civil Aeronautics Administration, Department of Commerce, August 1941.

"Flying Cadets," Pilot Training, Army Air Corps (recruitment brochure), Washington, Adjutant General, United States Army, 1940.

*Four-Engine Transition School, Outline of Flight Instruction*, Albuquerque, N.M. Transcontinental & Western Air Inc., 1941.

*Four-Engine Transition School, Outline of Ground Instruction*, Albuquerque, N.M. Transcontinental & Western Air Inc., 1941.

*History of Army Air Forces Training Command*, 1 January 1939 - V.J. Day, Barksdale Field, Louisiana, Headquarters Army Air Forces Training Command, June 15, 1946.

*History of Kirtland Field*, Albuquerque, New Mexico, Air Force Historical Branch, Maxwell Air Force Base, file No. 285.29.

*History of the Seventh Army Air Force Flying Training Detachment* (Oxnard June-December 1941), Air Force Historical Branch, Maxwell Air Force Base, file No. 234.541.

*History of Mather Field*, Sacramento, Calif., Air Force Historical Branch, Maxwell Air Force Base, file No. 286.24.

"Instructions for Aviation Cadet Examining Boards," Washington, Training Command, United States Army Air Forces, January 1942.

*Military Training Guide*, Plans and Training Office, Training Command, United States Army Air Forces, 1943.

Pilot logbooks of Harold Blackburn, Wayne Falk, Howard Kincheloe, Ralph Lessor, Robert Van Riessen, Jonas Ruff, and Harold "Hutch" Thurston.

Special Orders: Extracts from orders received by members of Class 42-B while stationed as aviation cadets at primary, basic and advanced flying schools, and subsequently as officers stationed at McChord Field, Salt Lake Army Air Base, and Kirtland Field.

*Standardization of Army Primary Flying Training* (Supplement to War Department Training Manual I-210), Training Command, United States Army Air Forces, January 1943.

*Take Off* (Official Pre-Flight Handbook), Training Command, United States Army Air Forces. 1942.

"Technical Report of the Aircraft Classification Committee" (Form 14), B-24D Serial Number 41-1133 Flying Accident, Headquarters, West Coast Air Force Training Center, May 11, 1942 (file No. WC.400.43M x 201).

"Thunderbird 50th Anniversary," Glendale, Arizona, The American Graduate School of International Management, 1996.

"Thunderbird Training Program," Air Force Training Detachment, Thunderbird Field, Glendale, Arizona, Western Air Training Command, 1944.

## Manuals

*B-24D Flight Manual*, Consolidated Aircraft, San Diego, September 1942.

*Basic Flying*, Army Air Forces, Western Flying Training Command, 1944.

*Basic Instrument Flying*, Technical Order No. 30-100A-1, Air Service Command, 1943.

*C-87 Cargo Transport Aircraft Operating Instructions*, Washington, D.C., Transcontinental & Western Air, Inc., March 8, 1943.

*Instrument Flying Technique in Weather*, Technical Order No. 30-100D-1, Air Service Command, Army Air Forces, 1943.

*Instrument Flying Trainer* (Link), Technical Order No. 30-10006-1, Air Service Command, 1942.

*Pilot Training Manual for the Vultee BT-13*, Technical Order No. 01-50BC-1-95, Training Command, Army Air Forces, 1943.

*Standard Beam Approach*, Technical Order No. 30-100E-1, Air Service Command, 1943.

## Articles

Bainbridge, John, "Captain Harold F. Blackburn," *New Yorker*, May 5, 1956.

Bainbridge, John, "Like a Homesick Angel," *New Yorker*, November 10, 1962.

Collins, Pat, "Wind In Its More Violent Forms," *Business Aviation Safety*, Volume Eight, Number One, 1992.

"Flight Crew Training Program," Washington, *Infantry Training Journal*, American War Training Institute, 1943.

Hyer, Charles R., "Thunderbirds," *AAHS Journal*, Volume 30, Number Three, 1985.

"Music Popularity Charts," *Billboard Magazine*, for the weeks ending 7/11/41, 9/26/41, 11/28/41 12/6/41, 2/20/42, 2/27/42, and 4/17/42.

## Personal Correspondence

Harold F. Blackburn

Lt. Charles O. Reynard, Jr.

Jonas G. Ruff

## Newspapers

*Albuquerque Journal*, Albuquerque, New Mexico, March 29 - May 12, 1942.

*Arizona Republic*, Phoenix, Arizona, July 15, September 30, 1941.

*The Californian*, Bakersfield, California, September 30, 1941 - December 10, 1941.

*East Oregonian*, Pendleton, Oregon, January 27, 1942.

*Kansas City Times*, Kansas City, Missouri, April 24 - May 10, 1942.

*Oxnard Press Courier*, Oxnard, California. July 10-16, 1941.

*Sacramento Bee*, Sacramento, California, December 9, 1941 - March 1, 1942.

*Salt Lake Tribune*, Salt Lake City, Utah, March 12, 1942.

*Tacoma News Tribune*, Tacoma, Washington., March 1, 1942.

# Suggested Reading with Commentary

From the following books, the reader will gain more insights into the times of the men who perished on Trail Peak and the lives of the pilots who trained 41-1133's crew.

WWII still dominates aviation literature by a wide margin, and the fighter pilot biography remains as the leading genre, followed by unit histories and aircraft type photo essays.

Lately, there has been an increase in the number of books written by WWII flyers. These men, most of them now in their late 70s and early 80s, and knowing they are well into the autumn of their years, are publishing recollections of the defining moments of their lives.

The "heavy brigades," as a subject, have been rather underdeveloped to date, but here are several significant works of which most delve into the lives of transport and heavy bomber pilots. Also listed are the key works on the Scouting connections with this narrative.

The benchmark work, *Fate is the Hunter*, was written by the late Ernest K. Gann, dean of American aviation writers and recognized by many as the finest pilot/author whose fingers ever graced both throttles and typewriter keys. That book is a marvelous journey through flight training, airline flying, and military transport aviation in the late 1930s and war years.

Gann, very much a contemporary of Blackburn, Carr, Thurston, and the other TWA pilots in this book, started as a private pilot in the 1930s, joined what would become American Airlines, and was on his way from the right seat to the left when the war came. He flew both the B-24 and its cargo version, the C-87. Gann trained on B-24s at Smyrna, Tennessee, and almost certainly flew some of the exact same Liberators which had previously been based at Kirtland Field during its CCTS days. Many pilots who appreciate really incisive aviation writing make it a point to re-read *Fate* every year or so.

*Wings of Morning* was written by University of Pennsylvania European History Professor, Thomas Childers. His subject is the crew of "Black Cat," the last American bomber, a B-24, shot down over Germany during WWII. The Black Cat's radio operator was the uncle whom the author never got to know. The book necessarily deals with aerial combat, but its excellence is in how it treats the crew's interrelationships, their good and bad times, training, fears, hopes, daily routines, diversions, and gritty determination that kept them going in the cold skies above Germany.

*Wings of Morning* is especially notable since it was written almost 50 years after the war, and involves so much of the digging into historical files and tracking down surviving relatives that preparing *The Last Flight of Liberator 41-1133* did (except, of course, Childers' task was much more complicated since Black Cat's crew was larger than 41-1133's).

*Flight to Everywhere*, by the well known 1940s photojournalist Ivan Dimitri, is that rarity: a color photo-dominated book produced during WWII. The book, published in 1944, is primarily about the Air Transport Command, but also covers front line flying in Asia, Africa, and the North Atlantic. Dimitri was a friend of Blackburn's, and readers will experience some of what it was like to fly the B-24 bomber and the C-87 Liberator Express by reading this book.

*Howard Hughes' Airline* is the definitive work on TWA including its predecessor, Trans Continental & Western Air, Inc. Capt. Hal Blackburn is one of the prominent figures in this book which traces TWA's origins just up to a point before the airline industry's consolidations of the mid to late 1980s.

British writers dominated aviation writing during and immediately after the war, and the one work which emerged as real literature is *The Last Enemy*, by Richard Hillary. He went from Oxford University's Trinity College in 1939 to a Battle of Britain Spitfire cockpit in 1940. Although he was a Royal Air Force fighter pilot, his book cuts across pilot categories and is really less about combat flying than it is a study of how he and his circle of friends adapted to their training, the war, death, and lasting, disfiguring injuries. Had they both lived to meet each other, a conversation between Flight Lieutenant Richard Hillary and Second Lieutenant Charles O. Reynard, Jr. would have been very, very much worth listening to.

Perhaps the best American early account of heavy bomber flying is *Serenade to the Big Bird*, by Bert Stiles who was later killed in action on a subsequent tour as a Mustang fighter pilot. Although Stiles' book, as edited by his mother from his diaries, includes battling German interceptors and AAA, it really excels in involving the reader with the emotions, outlooks, friendships, and fears of a 20 year-old copilot journeying from Colorado College to an operational bomber squadron in England.

The loss of Liberator 41-1133 brought grief to seven out of the several hundred thousand American families who lost loved ones in WWII. *With Wings As Eagles*, by Helen Chappell White, is one of few, if not the only, major work about how one family's faith helped them adjust to the death of a son (a B-17 navigator) in the Army Air Force.

Steve Zimmer's and Larry Walker's *Philmont, An Illustrated History* has the ideal blend of archival and contemporary photography and authoritative text to give the non-Philmont familiarized reader a good understanding of "the Ranch" and the many events, before and after the Trail Peak accident, which have influenced generations of staff and campers alike. This book is not strictly a coffee table book or an exhaustive history. Rather, it combines the best of both.

Minor Huffman was Philmont's first general manager. His *Magic Mountains* contains the complete chronology of Philmont's development from 1938 through the late 1980s.

*Beyond the Hills* is Waite Phillips' biography by Michael Wallis. From this book, readers will become well-acquainted with the man whose extraordinary gift of Philmont Ranch has had such a lasting impact on generations of Scouts, Scouters, and Philmont staffers.

The life of H. Roe Bartle has been the subject of many writers, but only one has the complete, insider's story. *Down Home With The Chief And Miss Maggie* is by the Chief's daughter, Jimmy Bartle Taylor. To read this book is to better understand one of the principal influences on Roland Jeffries' life.

One of the most ignored aviation history categories is 1930s/40s Army Air Corps/Force aviation cadet training which was a key, molding force in the lives of Blackburn, Redding, Jeffries, and Reynard. There are precious few first-hand accounts devoted solely to flying training in that era, and they are all very worthwhile reading. *Take 'er Up Alone, Mister* is long out of print (1943), but *Mister*, and *Look Proud Mister*, are currently available. A very readable alternative to the official USAF Training Command History is Errol Severe's, *The Last Of A Breed* which covers aviation cadet training from the 1960s back to WWI.

Childers, Thomas, *Wings of Morning*, Reading, Massachusetts, Addison Wesley Publishing Co., 1995.

Fletcher, Eugene, *Mister*, Seattle, University of Washington Press, 1992.

Gann, Earnest, *Fate Is the Hunter*, New York, Simon & Shuster Co., 1961.

Hibbits, John J., *Take 'er Up Alone Mister*, New York, McGraw-Hill, 1943.

Hillary, Richard, *The Last Enemy*, London, Macmillan & Co., 1942.

Huffman, Minor, *Magic Mountains*, Allendale, New Jersey, TIBS Inc., 1988.

Johnston, Lew, *Look Proud, Mister*, (To be published).

Serling, Robert, *Howard Hughes' Airline*, New York, St. Martin's/Marek Press, 1983.

Stiles, Bert, *Serenade to the Big Bird*, New York, W.W. Norton & Co., 1952.

Severe, Errol, *The Last of a Breed*, Eureka Springs, Arkansas, Lighthouse Productions Inc., 1997.

Taylor, Jimmy Bartle, *Down Home With The Chief And Miss Maggie*, Prairie Village, Kansas, Leathers Publishing, 1995.

Wallis, Michael, *Beyond the Hills*, Oklahoma City, Oklahoma Heritage Association, 1995.

White, Helen Chappell, *With Wings As Eagles*, New York, Rinehart & Company, 1953.

Zimmer, Stephen and Walker, Larry, *Philmont, An Illustrated History*, Irving, Texas, Boy Scouts of America, 1988.

# Acknowledgements

(P = personal interview, C = correspondence, T = telephone)

**The Crew's Families, Friends, and Hometown Residents**

Agee, Cecil, Windsor, Missouri, C,T.
Anderson, Ruth, Madelia, Minnesota, C,T.
Baskins, Darlene, Windsor, Missouri, C,T.
Burris, Odis, Moro Bay, California, C,T.
Crawford, Helen Ruff, San Jose, California, C,T.
Fullerton, Carolyn Van Hoozer, Santa Ana, California, C,T.
Gray, Fred, Jacksonville, Illinois, C,T.
Gunn, Walter, Mission, Kansas, C,T.
Hatfield, Eloise Macomber, Penney Farms, Florida, C,T.
Holt, Margaret, North Jay, Maine, P,C,T.
Homiller, William, Atlanta, Georgia, C.
Lewis, Peggy, Prairie Vilage, Kansas, C,T.
MacArthur, Mary Reynard, Morristown, New Jersey, P,C,T.
McPherron, Larry, Prairie Village, Kansas, P,C,T.
Moriarity, Ernest, Orange, Massachusetts, T.
Peterson, Bette, North Mankato, Minnesota, C,T.
Polson, Ruth K. Van Hoozer, Santa Ana, California, C,T.
Redding, Dale, Wichita Falls, Texas, C,T.
Reynard, George, Riverton, New Jersey, C.
Robertson, Gordon, Shawnee Mission, Kansas, C,T.
Sawyer, Joanne, Hiram, Ohio, C,T.
Spencer, Richard & Evelyn, Hiram, Ohio, P,C,T.
Tripp, Russell, Worthington, Minnesota, C.
Van Hoozer, David W., Bremerton, Washington, C, T.
Van Hoozer, William, Woodland, Calfifornia, C,T.
Van Hoozer, Louise, Savannah, Missouri, C.

Air Force Museum, Dayton, Ohio, P.
Ashcroft, Bruce, Randolph AFB, Texas, C,T.
Collings Foundation, Stow, Massachusetts, P.
Collins, John, 305th B.G., Alexandria, Virginia, C,T.
Day, David, Bakersfield, California, C,T.
Hegre, Thomas, Carmichael, California, C.
Hörst, Eric, Millersville, Pennsylvania, C.
Leigtenheimer, Thomas, Cedarville, Ohio, P,C,T.
McKillop, Jack, Edison, New Jersey, C.
Neef, Mel Jr., Harpers Ferry, West Virginia, C,T.
Province, Harold, 34th B.G. C,T.
Strong, Russell, 306th B.G., Charlotte, North Carolina, C,T.
Thole, Lew, Cincinnati, Ohio, C.T.

**TWA, Combat Crew Training School, Capt. Harold F. Blackburn**

American Heritage Center, University of Wyoming, Laramie, C.
Betts, Ed, Pacific Palisades, California, C,T.
Blackburn, Robert, Oakland, California. C,T.
Carr, Joseph, Fort Myers, Florida, C,T.
Carr, Stephanie, Eatontown, New Jersey, C,T.
Dafoe, Enid, Fort Myers Beach, Florida, C,T.
Davidson, Harry, Albuquerque, New Mexico, C,T.
Gratz, John, Chesterfield, Missouri, C,T.
Gunn, Walter, Mission, Kansas. C,T.
Keen, Patricia, Miami, Florida, C,T.
Kincheloe, Howard, Las Cruces, New Mexico. P,C,T.
Lincourt, Wayne, Richfield Springs, New York, C.
Thurston, Harold, Los Altos, California, C.T.
Tjossem, Betty Blackburn, Newtown, Pennsylvania, C,T.
Wheeler, James, Surprise, Arizona, C,T.
Woolsey, James, Washington, D.C., C.T.

**Philmont Scout Ranch, Heart of America Council,BSA, Tribe of Mic-O-Say, Sky Scout Troop 12, Scouting**

Archer, Barbara, Sioux Falls, South Dakota, C,T.
Blair, Frederick, Memphis, Tennessee, C,T.
Cederland, Kenneth, Mt. Dora, Florida, C,T.

Danger, Col. Charles W., St. James, Minnesota, C.
Dubill, Andy, Prairie Village, Kansas, C,T.
Gentry, Donald, Gering, Nebraska, C.
Hixson, Gail, Kansas City, Missouri, C,T.
Jung, David, Santa Fe, New Mexico, P,C,T.
Mills, Richard, Springfield, Illinois, C.
Moser, Mark, Windsor, Missouri, C.
Noel, Michael, Luverne, Minnesota, C.
Phillips, Chope, Amarillo, Texas, P,C.
Powell, Richard, Rancho Mirage, California, C,T.
Sperka, Scott, Tryon, North Carolina, P,C,T.
Taylor, Jimmy Bartle, Fort Worth, Texas, C,T.
Weis, Ted, Kansas City, Misssouri, C,T.
Zimmer, Stephen A., Cimarron, New Mexico, P,C,T.

**Former Army Air Force Pilots**

Once, when their country desperately needed them, these men were pilot-patriots. To a man, they still are. Unless otherwise noted, each was in Aviation Cadet Class 42-B; most were commissioned at Mather Field on February 20, 1942. Correspondence was exchanged with all, phone interviews were held with many, and several were interviewed in person. Without their recollections, photographs, orders, logbooks, memorabilia, and technical manuals, this book would have fallen far, far short of its intended mark.

Adams, Lyle M., Sarasota, Florida.
Arnold, Edison F., Wenatchee, Washington.
Berrier, John G., Allentown, Pennsylvania.
Briley, Carlus L., San Antonio, Texas.
Buyers, John W., Alagoas, Brazil.
Cole, Wayne, Silver Spring, Maryland. 43-A
Combs, John E., Oviedo, Florida.
Cooke, Robert R., San Francisco, California.
Cramer, Charles O., Silver Lake, Ohio.
Edwards, William H., Litchfield Park, Arizona.
Enggaard, Paul N., Oxford, New York, 42-I
Evans, Frank B., Sandpoint, Idaho.
Falk, Wayne W., Omaha, Nebraska.
Fauss, Ernest J., Cumberland, Maryland.
Gammon, William R., Aiea, Hawaii.

Garbarino, Angelo J., Knoxvile, Tennessee.

Gearhart, Robert A., Fort Wayne, Indiana.

Hadfield, Edward S., Ft. Walton Beach, Florida.

Haltom, Charles C., Bryan, Texas.

Hand, Clarence, B., Kansas City, Missouri.

Hennicke, Russell C., Maple Heights, Ohio.

Johnston, Lewis, San Francisco, California. 43-G

Kelly, Doran C., Sacramento, California.

Kelly, Jack, Austin, Texas.

Kroesen, Paul M., Irvine, California.

Lessor, Ralph H., Sapphire, North Carolina.

Maxson, William R., Hartsville, Pennsylvania.

McDonald, James, West Chester, Pennsylvania. 43-D

McDonald, David E., Circleville, Ohio.

Milam, Donald H., Ruston, Louisiana.

Monroe, Ralph E., Trabuco Canyon, California.

Newberry, William, Bensalem, Pennsylvania. 44-K

Nurre, Alvin H., St. Bernard, Ohio.

Nygaard, Denton J., Kansas City, Missouri.

Parker, Henry L., Kaneohe, Hawaii.

Radtke, W. Edward, Petaluma, California.

Readheimer, Thomas C., Shreveport, Louisiana.

Schleeh, Russell E., Irvine, California.

Skjersaa, Norman H., Orlando, Florida.

Smith, Jack, Alverado, Texas.

Van Riessen, Robert H., Grand Rapids, Michigan.

Wells, Trent H., Coulterville, California.

# Learn more about Philmont!

### *Return to the Summit of Scouting*
### *A Scouter's Midlife Journey Back to Philmont*

Enjoy Bill Cass' widely acclaimed predecessor book to
***The Last Flight of Liberator 41-1133.***

- 380 pages
- Soft cover
- 17 illustrations
- Two maps
- 23 photographs
- ISBN 0-923568-29-8
- $12.95

This unique glimpse of Philmont shows the Ranch through the eyes of a young staff member. Years later, he returns as a father in early middle age, and describes his experience from that perspective. ***Return to the Summit of Scouting*** shows the inner workings of Philmont in the ultimate crucible: adversity in the mountains. Conflict, humor, cooperation, awe, pride, exhaustion, apprehension, and achievement all come together on a Philmont expedition. Here at Philmont, the crown jewel in the Boy Scouts of America's High Adventure Program, young people learn apply everything Scouting has taught them — not so much how to put up a tent and read a compass — but how to gain confidence by overcoming the physical and mental challenges that come from a grueling, eleven-day mountain backpacking experience.